AF566706

CURRENT ADVANCES IN

DISTRIBUTED COMPUTING

AND

COMMUNICATIONS

ELECTRICAL ENGINEERING COMMUNICATIONS AND SIGNAL PROCESSING

ISSN 0888-2134

Raymond L. Pickholtz, Series Editor

Victor B. Lawrence, Joseph L. Lo Cicero, and Laurence B. Milstein, Editors
IEEE Communication Society's Tutorials in Modern Communications

Anton Meijer and Paul Peeters
Computer Network Architectures

Marvin K. Simon, Jim K. Omura, Robert A. Scholtz, and Barry K. Levitt
Spread Spectrum Communications, Volume I

Spread Spectrum Communications, Volume II

Spread Spectrum Communications, Volume III

William W Wu
Elements of Digital Satellite Communication: System Alternatives, Analyses, and Optimization, Volume I

Elements of Digital Satellite Communication: Channel Coding and Integrated Services Digital Satellite Networks, Volume II

Yechiam Yemini
Current Advances in Distributed Computing and Communications

ADVANCES IN TELECOMMUNICATION NETWORKS

ISSN 0888-2223

Dr. Wushow Chou, Series Editor

Raymond Pickholtz, Editor
Local Area and Multiple Access Networks

CURRENT ADVANCES IN

DISTRIBUTED COMPUTING

AND

COMMUNICATIONS

Yechiam Yemini, Editor
Columbia University

COMPUTER SCIENCE PRESS

Printed in the United States of America

Computer Science Press, Inc.
1803 Research Boulevard
Rockville, Maryland 20850

1 2 3 4 5 6 92 91 90 89 88 87

Library of Congress Cataloging-in-Publication Data
Current advances in distributed computing and communcations.

1. Electronic data processing—Distributed processing. I. Yemini, Yechiam.
QA76.9.D5C87 1987 004′.36 86-13512

ISBN 0-88175-128-6

Electrical Engineering, Communications, and Signal Processing Series
ISSN 0888-2134

CONTENTS

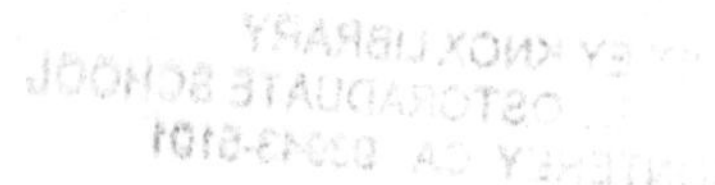

Preface

This book grew out of a series of seminars presented by the authors to the Distributed Computing and Communications (DCC) group and others at Columbia University. Seminal ideas were encouraged by seminar participants at the possible expense of full maturity. The value of the *concepts* and not their full refinement was the primary goal so that state-of-the-art research problems could be addressed.

The book is divided into two fairly loose sections. The first covers research in the area of performance analysis of distributed systems. The second deals with the areas of distributed processes and their communications, parallel systems and VLSI systems.

Many individuals and organizations have contributed to the success of this effort. The authors of the papers are to be thanked first, for having shared their research results with the seminar participants. Next, thanks go to my assistant, Ms. Abby Burton, whose long hours of devotion were essential to turning the project into a successful book. Many thanks go to Professor Michael Foster and other faculty of the Computer Science Department at Columbia University who helped coordinate the seminars. We are grateful to the editor of this series, Professor Raymond Pickholtz, who provided invaluable encouragement and support. Finally, we are indebted to our publisher, Computer Science Press, and the New York State CAT Program, without whose generous support the seminars would not have been possible.

Part One

Performance Analysis

Performance Analysis of Shared Response Systems

J. W. Wong
Department of Computer Science
University of Waterloo
Waterloo, Ontario, Canada N2L 3G1

M. H. Ammar
School of Information and Computer Science
Georgia Institute of Technology
Atlanta, Georgia 30332

Abstract

Two systems for delivering information to users are considered. The first system is *videotex* where information pages requested by users are retrieved by a service computer. If these pages are broadcast to all users, the response to one user would satisfy all other requests for the same page. This feature is referred to as *shared response*. Analytic results for the response time of shared response in videotex are derived. The second system under consideration is *teletext* where information pages are broadcast continuously to all users. The response time is affected by the order in which pages are selected for broadcast. A heuristic method to design a cyclic ordering of pages is presented.

1. Introduction

In conventional queueing systems, the service provided to a customer usually satisfies the requirement of that customer only. Theoretical studies of queueing systems are mostly concerned with this type of *individual response* systems, and results are available for a variety of customer arrival processes, service time distributions, and scheduling disciplines [1,2].

Another type of response to user requests is *shared response* where the service provided to one customer will satisfy the requirements of all customers in system who are requesting the same type of service. This is possible in certain interactive information systems if a broadcast medium (e.g., a coaxial cable) is used for information delivery. More specifically, in a *videotex* system [3], information is organized in units called *pages,* and information pages requested by users are retrieved by a service computer (see Figure 1). Shared response is observed if the retrieved pages are broadcast to all users. Due to its interactive nature, a videotex system requires a *two-way* communication network between the user terminals and the service computer.

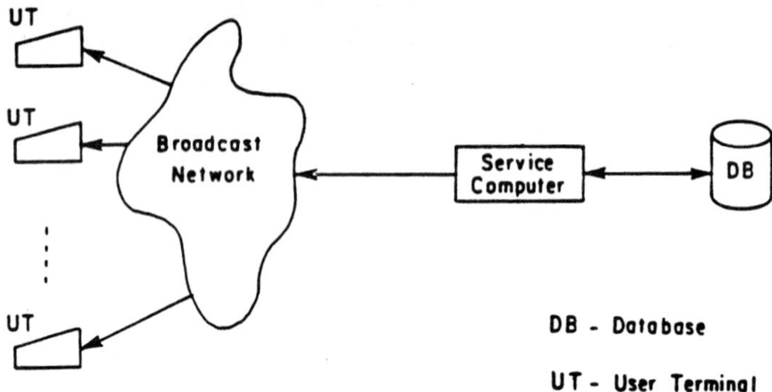

Figure 1. A Typical Videotex System

Another class of interactive information system is *teletext* where the available information pages are broadcast to all users in a continuous manner [3]. When a page of information is requested by a user, the terminal decoder examines the incoming stream of data until the desired page is detected. This page is then captured and then displayed. Note that in a teletext system, a user request does not propagate beyond the user-terminal; this feature is sometimes described as *pseudo-interactive*. Note also that only a *one-way* broadcast communication network is needed. Due to its one-way broadcast feature, teletext also provides shared response to its users.

Compared to individual response, shared response has the advantage of providing a lower response time, and more importantly, of being able to handle a traffic intensity significantly larger than one [4,5,6]. In this paper, we summarize our recent results on (a) performance analysis of videotex systems [4,6] and (b) the design of teletext broadcast cycles [5,6].

2. Performance Analysis of Videotex Systems [4,6]

2.1 Model

Our videotex system model is shown in Figure 2. Requests submitted by terminal users are processed by a service computer, resulting in the retrieval of the desired pages, and the broadcast of these pages to all users. We assume that the delay in the broadcast network is negligible compared to the processing time at the service computer.

The arrival process is assumed to be Poisson with parameter λ. This assumption is appropriate for the system under consideration because the number of users is normally large. There are N possible request types, each corresponds to a particular information page. The probability that a request is of type i is assumed to be q_i, $i=1, \cdots ,N$, where $\sum_{i=1}^{N} q_i = 1$. The service computer is modelled as a single-server, infinite-capacity queue with an exponential service time distribution. The service rate, μ, is assumed to be identical for all request types, and the queueing discipline is assumed to be first-come, first-served.

With shared response, a user's request is satisfied when a page of the same type is broadcast. If all requests are admitted into the system, some of the broadcasts may not satisfy any outstanding requests.

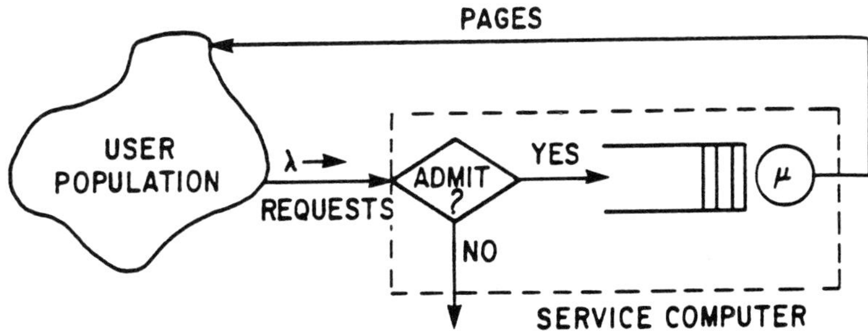

Figure 2. Model of Videotex with Broadcast Delivery

Such *broadcasts* are called *superfluous,* and they represent wastage of system resource. We therefore propose to discard a type i request if there is one already in the system (see Figure 2). Such a *request* is also called *superfluous.* Note that although a superfluous request is discarded, the user that generated it will still get served.

The performance measure of interest is the response time of type i requests, $i=1, \cdots ,N$. This is defined to be the elapsed time from when a request for page i is made to when page i is next broadcast.

2.2 Response time Analysis

We define the state of our model, to be $(n_1,n_2, \cdots ,n_N)$, where n_i, $i=1, \cdots ,N$ is the number of type i requests in the queueing system. Since superfluous requests are discarded, $n_i= 0$ or 1 for all i.

Let $P(n_1, \cdots ,n_N)$ be the probability that the system is in state $(n_1, \cdots ,n_N)$ at equilibrium. Using Lam's result [7], we have

$$P(n_1,n_2, \cdots ,n_N) = P(0,0, \cdots ,0)\rho^n \prod_{j=1}^{N} q_j^{\,n_j} \tag{1}$$

where $n = \sum_{j=1}^{N} n_j$ and $\rho = \dfrac{\lambda}{\mu}$.

Let $P(n)$ be the equilibrium probability that there are n requests in the system, regardless of type. By summing over all the state probabilities in (1) where $\sum_{j=1}^{N} n_j = n$ we get

$$P(n) = n!\rho^n P(0)g(N,n) \tag{2}$$

where

$$g(N,n) = \sum_{\substack{n_1+ \cdots +n_N=n \\ n_j\leq 1,\ j=1, \cdots ,N}} \prod_{l=1}^{N} q_l^{\,n_l} \tag{3}$$

Since $\sum_{n=0}^{N} P(n) = 1$ we have

$$P(0) = \left[\sum_{n=0}^{N} n!\rho^n g(N,n)\right]^{-1} \tag{4}$$

To derive the mean response time we define the following events

$$A_i(n) = \{\, n \textit{ requests in system and none of type } i \,\}\,,$$
$$\text{for } n=0, \cdots, N-1, \text{ and } i=1, \cdots, N,$$

and

$$B_i(n,k) = \{\, n \textit{ requests in system, kth request of type } i \,\}\,,$$
$$\text{for } n=1, \cdots, N,\ k=1, \cdots n, \text{ and } i=1, \cdots, N.$$

It can be shown that [6]

$$Prob[A_i(n)] = n!\rho^n P(0) g^{-i}(N,n) \tag{5}$$

and

$$Prob[B_i(n,k)] = (n-1)!\rho^n P(0) q_i g^{-i}(N,n-1) \tag{6}$$

where

$$g^{-i}(N,n) = \sum_{\substack{n_1+\cdots+n_N=n \\ n_i=0;\ n_j\le 1, j\ne i}} \prod_{l=1}^{N} q_l^{\,n_l} \tag{7}$$

If at the moment of the arrival of a type i request event $A_i(n)$ is satisfied, then the request is accepted and its mean response time will be $\frac{n+1}{\mu}$. If , on the other hand, event $B_i(n,k)$ is satisfied, the request is discarded and its mean response time will be $\frac{k}{\mu}$. The mean response time for a page i request is then given by

$$S_i = \frac{P(0)}{\mu} \sum_{n=0}^{N} (n+1)!\rho^n \left[g^{-i}(N,n) + \frac{q_i}{2} g^{-i}(N,n-1) \right] \tag{8}$$

where $P(0)$ is given by (4) and $g^{-i}(N,-1) = g^{-i}(N,N) = 0$. The mean response time over all page types is

$$S = \sum_{i=1}^{N} q_i S_i$$

As mentioned in the introduction, a shared response system can handle a traffic intensity significantly larger than one. It is therefore of interest to investigate the limit of S_i as ρ approaches infinity. Note that the maximum queue length is N because superfluous requests are discarded. The system is thus stable, and it can be shown using L'Hospital's rule on (8), that

$$\lim_{\rho \to \infty} S_i = \frac{N+1}{2\mu} \qquad \textit{for all } i=1, \cdots, N \tag{9}$$

We interpret the above limit by observing that as ρ increases the probability that there are N requests in the system approaches 1. All these requests are distinct, and the probability of finding a request (of any type) in the kth position approaches $\frac{1}{N}$. Hence

$$\lim_{\rho \to \infty} S_i = \sum_{k=1}^{N} \frac{k}{\mu} \left(\frac{1}{N} \right) = \frac{N+1}{2\mu}$$

For $\rho < \infty$, the computation of S_i relies on the ability to compute $g(N,n)$ and $g^{-i}(N,n)$ efficiently. An efficient algorithm was presented in [4,6]; it is based on the following two relationships:

$$g(N,n) = g(N-1,n) + q_N g(N-1,n-1) \tag{10}$$

$$g^{-N}(N,n) = g(N-1,n) \tag{11}$$

Using (10), we develop the following algorithm to calculate $g(N,n)$, $n=0, \cdots, N$, for an arbitrary request probability vector $(q_1, \cdots, q_N)$.

```
Declare G( 0 → N ) Array of Reals
G(0) ← 1
G(1) ← q1
G( 2 → N )←0
For i = 2 to N
  For j = i to 1 by −1
    G(j) ← G(j) + qi * G(j−1)
  End
End
```

The required functions are contained in the array G at the end of the algorithm, i.e., $g(N,n) = G(n)$.

The above algorithm can also be used to calculate $g^{-N}(N,n)$, since by (11) it is equal to $g(N-1,n)$. To calculate $g^{-i}(N,n)$ for an arbitrary i, we use the algorithm with the rearranged request probability vector $(q_1, \cdots, q_{i-1}, q_N, q_{i+1}, \cdots, q_i)$ as input. The amount of computation is $O(N^3)$.

2.3 Numerical Example

For simplicity, we consider the case where each page is equally likely to be requested, i.e., $q_i = \frac{1}{N}$ for all $i=1, \cdots, N$. Note that, for this case, $S = S_i$ for any i.

Figure 3 shows how S varies as a function of N for various values of ρ. We observe that (a) the mean response time is a linear function of N as $\rho \rightarrow \infty$ and (b) for $\rho<1$, the mean response time approaches a constant (equal to that of an M/M/1 model [1,2]) as N increases. Results for other settings of parameters values can be found in [6].

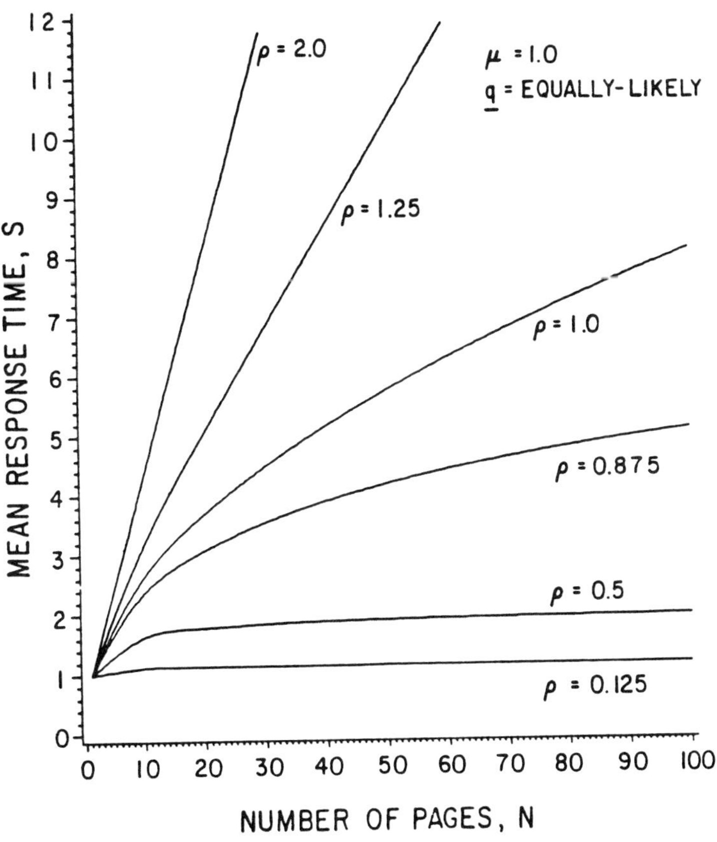

Figure 3. Mean Response Time vs. Number of Pages

3. The Design of Teletext Broadcast Cycles [5,6]

3.1 Model

We use essentially the same model as that for videotex systems. For convenience, two of the assumptions used in the videotex model are modified slightly. Specifically, the service time is assumed to be constant instead of exponentially distributed, and a type i request arriving during a broadcast of page i must wait for the next instance of a page i broadcast.

The differences in assumptions used are of concern when one tries to compare the performance of teletext to that of videotex. However, due to the major differences in the capabilities and architectures of the two systems, we feel that such a comparison is of secondary importance when compared to the performance characteristics of each system individually.

3.2 Response Time Analysis

Without loss of generality, we will use the page broadcast time as our time unit. To motivate our investigation of broadcast cycles, consider Gecsei's result [3] on the mean response time of probabilistic page broadcasting. At each broadcast instance, let p_i be the probability that page i is selected for broadcast. The mean response time for page i is now the elapsed time from when a request for page i is made to when the next broadcast of page i is complete. It is given by

$$S_i = \frac{1}{p_i} + \frac{1}{2} \tag{12}$$

and the mean response time over all requests is

$$S = \sum_{i=1}^{N} \frac{q_i}{p_i} + \frac{1}{2} \tag{13}$$

S is minimized when $\frac{p_i}{p_j} = \frac{\sqrt{q_i}}{\sqrt{q_j}}$, for all i, j [3]. Since $\sum_{i=1}^{N} p_i = 1$, we have

$$\min S = \left(\sum_{i=1}^{N} \sqrt{q_i} \right)^2 + \frac{1}{2} \tag{14}$$

As Gecsei remarked, one drawback to generating a random

sequence of pages for broadcast, is that the response time may become unbounded. This can be avoided by utilizing a fixed broadcast cycle.

A simple example of a broadcast cycle is $(1,2, \cdots ,N)$. In this example each page appears once and the mean response time is $\frac{N}{2}+1$, for any page i, $i=1, \cdots ,N$. In general, the broadcast cycle under consideration has the following two properties:

(i) The cycle length, L, is finite.

(ii) Each page appears at least once in the cycle; this implies that $L \geq N$.

For a given broadcast cycle, the following useful parameters are identified:

(i) Page Frequencies, k_i, $(i=1, \cdots ,N)$ - the number of appearances of page i in the broadcast cycle $(\sum_{i=1}^{N} k_i = L)$.

(ii) Inter-appearance Gaps, T_r^i, $(r=1, \cdots ,k_i$, and $i=1, \cdots ,N)$ - the number of pages between the beginning of the rth and the $(r+1)$st appearances of page i in the cycle, $r=1, \cdots ,k_i-1$ (see Figure 4). $T_{k_i}^i$ is the number of pages between the beginning of the k_ith appearance of page i in the cycle and the beginning of its 1st appearance in the next cycle. Note that $\sum_{r=1}^{k_i} T_r^i = L$.

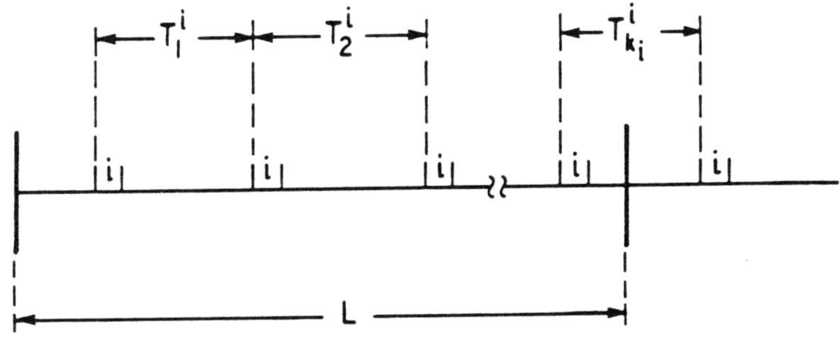

Figure 4. A Teletext Broadcast Cycle

We first analyze the mean response time of a *given* broadcast cycle. Since the parameters T_r^i are known for $r=1, \cdots, k_i$, and $i=1, \cdots, N$, we have the following expressions for S_i and S [5,6]:

$$S_i = \sum_{r=1}^{k_i} \frac{T_r^i}{L} \left(\frac{T_r^i}{2} + 1 \right) = \frac{1}{2L} \sum_{r=1}^{k_i} \left(T_r^i \right)^2 + 1 \tag{15}$$

and

$$S = \sum_{i=1}^{N} q_i S_i = \frac{1}{2L} \sum_{i=1}^{N} q_i \sum_{r=1}^{k_i} \left(T_r^i \right)^2 + 1 \tag{16}$$

It is important to note that the mean response time is only affected by the cycle used, and is independent of the traffic intensity.

We next study the properties of an ideal cycle and obtain a lower bound for the mean response time. Consider the case where the cycle length L and the page frequencies k_i, $i=1, \cdots, N$ are given. (15) is minimized when all the T_r^i's are equal, i.e.,

$$T_r^i = \frac{L}{k_i} \qquad r=1, \cdots, k_i \tag{17}$$

Note that this is the ideal condition and may not be achievable because the T_r^i's are required to be integers. Substituting (17) into (16), we get the following bound for the mean response time S:

$$S \geq \frac{1}{2L} \sum_{i=1}^{N} q_i \sum_{r=1}^{k_i} \left(\frac{L}{k_i} \right)^2 + 1 = \frac{L}{2} \sum_{i=1}^{N} \frac{q_i}{k_i} + 1 \tag{18}$$

The right hand side of (18) is smallest when we choose the k_i's such that [5,6]:

$$\frac{k_i}{k_j} = \frac{\sqrt{q_i}}{\sqrt{q_j}} \tag{19}$$

Substituting (19) into (18) and noting that $\sum_{i=1}^{N} k_i = L$, we get

$$S \geq \frac{1}{2} \left(\sum_{i=1}^{N} \sqrt{q_i} \right)^2 + 1 \tag{20}$$

The lower bound in (20) is very useful for evaluating the relative performance of any particular cycle because it is independent of k_i, $(i=1,2,\ldots,N)$ and L.

3.3 Cycle Design Procedure

Our discussion of cycle design is based on the following considerations:

(i) The cycle length L must not exceed a pre-specified value L^*. This maximum cycle length is determined by the amount of memory used to store the broadcast cycle.

(ii) The response time of any given request must not exceed $T^* + 1$. This implies that the inter-appearance gaps T_r^i must not exceed T^* for all r and i.

(iii) The mean response time over all requests is to be minimized.

Note that L^* and T^* must not be smaller than N, the total number of pages.

For a given frequency vector $\underline{k} = (k_1, \cdots, k_N)$ where $\sum_{i=1}^{N} k_i = L$, the number of possible broadcast cycles is $J(\underline{k}) = \dfrac{L!}{k_1! \cdots k_N!}$. It is not possible to enumerate all the cycles and determine the one that satisfies the conditions mentioned above. We have therefore developed a heuristic algorithm to design a near-optimal cycle. Our algorithm is based on the results in (17) and (19). A brief description of this algorithm is given below (for a detailed description, see [5,6]).

For a given cycle length L, perform the following steps:

(i) Select the k_i's such that $\sum_{i=1}^{N} k_i = L$, and that $\dfrac{k_i}{k_j}$ is as close as possible to $\dfrac{\sqrt{q_i}}{\sqrt{q_j}}$.

(ii) Ideally, allocate cycle position to pages such that for any given page i, the inter-appearance gaps of page i in the cycle are equal. Where this is not possible, the pages with higher request probabilities are given priority.

Consider now the range of feasible cycle lengths $N \leq L \leq L^*$, use the two steps above repeatedly and choose the cycle where the overall mean response time, S, is smallest, and where the maximum inter-appearance gap of any page is not larger than T^*.

3.4 Numerical Examples

Consider a teletext system with a 100 pages. The broadcast cycle length is restricted to be not more than 1000, and the maximum acceptable response time is 301. The request probabilities for the pages are assumed to follow Zipf's law [8]. That is, if the pages are ordered such that $q_1 \geq q_2 \geq \cdots \geq q_N$ then $q_i = \frac{c}{i}$ where c is a normalization constant. This particular distribution has been shown to closely approximate real user behaviour in teletext systems [3]. The lower bound mean response time for this case, as given by (20), is 34.3.

In Figure 5, we show the results of applying the heuristic algorithm outlined above. The best cycle obtained is the one with length L=743. The overall mean response time of this cycle is S = 34.4 which is only 0.29% higher than the lower bound. In Figure 6, we show the page frequencies and inter-appearance gaps of the cycle of length 743 for selected pages. The maximum inter-appearance gap of any page is 223.

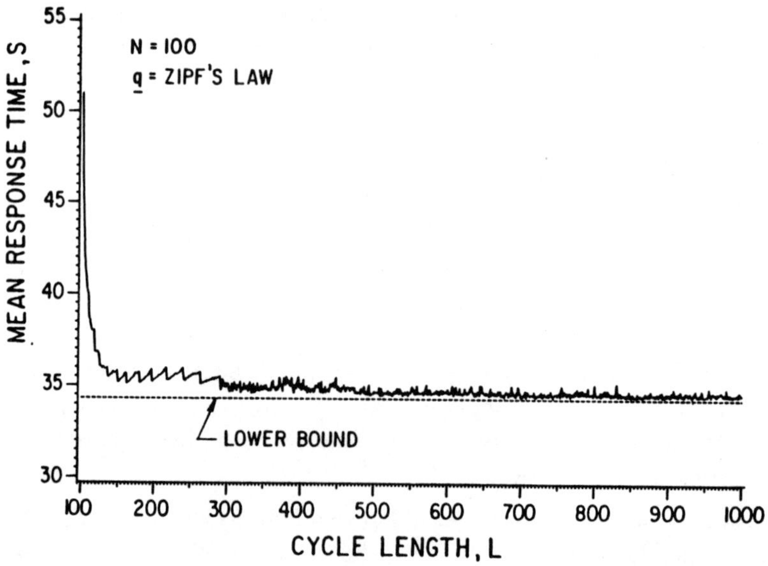

Figure 5. Mean Response Time vs. Cycle Length

i	k_i	T_r^i, $r = 1, \cdots, k_i$
1	41	19 19 19 19 19 18 18 18 18 18 18 18 18 18 18 18 18 18 18 18 18 18 18 18 18 18 18 18 18 18 18 18 18 18 18 18 18 18 18 18 18
10	13	57 57 57 57 57 57 58 58 57 57 57 57 57
20	9	82 82 82 82 83 83 83 83 83
30	7	107 106 107 105 106 106 106
40	6	123 125 124 124 124 123
50	6	122 124 124 123 124 126
60	5	149 148 146 151 149
70	5	149 140 161 145 148
80	4	185 186 190 182
90	4	169 203 178 193
100	4	168 213 195 167

Figure 6. Page Frequencies and Inter-appearance Gaps (Cycle Length = 743)

It is also instructive to compare probabilistic page broadcasting with the broadcast cycle approach. With probabilistic broadcasting, the optimal mean response time, as given by (14), is 67.1. Using a simple cycle of the form (1,2, · · · ,100) the overall mean response time would be $S = 51.0$. On the other hand, our heuristic algorithm yields a cycle with mean response time 34.4.

4. Conclusion

We have considered two classes of interactive information systems, called videotex and teletext, and presented analytic results for the mean response time of these systems under broadcast delivery. For teletext, the mean response time is affected by the broadcast cycle used, and an algorithm to design a near-optimal cycle is discussed. For a more complete treatment of the subject in this paper, the reader is referred to [4,5,6].

5. Acknowledgement

This research has been supported in part by the Natural Sciences and Engineering Research Council of Canada.

6. References

[1] Kleinrock, L., *Queueing Systems Volume 1: Theory,* Wiley-Interscience, 1975.

[2] Conway, R.W., Maxwell, W.L., and Miller, L.W., *Theory of Scheduling,* Addison Wesley, 1967.

[3] Gecsei, J., *The Architecture of Videotex Systems,* Prentice-Hall, 1983.

[4] Wong, J.W. and Ammar, M.H. "Analysis of Broadcast Delivery in a Videotex System," IEEE Transactions on Computers C-34 (9), Sept. 1985, 863-866.

[5] Ammar, M.H. and Wong, J.W. "The Design of Teletext Broadcast Cycles," to appear in Performance Evaluation.

[6] Ammar, M.H. "Performance Analysis of Information Systems Using Broadcast Delivery," Ph.D Thesis, Department of Electrical Engineering, University of Waterloo, 1985.

[7] Lam, S. S., "Queueing Networks with Population Size Constraints," IBM Journal of Research and Development 21 (7), July 1977, 370-378.

[8] Zipf, G.K., *Human Behaviour and the Principle of Least Effort,* Addison-Wesley, 1949.

Modelling the Delay in 'Moving Server' Random Access Protocols

Mart L. Molle
Computer Systems Research Institute
University of Toronto
Toronto, Canada M5S 1A4

Abstract — Several methods for controlling access to a distributed multiaccess communications channel can be modelled as 'moving server' queueing systems. Here the server marches down the time axis at some fixed rate, searching for the arrival of the next customer in need of some service. When he finds one, he pauses to offer service to that customer and then resumes his march down the time axis. The difference between this moving server model and ordinary queueing systems is in the walking time overhead. First we show how to derive the exact value of the mean customer delay for the M/G/1 queue with moving server overhead in both discrete and continuous time. Then we apply this result to the analysis of two random access protocols that fit the model and for which no delay models previously existed. First, we find approximate results for the mean packet delay in the Virtual Time CSMA protocol, with and without Head-of-the-Line priority classes. These results are approximations because our model does not explicitly include the backoff algorithm. Second, we can find the exact expression for the mean packet delay in a variation of Capetanakis' Dynamic Tree Conflict Resolution Algorithm that uses a sliding window to admit packets to each conflict resolution epoch.

I. The Model: 'Moving Server' Queueing Systems

Consider the following variation on ordinary queueing systems of the type M/M/1, M/G/1, etc. Instead of asking the customers to come to the server (and join a central queue to obtain his service), we require the server to come to the customers. Customers 'arrive' to points on the time axis, and then wait there until the server reaches that point in his walk down the time line. The actions of the server consist of walking down the time line at a fixed rate, pausing to offer service to each customer as he encounters them. Our model is similar to the well-known literature on cyclic multiqueue systems (used to model polling systems or token ring LANs) [6, 3] and to the classical 'machine repairman' problem in Operations Research. However, the novelty on our work is that the server traverses an *open* path (i.e., the time line) rather than a closed cycle. As a consequence, the customer arrival process resembles that in an open queueing network model [7] in the sense that the distribution of the number of customers (or, equivalently, their aggregate total service requirements) encountered by the moving server in one segment of the time line is unaffected by the time he spent traversing any earlier segments of the time line. This is quite different from cyclic queue systems, where the number of customers encountered at each queue (or per unit distance in the continuous case [2]) depends on the time that has elapsed since his last visit to this queue. As will become clear below, this difference allows us to solve for the mean delay in such moving server systems in an elementary way by transforming the system into a *synthetic queueing problem* as defined below.

We permit both discrete and continuous time operation in our moving server queueing system so that both synchronous ('slotted') and asynchronous ('unslotted') protocols, respectively, can be modelled. In continuous time, we assume that the interarrival times are exponential. In discrete time, possible arrival points are regularly spaced once every ω time units. The number of arrival points between successive customer arrivals is geometrically distributed. It should be clear that we have a *memoryless* arrival process in both cases. We also assume that customers' service times are independent and either generally distributed in the continuous time model, or else drawn independently (based on a general pdf) from a countable set of allowable values in the discrete time model. (The restriction to a particular set of allowable service times in discrete time is necessary to ensure that events, such as customer's entries into service and departures from service, only occur at multiples of ω — more on this below.)

The model of a moving server system described above differs only slightly from the familiar M/G/1 queueing system [4]. This difference is in the actions of the server. Whenever he is *not* offering service to some customer, we require him to walk down the time line looking for customers to serve instead of simply waiting for the next customer to come to him. And while he is walking, he either walks at an *accelerated* rate (say η times faster than the advance of real time) if he has fallen behind real time, or else in lock step with real time otherwise. We note that in the first case, some time will elapse between the completion of service for kth customer and the start of service for the k+1st customer even if the k+1st customer arrived *before* the completion of service for the kth customer. However, the system reduces to an "ordinary" M/G/1 queue in the limit as $\eta \rightarrow \infty$.

II. Finding the Waiting Time using a Synthetic Queueing System

Ordinary queueing systems are said to be *work conserving* in the sense that whenever there is work to be done, the server is busy performing useful work [4]. If we consider only service to customers as work, then our moving server queueing systems are clearly *not* work conserving because waiting customers may be delayed while the otherwise-idle server walks down the time line to the next customer's arrival point. (It should be clear that the time he spends walking in lock-step with real time does not delay the entry of any customer into service and hence need not be viewed as work.)

Thus, for ease of analysis, we shall *define* our moving server system to be work conserving by treating the time that the server spends "catching up" at rate η as work, and charging this catch-up time to the service times of the customers responsible for delaying him. In view of the discussion above, we see that the total work attributed to a customer consists of two components (which map onto the two categories of work mentioned before), namely a 'resting' component, X_R (during which the server is stopped at the customer's arrival point, offering him service), and a 'scanning' component, X_S (during which the server is moving at rate η in an effort to regain the time lost while he was resting). Since $X_S = X_R/(\eta - 1)$, we have that the total work attributed to the customer is

$$\Phi(X_R) = X_R \frac{\eta}{\eta - 1}. \tag{1}$$

Obviously, in continuous time, X_R is simply the customer's service time. However, in discrete time the calculation of X_R requires some care. Recall that while he is trying to catch up, the server 'steps' across the idle arrival points at a rate η times faster than the advance of real time. Now since successive arrival points are separated by a distance ω on the time line, *real* time must be advancing at the rate of one 'step' every ω time units and hence the moving server must be spending ω/η on each step ***even in the absence of a customer.*** But when a customer is encountered, one such a step will already have taken place, to trigger his entry into service. Therefore in discrete time, X_R must represent the *excess* customer service time beyond the ω/η time units expended on the server's initial advance.

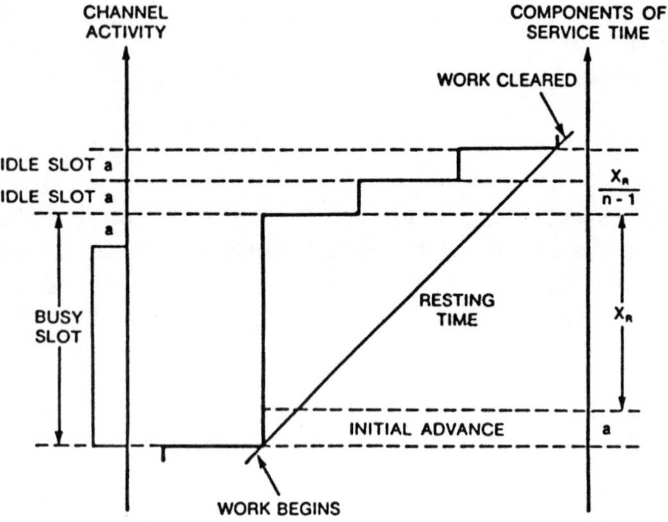

Figure 1: The work associated with serving a customer in the discrete time model.

Unfortunately, even this broadened definition of work does not make the moving server system any easier to analyze, because the catch-up time exhibits some odd properties. Its 'service' will be *preempted* in favour of service to real customers whenever possible (i.e., whenever the server reaches the arrival point of another customer in his walk). And consequently, the catch-up time overhead attributed to a given customer continues to delay subsequent customers long after his departure. Fortunately, it is a simple matter to (temporarily) define away these complications by transforming the problem into a *synthetic queueing system* in which the service (inflated to include catch-up time) for the same sequence of customers is carried out *non-preemptively*. In other words, if the jth customer (within a single busy period, say) were to arrive to the moving server system at time $a^{(j)}$, then the corresponding customer in the synthetic system would also arrive at $a^{(j)}$. And if his actual service time in the moving server system were $X^{(j)}$, then his service time in the synthetic system would be $\Psi(X_R^{(j)})$, where $X_R^{(j)}=X^{(j)}$ in the continuous time model, and $X_R^{(j)}=X^{(j)}-\omega/\eta$ in discrete time. Clearly the waiting times in the synthetic queueing system upper bound

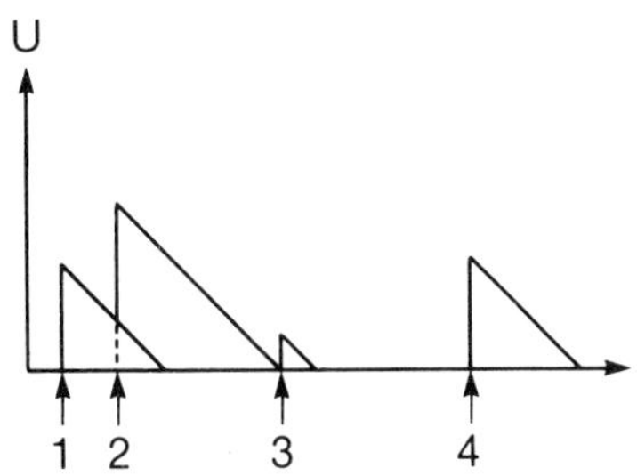

2 (a): An Ordinary Queueing System showing the Unfinished Work

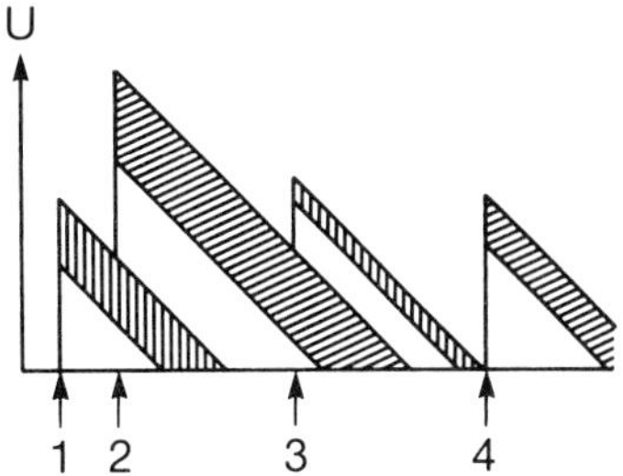

2(d): The Synthetic Queueing System for the same set of arrivals. (The scan-time component of service is shaded.)

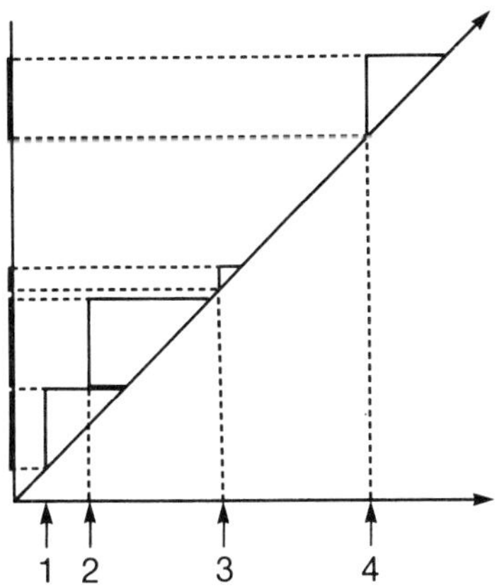

2(b): Unfinished Work Redrawn so that time advances up the page. (The upper edge of the blocks of 'work' may be interpreted as position of the server as a function of time.)

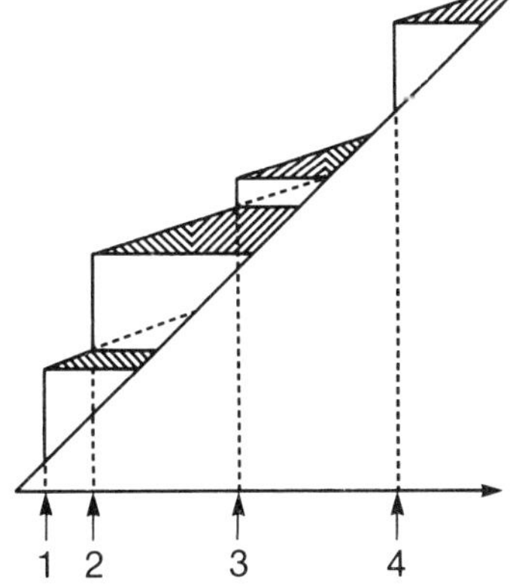

2(c): Figure 1(b) redrawn to add moving server overhead.

Figure 2: Ordinary, moving server, and synthetic queueing systems.

the waiting times in the corresponding moving server system. We will see below that the relationship between the moving server and synthetic systems may be exploited to give us the *exact* expression for the mean waiting time in the moving server system in terms of the mean waiting time in the synthetic system.

At this point we observe that the synthetic queueing system is nothing more than an ordinary M/G/1 queue. (Note that for this to be true in discrete time, the *inflated* service times, $\Psi(X_R)$, must be evenly divisible by ω so that every customer's service will begin and end at an arrival point.) It is well known [4,9] that the mean waiting time in an M/G/1 queueing system is

$$W = \frac{W_0}{1-\lambda\overline{X}} = \begin{cases} \overline{X}\omega\dfrac{\rho(C_b^2+1)}{2(1-\rho)} & \text{continuous time} \\ \overline{X}\omega\dfrac{\rho(C_b^2+1)-p}{2(1-\rho)} & \text{discrete time} \end{cases} \tag{2}$$

where $\overline{X}$ is the average service time, $C_b^2=\overline{X^2}/(\overline{X})^2-1$ is the squared coefficient of variation of service time, $\rho=\lambda\overline{X}$ is the utilization of the server, and p is the probability that a customer arrives at an arrival point in discrete time. Thus to find the mean waiting time in the synthetic queueing system, say W, we need only substitute $\Psi(\overline{X_R})$ for $\overline{X}$ and $\lambda\Psi(\overline{X_R})$ for ρ in Eq. (2). It remains to show how the the mean waiting time for the moving server system, $\widetilde{W}$, can be expressed in terms of W, $\Psi(\cdot)$, etc. The key step is outlined in the following paragraph.

Let $\tau^{(j)}$ be the *departure* time of the jth customer of the busy period in the synthetic queueing system, and let $\tau^{(0)}$ be the time at which the busy period began (i.e., the departure time of the "zeroth customer"). Then obviously

$$\tau^{(j)}-\tau^{(j-1)} = \Psi(X_R^{(j)})$$

because of the definition of the synthetic queueing system. However, it is also true (but far less obvious!) that in the moving server system, the server moves *exactly* from $\tau^{(j-1)}$ to $\tau^{(j)}$ along the time line while his working on the 'walk time' overhead attributed to the jth customer.

Let us now compare the waiting times in the two systems for the kth customer of the busy period, assuming that his arrival time, $a^{(k)}$ falls within the interval $\left(\tau^{(j-1)},\tau^{(j)}\right]$ for some $j<k$. In the synthetic

queueing system, his waiting time will be the sum of the remaining service time for the jth customer plus the total service times for the $k-j-1$ customers ahead of him in the queue on his arrival. But $1/\eta$th of this waiting time is actually 'walk time' overhead — enough time for the server to walk from $a^{(k)}$ to $\tau^{(k-1)}$, *and all of this would have been avoided by the customer in the moving server system.* Hence

$$\tilde{W} = \Psi^{-1}(W).$$

In other words, we can obtain $\tilde{W}$ directly from Eq. (2) merely by substituting $\overline{X_R}$ for $\overline{X}$ and $\lambda\,\Psi(\overline{X_R})$ for ρ in Eq. (2), i.e.,

$$W = \frac{W_0}{1-\Psi(\overline{X_R})\lambda}, \tag{3}$$

where $\Psi(W_0)$ is the average delay due to the customer in service in the synthetic queueing system.

Now consider the generalization of the problem to a moving server system with P Head-of-the-Line (HOL) priority classes. In this case, we need P separate time lines — one for the arrivals of each class — with a moving server walking along each one. Whenever *any* of the servers encounters a customer, *all* of them stop until the service is complete. Thereafter, only the class P server begins walking at rate η_P, and when he has caught up with real time the class $P-1$ server begins walking at rate η_{P-1}, and so on. We say that the class p server is *busy* whenever he is stopped (either because some customer is being served, or because the class $p+1$ server is still busy) or walking at rate η_p, and that he is *idle* otherwise. Thus, from the point of view of class p, any customer from any priority class with an actual service time (excluding the initial advance in the discrete time case) of X_R actually represents

$$\Psi(X_R,p) \equiv X_R \prod_{i=p}^{P} \frac{\eta_i}{\eta_i - 1} \tag{4}$$

units of 'work' to the class p server, out of which the class p server is stopped (and seemingly offering service to the customer) for $\Psi(X_R,p+1)$ time units, and moving at rate η_p for the rest.

In the case of the synthetic queueing system with P HOL priority classes, we assume that the kth class p customer of the busy period arrives at time $a^{(k,p)}$, which falls within the jth service interval (regardless of class) in the busy period, $j \le k$. Then this customer's waiting time is the sum of the remainder of the jth service interval (i.e., $\tau^{(j)} - a^{(k,p)}$), the entire service times for the $n_{i,p}^{(j)}$ class i customers in the queue on his arrival, $i=p,p+1,\ldots,P$, and the $m_{i,p}^{(j)}$ class i customers that arrive during his waiting time but are served before him, $i=p+1,\ldots,P$. Taking expectations, we have

$$W_p = W_{0,p} + \sum_{i=p}^{P} \Psi(\overline{X_i},p)\lambda_i W_i + \sum_{i=p+1}^{P} \Psi(\overline{X_i},p)\lambda_i W_p, \tag{5}$$

where

$$W_{0,p} = \frac{1}{2}\sum_{i=1}^{P}\lambda_i \Psi(\overline{X_i^2}). \tag{6}$$

Now consider the waiting time for the kth class p customer in the corresponding P-class HOL moving server priority queueing system. First, even though $\{\tilde{m}_{i,p}^{(j)}\}$ may be differ from $\{m_{i,p}^{(j)}\}$ because class i customers are allowed to preempt the 'walk time' overhead that is needed to cover the motion of the class p server for all $i \geq p$, it should be clear that

(a) the same set of class i customers arrived between $\tau^{(0)}$ and $a^{(k,p)}$ in both systems, for all $1 \leq i \leq P$,

(b) the server has accomplished the same total amount of work between $\tau^{(0)}$ and $a^{(k,p)}$ in both systems, and hence

(c) the total amount of work remaining in the system at $a^{(k,p)}$ must be the same in both systems.

Out of this total, the only savings in waiting time for the kth class p customer in the moving server system over the synthetic system is the time for the class p server to walk from $a^{(k,p)}$ to what would have been the beginning of his service time in the synthetic queueing system.

Next, consider the contribution to the waiting time for the kth class p customer from customers that arrive after him but enter service before him because they belong to strictly higher priority classes. Since the 'walk time' overhead added to their service times would be used to move the class p server even further along the time line beyond $a^{(k,p)}$, only that part of these subsequent customers' service times that represents actual service or the 'walk time' overhead due classes $p+1,\ldots,P$ matters to our class p customer. Thus, letting $\{W_p\}$ and $\{\widetilde{W}_p\}$ represent the mean waiting times for each class in the synthetic system and moving server system, respectively, we have that

$$\widetilde{W}_p = W_{0,p+1} + \sum_{i=p}^{P} \Psi(\overline{X_i},p+1)\lambda_i W_i + \sum_{i=p+1}^{P} \Psi(\overline{X_i},p+1)\lambda_i \widetilde{W}_p, \tag{7}$$

or as one can easily verify, that

$$\tilde{W}_p = \frac{W_{0,p+1}}{\left(1-\sum_{i=p}^{P}\Psi(\overline{X_i},p)\lambda_i\right)\left(1-\sum_{i=p+1}^{P}\Psi(\overline{X_i},p+1)\lambda_i\right)} \tag{8}$$

III. Application to Virtual Time CSMA

Virtual time CSMA [9,10] is an alternative to the well-known Non-Persistent, 1-Persistent and p-Persistent CSMA protocols [5]. In Virtual Time CSMA, the method of selecting packets for transmission involves having all stations simulate the actions of a moving server in a distributed way through the use of 'virtual time' clocks. These virtual clocks remain stopped when the channel is sensed busy and run (at rate η if they are behind real time or at rate unity otherwise) when the channel is sensed busy. A station transmits each packet as soon as its virtual time clock passes that packet's arrival time.

Although the moving server model makes no provision for the effect of collisions and retransmissions on the mean packet delay (which is unavoidable in all CSMA protocols, including Virtual Time CSMA), it can certainly be used to model the *initial delay*, T_0, from the generation of each packet to its first transmission. We can approximate the remainder of the delay using the standard 'equilibrium' formula

$$T = T_0 + \left(\frac{G}{S} - 1\right) T_R + 1 + a, \tag{9}$$

where $G/S-1$ is the average number of retransmissions, T_R is the mean delay imposed by the backoff algorithm, and $1+a$ is the transmission and propagation time during its final (successful) transmission.

It is worth noting here that in neither the synchronous (slotted) nor the asynchronous (unslotted) versions of the protocol is it the case that every packet transmitted by some station becomes a customer in the moving server system. In the synchronous case, all packets that arrived within a 'window' of duration $\omega = \eta a$ are treated as a single customer whose service time depends on the number of packets in that window. If we let the slot lengths be a for idle slots, $1+a$ for successful transmissions and $b+a$ for collisions (where we use $b<1$ to represent collision detection), then the respective customer service times become 0, $1/(\eta-1)$ and $b/(\eta-1)$. In the asynchronous case, only the *first* transmission following each channel idle period represents a customer in the moving server system. The packets (if any) whose transmissions begin within the next a time units merely collide with the first transmission, changing his service time. Note that this propagation time effect

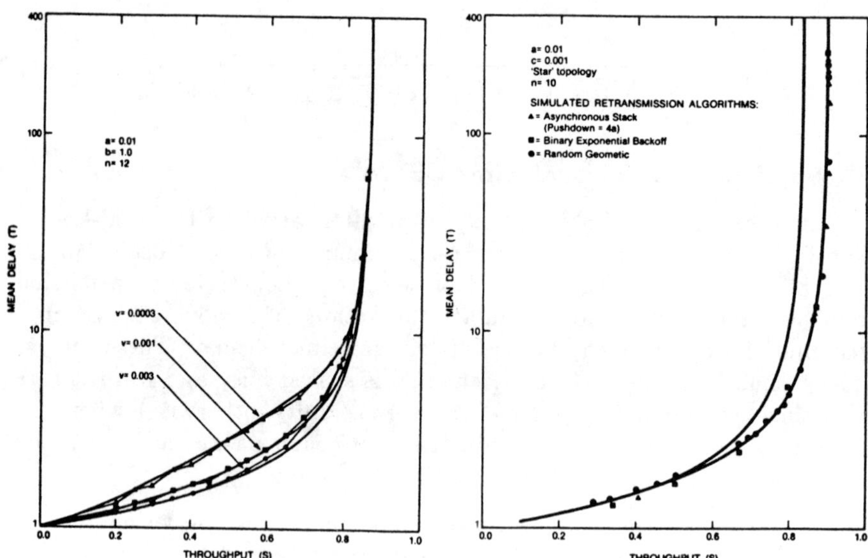

Figure 3: Simulation and analysis of the delay in Virtual Time CSMA, (a) Synchronous operation with three retransmission rates, and (b) Asynchronous operation with three backoff algorithms.

introduces an inaccuracy in the model, since the customer interarrival times now consist of a small "gap" that *cannot* contain any customer arrivals (i.e., the *vulnerable period* for the previous transmission) followed by an exponential inter-packet generation time with mean $1/G$. Furthermore, the size of the gap may be either a if the virtual clocks are caught up with real time when the first transmission begins, or ηa if they are behind. Thus our results in the asynchronous case show upper and lower bounds on T_0 based on exponential customer interarrival times with the same means as the two extreme cases, namely $1/G+a$ and $1/G+\eta a$, respectively. In all cases, these analytical results agree with our detailed simulations remarkably well.

IV. Application to Prioritized Virtual Time CSMA

There is an elegant way to incorporate P-class Head-of-the-Line priorities into Virtual Time CSMA through the use of P virtual clocks (moving servers), one for each class [9,11]. Here the class p virtual clocks at each station can only move (at rate η_p, say) when the channel is idle *and* the virtual clocks from classes $p+1, p+2, \ldots, P$ have all caught up with real time.

It is interesting to note that this HOL priority scheduling comes essentially "for free" (i.e., it imposes no additional channel overhead), and that with proper choice of $\{\eta_p\}$ it need not have any influence on the overall average packet delay across all classes. All that happens is that the order in which the packets are transmitted is permuted. In Figure 4, for example, we have managed to add HOL priority queueing with two classes to the Virtual Time CSMA system without changing the length of the busy period. This happened because we let $\eta_2 = 2\eta$ and $\eta_1 = 2\eta - 1$, so that total amount of work (including 'moving server' overhead) for each packet is the same in both systems, i.e.,

$$\Psi(X) = X \frac{\eta}{\eta - 1} = X \frac{(2\eta)}{(2\eta) - 1} \frac{(2\eta - 1)}{(2\eta - 1) - 1} = \Psi(X, 1)$$

And furthermore, if half the traffic were to originate from each class, then the apparent offered load during a busy period would be ηG for the entire time if there were no priority classes, and either $(2\eta)\, G/2 = \eta G$ when only the high class is active or $G/2 + (2\eta - 1)\, G/2 = \eta G$ when both classes are active.

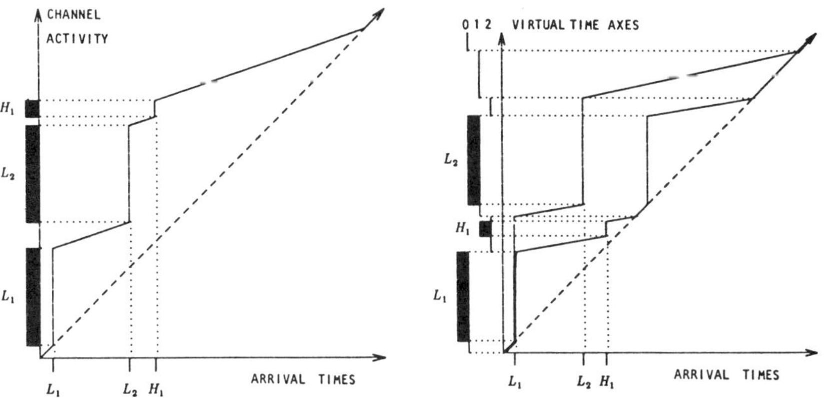

Figure 4: A single busy period in (a) Virtual Time CSMA, and (b) Prioritized Virtual Time CSMA.

To find the mean waiting time for class p packets, we can once again estimate the initial delay from the result for the moving server system (i.e., Eq. (8) in this case). Here too, we must be content with upper and lower bounds on the delay as a function of throughput, because of the state dependence in service times (depending on which priority classes are enabled) and arrival rates (because of the state dependence in apparent load and virtual clock speed for the given priority class — and hence probability of being "erased"). Thus, to get an upper bound to delay, we use the highest state-dependent arrival rate and packet transmission times, and to get a lower bound to delay we use the opposite extreme values. Obviously, the resulting upper and lower bounds are somewhat weaker than the corresponding bounds in the non-priority case. But at least the model is still easy to solve for any number of priority classes, different packet lengths per class, different arrival rates per class, and different virtual clock rates per class.

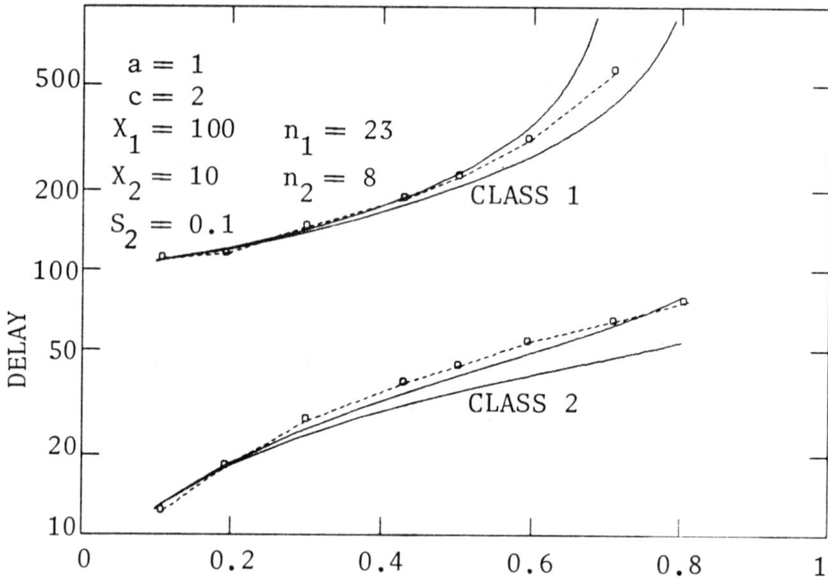

Figure 5: Simulation and analysis of the delay in Prioritized Virtual Time CSMA with two classes.

V. Application to a 'Sliding Window' Capetanakis-type Tree Algorithm

Tree Conflict Resolution Algorithms differ from Aloha- and CSMA-type algorithms in that they resolve collisions algorithmically as they are encountered before continuing on with the transmission of subsequent packets [1,8]. The protocol we consider here uses a 'sliding window' to admit packets to the current *epoch*: all packets whose arrival times fall between $(k-1)\omega$ and $k\omega$ are transmitted in the kth epoch. All packets admitted to an epoch are transmitted in the first slot of that epoch; the epoch continues until it becomes clear to all stations that all those packets have been transmitted successfully. This is accomplished by arranging for all stations to perform in lock-step a preorder traversal of a *conflict resolution tree,* where all collision slots represent non-terminal nodes having exactly two successors, and all idle slots and successful transmissions represent terminal nodes. We note that since conflict resolution trees are clearly *binary trees,* they can contain only an odd number of nodes, and hence the duration of an epoch (in slots) can be any odd integer.

The mean packet delay can be found exactly for this protocol as the sum of the waiting time up to the point where the packet gets admitted into an epoch, and the time from the start of that epoch to the successful transmission of the packet [12]. If we view *windows* as the customers, each having a complete conflict resolution epoch's worth of slots as its service requirement, it is clear that the first component of delay can be found as a moving server queueing system in discrete time. The second component can be found using other techniques that exploit the recursive structure of the conflict resolution algorithm [12]. (This same analysis is also used to give us the first two moments of the conflict resolution epoch lengths for use in the M/G/1 formula.)

Recall that in the discrete time analysis, we required all inflated customer service times to be divisible by ω. But here we are considering a slotted system, where each 'step' of the algorithm (idle slot, success or collision) requires one unit of time. Thus the initial advance at the start of a customer's service should last for one slot and advance the server by ω slots. Hence, to satisfy the service time restriction we require

$$(K-1)/(\omega-1) \in I^{+}, \quad K=1,3,5,\ldots \tag{10}$$

which is clearly true for $\omega=1+2/N$, $N \in I^{+}$, and for which window sizes of 3 and 2 are the most useful.[1] It is interesting to note that non-conflict epochs do not appear as customers in the synthetic queueing system, even though many of them represent epochs in which a single successful packet transmission took place! This is because the *excess* service time for such 'customers' beyond the time required by the moving server to walk past that arrival point is zero.

---

[1] Actually, maximum capacity occurs at $\omega \approx 2.67$, but $\omega=3,2$ differ in capacity from this maximum by only one unit in the third and second decimal places, respectively.

In Figure 6, we show the resulting delay curves for the sliding window tree algorithm with window sizes of 3 and 2, together with some simulation points for ω=3 and Capetanakis' upper and lower bounds for the Dynamic Tree protocol, a slightly different protocol that exhibits the same behaviour under heavy load.

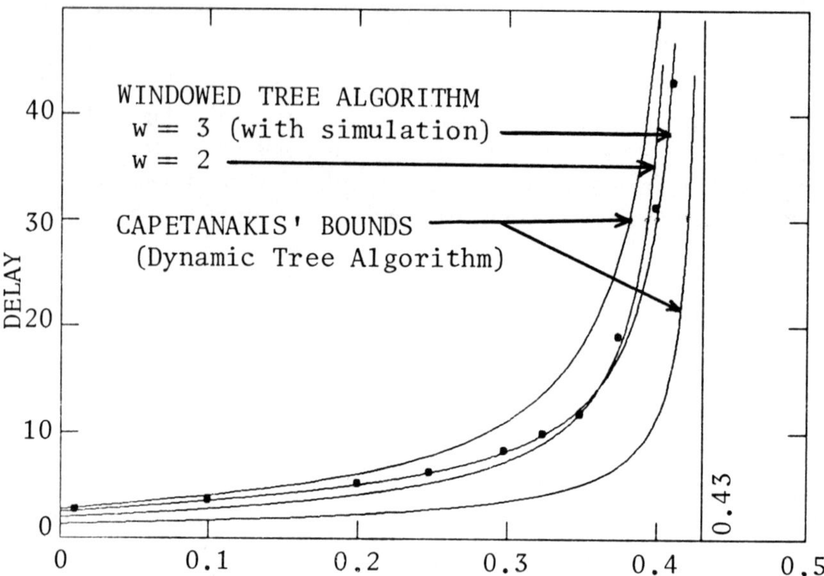

Figure 6: Simulation and analysis of the delay in the Windowed Tree Conflict Resolution Algorithm

VI. Conclusions

We have outlined a general method for finding the mean customer waiting time in M/G/1 queueing systems with 'moving server' overhead. The method uses a novel transformation of the moving server problem into an ordinary M/G/1 'synthetic queueing' problem that allows us to write down the solution almost by inspection. The results are quite interesting because they can be used to model the delay in a variety of 'sliding window' type random access protocols for which there was no previous analytical model of delay.

Several extensions of this work come immediately to mind. These include further applications to other random access protocols, for example Virtual Time CSMA with other types of priority structure such as *time-dependent* priorities, and sliding window tree algorithms using the more efficient 'level skipping' conflict resolution. We are also pursuing generalizations of the underlying moving server queueing model to the case of M/G/1 with generalized busy periods.

References

[1] J. I. Capetanakis, "Tree Algorithms for Packet Broadcast Channels," *IEEE Transactions on Information Theory* **IT-25**, pp.505-515 (September 1979).

[2] E. G. Coffman, Jr. and E. N. Gilbert, "A Continuous Polling System with Constant Service Times," *Abstracts of Papers, 1985 IEEE International Symposium on Information Theory* (June 23-28, 1985).

[3] M. J. Ferguson and Y. J. Aminetzah, "Exact Results for Nonsymmetric Token Ring Systems," *IEEE Transactions on Communications* **COM-33**(3), pp.223-231 (March 1985).

[4] L. Kleinrock, *Queueing Systems, Vol I., Theory,* Wiley-Interscience, New York (1975).

[5] L. Kleinrock and F. A. Tobagi, "Packet Switching in Radio Channels: Part I — Carrier Sense Multiple-Access Modes and Their Throughput-Delay Characteristics," *IEEE Transactions on Communications* **COM-23**(12), pp.1400-1416 (December 1975).

[6] A. G. Konheim and B. Meister, "Waiting Lines and Times in a System with Polling," *Journal of the ACM* **21**(3), pp.470-490 (July 1974).

[7] E. D. Lazowska, J. Zahorjan, G. S. Graham, and K. C. Sevcik, *Quantitative System Performance: Computer System Analysis using Queueing Network Models,* Prentice-Hall, Englewood Cliffs (1984).

[8] J. L. Massey, "Collision-Resolution Algorithms and Random-Access Communications," in *Multi-User Communications,* ed. G. Longo, Springer-Verlag, New York (1981). (preprint: UCLA Report no. UCLA-ENG-8016, April 1980).

[9] M. L. Molle, "Unifications and Extensions of the Multiple Access Communications Problem," CSD Report No. 810730 (UCLA-ENG-8118), Computer Science Department, University of California, Los Angeles (July 1981). Ph.D. Dissertation.

[10] M. L. Molle and L. Kleinrock, "Virtual Time CSMA: Why Two Clocks are Better than One," *IEEE Transactions on Communications* **COM-33**(9), pp.919-933 (September 1985).

[11] M. L. Molle and M.-W. Wu, "Prioritized Virtual Time CSMA: Head-of-the-Line Priorities Without Channel Overhead," *IEEE International Conference on Communications*, pp.35.4.1-35.4.6 (June 1985).

[12] G. C. Polyzos, *Tree Conflict Resolution Algorithms: The Non-Homogeneous Case,* Department of Electrical Engineering, University of Toronto, Toronto (December 1984). (M.A.Sc. Thesis).

Capacitated Facility Location

Aaron Kershenbaum
Polytechnic Institute of New York

Abstract

The problem of locating capacity limited facilities in a network is considered. At each potential site, one of a given set of facilities may be placed. We are given the facility cost and capacity alternatives at each site and the cost of connecting terminals to these facilities. The objective is to select the size (possibly none) of the facility at each location and to select the association of terminals to facilities, minimizing the overall cost without violating any of the capacity constraints. An algorithm for the solution to this problem is presented and its effectiveness and computational complexity are discussed.

1. Introduction and Problem Statement

The problem of locating facilities arises in the design of most types of communication networks. In centralized networks, where terminals communicate with or through a single central site, the problem arises in locating concentrators. In distributed networks, both telephone networks and computer communication networks, the problem arises in the location of switches. In broadcast radio networks and satellite networks, the problem arises in the location of repeaters and earth stations. In all of these situations, the facility location problem is only part of the overall network design problem. There are no known procedures for carrying out an entire design of such networks reliably with a single procedure. It is therefore necessary to use a design methodology which decomposes the overall problem into subproblems and solves these subproblems individually using as input assumptions about the solutions to the remaining subproblems. After solutions to all the subproblems are obtained, the process is iterated until the input assumptions converge.

Realistic problems often contain hundreds of terminal sites, many of which can be potential facility locations. The large size of the problems encountered and the iterative design methodology described above, requires that we develop efficient and reliable algorithms for the solution of the subproblems. Ideally, we would like to develop algorithms which guarantee optimal solutions and also guarantee modest running times. Unfortunately, even after making simplifying assumptions, these subproblems are still intractable from this idealized point of view. We thus seek heuristics which will perform reliably, i.e., which have reasonable running time and which produce solutions within some reasonable bound of the optimum most of the time. There is generally no guarantee either on the running time or on the solution quality, but both can be verified empirically. In particular, it is desireable that the algorithm produce as a by-product a bound on the optimal solution so that it is at least possible to verify the quality of the solution obtained. The algorithm described here has this desireable property.

We now turn to the formal specification of the facility location problem. We are given a set of potential facility locations, i=1,...M, and a set of terminal locations, j=1,...N. In general the terminal and facility locations may overlap. Each terminal, j, has b_j units of traffic. The cost of connecting the terminal at location j to a facility at location i is a_{ij}. We are also given the cost, c_{ik} of placing a facility of size k at location i and the capacity, p_k, of a facility of size k. Every terminal must be assigned to a facility and the total traffic of all terminals assigned to a facility may not exceed its capacity. The problem can thus be stated as:

$$\text{minimize} \sum_{i,j} a_{ij}\, x_{ij} + \sum_{i,k} c_{ik}\, y_{ik}$$

subject to:

$$\sum_i x_{ij} = b_j$$

$$\sum_j x_{ij} <= \sum_k p_k\, y_{ik}$$

$$x_{ij} <= b_j \sum_k y_{ik}$$

$$\sum_k y_{ik} <= 1$$

$$x_{ij},\ y_{ik} = 0 \text{ or } 1$$

where x_{ij} is 1 if terminal j is connected to facility i and y_{ik} is 1 if a facility of size k is selected at location i. Initially, we will discuss the case where $b_j = 1$ and then later describe how the procedure can be extended to the more general case.

The problem description above is fairly general and adequately models many realistic problems which arise in practice. It is possible to model the cost of a trunk connecting a facility to a central site simply by adding this cost to the facility cost and to reflect the cost of different speed trunks associated with different capacity facilities in the separate c_{ik}. A cost per port on a facility can be added to the a_{ij}. The model is not, however, totally general. It does not take into account the cost of directly connecting facilities to one another, which is typically part of distributed network design. It also only approximately models the cost of multipoint lines connecting a group of terminals to a facility in centralized networks. Thus, this model is, as described above, capable in general of describing a subproblem within the overall context of a network design problem.

Problems similar to this have been much studied. The simplest such problem is the set covering problem. In this case, we are given a set, S, and a collection of subsets of S. The object is to find a minimum cardinality collection of subsets covering (i.e., containing all the elements of) S. A slightly more general form of this problem is to associate weights with the subsets and to minimize the total weight of the selected subsets rather than the cardinality. Garfinkel and Nemhauser [4] and Christophides [1] describe algorithms for the solution of the set covering problem. Another approach to the set covering problem is given by Jeroslow [7].

Another even more closely related problem is the uncapacitated facility location problem. In this case, we are given a set of terminals and potential facility locations, exactly as we are given here. The facilities are assumed to have infinite capacity and hence, there is no need to consider a capacity constraint or more than one type of facility. Uncapacitated facility location problems, while generally structurally similar to the capacitated facility location problem studied here, are easier to solve. Erlenkotter [2] gives an algorithm which works well in practice for the soluton to the uncapacitated facility location problem. The procedure here can be considered to be a generalization of his procedure. Handler [6] also describes algorithms which can be applied to this problem.

There has been work done on heuristics for the solution of the capacitated facility location problem in the context of finding concentrators in centralized teleprocessing networks. Tang [12] and McGregor [8] have described algorithms capable of handling problems of realistic size efficiently. Both procedures deal only with a single facility size, however, and neither offers a bound on performance.

Finally, the exact solution of the capacitated facility location problem itself has received some attention. Guignard and Spielberg [5] describe a procedure, also based on Erlenkotter's approach and more recently, Mirzaian [10] has proposed a procedure based on Lagrangean relaxation. Mendelson [9] has also recently proposed an approach based on cutting planes. In all of these cases, however, only a single type of facility is considered and both procedures have thus far been applied only to problems of modest size, with less than one hundred nodes. The algorithm described here is capable on treating problems with multiple facility sizes and has been successfully used, within an interactive network design tool, on problems with up to 1000 nodes.

2. Algorithm Description

The capacitated facility location problem, as stated formally above, is an integer programming problem and is not amenable to exact solution by an algorithm with reasonable running time. If we relax the problem by ignoring the integrality constraints on the x_{ij} and y_{ik}, however, it becomes a linear programming problem which can be dealt with more efficiently. We can then form the dual of this linear programming problem, yielding the following formulation (for the case $b_j=1$):

$$\text{Maximize } \sum_j v_j - \sum_i t_i$$

subject to:

(1) $a_{ij} + w_{ij} + u_i \quad >= \quad v_j$ for all j

(2) $\sum_j w_{ij} + p_k u_i \quad <= \quad c_{ik} + t_i$ for all i, k

(3) $v_j, w_{ij}, u_i, t_i >= 0$

The dual variables can be interpreted as follows. The v_j are the costs associated with satisfying the requirement at terminal j. Alternatively, they can be though of as the revinue derivable from terminal j if it were to be charged for service. The w_{ij} are penalties associated with connecting terminal j to facility i. Alternatively, they can be thought of as how much terminal j is willing to contribute to the purchase of a facility at location i in order to avoid having to connect to another more distant facility. The u_i are per unit of capacity costs associated with usage of a facility at location i. The t_i are costs associated with purchasing additional capacity at location i. Thus, the original (primal) optimization problem can be considered from the point of view of a network designer who is trying to minimize cost while the dual problem can be considered from the point of view of a network manager who is trying to maximize revenue. Indeed, Erlenkotter considers a similar analogy in [3] where he describes an extension to the uncapacitated facility location problem where there is a revenue associated with each terminal as well as a cost and the objective is to maximize the profit; i.e., the difference of the revenue and the cost.

2.1 W-Ascent

The algorithm proceeds in several phases. Initially, the u_i and t_i are set to 0. The first phase of the algorithm attempts to maximize the sum of the v_j without changing the current values of the u_i or t_i. Constraint (1) in the dual formulation above forces v_j to be no greater than the sum of the three terms on the left hand side. For any terminal, j, this constraint must hold for all facilities, i. The a_{ij} are input and the u_i are held constant throughout this phase of the algorithm. Thus, constraint (1) can be rewritten as:

$$v_j <= \min_i (d_{ij} + w_{ij})$$

where $d_{ij} = a_{ij} + u_i$, which is a constant during this phase of the algorithm.

We begin this phase with $w_{ij} = 0$ for all i and j and

$$v_j = \min_i (d_{ij})$$

and we seek to increase the v_j by increasing the w_{ij}. Constraint (2), however, limits the amount by which we can increase the w_{ij}. Using (2), we define s_i, the slack available for use in increasing the w_{ij}, to be:

$$s_i = \min_k (c_{ik} + t_i - p_{ik}\, u_i)$$

Constraint (2) then becomes:

$$\sum_j w_{ij} <= s_i$$

This W-ascent procedure then proceeds to carefully increase the v_j by increasing the w_{ij}. In doing so, it attempts to avoid wasting the w_{ij}. The algorithm does this by not increasing any w_{ij} unless it will result in an immediate increase in some v_j and furthermore, it attempts to increase the smallest possible number of w_{ij} at each step. We let m be the "level" number, i.e., the number of w_{ij} we are willing to simultaneously increase in order to increase a v_j. The w-ascent procedure follows.

Step 0: Compute s_i an d_{ij} as described above.
For each j, sort the d_{ij}. Let ds_{nj} be the nth smallest d_{ij} for a given j and ps_{nj} be the corresponding facility, i.
Set $ds_{M+1,j}$ = C, a very large number.
(Recall that M is the number of potential facility sites).
Set $w_{ij} = 0$ for all i and j.
Set m = 1
Set $v_j = ds_{ij}$

Step 1: Set $delta_1 = ds_{m+1,j} - ds_{mj}$
Set $I = \{i \mid ps_{nj} = i \text{ for } n <= m\}$
Set $delta_2 = \min_{i \varepsilon I} (S_i)$
Set delta = min ($delta_1$, $delta_2$)

Step 2: Set $v_j = v_j$ + delta
For all $i \varepsilon I$:
Set $w_{ij} = w_{ij}$ + delta
Set $s_i = s_i$ - delta

Step 3: If m < M and any S_i are still > 0:
Set m = m + 1 and return to Step 1
Otherwise, stop.

In the above procedure, I is the set of the m nearest potential facility sites, where near is measured by d_{ij} which includes u_i as well as a_{ij}. Delta is the maximum we can increase v_j by without increasing more than m w_{ij} and without violating any slack constraints.

The w-ascent procedure has a computational complexity which is $O[NM^2]$, due to Step 2. It is possible to improve the average complexity of this procedure (although not its worst case complexity) by observing that once $delta_2$ is 0 for a given j, it remains 0 for the rest of this iteration of the w-ascent procdure (but not later iterations). Such j can be flagged and skipped for the remainder of this pass through the w-ascent procedure.

This w-ascent procedure is itself a heuristic. It is possible to obtain an exact solution to the problem of maximizing the sum of the v_j given the current values of u_i and t_i by using linear programming techniques. The effort in doing so, however, is far greater than that involved in carrying out the above procedure and since this is only a single step in the overall iterative algorithm, this additional effort does not appear warranted.

Erlenkotter, in presenting his original procedure for the uncapacitated facility location algorithm [2], gives a procedure for adjusting the w_{ij} and v_{ij} by searching for situations where one v_j can be decreased and two or more others increased. In the uncapacitated case, where there are no u_i or t_i and hence no iteration, this effort was warranted but here it is not.

We can think of the w-ascent procedure as identifying terminals which are willing to contribute to the cost of a facility. In particular, terminal j is willing to contribute w_{ij} towards the purchase of a facility at location i. If each terminal contributed to the cost of only one facility and if the total traffic demand from all terminals contributing to the cost of a facility did not exceed the capacity of that facility, we could choose precisely those facilities whose cost is entirely paid for by the terminals; such facilities are identified by their s_i being 0 at the end of the w-ascent procedure. Since we are solving relaxation of the original problem, we are guaranteed that this feasible solution is optimal and the entire algorithm could terminate right here.

Unfortunately, we cannot guarantee that any of this will happen. First, in general terminals will contribute to more than one facility's cost; i.e., more than one w_{ij} will be non-zero for a given j. The w-ascent procedure above tries to minimize this problem by increasing as few w_{ij} as possible at each iteration, but it cannot guarantee success in avoiding situations where a terminal contributes to 2 or more facilities. This problem only matters if w_{ij} is not zero for more than one i which corresponds to a facility picked for inclusion in the solution. The overall procedure is to pick only facilities which have justified their inclusion by virtue of their s_i being 0. It is not, however, required that we pick all such facilities. The problem of selecting which facilities to pick among those with s_i equal to 0 is discussed below.

Another problem is that in general a facility may appear attractive to a very large number of terminals, too many for it to hold without violating its capacity constraint. The u-ascent procedure below helps to deal with this problem.

2.2 U-ascent

The u_i reflect the facility capacity constraints. Implicitly, in the w-ascent procedure above, terminals are being associated with facilities whose cost they contributing to. In a situation where too many terminals are contributing to the cost of a facility, violating its capacity constraint, we wish to make that facility appear less attractive. Alternatively, we can think of this process as increasing the revinue, reflected in the sum of the v_j, by selling space on a facility on a per unit of capacity basis rather than on a terminal by terminal basis.

The u-ascent procedure seeks out facilities which are overloaded, and seeks to increase the available slack in these facilities (which can then be used by the w-ascent procedure to increase the v_j). Looking again at constraint (1), we see that if w_{ij} is decreased by some quantity, q, and u_i is increased by q, then v_j is unchanged. Looking at constraint (2), we see that if the number of non zero w_{ij} for a given i is larger than the dominant p_k, then it is possible to increase u_i, decrease all these w_{ij} and generate slack in the constraint. Conversely, if the number of non zero w_{ij} is less than p_k, it is possible to generate additional slack by decreasing u_i.

This is exactly what the u-ascent procedure does. In carrying out the calculations, all relevant values of k (the facility size) must be checked. In some cases, specifically when then number of non zero w_{ij} is exactly equal to p_k for the dominant constraint of type (2), altering u_i has no effect on the slack. In this case, we have found it empirically best to let u_i take the largest values possible.

Note that increasing the value of u_i and decreasing the values of w_{ij} will in general decrease the number of non-zero w_{ij}. Thus, we continue decreasing (or increasing) the number of non-zero w_{ij} until it is exactly equal to p_k or until u_i is zero. The u-ascent procedure follows.

[These steps are carried out for each facility, i.]

Step 1: Let n be the number of non-zero w_{ij}
Sort the w_{ij} and let ws_j be the jth smallest w_{ij}
Set $ws_o = 0$
Set $wsum_o = \sum_j w_{ij}$

Step 2: For j = 1 to n
Set $wsum_j = wsum_{j-1} - (n+1-j)\ (ws_j - ws_{j-1})$

Step 3: For k = 1 to K (Recall, K is the number of facility sizes)
For j = 0 to n
Set $slack_{kj} = c_{ik} - wsum_j - ws_j\ p_k$

Step 4: Find the j for which $\min_k (slack_{kj})$ is as large as possible.

Step 5: The desired values of u_i lies between ws_{j-i} and ws_{j+i}. Find the appropriate values by interpolation of the $slack_{kj}$ in this range. Set u_i to this value.

Step 6: For j = 1 to n
Set $w_{ij} = \max (0,\ w_{ij} - u_i)$

The interpolation process in Step 5 is straightforward since the $slack_{kj}$ are linear functions of u_i.

The above procedure has a worst case computational complexity of O[NMK], where N is the number of terminals, M is the number of potential facility sites, and K is the number of facility sizes. In practice, the complexity of the procedure is proportional to the number of non-zero w_{ij} times the number of facility sizes and so a more reasonable estimate of the complexity is O[NK].

There are several refinements which can be made to this basic procedure. First, it is not necessary to set u_i for any i which has non-zero s_i at the end of the w-ascent procedure, since we do not need any additional slack from that facility. Also, as mentioned above, the interpolation process in Step 5 will usually reveal that a range of values maximizes the slack. In this case, we prefer the largest values of u_i.

2.3 Iteration of the Ascent Procedures

The w-ascent and u-ascent procedures are iterated, alternating between them. There are several options in this regard. One is to begin with all u_i set to 0 and to begin with the w-ascent procedure. This tends to create a small number of large w_{ij} since any terminal much closer to one facility than any other will receive a large w_{ij}.

Another alternative is to begin with

$$u_i = \min_k (c_{ik}/p_k)$$

This is the maximum value possible for u_i and generally corresponds to the largest value of k, since facilities ordinarily exhibit an economy of scale. This will tend to produce a tighter bound in most cases, and is generally the preferred way to start the procedure.

Another choice to consider in implementing this procedure is how to start the second and later iterations of the w-ascent procedure. One possibility is to begin with all w_{ij} at 0 as was indicted above. This sometimes leads to anomolous behavior where the sum of the v_j decreases on later iterations. One way to avoid this is to not reset the values of the v_j or the w_{ij} at the start of the w-ascent procedure. This will start the w-ascent procedure off with the slack created by the u-ascent procedure. This method often works better than resetting the w_{ij} to 0.

The ascent procedures are iterated until no further progress is made. This can be measured in several ways. The safest way of measuring progress is by noting the values of the u_i. If they have not changed, no further progress will be made.

2.4 Facility Selection

The above procedure produces a lower bound on the optimal solution value, given by the sum of the v_j. It also produces information, in the form of the s_i and u_i, which is useful in selecting the locations and sizes of the facilities to be included in the solution. Ideally, we would select all facilities which have s_i equal to 0 at the end of the above iteration. The size of the facilities being determined by which value of k gives rise to a tight constraint of type (2). We first attempt to do exactly this. If a feasible solution is obtained and the value of this solution is equal to (or sufficiently close to) the lower bound, then we have obtained an optimal (or provably near-optimal) solution and we need go no further with the facility selection.

Unfortunately, this ideal situation need not prevail. While the set of facilities with s_i equal to 0 usually correlates well with the best set of facility locations, the two sets need not be identical. The presence of multiple facility sizes further complicates the situation as even when the right sites are chosen, there may be some discrepancies in the facility sizes.

There are three possible directions for improvement. First, an aggressive application of the above w-ascent and u-ascent procedures may lead to too many facility sites having s_i equal to 0. In this case, it is necessary to select a subset of those sites. A second possibility is that too few sites have s_i equal to 0, in which case additonal sites must be picked. A third possibility is that the facility sizes may need to be adjusted, either upward or downward. There is, theoretically, also the possibility of picking somewhat different sites but there is little empirical evidence leading to the conclusion that this occurs often. All of these perturbations are handled within the context of the following general procedure.

We begin by tentatively selecting the set of facilities and facility sizes as described above. We then determine the direction of perturbation based upon the total capacity of all selected facilities and the total demand from all terminals. If the demand exceeds the selected capacity, clearly more capacity must be obtained, either by increasing the size of some of the selected facilities or by selecting additional facilities. We use the slacks, s_i, to guide our selection, choosing those facilities with the smallest slacks. In the case of selecting additional sites, we use the actual s_i. In the case of increasing the size of a given facility, we consider the slack associated with the larger facility size. In particular, if s_i

equal to 0, then there exists some k for which constraint (2) is tight. For larger values of k, this constraint loosens, creating slack at the current values of v_j and u_i. We compare the slack of the appropriate type associated with each facility site, and select additional sites (or larger facilities) picking those with the smallest slack.

It is somewhat more difficult to recognize the situation where there is too much capacity. In general, we expect the total capacity of the selected facilities not too exceed the total demand by a large factor. Typically, the ratio of capacity to demand should be around 1.2. There is no hard rule, however. A similar question exists with respect to adding capacity; we will generally want to add capacity until this ratio is achieved. The most direct way of determining whether we need to add or remove capacity is to attempt to do so and to see what happens to the total network cost. We will discuss this issue further in the next section when the problem of assigning terminals to selected facilities is discussed.

A general approach which can result in adding or removing capacity relative to the amount which would be selected by the s_i equal to 0 rule, is to select facilities one at a time, starting first with those with s_i equal to 0 and proceeding to those with remaining slack, if necessary. In selecting among those with the same slack, an assignment of terminals to the facility is made, and the facility saving the most is selected first. The savings are computed based on the cost of connecting the assigned terminals to the facility versus the cost of connecting them to the next closest facility. Specifically, we compute for each potential facility site, i, with s_i less than a given threshold (initially 0), the cost of placing the smallest sized facility (or next largest sized facility, in locations where a facility has already been selected):

$$P_i = \min_k \left(\sum_{j \varepsilon J_k} (a_{ij} - a_{i2(j),j}) - c_{ik} \right)$$

where J_k is the set of terminals which save the most by connecting to location i and i2(j) is the facility site second nearest to j. Thus P_i is a measure of the profit associated with selecting (or inreasing the size of) a facility at location i.

This is an "add" algorithm as described in [8], but with the important addition that it is guided by the slacks produced by the above procedure. After selecting a facility using this procedure, the associated terminals are removed from further consideration and the next facility is selected.

A more time consuming but even more reliable procedure

is to select a single facility using this procedure and then to redo the w- and u-ascent procedures, with the assigned terminals removed and with the cost and capacity of the selected facility adjusted to reflect the selection; i.e., the cost and capacities of all larger size options are adjusted downward by the cost and capacity of the selected option. This latter procedure has worked very well in practice.

2.5 Terminal Assignment

If the procedure above is used to modify the facility selection, it also produces a terminal assignment and no futher work need be done. However, it is often not necessary to resort to such modification and it is much faster, and often better, to simultaneously assign all terminals to facilities. Also, the desireability of increasing or decreasing the total capacity selected is made clearer by doing a terminal assignment. In particular, we can do a terminal assignment with the current capacity, modify the capacity and then redo the terminal assignment. If the cost goes down, we continue to modify the capacity in the same direction.

The terminal assignment problem has been much studied [11] and efficient algorithms exist for its optimal solution in the case where all terminal demands are the same, which is the situation we are currently discussing. It is possible to use an exact algorithm to solve this problem or, alternatively, to use the following heuristic, which is much faster and in practice has yielded excellent results. In particular, when the terminal assignment is being iterated during facility selection, the use of this heuristic is clearly recommended.

Step 1: Let $I = \{i \mid \text{a facility has been selected at location } i\}$
For each terminal, j
Find i1(j) and i2(j), the facilities in I which are nearest and second nearest to j, respectively.
Compute $d_j = a_{i2(j),j} - a_{i1(j),j}$
Place the d_j in a heap, with the largest d_j at the top.

Step 2: Consider the d_j currently at the top of the heap.
Assign j to i1(j).

Step 3: If this assignment fills the facility at location i1(j):
Recompute d_j for all terminals, t, with i1(t) or i2(t) = i1(j) and bubble the new values of d_j to where they belong in the heap.

Step 4: If any terminals remain to be assigned, remove d_j from the heap and return to Step 2; otherwise, continue to Step 5.

Step 5: For each terminal not associated with the nearest facility in I, consider exchanging it with a terminal at a closer facility. Consider all such exchanges, and make the one which saves then most. Repeat this step until no further progress is made.

Step 5 is potentially the most time consuming part of this procedure. If done naively, a single iteration of the step involves looking at all pairs of terminals. A careful implementation, however, is much faster. If a list of all terminals associated with each facility is kept, then only the terminals associated with given facilities need be searched and only facilities loaded to capacity need be considered. This reduces the search to a fraction of the terminals at each step. Experiments were run comparing the results obtained using this procedure with those obtained using an optimal algorithm and while this heuristic does not guarantee an optimal solution it almost always found one.

2.6 General Terminal Demands

The above procedure can be extended to the case where the terminal demands are not all equal to 1. In this case, the dual problem becomes:

$$\text{Maximize } \sum_j b_j v_j - \sum_i t_i$$

subject to:

(1) $a_{ij} + w_{ij} + u_i >= v_j$ for all j

(2) $\sum_j b_j \; w_{ij} + p_k \; u_i <= c_{ik} + t_i$ for all i,k

(3) $v_j, w_{ij}, u_i, t_i >= 0$

The presence of the b_j in the objective function and in constraint (2) has several effects on the overall procedure. First, the w-ascent procedure must be modified slightly. In order to increase v_j by one unit, the facility slack must be reduced by b_j units because of the change in constraint (2). The objective function, however, also increases by b_j units because of the change in the objective function. Thus, the net effect is that a unit of slack is converted into a unit of increase in the objective function as it was before and the overall w-ascent performs as it did before. Similarly, the u-ascent procedure must be modified slightly to reflect the presence of the b_j but the alogrithm is essentially the same.

The only significant change brough about by the generalized demands is in the terminal assignment problem. The terminal assignment problem with generalized demands is a much harder problem than the corresponding problem with unit demands. There are no known algorithms for the former problem which guarantee both an optimal solution and reasonable running time. Furthermore, the heuristic described above, while still effective, must take into account the fact that terminals with different demands may not be able to be exchanged for one another without violating a capacity constraint. Thus, the exchange procedure described above as the final phase of the terminal assignment heuristic is somewhat more complex and somewhat less effective. Nevertheless, we believe that the procedure as a whole is still reasonably effective. We are currently experimenting with this extension.

3. Implementation and Computational Experience

There are currently two implementations of this procedure. The first is a prototype implementation at the Network Design Laboratory at the Polytechnic Institute of New York. The major function of this prototype is to test and further develop the algorithm itself. This implementation allows the user to interact closely with the algorithm at many levels. The user can run the entire procedure automatically and see the resulting network on an interactive graphic display. The user can also see the percentage difference between the lower bound and the actual solution obtained. The user is also able to modify all or part of the network design. In particular, one can change the locations and sizes of the facilities and rerun the terminal assignment algorithm. One can also modify the terminal assignments, but in practice this is almost never necessary.

In addition to this, the user can interact with the lower bounding procedure, running separate iterations of the w-ascent and u-ascent procedures and even modifying individual values of w_{ij}, v_j, and u_i. The user can also experiment with modifying the t_i, but this has not proved fruitful in practice as yet and so no automated procedure has yet been implemented to modify the t_i. Thusfar, only relatively small problems with up to 50 nodes have been run on this prototype. Results have been encouraging, with near optimal (less than 5% from the lower bound) results produced in most instances. We are currently experimenting with larger problems.

The other implementation is part of a full scale network design package. This implementation is more fully automated and is set up to handle larger networks and more realistic problems. Thus, actual tariff information and actual network design problems with up to 1000 nodes have been fed into a procedure based upon the description above. Results to date have been quite positive with highly satisfactory designs coming oiut of the system.

4. Conclusions and Areas for Further Research

We have presented a family of procedures for the solution of the capacitated facility location problem and the associated terminal assignment problem. We have implmented some of these procedures and found that they generally produce near optimal results.

As mentioned above, we are continuing to experiment with and refine the above procedure. The most active area of research concerns more efficient ways to automate the selection of facility sites. The iterative method where the facilities are picked individually and the lower bounding procedure is rerun has proven thusfar to be very effective but we are still trying to find a faster and even more reliable procedure. Another area of investigation is how to tighten the lower bound.

Bibliography

[1] N. Christophides, Graph Theory: An Algorithmic Approach, Academic Press, 1975.

[2] D. Erlenkotter, "A Dual-Based Procedure for Uncapacitated Facility Location," Operations Research 26, p. 992-1009, 1978.

[3] D. Erlenkoter, "Facility Location with Price-Sensitive Demands: Private, Public, and Quasi-Public," Management Science 24, p. 378-386, 1977.

[4] R.S. Garfinkel and G.L. Nemhauser, Integer programming, Wiley, 1972.

[5] M. Guignard and K. Spielberg, "A Direct Dual Method for the Mixed Plant Location Problem with Some Side Constraints," Mathematical Programming 17, p. 198-208, 1979.

[6] G.Y. Handler and P.B. Mirchandani, Location on Networks, MIT Press, 1979.

[7] R. Jeroslow, "An Introduction to the Theory of Cutting Planes," Annals of Discrete Mathematics 5, p. 71-95, 1979.

[8] P. McGregor and D. Shen, "Network Design: An Algorithm for the Access Facility Location Problem," IEEE Trans. on Communications COM-25 No. 1, p. 61-73, 1977.

[9] R. Mendelson, "A Cutting Plane Approach to the Concentrator Location Problem," Ph.D. Thesis, Polytechnic Institute of New York, 1983.

[10] A. Mirzaian, "Lagrangian Relaxation for the Star-Star Concentrator Location Problem: An Approximation Algorithm and Bounds," NETWORKS 15 No. 1, p. 1-20.

[11] C. Papadimitriou and K. Steiglitz, Combinatorial Optimization: Algorithms and Complexity, Prentice Hall, 1982.

[12] D.T. Tang, L.S. Woo, and L.R. Bahl, "Optimization of Teleprocessing Networks with Concentrators," Proc. of the national Telecommunications Conference, Atlanta, p. 37C1-37C5, 1973.

Recent Results in Performability Analysis

Balakrishna R. Iyer
IBM Thomas J. Watson Research Center
P.O. Box 218,
Yorktown Heights, New York 10598

Abstract

The emergence of multi-processor based fault tolerant distributed systems impacts the way systems are evaluated and analyzed. In particular, many systems exhibit trade-off's between performance and reliability both in their design and operation. Performability (Meyer(1982)) is a composite measure for the performance and reliability of a system observed over a finite mission time t. Performability may be interpreted as the probability distribution of the accumulated reward obtainable from a system during its mission time. The computation of performability requires new methodology because of the need for transient analysis in estimating the accumulated reward for a finite mission time. Also, since the notion of performability is new there is insufficient understanding of the proper application of performability modelling and analysis to solve realistic problems in system design and evaluation. Recent advances in both the areas of computational methodology and applications are surveyed in this paper.

1. Introduction

Classical performance and/or reliability analysis is used for quantitative evaluation of computer and communication systems. Simulation and analytical methods have been used extensively for performance analysis (e.g. Lavenberg (1983) or Heidelberger and Lavenberg (1984) and the references therein). In reliability analysis knowledge or estimates of failure rates of individual components are used to project the reliability of a system composed of many components (Barlow and Proschan (1981)). In the past, performance and reliability of computer systems were usually analyzed separately (Trivedi (1982)). The emergence of fault-tolerant multiple processor based distributed systems (Siewiorek and Swarz (1982) and

Kim(1984)) that are subject to reconfiguration and graceful degradation on failure of components, makes it meaningful to consider composite performance and reliability measures (Meyer (1980A), Gay and Ketelson (1979), Castillo and Siewiorek (1981), Beudry (1978), Huslende(1981)). Often, reliability is obtained at the cost of performance, as we illustrate in the following examples. (i) Frequent check-pointing in a computer system degrades the performance during normal operation but aids in recovery upon component failure. (ii) Processors with store-through caches have worse performance than those with store-in caches. However if a transient hardware error is detected to have destroyed cache data then it is the processor with the store-through cache rather than the processor with the store-in cache that is more likely to find that data backed up in main storage and restore it. (iii) In a multiple-processor system, one processor may be designated as a spare and made to idle or track the computations of the other processors during normal operation (losing performance), in order to have the capability of taking over the workload of any failing processor. Sparing was the technique employed in the 60's by the telephone industry to provide very high reliability for electronic switching systems. Examples of this kind are found in the ESS systems and the more recent 3B20D of ATT (Serlin (1984) and Toy and Gallaher (1983)). (iv) The technique of back-up checkpointing first exploited commercially by Tandem creates a back-up process for every process that is to be made fault-tolerant. By periodically passing state information the back-up process has the capability of taking over on failure of the primary process. Siewiorek (1984) suggests that the effective power of a pair of Tandem processors is reduced by 15 to 30 percent due to checkpointing. (v) Real estate on silicon may be used for implementing error-detection and correction functions (Carter (1984) and the references therein) instead of being used to increase the raw instruction execution speed of a processor. Performance, therefore, can be traded off not only for decreased failure rate but also for decreased outage time. Composite performance and reliability measures are useful in evaluating the performance reliability trade-off.

Meyer (1980A) formally defined the performability of a system as the probability that the system reaches an accomplishment level of y or less over a utilization interval of $(0,t)$. Informally, we may regard performability as the probability that the system does up to a certain amount of useful work over a mission time t. We restrict ourself to systems where the rate at which work is done, and the failure and repair rates are only a function of the system state. In the case of computer systems, this assumption is valid if the performance measures involved are for jobs whose processing times are small relative to the average time between system failures and repairs. Composite performance reliability analysis without this assumption is quite involved even for the simple M/G/2 queueing system model (Baccelli and Trivedi (1983)).

It is important to consider finite mission times and carry out transient analysis because of the following two reasons:

1. Failures occur so infrequently in well-designed systems that there may be considerable difference between steady state results and results from transient analysis.
2. There may be scheduled outages for computer systems and we are actually only concerned with what happens between these scheduled outages.

Examples of mission times are one week, in the case of systems that undergo preventive maintenance and re-initialization weekly, the blast-off to earth-landing time interval, in the case of systems aboard a space craft, etc. We will point to certain limit theorems to determine distribution of performability for large t.

We define an N configuration fault-tolerant system by the process $\{X_s, 0 \leq s\}$, where X_s describes the configuration (state) of the system at time s. System failures and repairs cause system reconfigurations. We assume that a reward function f_i may be associated with configuration i. The reward function is intended to be a measure of performance per unit time. We will sometimes write $f(i)$ for f_i. We define τ_i to be the time spent by the system in configuration i over the mission time t ($\sum_{i=0}^{N} \tau_i = t$). Due to our assumption, f_i is independent of τ_i.

We assume that the average time between a system going into state i and changing configuration as a result of a fault is generally distributed with mean $\frac{1}{c_i}$. We also assume that a failure or repair action causes a system in state i to reconfigure itself into state j ($j \neq i$) with probability p_{ij}, $\sum_{j=0}^{N} p_{ij} = 1$.

We define $\{X_s, s \geq 0\}$ as a process with state space $\{0, 1, 2, \ldots, N\}$. Due to the above assumptions $\{X_s, s \geq 0\}$ is a semi-Markov process.

The performability of the system over the mission time t is the distribution of the accumulated reward

$$Y_t = \sum_{i=0}^{N} f_i \tau_i = \int_{s=0}^{t} f(X_s) ds. \tag{1.1}$$

Y_t is the definite integral of a function of the semi-Markov process X_s.

Let us consider some interesting reward functions. If we set $f_i = J_i$, the throughput of the system in configuration i, then $Y_t = \sum_{i=0}^{N} J_i \tau_i$ is the number of jobs processed in time t, $\frac{Y_t}{t}$ is the average throughput over time t, $\frac{d}{dt} Y_t$ is the instantaneous throughput at the end of the mission time interval t. To calculate the probability that the average response time is less than or equal to a threshold R, we want

$$P\{\text{average response time} \leq R\} = P\left\{ \frac{\sum_{i=0}^{N} r_i J_i \tau_i}{\sum_{i=0}^{n} J_i \tau_i} \leq R \right\} \tag{1.2}$$

where J_i and r_i are respectively the average throughput and response time in configuration i. Rearranging terms we can write

$$P\{\text{average response time} \leq R\} = P\{ \sum_{i=0}^{n} (r_i - R) J_i \tau_i \leq 0 \} \tag{1.3}$$

and hence we would be interested in the reward function $f_i = (r_i - R) J_i$.

Huslende (1981) proposed that the probability of a fault tolerant system residing in states i with reward function $f_i > f$ over the entire mission time t be regarded as a composite measure of performance and reliability. He computed this measure for a non-repairable system with rewards f_i non-increasing in i. We make the observation that if we set

$$\hat{f}_i = I(\{i \mid f_i > f\}), \tag{1.4}$$

where $I(E)$ is the indicator function for the event E, and we define performability in terms of $\hat{f}_i$, as $Y_t = \sum_{i=0}^{N} \hat{f}_i \tau_i$, then $P\{Y_t \geq t\}$ reduces to Huslende's performance reliability measure. Since we will not make any assumptions about the monotonicity of our reward function, computation can proceed even when f_i is not non-increasing in i.

Kulkarni et. al. (1984a) pointed out the relationship between the distribution of performability and the distribution of work-completion time (Krishna and Shin (1983)) in a fault-tolerant system. They looked at work-completion times for systems where all or no previous work is lost at reconfigurations. Performability corresponds to the case where no previous work is lost during a reconfiguration.

For Markovian models of systems without repair, both the performability distribution and all of it's moments can be found analytically. Markovian models of repairable system yield analytical solutions for all the moments of performability and a Laplace transform solution for performability itself. The transform has been shown to be numerically invertible. For a simple two state Markovian model a closed form solution is available for the distribution. In limiting cases the distribution is derivable from a normal distribution. Easily computable approximations have been found for the first moment. Only transform results and numerical solutions are available for semi-Markovian models. Interesting applications of performability are also surveyed in this paper.

2. Performability Results

This section lists the advances in the methodology for performability analysis over the past few years. Since the moments as well of the performability distribution may be used in systems analysis the results focus on obtaining the distribution and (if that fails) on obtaining the moments. The discussion is divided into two parts: a) Non-repairable systems and b) Repairable systems. Non-repairable systems are of interest in applications on board space vehicles, for computer systems in locations too remote to be attended to on failure, or for some systems with a declared repair policy that repairs (due to economical reasons) may be provided only at the end of fixed time intervals. If the reward rates of states into which a transition occurs for a non-repairable system is never greater than the rewards in states from which the transition occurred, then that system is called a degradable system. Non-repairable systems are considerably easier to analyze. Analysis makes use of the fact that a non-repairable system will not re-enter a state once it has made a transition out of that state. The state space and the transitions of the system may be modelled by a directed acyclic graph. Since a large class of computer and communication systems are serviced by maintenance personnel, repairable systems are also of interest. Repairable system models may no longer be represented by an acyclic graph and their analysis is more difficult. Performability solutions obtained for repairable systems rely on the eigenanalysis of the generator matrix, in case the model is Markovian.

2.1. Non-repairable Systems

If we assume that the time between state transitions is exponentially distributed then $\{X_s, 0 \leq s \leq t\}$ is a Markov process. Two approaches have been used to compute the distribution for performability for Markovian models of non-repairable systems. The first was proposed by Meyer (1982) where performability was written in terms of an $N+1$ fold integral

$$P(Y_t \leq y) = \int\int..\int_{(t_0, t_1, ..., t_N): \sum_{i=0}^{N} f_i t_i \leq y} p(t_0, t_1, ..., t_N) dt_0 dt_1 .. dt_N, \quad (2.1)$$

where $p(t_0, t_1, ..., t_N)$ is the joint (unconditional) density of the times spent in the different states 0 , 1 to N.

The joint density is expressible as a product of exponential terms. This approach requires that we identify the regions in the N+1 dimensional space of time variables (times spent in each state) for which $\sum_{i=0}^{N} f_i t_i \leq Y_t$. The most difficult part is to determine the region of integration. Meyer (1982) determined the region of integration by enumeration for a three state model. Furchgott and Meyer (1984) described an algorithm that automatically determines the region of integration by enumerating all the state trajectories of the system (same as the different realizations of the Markov process $\{X_s, 0 \leq s \leq t\}$). Once the regions of integration are determined the integration may proceed analytically. In case the residence times in the different states is generally distributed, instead of being exponentially distributed, the integration may still be done, though numerically. The complexity of the algorithm determining the regions of integration is linear in the number of state trajectories, which can be exponential in the number of states, in general.

An alternative approach proposed by Donatiello and Iyer (1984) exploits the acyclic property of the process modelling the non-repairable system. Their results are summarized below. The key idea is that performability starting from a state N can be written in terms of reward accumulated in that state and performability starting from states that can be reached from N in a single transition. This renewal theoretic argument (Smith (1958)) is encapsulated in the following relation for performability.

$$P(Y_t(N) < y) = I_{\{f_N t < y\}} e^{-c_N t} + \sum_{i=0}^{N-1} \int_0^t e^{-c_N \tau} p_{Ni} P(Y_{t-\tau}(i) < y - f_N \tau) d\tau, \quad (2.2)$$

where $I_{\{E\}}$ is the indicator function for the event E, p_{Ni} is the probability that the system makes a transition to state i given that a transition out of state N occurs, and $Y_t(N)$ is the accumulated reward during the mission time t, starting out from state N.

If we let $S_N(s,t)$ be the Laplace-Stieljes transform of the distribution $P(Y_t(N) \leq y)$ and $L_N(s, \delta) = \int_{t=0}^{\infty} e^{-\delta t} S_N(s,t)dt$, be the Laplace transform of $S_N(s,t)$ then the above relation for performability may be written in the transform domain as:

$$L_N(s, \delta) = \frac{1}{c_N + sf_N + \delta} + \sum_{i=0}^{N-1} \frac{c_N}{c_N + sf_N + \delta} p_{Ni} L_i(s, \delta) \tag{2.3}$$

Using mathematical induction on the above relation and partial fraction expansion the recursion may be expanded to give

$$L_N(s, \delta) = \sum_{i=0}^{N} \sum_{\substack{m=0 \\ m \neq i}}^{N} \frac{\dfrac{h_N(m,i)}{(c_m - c_i) + s(f_m - f_i)}}{c_i + sf_i + \delta} + \frac{1}{c_N + sf_N + \delta}, \tag{2.4}$$

in terms of the coefficients $h_N(m,i)$. Inversion of the double Laplace transform gives the following analytical result for performability

$$P(Y_t(N) < y) = 1 - \sum_{i=0}^{N} \sum_{\substack{m=0 \\ m \neq i}}^{N} \frac{h_N(m,i)}{c_m - c_i} e^{-c_i t} e^{-\frac{c_m - c_i}{f_m - f_i}(y - f_i t)} I_{\{y > f_i t\}} - e^{-c_N t} I_{\{y \leq f_N t\}}, \tag{2.5}$$

where the following assumptions are needed to avoid degeneracies:
(*i*) $c_i \neq c_j$ and $f_i \neq f_j$ whenever $i \neq j$ and $i, j \in \{0,1,2, ..., N\}$,
(*ii*) $\dfrac{c_i - c_j}{c_k - c_j} \neq \dfrac{f_i - f_j}{f_k - f_j}$, whenever $i,j,k \in \{0,1,2, ..., N\}$ and, $i \neq k$ and $i,k \neq j$.

The coefficients $h_n(m,i)$ and $w_n(i)$ are independent of y and t are found by recursive expressions in Donatiello and Iyer (1984). An algorithmic solution based on a similar recursion models for degradable systems is indicated in Goyal and Tantawi (1984).

There has been considerable recent focus on a specific example of a buffered multi-processor system model due to Meyer (1982), which is modelled as a non-repairable system with failures that either cause the loss of a single processor or the whole multi-processor system. In terms of the transition probabilities this may be expressed by the relation that $p_{Ni} = 0$, for all i except for $i = 0$ or N-1. For this special case the recursion in Laplace transforms in Equation (2.3) may be expanded to give:

$$L_N(s, \delta) = \sum_{i=0}^{N} \frac{1}{c_i + sf_i + \delta} \prod_{j=i+1}^{N} \frac{p_{jj-1} c_j}{c_j + sf_j + \delta}$$

$$+ \sum_{i=2}^{N} \frac{c_i p_{i0}}{(c_i + sf_i + \delta)(c_0 + sf_0 + \delta)} \prod_{j=i+1}^{N} \frac{p_{jj-1} c_j}{c_j + sf_j + \delta} \tag{2.7}$$

Using partial fraction expansion and then inverting the expanded Laplace transform Donatiello and Iyer (1984) obtained the following closed form expression for the performability distribution:

$$P(Y_t(N) < y) = 1 - \sum_{i=0}^{N} \sum_{\substack{m=0 \\ m \notin S_i}}^{N} \frac{h_N(m,i)}{c_m - c_i} e^{-c_i t} e^{-\frac{c_m - c_i}{f_m - f_i}(y - f_i t) I_{\{y > f_i t\}}} - \sum_{i=0}^{N} w_N(i) e^{-c_i t} I_{\{y \leq f_i t\}},$$

assuming that

(i) $\{c_i \neq c_j\}$ whenever $i \neq j$ and $i, j \in \{0,1,2, ..., n\}$,

(ii) $\dfrac{c_i - c_j}{c_k - c_j} \neq \dfrac{f_i - f_j}{f_k - f_j}$, whenever $i,j,k \in \{0,1,2, ..., N\}$ and, $i \neq k$ and $i,k \notin S_j$, where $S_j = \{l \ni (f_l - f_j) = 0, 0 \leq l \leq N\}$.

Closed form expressions are given for $h_N(m,i)$ and $w_N(i)$ are independent of y and t. Recursive expressions are also given as an alternative for the computation of these coefficients.

For this special case the n'th moment of performability may be obtained by differentiating the Laplace transform of the distribution in equation (2.3) n times. If we denote this n'th moment starting from state N as $m_{N,n}(t) = E(Y_t^n(N))$, and it's Laplace transform as $M_{N,n}(\delta)$, then

$$M_N^n(\delta) = \sum_{i=0}^{N} \sum_{j=0}^{n} \frac{v_{Nn}(i,j) j!}{(c_i + \delta)^{j+1}}, \tag{2.8}$$

$$v_{Nn}(i,j) = \sum_{\substack{m=0 \\ m \notin S_i}}^{N} \frac{h_N(m,i)(f_m - f_i)^{N-j} f_i^j N!}{(c_m - c_i)^{N-j+1} j!} + w_N(i) \frac{n!}{j!} f_i^n I_{\{j=n\}} \tag{2.9}$$

Inverting (2.9) we get the expression for the n'th moment in the time domain the closed form solution for moments is written as

$$m_{N,n}(t) = \sum_{i=0}^{N} \sum_{j=0}^{n} v_{Nn}(i,j) t^j e^{-c_i t} \tag{2.10}$$

To avoid degeneracies it must be assumed that $c_m \neq c_i$ for $m \neq i, 0 \leq m,i \leq n$.

In the general case of Markovian models for non-repairable systems (acyclic graphs) the n'th moment may be written in the same form as Equation (2.10). If we differentiate Equation (2.3) n times to generate a recursion for the transform of the moments and substitute the expression from Equation (2.10) there, we will be able to derive recursions for the coefficients $v_{Nn}(i,j)$ for the general case.

2.2. Repairable Systems

The transform solution for the performability distribution for Markovian models has been obtained previously by Puri (1971). Iyer et. al. (1984) extended the result in a straight forward manner to semi-Markovian models as described below. For Markovian models the Laplace transform can be analytically inverted in one parameter, thus setting up the basis for numerical Laplace transform inversion in the other parameter.

Let us define $P_i(t,y) = \text{Prob}\{Y_t(i) \le y = i\}$ and let $p_i(t,y) = \frac{\partial}{\partial y}P_i(t,y)$ be the probability density function of $Y_t(i)$, the accumulated reward starting from state i. Let the density function for the time to first transition from state i be denoted as $r_i(t)$ and $w_i(t)$ = Prob(time to first transition from state $i > t$). Let **P** be the matrix of transition probabilities with entries p_{ij}. From renewal theoretic arguments (e.g. Smith(1958)):

$$P_i(y,t) = I_{\{f_i t \le y\}} w_i(t) + \int_0^t r_i(\tau) \sum_{j=0}^{N} p_{ij} P_j(y - f_i \tau, t - \tau) d\tau. \tag{2.11}$$

Taking the Laplace-Stieltjes transform in the y variable and the Laplace transform in the t variable and rearranging yields:

$$\mathbf{L}(s, \delta) = (\mathbf{I} - \text{Diag}\{\mathbf{R}(\delta + s\mathbf{f})\}\mathbf{P})^{-1}\mathbf{W}(\delta + s\mathbf{f}). \tag{2.12}$$

If, in addition, the time between reconfigurations is exponentially distributed, then $\{X_s, s \ge 0\}$ is a Markov process with $R_i(\delta) = c_i/(c_i + \delta)$ and $W_i(\delta) = 1/(c_i + \delta)$. The Markov generator matrix **Q** for $\{X_s, s \ge 0\}$ is given by $\mathbf{Q} = \mathbf{C}(\mathbf{P} - \mathbf{I})$ where **C** is the diagonal matrix with entries c_i. Equation (2.5) can be reduced to

$$\mathbf{L}(s, \delta) = (\delta\mathbf{I} + s\mathbf{F} - \mathbf{Q})^{-1}\mathbf{e} \tag{2.13}$$

where **F** is the diagonal matrix with entries f_i and **e** is the column vector of all ones. This is the result obtained by Puri (1971) using a quantal response approach. The double Laplace transform $\mathbf{L}(s, \delta)$ may be directly inverted in the δ parameter to give the single Laplace transform $\mathbf{S}(s,t)$ as follows:

$$\mathbf{S}(s, t) = \exp(\mathbf{Q}t - s\mathbf{F}t)\mathbf{e}. \tag{2.14}$$

Standard numerical techniques for Laplace transform inversion could be used to obtain the performability distribution.

Kulkarni et. al. (1984,1985) invert the Laplace transform $\mathbf{L}(s, \delta)$ in a different way. The i'th component $\mathbf{L}_i(s, \delta)$ may be written from Equation (2.13) as

$$L_i(s, \delta) = N_i(s, \delta) / \det(\delta\mathbf{I} + s\mathbf{F} - \mathbf{Q}), \tag{2.15}$$

where $N_i(s, \delta)$ is the determinant of $(\delta\mathbf{I} + s\mathbf{F} - \mathbf{Q})$ with the i'th column replaced by the vector **e**. $N_i(s, \delta)/\det(\delta\mathbf{I} + s\mathbf{F} - \mathbf{Q})$ is a rational function in δ for a fixed value of s. The roots for the polynomial $\det(\delta\mathbf{I} + s\mathbf{F} - \mathbf{Q})$ in δ may be found in terms of s and denoted as $\delta_0(s), \delta_1(s), \ldots, \delta_N(s)$. The roots are the eigenvalues of $(\mathbf{Q}\text{-}s\mathbf{F})$. Let $\det(\delta\mathbf{I} + s\mathbf{F} - \mathbf{Q}) = \prod_{i=0}^{d} (\delta - \delta_i(s))^{k_i(s)}$ where each of its distinct roots $\delta_i(s)$ is assumed to have a multiplicity $k_i(s)$. Kulkarni et. al. (1984,1985) write the partial fraction expansion of $L_i(s, \delta)$ as follows:

$$L_i(s, \delta) = \frac{N_i(s, \delta)}{\det(\delta\mathbf{I} + s\mathbf{F} - \mathbf{Q})} = \sum_{i=0}^{d} \sum_{j=1}^{k_i(s)} a_{i,j}(s)(\delta - \delta_i(s))^{-j} \tag{2.16}$$

By choosing n values of δ that are not close to any $\delta_j(s)$, they set up linear equations to determine $a_{i,j}(s)$. Inverting in the δ parameter:

$$S(s,t) = \sum_{i=0}^{d} \sum_{j=1}^{k_i(s)} \frac{a_{i,j}(s)}{(j-1)!} t^{j-1} e^{\delta_i(s)t}. \tag{2.17}$$

Thus for every value of s, $S(s,t)$ may be evaluated from Equation (2.17). These values are used in a numerical Laplace inversion procedure outlined by Kulkarni et. al. (1985).

The following result is from Iyer et. al. (1984). If $\{X_s, 0 \leq s\}$ is a finite state space irreducible semi-Markov process, then there is a central limit theorem for Y_t (e.g., Smith (1958) or Crane and Iglehart (1974)) which proves that for large values of t, Y_t is approximately normally distributed with mean rt and standard deviation $\sigma\sqrt{t}$. Both r and σ can be evaluated by solving sets of linear equations (Hordijk et al. (1976)). To be valid, t must be large enough so that there are many entrances to any fixed state of the system.

In what follows, we must define some notation. All vectors shall be understood to be column vectors. Let **f** be the vector with entries tries f_i. Let $\mathbf{m}^n(t)$ be the vector with entries $m_i^n(t)$ where $m_i^n(t) = E(Y_t^n(i))$. Note that $m_i^0(t) = 1$. Let $\mathbf{M}^n(\delta)$ be the Laplace transform of $\mathbf{m}^n(t)$ and $\mathbf{P}(t)$ be the matrix of transition probabilities with entries $P_{ij}(t) = P\{X_t = j \mid X_0 = i\}$. Then $\mathbf{P}(t) = e^{\mathbf{Q}t}$ (Karlin and Taylor (1975)). By rearranging Equation (2.13), differentiating it $n+1$ times with respect to s, using Leibnitz's rule and setting $s=0$

$$\mathbf{M}^{n+1}(\delta) = (n+1)(\delta\mathbf{I} - \mathbf{Q})^{-1}\mathbf{F}\mathbf{M}^n(\delta). \tag{2.19}$$

An explicit recursive computational formula for $\mathbf{m}^n(t)$ is derived by Iyer et. al. (1984) in the following theorem.

Theorem

If $\{X_s, s \geq 0\}$ is a finite state space, continuous time Markov chain with finite generator matrix **Q** having distinct eigenvalues $(\lambda_0, \lambda_1, \ldots, \lambda_N)$ and if **F** is finite, then there exist vectors $\mathbf{v}_n(i,j)$ such that

$$\mathbf{m}^n(t) = \sum_{i=0}^{N} \sum_{j=0}^{n} \mathbf{v}_n(i,j) e^{\lambda_i t} t^j. \tag{2.20}$$

Furthermore, the vectors $\mathbf{v}_n(i,j)$ are defined by the following recursion:

$$\mathbf{v}_0(i,j) = \begin{cases} \mathbf{e} & i = j = 0 \\ \mathbf{0} & \text{otherwise,} \end{cases} \tag{2.21}$$

$$\mathbf{v}_{n+1}(i,n+1) = \mathbf{Z}_i\mathbf{F}\mathbf{v}_n(i,n) \quad 0 \leq i \leq N, \quad n \geq 0 \tag{2.22}$$

$$\begin{aligned} \mathbf{v}_{n+1}(i,j) = {} & (n+1)\sum_{l \neq i} \sum_{k=j}^{n} \mathbf{Z}_l\mathbf{F}\mathbf{v}_n(i,k)c(j,i,l,k) \quad 0 \leq j \leq n, \ 0 \leq i \leq N, \ n \geq 0 \\ & + I(j=0)(n+1)\sum_{l \neq i} \sum_{k=0}^{n} \mathbf{Z}_i\mathbf{F}\mathbf{v}_n(l,k)d(i,l,k) \\ & + I(j \neq 0)((n+1)/j)\mathbf{Z}_i\mathbf{F}\mathbf{v}_n(i,j-1) \end{aligned} \tag{2.23}$$

where e is a vector of ones, **0** is a vector of zeros, $I(j=0) = 1$ if $j = 0$ and 0 otherwise, $I(j \neq 0) = 1 - I(j=0)$, $d(i,l,k) = k!/(\lambda_i - \lambda_l)^{k+1}$ and $c(j,i,l,k) = (-1)k!/(j!(\lambda_l - \lambda_i)^{k+1-j})$, $\mathbf{Z}_i$'s are component matrices of Q and $e^{\mathbf{Q}t} = \sum_{i=0}^{N} \mathbf{Z}_i e^{\lambda_i t}$.

If the eigenvalues of Q are distinct then Lancaster (1969) shows that:

$$\mathbf{Z}_i = \prod_{l=1}^{N} (\mathbf{Q} - \lambda_l \mathbf{I}) / \prod_{\substack{l=1 \\ l \neq i}}^{N} (\lambda_i - \lambda_l). \tag{2.24}$$

From a computational viewpoint it is useful to deduce from Equation (3.2) of Stewart (1973) that $\mathbf{Z}_i = \mathbf{x}_i \mathbf{y}_i^T$, where $\mathbf{x}_i$ and $\mathbf{y}_i$ are right and left eigenvectors, respectively, corresponding to eigenvalue λ_i of Q . A standard package like EISPACK (Smith et. al. (1976) and Garbow et. al. (1977)) may be used to generate both the eigenvalues and eigenvectors of Q . Routines in this package can also make use of special properties of the Markov generator Q , if any.

The theorem is proved by induction, substituting the Laplace transform of the moments from Equation (2.20) into Equation (2.19). The assumption that the generator matrix Q has distinct eigenvalues is made primarily for simplicity of notation and derivation. In practice, it is not a severe restriction. When the eigenvalues are not distinct, $\mathbf{P}(t) = e^{\mathbf{Q}t}$ will have a different representation than is given in Equation (3.1). More specifically, if there are $(d + 1)$ distinct eigenvalues with eigenvalue i having multiplicity k_i, then by Theorem 5.4.1 of Lancaster (1969):

$$\mathbf{P}(t) = e^{\mathbf{Q}t} = \sum_{i=0}^{d} \sum_{j=1}^{k_i} \mathbf{Z}_{ij} e^{\lambda_i t} t^{j-1}. \tag{2.25}$$

It is straightforward to show (by induction) that:

$$\mathbf{m}^n(t) = \sum_{i=0}^{d} \sum_{j=0}^{nK} \mathbf{v}_n(i,j) e^{\lambda_i t} t^j \tag{2.26}$$

where $K = \max\{k_0, k_1, \ldots, k_d\}$. It is possible to derive recursions for the $\mathbf{v}_n(i,j)$'s, although the algebra will be significantly more complicated.

We now focus on the computation of the first moment of performability $\mathbf{m}_1(t)$. We note that the steady state analysis for the computation of $\overline{\mathbf{m}}(t) = \lim_{t \to \infty} \frac{\mathbf{m}_1(t)}{t}$ is straight forward, while transient analysis requires complex eigenanalysis. A method based on randomization to compute the first moment is given in Gross and Miller (1984). The randomization technique has been used by de Souza e Silva and Gail (1985) to evaluate availability distribution for Markovian models. We discuss an approximate method to compute $m_{N,1}(t)$ from the steady state measure $\overline{m}_N$. Details may be found in Iyer et. al. (1985). For computing $\overline{m}_N$, the time axis can be divided into intervals, each of length equal to the mission time t, and averaging over this ensemble. For a Markov failure and recovery process (i.e. an exponentially distributed time in each state), $\overline{m}_N$ (in the limit $\overline{m}_j = \overline{m}_i$ and can be written as just $\overline{m}$) can be written as:

$$
\begin{aligned}
m_{N,1}(t) - \overline{m}t &= m_{N,1}(t) - \pi_N m_{N,1}(t) - \sum_{i=0}^{N-1} \pi_i m_{i,1}(t) \\
&= \sum_{i=0}^{N-1} \pi_i \,(m_{N,1}(t) - m_{i,1}(t)) \\
&\leq \sum_{i=0}^{N-1} \pi_i \,(f_N - f_i)\, T_i
\end{aligned}
\tag{2.27}
$$

where, π_i is the probability of being in state i at the start of the interval, f_i is the reward in state i, T_i is the mean time to get from state i to state n , and t is the mission time. The final inequality in equation (2.27) assumes that the reward in intermediate states in returning from a state i to state N is a non-decreasing reward function.

The bound in equation (2.27) can be tightened by considering the rewards and times spent in intermediate states between states i and N. Suppose that the system (given that a transition occurs) goes from a failure state i to state N through intermediate states. The concomitant loss in reward (over being in state N) will be denoted by Δ_i for the loss in state i. Then, for exponential failure and repair times,

$$
\Delta_i = \sum_{j=0}^{N-1} \Delta_j p_{ij} + (f_N - f_i)\, t_i \ , \tag{2.28}
$$

where t_i is the mean time spent in state i and $f_N - f_i$ is the loss in reward in state i compared with the "up" state N. Thus,

$$
\begin{bmatrix} 1 & . & . & . & . \\ . & 1 & . & -p_{ij} & . \\ . & . & . & . & . \\ . & . & -p_{ij} & 1 & . \\ . & . & . & . & 1 \end{bmatrix}
\begin{bmatrix} \Delta_0 \\ \Delta_1 \\ . \\ . \\ \Delta_{N-1} \end{bmatrix}
=
\begin{bmatrix} (f_N - f_0)\, t_0 \\ . \\ . \\ . \\ (f_N - f_{N-1})\, t_{N-1} \end{bmatrix}
$$

Writing this equation as $\mathbf{P}\,\underline{\Delta} = \mathbf{R}$,

$$
\underline{\Delta} = \mathbf{P}^{-1}\mathbf{R}. \tag{2.29}
$$

Now, we may rewrite equation (2.27) as,

$$
\begin{aligned}
m_{N,1}(t) - \overline{m}t &= \sum_{i=0}^{N-1} \pi_i \,(m_{N,1}(t) - m_{i,1}(t)) \\
&\leq \sum_{i=0}^{N-1} \pi_i \Delta_i = \underline{\pi}^T \mathbf{P}^{-1} \mathbf{R}
\end{aligned}
\tag{2.30}
$$

While Equation (2.30) expresses a solution for the general case, for most systems, $\underline{\Delta}$ reduces to a simple summation and can be written directly by inspection. Iyer et. al. (1985) discuss the evaluation of tighter upper and lower bounds for the first moment of performability a specific class of Markovian models.

For a simple two state Markovian model of the system (exponential distributions for failure and repair times), the performability distribution may be written in closed form in terms of modified Bessel functions (Donatiello and Iyer(1985)). An approach based on numerical integration is given for a two state semi-Markov model by Goyal and Tantawi (1985).

Kulkarni et. al. (1984, 1985) have extended the notion of performability to handle system models where the amount of work done (reward accumulated) may be all lost on transitions to some states. The extension may be used to model a job that has to be restarted from the beginning after a failure.

3. Applications

Since the methodology for performability analysis is still new, there are relatively few applications of performability analysis published in the literature. In this section we will highlight some of the applications that have appeared in recent years.

Meyer et. al. (1980B) modelled the SIFT computer by a two dimensional Markov process - the two dimensions representing processors and busses, respectively. The SIFT computer is modelled as an n processor b bus system. They defined five accomplishment levels to be attained during the course of a mission - a transatlantic flight aboard an airplane. Based on a hierarchical model they evaluated the performability for different SIFT computer configurations consisting of different number of processors and busses. Goyal and Tantawi (1984) proposed a similar performability model an n processor m memory and b bus computer system.

Meyer (1982) modelled the performance of a buffered n processor system as an $M/M/N/N+b$ queueing system (Allen (1978)). There are b buffers in the system to hold b waiting jobs. Jobs arriving when the buffers are full are lost. Thus the throughput of the system increases with the number of buffers. The system is subject to processor failures. Failures of the buffer cause the loss of the entire system. The contribution to the failure rate due to buffer failure is modelled to be linear in the size of the buffer. Hence increasing the buffer size decreases system reliability. Meyer (1982) used performability to determine the optimum buffer size for a fixed mission time t. This model was extended to include processor and buffer repairs by Iyer et. al. (1984) and Kulkarni et. al. (1985).

Iyer et. al. (1985) built a performability model of a configurable duplex system. A configurable duplex system is a dual processor system which may be run under two operation modes. Under the first mode called the 'single image mode' the two processors are run under a single operating system as a tightly coupled dual processor. Under the second mode called the 'partitioned mode' the two processors run under two different operating systems as two independent uni-processors. Each processor has associated with it several components, e.g. a memory controller, an i/o controller, etc.. A controller failure causes the outage of one of the processors if operating under partitioned mode. Depending on the interconnections and the system structure a controller failure may be masked in single image mode (since there are two of each controller in the configuration). On the other hand, an operating system failure brings down one processor in the partitioned mode while it brings down both processors in the single image mode. Simple reliability analysis (based on a binary valued function) is inadequate to characterize the mode selection problem. Mode selection based on performability consideration is discussed in Iyer et. al. (1985). Since single image outages are sensitive to system structure and interconnections, their impact on performability is also evaluated in Iyer et. al. (1985).

Dias et. al. (1985) model a multi-processor database transaction processing system. They look at the trade-offs involved in constructing a high performance transaction processor from either a small number of large processors or a large number of small processors. Disadvantages of having smaller processors are (a) increased coupling overhead and (b) increased overall processor failure rate (because there are more processors). The advantages are (a) lower cost per MIPS for smaller processors and (b) smaller loss of processing power on a single processor failure. The paper provides a comprehensive analysis of the performance penalties of coupling transaction processors. Again reliability analysis based on a binary valued variable is inadequate to capture the impact of failures. Performability analysis is hence used to determine an optimal cost system.

4. Conclusions

It is becoming increasingly clear that both distributed computer system designers and evaluators will be increasingly faced with trade-off's involving performance and reliability. The need to have good measure to evaluate this trade-off is already being felt. Performability qualifies for this task. Considerable computational methodology has been recently developed for performability evaluation. The methodology has been useful in helping understand the trade-off's for numerous applications. There are still open problems in this area. The closed form solution for the performability distribution is still unknown. On the practical side, there are open questions regarding the appropriate choice of reward rates for different configurations of the system.

References

1. Allen, A. O. (1978). *Probability, Statistics, and Queueing Theory - With Applications,* Academic, New York.
2. Baccelli, F. and Trivedi, K.S. (1983). Analysis of M/G/2 - Standby Redundant System, *Performance '83*, A.K. Agrawala and S.K. Tripathi (Editors), North-Holland, Amsterdam, 457-476.
3. Barlow, R.E. and Proschan, F. (1981) *Statistical Theory of Reliability and Life Testing Probability Models,* Holt, Reinhart and Winston, Silver Spring, Maryland.
4. Beaudry, M. D. (1978) Performance-Related Reliability Measures for Computing Systems, *IEEE Trans. on. Computers 27, 6*, C-27(6), 540-547.
5. Carter, W. C. (1984) A Short Survey of Some Aspects of Hardware Design Techniques for Fault Tolerance, IBM Research Report RC 10811, Yorktown Heights, New York.
6. Castillo, X. and Siewiorek, D.P. (1981). A Performance Reliability Model for Computing Systems, *Proceedings of the International Symposium of Fault-Tolerant Computing,* 187-192.
7. Crane, M.A. and Iglehart, D.L. (1974). Simulating Stable Stochastic Systems, II: Markov Chains. *J. Assoc. Comput. Mach.* **21**, 114-123.

8. de Souza e Silva, E. and Gail, H. R. (1985). Calculating Cumulative Operational Time Distributions of Repairable Computer Systems, IBM Research Report RC11253, Yorktown Heights, New York,
9. Dias, D. M., Iyer, B. R. and Yu, P. S. (1985). The Myth of Coupling Many Small Processors for Transaction Processing, IBM Research Report, Yorktown Heights, NY (To be published).
10. Donatiello, L. and Iyer, B.R. (1984). Analysis of a Composite Performance Reliability Measure for Fault-tolerant Systems, IBM Research Report RC10325, Yorktown Heights, New York, To appear in *J. ACM.*
11. Donatiello, L. and Iyer, B.R. (1985). Closed Form Solution for System Availability Distribution, IBM Research Report RC11169, Yorktown Heights, New York,
12. Furchtgott, D.G. and Meyer,J.F. (1984). A Performability Solution Method for Degradable Nonrepairable Systems, *IEEE Transactions on Computers,* C-33, 550-554.
13. Gay, F. and Ketelson, M.L. (1979). Performance Evaluation for Gracefully Degrading Systems, *FTCS-9*, 51-57.
14. Goyal, A. and Tantawi, A.N. (1984). Evaluation of Performability in Acyclic Markov Chains. IBM Research Report RC 10529, Yorktown Heights, New York.
15. Goyal, A. and Tantawi, A.N. (1985). Numerical Evaluation of Guaranteed Availability, *Proceedings of the 15'th Intl. Fault Tolerant Computing Symposium* , Ann Arbor, Michigan, 324-329.
16. Garbow, B. S., Boyle, J. M., Dongarra, J. J., and Moler, C. B. (1977). Matrix Eigensystems Routines - Eispack Guide Extensions, *Lecture Notes in Computer Science - Volume 51*, Springer-Verlag.
17. Gross, D. and Miller, D.R. (1984). The Randomization Technique as a Modeling Tool and Solution Procedure for Transient Markov Processes. Operations Research 32, 343-361.
18. Heidelberger, P. and Lavenberg, S.S. (1984). Computer Performance Evaluation Methodology, *IEEE Transactions on Computers*, C-33, 1195-1220.
19. Hordijk, A., Iglehart, D.L. and Schassberger, R. (1976). Discrete Time Methods for Simulating Continuous Time Markov Chains. *Adv. Appl. Prob.* **8**, 772-788.
20. Huslende, R. (1981). A Combined Evaluation of Performance and Reliability for Degradable Systems, *Perf. Eval. Rev.*, **10**(3), 157-164
21. Iyer, B. R., Donatiello, L. and Heidelberger, P. (1984). Analysis of Performability for Stochastic Models of Fault-tolerant Systems, IBM Research Report RC 10719, Yorktown Heights, New York.
22. Iyer, B. R., Dias, D. M. and Yu, P. S. (1985). Performability Comparison of Configurable Duplex System Structures, IBM Research Report RC 11316, Yorktown Heights, New York.
23. Karlin, S. and Taylor, H.M. (1975). *A First Course in Stochastic Processes* (Second Edition). Academic Press, New York.
24. Kim, W., (1984). Highly Available Systems for Database Applications, *Computing Survey*, 16(1).
25. Krishna, C.M. and Shin, K.G. (1983). Performance Measures for Multi-Processor Controllers, *Performance '83*, A.K. Agrawala and S.K. Tripathi (Editors), North-Holland, Amsterdam, 229-250.

26. Kulkarni, V.G., Nicola, V.F. and Trivedi, K.S. (1984). On Modelling the Performance and Reliability of Multi-Mode Computer Systems, in: M. Becker (ed.), *Proceedings of the International Workshop on Modelling and Performance Evaluation of Parallel Systems,* North Holland.
27. Kulkarni, V.G., Nicola, V.F., Trivedi, K.S. and Smith, R. M. (1985). A Unified Model for the Analysis of Job Completion Times and Performability Measures in Fault-Tolerant Computer Systems, Technical Report CS-1985-13, Dept. of Computer Science, Duke University. Durham, North Carolina.
28. Lancaster, P. (1969). *Theory of Matrices.* Academic Press, New York.
29. Lavenberg, S.S. (Editor) (1983). *Computer Performance Modeling Handbook*, Academic Press, New York.
30. Meyer, J.F. (1980A). On Evaluating Performability of Degradable Computing Systems, *IEEE Trans. on Computers,* **C-29**, 720-731.
31. Meyer, J.F., Furchtgott, D. G. and Wu, L. T. (1980B). Performability Evaluation of the SIFT Computer, *IEEE Trans. on Computers,* **C-29(6)**, 501-509.
32. Meyer, J.F. (1982). Closed-form Solutions of Performability, *IEEE Trans. on Computers,* **C-31**, 648-657.
33. Puri, P.S. (1971). A Method for Studying the Integral Functionals of Stochastic Processes with Applications: I. Markov Chain Case, *J. Appl. Prob.* **8**, 331-343.
34. Serlin, 0. (1984). Fault-tolerant Systems in Commercial Applications, *IEEE Computer*, **17(8)**, 19-30.
35. Siewiorek, D.P. and Swarz, R.S. (1982). *The Theory and Practice of Reliable System Design,* Digital Press, Bedford, Massachusetts.
36. Siewiorek, D. P. (1984). Architecture of Fault-Tolerant Computers, *IEEE Computer*, **17(8)**, 9-18.
37. Smith, B. T., Boyle, J. M., Dongarra, J. J., Garbow, B. S., Ikebe, Y, Klema, V. C. and Moler, C. B. (1976). Matrix Eigensystems Routines - Eispack Guide, Second Edition, *Lecture Notes in Computer Science - Volume 6*, Springer-Verlag.
38. Smith, W.L. (1958). Renewal Theory and its Ramifications. *J. Roy. Statist. Soc. Ser. B.* **20**, 243-302.
39. Stewart, G. W. (1973). *Introduction to Matrix Computations*, Academic Press, New York and London.
40. Toy, W. N. and Gallaher, L. E. (1983). Overview and Architecture of the 3B20D Processor, *Bell Systems Tech. Journ.*, **62(1)** Part 2, 181-190.
41. Trivedi, K.S. (1982). *Probability and Statistics with Reliability, Queueing, and Computer Science Applications*, Prentice-Hall, Englewood Cliffs, New Jersey.

Flow Control in Local-Area Networks of Interconnected Token Rings

Werner Bux and Davide Grillo*
IBM Zurich Research Laboratory, 8803 Rüschlikon

Abstract - We investigate flow-control issues in local-area networks consisting of multiple token rings interconnected through bridges. To achieve high throughput, bridges perform only a very simple routing and store-and-forward function, but are not involved in error- or flow-control. In case of congestion, bridges discard arriving frames which will be recovered through an appropriate end-to-end protocol between the communicating stations. The end-to-end protocol considered is the IEEE 802.2 Type-2 Logical-Link-Control (LLC) protocol. Extensive simulations show that performance can be severely degraded if in such a network, the LLC protocol is employed as defined today. Therefore, we suggest an enhancement to this protocol in the form of a dynamic flow-control algorithm. As our results demonstrate, this enhancement guarantees close-to-optimal network performance under both normal traffic load and overload conditions.

1. INTRODUCTION

Local-area networks must be capable of interconnecting a large number of stations over distances of several kilometers. Whenever

---

*D. Grillo was on leave from the Fondazione Ugo Bordoni, Rome, Italy

the limitations of a single ring or bus subnetwork are reached with respect to the maximum number of attachments or maximum distance, means to interconnect subnetworks become necessary.

In this paper, we consider a network of interconnected token rings. Rings operate as specified in the ECMA and IEEE Standards [1],[2]. Ring interconnection is provided by nodes called bridges [3]. To meet the high throughput requirements for interconnecting high-speed rings at reasonable costs, the bridge functions have to be simple which excludes their performing any complex flow or error control. In case of congestion, bridges simply discard frames they cannot handle momentarily. Discarded frames will be recovered through the end-to-end protocol between the communicating stations. We consider a network architecture in which Type 2 of the IEEE 802.2 Logical-Link-Control (LLC) Standard [4] is employed as end-to-end protocol.

A potential problem in such a network is that recovery of frames lost in congested bridges may worsen congestion, but, without a detailed analysis, it is very difficult to predict how severe this problem will be. Therefore, we developed a detailed model of a multi-ring network including all the relevant medium-access-control and logical-link-control functions. Since the complexity of such a model is far beyond the one of queueing models that can be analytically treated today, we employed simulation. Specifically, we used the RESQ2 simulation tool [5] which for our modeling purposes turned out to be a very flexible and powerful instrument. Our simulations show that network performance can be severely degraded in case of congestion. To overcome this problem, we suggest providing a dynamic flow-control mechanism in the LLC protocol which in case of congestion throttles the input traffic to the network.

In the next section, the elements of the multi-ring network are described. Section 3 shows how this network performs when the IEEE 802.2 Type-2 LLC protocol as defined today is employed. In Section 4, we introduce a new flow-control mechanism in this protocol, and show the improvement attained. Section 5 summarizes our findings.

2. ELEMENTS OF THE MULTI-RING NETWORK

The network topology underlying our study is depicted in Fig. 1. Several token rings are interconnected through bridges and a "backbone" token ring, the latter serving to interconnect bridges.

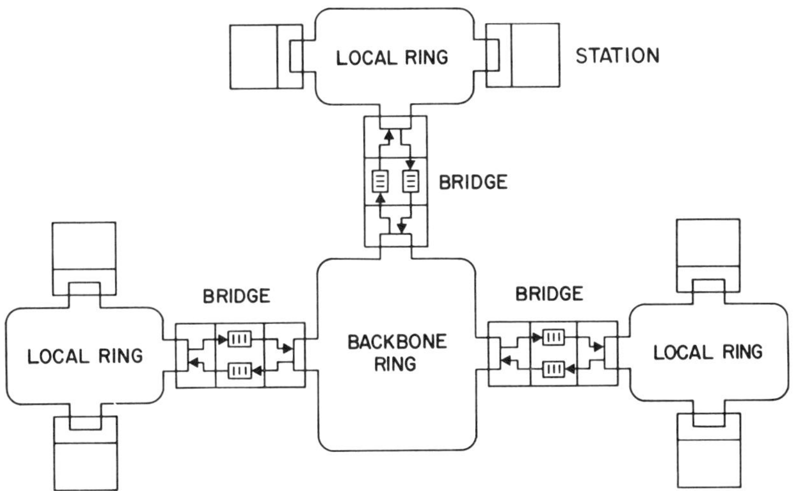

Fig. 1. Network topology.

2.1. Token Rings

The token-ring standards [1], [2] define a priority mechanism by which eight levels of priorities can be provided. We study two different kinds of ring operation. The so-called "non-priority mode" assumes that all stations and the bridges operate at the same ring-access priority level and are only allowed to transmit a single frame per token. In "priority mode", bridges operate at a higher ring-access priority level than normal stations. Whenever a bridge has a frame ready for transmission on a local ring, it will either seize the low-priority token, if available, or make a reservation for high-priority access. This forces the currently transmitting station to issue a priority token which will then be used by the bridge. After the bridge has completed transmission, circulation of the low-priority token is resumed at the next station downstream from the one which last transmitted. In priority mode, bridges are allowed to transmit continuously until their transmit buffer has been emptied, i.e., we assume a very long token-holding timeout. Stations transmit only one frame per token. On the backbone, priority access is not employed and each bridge transmits a single frame per token.

For simplicity, we assumed that both token-passing overhead and transmission errors can be neglected.

2.2. Bridges

Bridges provide a basic routing and store-and-forward function [3]. Frames are buffered in a bridge until they can be transmitted on the local or backbone ring. We assume that the bridge memory space is partitioned into two separate buffer pools, one for each data-flow direction, see Fig. 2. The buffer pools are structured in segments of a fixed size. Frames which do not find a sufficient number of free segments upon their arrival at a bridge are lost.

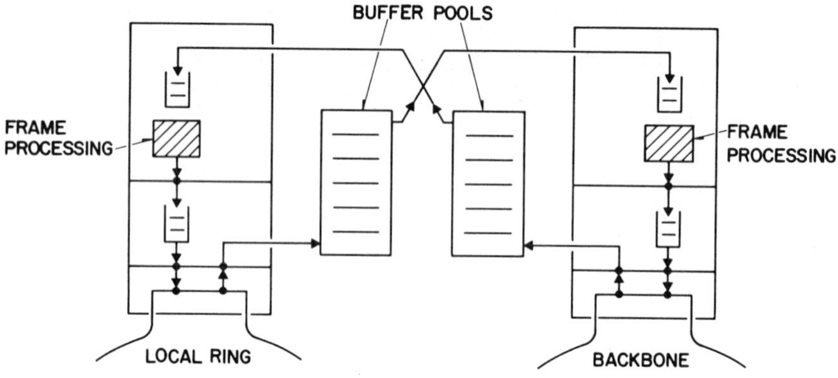

Fig. 2. Bridge.

A bridge is controlled by two processors, each of which handles one direction of data flow. These processors are modeled by two independent single servers which process all frames on a first-come, first-served basis.

2.3. Stations

A conceptual representation of a user station is shown in Fig. 3.

Application and Higher Layers: An application is represented by a traffic source in the sending station which generates messages with given length and interarrival-time distributions and a corresponding sink at the receiving station. The following two functions pertaining to the "higher layers", i.e., layers above LLC are modeled in detail: 1) segmentation/reassembly of messages when the maximum frame length specified for LLC is exceeded, and 2) the "higher-layer interface" on top of LLC which works as follows. Data units provided by users of the LLC service are transmitted by LLC in the form of Information (I-) frames. If LLC cannot transmit I-frames at the rate data units are supplied, it will apply backpressure on the

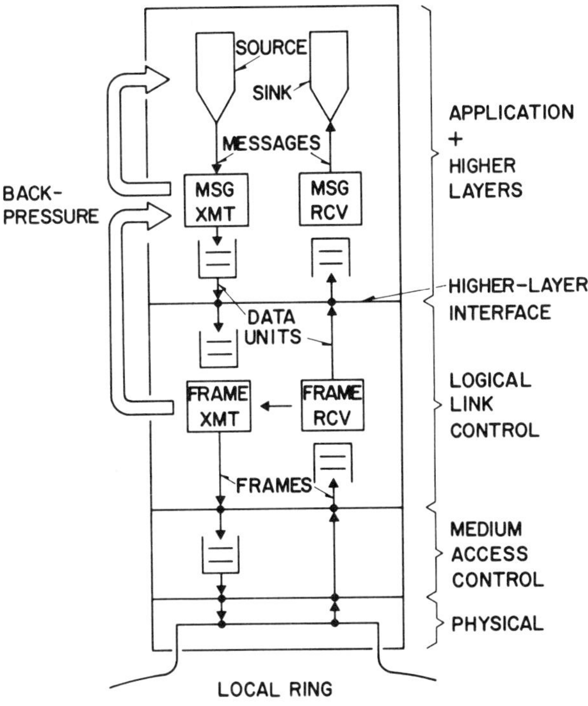

Fig. 3. Station.

higher layers. Specifically, a data unit supplied by a higher-layer entity is not accepted by LLC, when the total number of I-frames and data units being currently handled by the LLC entity has reached a threshold value B. This number encompasses: 1) the number of I-frames already transmitted but not yet acknowledged; 2) the number of I-frames waiting to be transmitted, and 3) the number of accepted data units not yet processed, i.e., formatted as I-frames. An unaccepted data unit together with all subsequent data units pertaining to the same message are queued by the higher-layer entity. At the same time, the generation of further messages is halted. When LLC service again becomes available, queued data units, if any, are handled first and the application resumes generation of new messages.

Logical Link Control: Particular emphasis was placed on a complete and detailed representation of all LLC functions. We subsequently give a brief outline of these functions; for a detailed specification, the reader is referred to [4].

Flow Control: Flow control is realized by a window mechanism, i.e., a sender is permitted to transmit up to a fixed number W (the window size) I-frames without having to wait for an acknowledgment. In our LLC implementation, for each I-frame successfully received, one Receive-Ready (RR) frame is transmitted back carrying the acknowledgment. We do not make use of the Receive-Not-Ready (RNR) function provided in [4].

Error Recovery: If the send sequence number of a received I-frame is not equal to the one expected, the receiver will return a Reject (REJ-) frame. It then discards all I-frames until the expected one has been correctly received. The sender, upon receiving a REJ-frame, retransmits I-frames starting with the sequence number received within the REJ-frame.

In addition to reject recovery, a time-out mechanism is provided. At the instant of transmission of an I-frame, a timer is started when not already running. When the sender receives an acknowledgment, it restarts the timer when there are still unacknowledged I-frames outstanding. When the timer expires, the station performs a "checkpointing" function by transmitting an RR-frame with a dedicated bit (the "P-bit") set to one. The receiver, upon receiving this frame, returns an RR-frame with the "F-bit" set to one. When this RR-frame is received by the sender, it either proceeds with transmitting new I-frames or retransmits previous I-frames, depending on the sequence number contained in the RR-frame received. The checkpointing function itself is protected by timeout. The timer is started upon transmission of the P-bit, and stopped when the F-bit is received. When the timer expires, transmission of an RR-frame with the P-bit set is repeated.

Medium-Access Control: User systems are attached to the rings through ring adapters which implement the medium-access control functions described in Section 2.1. We assume that ring adapters do not cause any noticeable increase in delay or decrease in throughput.

3. NETWORK PERFORMANCE FOR IEEE 802.2 TYPE-2 LLC

In this section, we first define the performance measures and list the assumptions underlying our examples. We then discuss simulation results pertaining to a network in which the IEEE 802.2 Type-2 LLC as defined in [4] is employed.

3.1. Performance Measures

We shall restrict the discussion to two basic performance measures, throughput and end-to-end-delay, both measured at the higher-layer interface, because there, data units are delivered without errors and in the proper sequence.

Throughput of a connection is defined as the mean number of bits received at both ends across the higher-layer interface per unit time. In the subsequent examples, we shall usually show the total throughput of all connections in the network.

End-to-end delay is defined as the time elapsed between supplying a data unit to LLC at the higher-layer interface in the source node until receiving it across this interface at the sink node.

For the subsequent discussion, we need to specify a further quantity called "offered data rate". This is defined as the mean number of bits generated by an application for transmission per unit time under the condition that the application is not halted because of backpressure (c.f. Section 2.3).

3.2. Assumptions

The choice of values for the simulation parameters given below is based on the parameters specified in [1], [2], [4], and on experience gained in experimental implementations [6].

The transmission rates investigated are 4 Mbps for the local rings and 4 or 16 Mbps for the backbone. Bridges are assumed to need 300 μs to process one frame, unless otherwise specified. The default size of each of the two bridge buffer pools is assumed to be 4 kbyte. The maximum I-field length is 0.5 kbyte; the framing overhead of I-frames and the length of S-frames is 24 bytes. The time intervals between generation of messages are assumed to be exponentially distributed. The mean message length is 1 kbyte; the coefficient of variation 1.5. This message-length distribution together with the effect of message segmentation and the superposition of S-frames results in an overall frame-length distribution that resembles the bimodal distribution observed in measurements [7] with a mean of about 250 bytes.

Execution of the LLC protocol is assumed to require the following processing times: a) transmit I-frame (first time): 2 ms; b) receive in-sequence I-frame and transmit RR-frame: 2.5 ms; c) receive RR-frame and delete I-frame(s): 0.75 ms; d) receive out-of-sequence I-frame and transmit REJ-frame: 1 ms; e) receive REJ- or RR-frame with F-bit and retransmit I-frame(s): 1 ms; f) receive out-of-sequence I-frame and transmit nothing: 0.5 ms; g) handle timer interrupt and transmit RR-frame: 1 ms; h) receive RR-frame with P-bit and transmit RR-frame with F-bit: 1 ms.

The LLC timeout value chosen is 250 ms. The backpressure threshold value B defined in Section 2.3. is set to the window size plus four. This gives a source node sufficient flexibility to prepare I-frames for later transmission also during times when the LLC window is closed.

3.3. Results

Fig. 4 shows the total throughput as a function of the total offered data rate. Each of the 12 stations attached to a ring is assumed to generate the same amount of traffic and to have a logical link set up to a station on a different ring. I-frame transmission on each logical link is two-way. The backbone transmission speed is 4 Mbps. Bridges operate in non-priority mode.

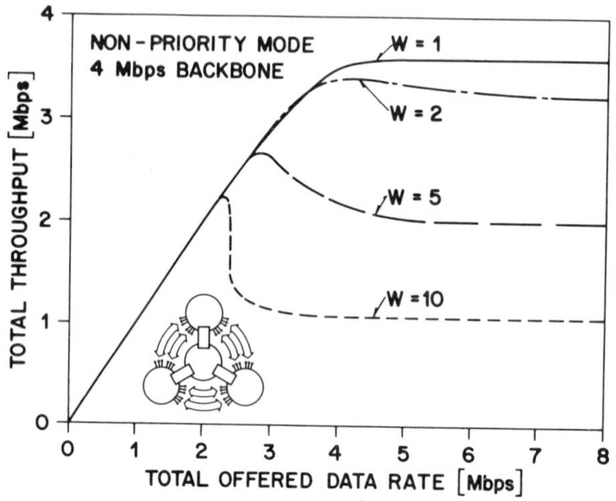

Fig. 4. Total throughput vs total offered data rate for different window sizes W.

When the offered data rate is increased from zero, throughput initially follows linearly. As the backbone becomes noticeably loaded, queues of frames waiting to enter the backbone build up in the bridges, and eventually buffer overflow occurs. Loss of an I-frame leads to the retransmission of one or more I-frames depending on the number of I-frames a station has outstanding when it receives a REJ or has performed checkpointing. Since the window size sets an upper limit to the number of frames to be retransmitted per lost frame, the additional traffic created by retransmissions decreases with smaller window sizes. This explains the significant differences between the throughput values pertaining to different window sizes.

For the same example, Fig. 5 shows the mean end-to-end delay as a function of the total throughput. At small throughput values, the message delay is higher for small window sizes. This is caused by the time periods during which stations cannot transmit pending I-frames because the window is closed. As throughput increases, delay also increases, owing to contention at the various network resources. When the throughput approaches the maximum value attainable, delays increase very steeply. Further increase of the offered data rate leads to both a decrease in throughput and an increase in delays. In the traffic-load range beyond the maximum throughput, delays grow to unacceptably high values. Taking into account possible fluctuations in the traffic, it is advisable to configure the network such that the offered data rate is sufficiently smaller than the maximum throughput. However, given the peakedness of data traffic, it is an

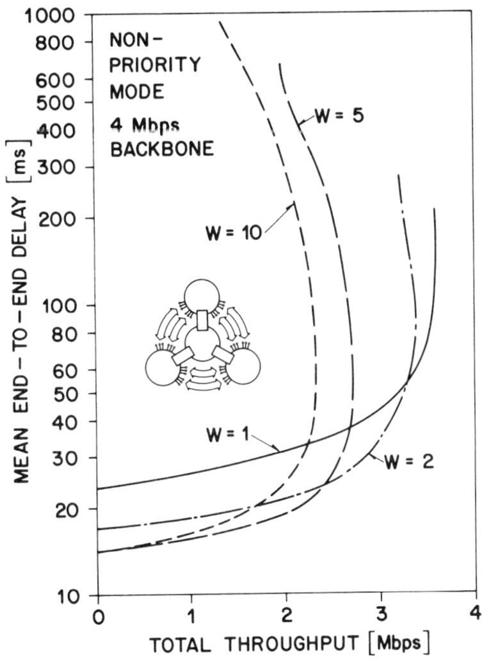

Fig. 5. Mean end-to-end delay vs total throughput for different window sizes W.

open question whether this can always be guaranteed in a real installation.

We next consider the network performance under the same assumptions as above, except for a significantly faster backbone, i.e., 16 Mbps, see Fig. 6. In contrast to the previous example, here the system bottleneck is not the backbone but the local rings. At higher ring utilizations, queues of frames waiting to enter the local rings build up in the bridges, and eventually overflow of the buffer pools in direction backbone to local rings occurs. Frame losses have the same effect as described in the context of Fig. 4; hence, we obtain a similar throughput characteristic.

Fig. 7 shows the delay-throughput characteristic for the same scenario. Except for smaller absolute delay values, we observe the same tendencies as for the lower backbone speed.

In both of the above examples, bridges do not make use of priority access to the local rings. In Fig. 8, we consider the same scenario as in the previous example, however, bridges employ priority

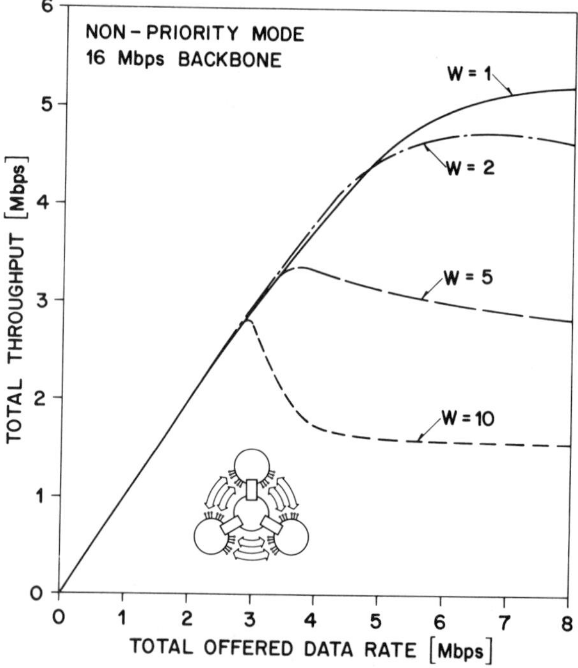

Fig. 6. Total throughput vs total offered data rate for different window sizes W.

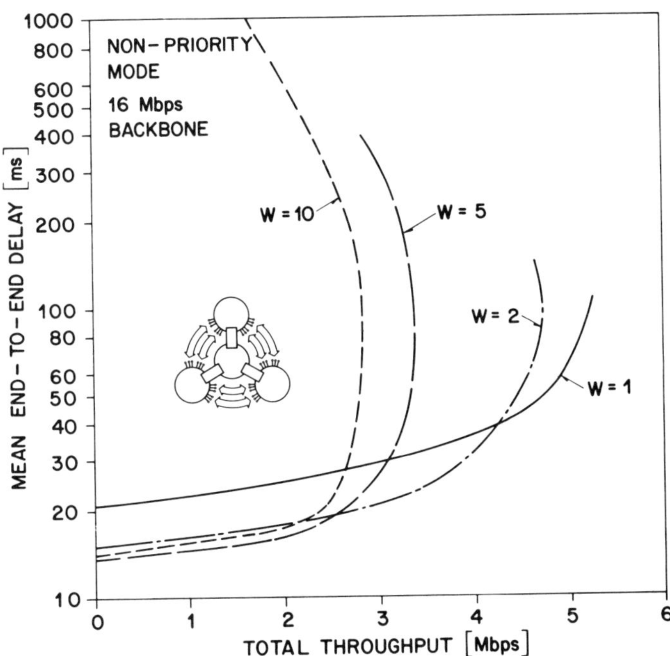

Fig. 7. Mean end-to-end delay vs total throughput for different window sizes W.

access to the local rings. We observe substantial improvement compared to non-priority mode (Fig. 6). In fact, for all the window sizes investigated, no or negligibly few frame losses were observed. The explanation of this remarkable effect is as follows. When priority access for bridges is employed, access of stations to their local ring is delayed slowing down both the injection of new I-frames into the network and the returning of acknowledgments. Delayed acknowledgments, in turn, further throttle the transmission of I-frames because of the LLC window flow-control mechanism. The overall effect is similar to that of flow-control schemes suggested for wide-area packet-switching networks, in which packets are handled with higher priority the closer they are to their destination [8]-[10].

Fig. 9 shows the corresponding delay-throughput characteristic. It should be pointed out that [as will become clear from a subsequent example (Fig. 13)] the effectiveness of the priority-mode operation is due to a great extent to the symmetry of the traffic pattern assumed in this example.

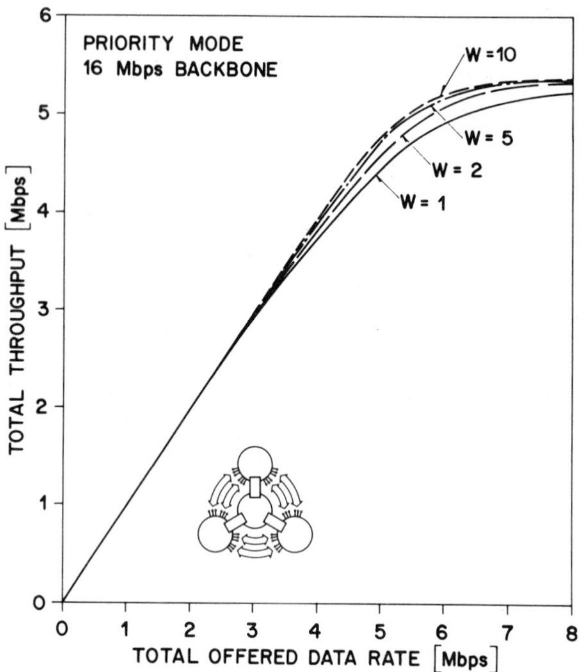

Fig. 8. Total throughput vs total offered data rate for different window sizes W.

A discussion of priorities for bridges would be incomplete without considering their impact on how fair local-ring bandwidth is shared between intra-ring and inter-ring connections. Fig. 10 addresses this question for the following scenario: 24 stations are attached to each ring; 12 of them communicate with 12 stations attached to two other rings; each of the other 12 stations has a logical-link set up with a station on the same ring. I-frame flow is two-way on each connection. All stations generate the same amount of traffic. The figure shows the throughput of all inter-ring and all intra-ring connections as the offered data rate is varied. When priority mode is employed, we observe a fair sharing of the bandwidth between the two connection types in the sense that the total throughput of both is equal, almost completely independent of the traffic load and the LLC window size. In non-priority mode, throughput becomes very unbalanced when the local rings are heavily utilized: High throughput for intra-ring connections, low throughput for inter-ring connections. The explanation for this effect is as follows. In non-priority mode, the intra-ring connections as a whole

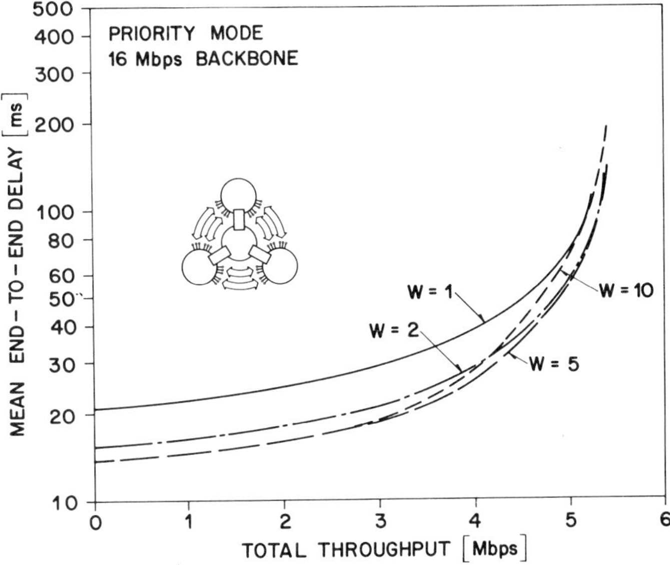

Fig. 9. Mean end-to-end delay vs total throughput for different window sizes W.

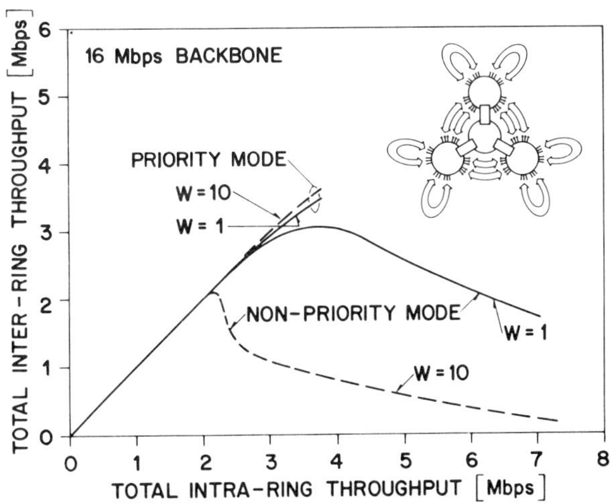

Fig. 10. Total inter-ring vs total intra-ring throughput for different window sizes W.

obtain much better service than the inter-ring connections, because the latter have to share the single-access points of the bridges to the local rings. Furthermore, at larger window sizes, a significant portion of the bandwidth available for inter-ring traffic is lost owing to retransmissions; therefore, unfairness between inter- and intra-ring connections is even more pronounced.

Figures 11 and 12 present further results for a network carrying both inter- and intra-ring traffic. The situation considered here is that 12 stations attached to two rings transmit information frames to 12 stations on the third ring. Further connections are set up among 12 additional stations on the third ring. We consider both priority and non-priority modes for a window size of ten. Fig. 11 shows the throughput on the inter- and intra-ring connections and the total network throughput as a function of the total offered data rate; Fig. 12 gives the corresponding end-to-end delay results. In non-priority mode, we again observe unfair sharing of the ring bandwidth between intra- and inter-ring connections. It is interesting that this unfairness already exists at relatively small offered data rates, and becomes very pronounced at high loads. In priority mode, fair ring bandwidth sharing is achieved up to rather high offered data rates. At very high traffic loads, priority mode tends to favor the inter-ring connections and then delays on both connection types deviate distinctly. However, this unfairness effect is by far less severe than the one in non-priority mode. Furthermore, Fig. 11 reveals that also from

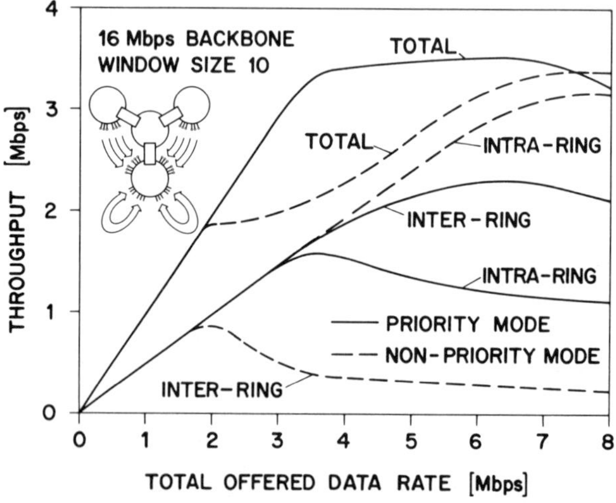

Fig. 11. Inter-ring, intra-ring, and total network throughput vs total offered data rate.

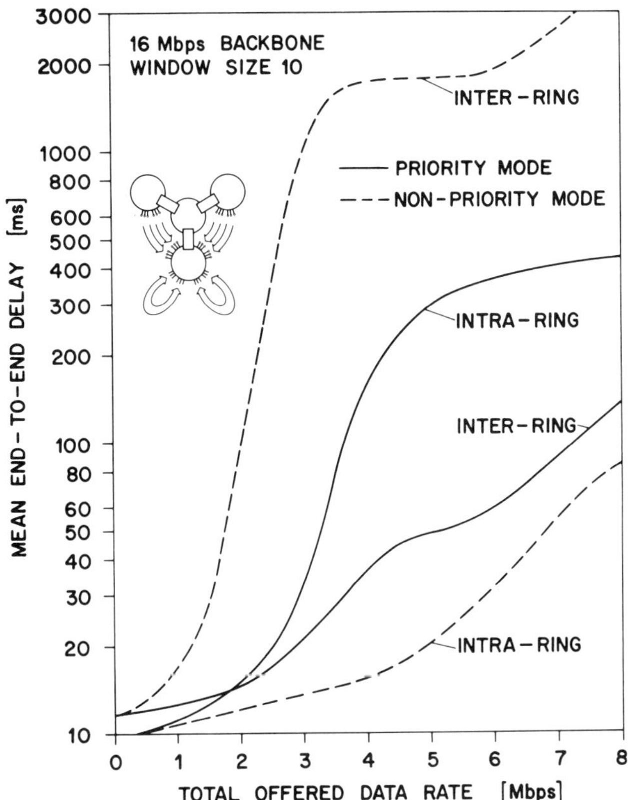

Fig. 12. Mean inter-ring and intra-ring end-to-end delay vs total offered data rate.

a total network throughput point of view, priority mode is superior to non-priority mode.

The conclusion from the examples shown so far is that use of priority ring access for bridges has two distinct advantages. It yields better overall efficiency and fairer sharing of the ring bandwidth.

It is important, however, to understand that priority mode does not avoid congestion problems under all circumstances, as the following two examples demonstrate.

1) When in the scenario of Figs. 4 and 5, priority mode is employed, we observe basically the same throughput and delay characteristics as for non-priority mode. This is not surprising, since the network bottleneck is the backbone, and hence providing bridges

with priority access to their local rings cannot change performance significantly.

2) Even the combination of a fast backbone with ring-access priority for bridges is not always sufficient to avoid congestion problems, as our next example in Fig. 13 demonstrates. Six stations attached to one ring and the same number of stations attached to a second ring transmit I-frames to 12 stations on the third ring. For larger window sizes, we observe the typical throughput characteristic indicating congestion in the bridge connecting the backbone with the third ring when the offered data rate exceeds a certain value.

A further important question is to what extent the bridge-buffer size affects performance. Fig. 14 shows the throughput characteristic for the same scenario as in Fig. 13, except that bridges now have twice as much buffer space as before. Comparison of Figs. 13 and 14 indicates that there is some gain in throughput by enlarging the bridge-buffer size from two times 4 kbyte to two times 8 kbyte. However, the gain is modest, especially in an overload situation, for the following reason. When the input traffic to a bridge approaches its output capabilities, its buffers tend to fill up completely, irrespective of the absolute buffer size, and therefore, frame losses cannot be reduced by increasing the bridge-buffering capacity.

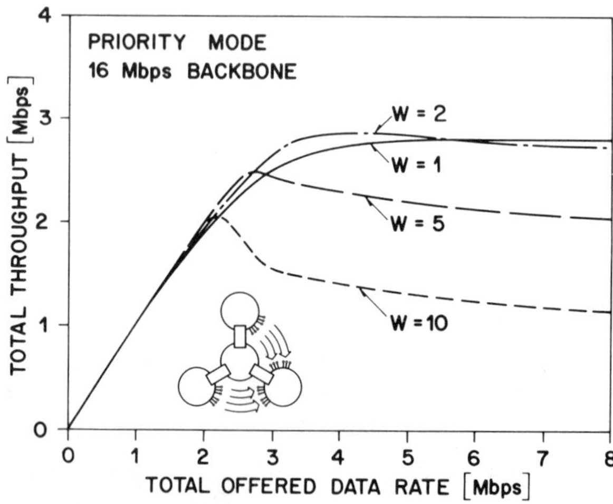

Fig. 13. Total throughput vs total offered data rate for different window sizes W. 2 × 4-kbyte bridge buffer.

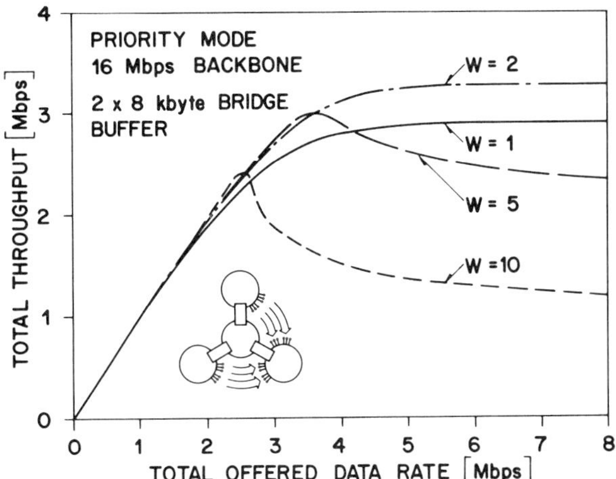

Fig. 14. Total throughput vs total offered data rate for different window sizes W. 2 × 8-kbyte bridge buffer.

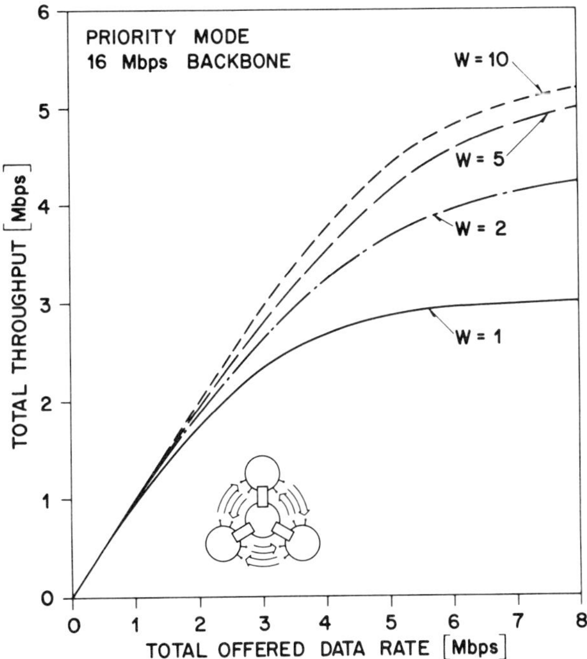

Fig. 15. Total throughput vs total offered data rate for different window sizes W.

All the results shown so far have indicated that a small window size is an effective means of minimizing congestion. However, a small window size can also be a disadvantage, e.g., when only a small number of stations is simultaneously active. In Fig. 15, we show the throughput characteristic of a network in which only two stations on each ring communicate with two stations attached to a different ring. We observe that the total throughput can be substantially improved by increasing the window size. This indicates that at small window sizes, a small number of stations is not able to make full use of the available bandwidth, because acknowledgments do not return sufficiently fast.

4. DYNAMIC FLOW CONTROL

4.1. Concept

The results shown in the previous section demonstrate that in case of congested bridges, network performance can be severely degraded. This suggests that the architecture should be enhanced by providing an effective flow-control mechanism to ensure efficient operation under both normal traffic load and overload.

Our specific proposal is to introduce the following dynamic flow-control algorithm into the IEEE 802.2 Type-2 protocol. Initially, stations use the window size as defined during the set-up of the logical link. Whenever a station needs to retransmit an I-frame (either because of a received Reject frame or after checkpointing) it sets its window size to one. Afterwards, the window size is increased by one (up to the initial value) for every n-th successfully transmitted (i.e., acknowledged) I-frame.

The rationale behind this algorithm is as follows. Under normal conditions, i.e., no congestion, the actual window size used is the one initially chosen by the communicating stations. By reducing the window size to one, whenever there is an indication of a possible congestion, we achieve a high responsiveness of the flow-control mechanism in the sense that an immediate and very effective throttling of the network input traffic is performed. Subsequent to reduction, stations again attempt to increase their window sizes. This process is tightly coupled to the reception of acknowledgments. Hereby, we achieve control of the speed by which the window size is increased, by the momentary ability of the network to transport frames successfully.

We subsequently show how the multi-ring network performs when this enhanced LLC protocol is employed.

4.2. Results

We first address the question of selecting an appropriate value for the parameter n in the dynamic window-size algorithm. The value of n specifies how many I-frames a station needs to transmit successfully (following a window-size reduction) before it increases its window size by one.

For the scenario previously studied in Figs. 4 and 5, in Fig. 16 we show the total network throughput as a function of the total offered data rate for different values of n. The initial window size is ten. We observe substantial improvement in throughput when the window size is dynamically adjusted; the gain is the higher the larger n. The incremental gain in throughput decreases, however, as n increases, see, e.g., the small difference between n = 8 and n = 16. For small values of n, the window is opened too rapidly, i.e., the throttling effect does not last long enough.

For the same example, Fig. 17 shows the end-to-end delay as a function of the total throughput. It can be seen that the delay characteristic is the better the larger the parameter n; in particular for n = 8 or greater, the behavior is almost ideal.

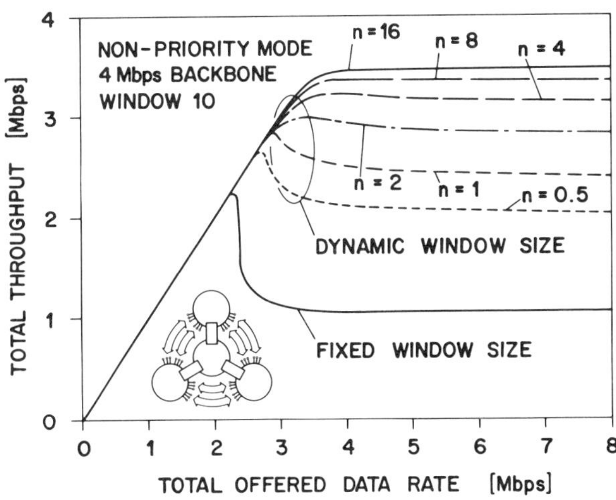

Fig. 16. Total throughput vs total offered data rate for dynamic window-size LLC with initial window size ten. (Note: n = 0.5 means that the window size is increased by two per acknowledgment.)

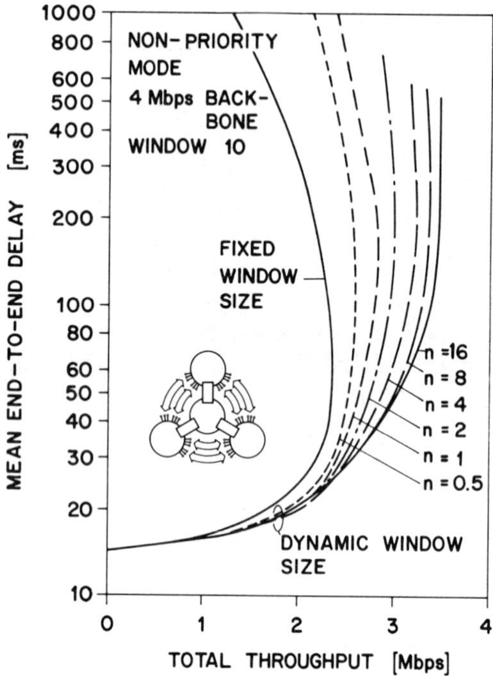

Fig. 17. Mean end-to-end delay vs total throughput for dynamic window-size LLC with initial window size ten. (Note: n = 0.5 means that the window size is increased by two per acknowledgment.)

For the scenario previously considered in the context of Fig. 13 where the entire I-frame traffic is flowing to one ring, Fig. 18 shows the improvement attained through the dynamic window algorithm. Again, a value of n = 8 already yields excellent performance. A general observation from numerous simulations has been that, even under extreme overload, the frame-loss frequencies in bridges is never substantially greater than one percent, when the dynamic window-size algorithm with n > 8 is employed. Under this condition, only a very small fraction of the bandwidth is lost for retransmissions, and hence performance is excellent. For this reason, we chose to use n = 8 in the subsequent examples, intended to show further interesting aspects of the dynamic flow-control algorithm.

The first question we address is whether the dynamic window-size algorithm has an impact on fairness. We consider the same example as in Fig. 11. For the dynamic window-size algorithm with an initial window of 10 and n = 8, Fig. 19 shows the throughput of the inter- and intra-ring connections and the total network throughput for both priority and non-priority modes. The figure demonstrates that the overall efficiency in terms of the total throughput is excellent for both modes when the dynamic window-size algorithm is employed. In the case of non-priority mode, throughput of the inter-ring connections is significantly improved compared to the fixed-window LLC; at medium and high traffic loads, however, there still exists a distinct unfairness between the two connection types in non-priority mode. In priority mode, fairness is good for offered data rates up to the ring transmission rate of 4 Mbps. At high overload, priority mode tends to favor the inter-ring connections.

For the scenario underlying Figs. 13, 14, and 18, we compare in Fig. 20 the throughput characteristics of the dynamic window-size LLC and the fixed window-size LLC for three different bridge-buffer sizes. We have already observed (see Figs. 13 and 14) that for larger fixed window sizes, the overload behavior is not improved through bigger bridge buffers. On the other hand, the dynamic window-size algorithm yields a stable throughput behavior even for relatively small bridge-buffer sizes in the sense that throughput never decreases with increasing offered data rate. With the dynamic window, throughput is improved by bigger bridge buffers, but, increasing the buffer size beyond the two times 8 kbyte shown in the figure, does not yield any noticeable further improvement.

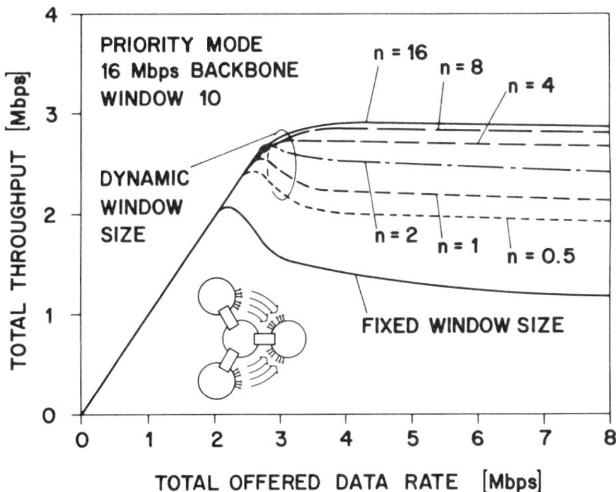

Fig. 18. Total throughput vs total offered data rate for dynamic window-size LLC with initial window size ten. (Note: n = 0.5 means that the window size is increased by two per acknowledgment.)

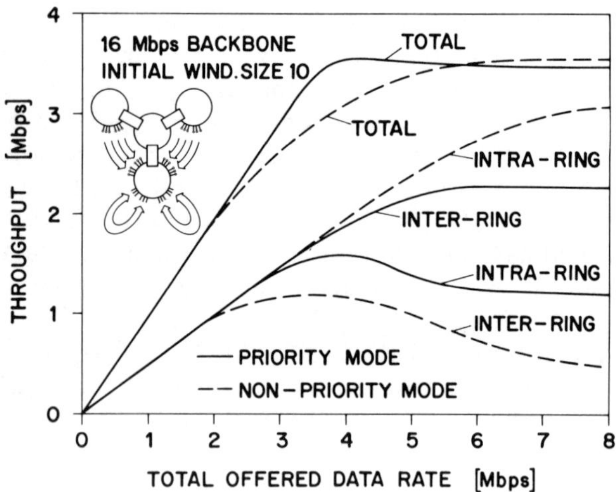

Fig. 19. Inter-ring, intra-ring, and total network throughput vs total offered data rate.

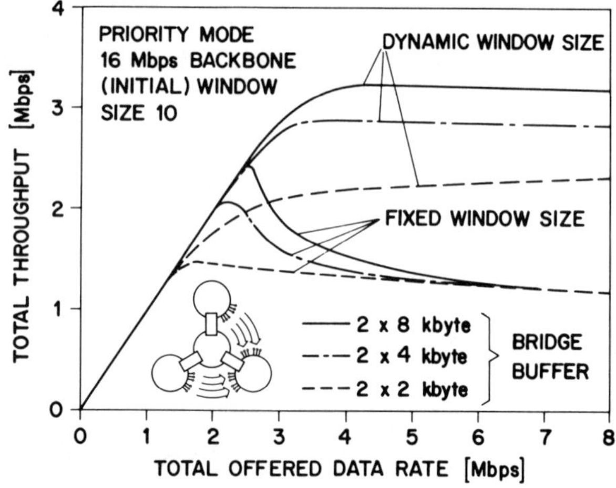

Fig. 20. Total throughput vs total offered data rate for different bridge-buffer sizes.

For both fixed and dynamic window-size LLC, Fig. 21 shows the total throughput of the network with a 16-Mbps backbone ring and priority ring access for bridges. For the case of 0.3 ms mean bridge-processing time per frame, we have already seen from Fig. 8

that performance is excellent even with the fixed window-size LLC. Consequently, the dynamic window-size algorithm yields equally good results in this case. If the frame-processing times in the bridges are substantially longer, i.e., 1.2 ms on the average, the bridge processors become the system bottlenecks at larger values of the offered data rate; hence, we again observe the negative effects of frame losses and retransmissions. The dynamic window helps to improve performance also in this case. The algorithm works in such a way that the bridge processors are very highly utilized, but at the same time, the frame-loss frequency remains small, typically on the order of one percent.

In our last example, we reconsider the scenario of a 4-Mbps backbone ring and completely symmetrical traffic, however, the number of active stations is varied. For the fixed-window protocol, we observe from Fig. 22 that congestion generally becomes worse when the number of stations increases. In contrast, network performance is no longer sensitive to the number of stations, when the

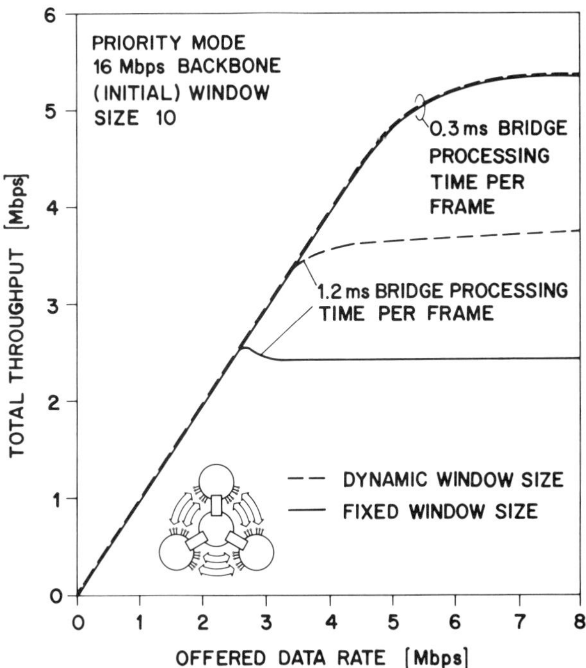

Fig. 21. Total throughput vs total offered data rate for different bridge-processing times.

dynamic window-size algorithm is employed. These observations shed additional light onto the necessity of a dynamic flow-control scheme in multi-ring networks. We conclude the discussion of the dynamic flow-control scheme with two final remarks:

1) In all cases where the fixed window-size protocol works without congestion problems, the dynamic flow-control algorithm yields equally good performance since the window size is never or only very rarely reduced. A typical example is the one of Fig. 15 for which the throughput characteristic of the dynamic-window LLC with an initial window size of ten is identical to the result for the fixed window of ten, namely, almost ideal.
2) If I-frames are lost owing to transmission errors and not congestion, the window will be unnecessarily reduced. However, for normally functioning rings with bit error rates of, e.g., 10^{-9} or less, this will not cause any noticeable performance degradation. On the other hand, in failure situations, e.g., transient periods with high error rates or short ring interruptions, our flow-control method may be very helpful. After a failure, heavy overload can occur owing to back-logged traffic and increased recovery activity. Initial experiments suggest that this overload can be very effectively controlled by the dynamic window mechanism. This is the subject of an ongoing study.

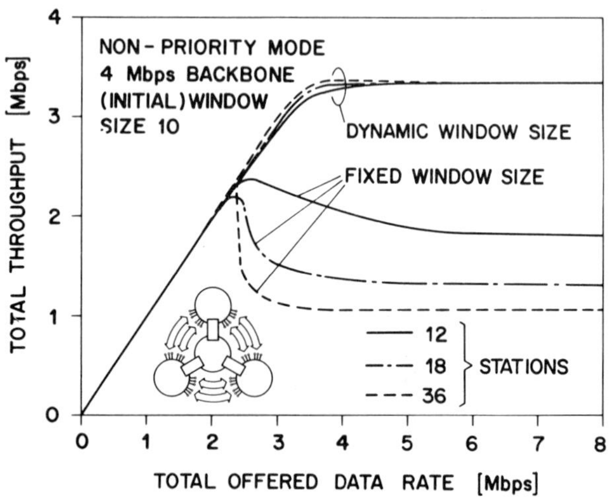

Fig. 22. Total throughput vs total offered data rate for different number of active stations.

5. CONCLUSION

In this paper, we have investigated the performance of local networks consisting of interconnected token rings. We first considered networks in which the IEEE 802.2 Type-2 LLC protocol as defined today is employed end-to-end. The key observations of this part of the study are: 1) in a congested network, large fixed window sizes can lead to severe performance degradation. On the other hand, small windows are unnecessarily restrictive and can lead to poor performance if the network is not congested. 2) If bridges are provided with priority to access the local rings, significant improvements both with respect to overall efficiency and fair sharing of bandwidth can be achieved. 3) To a limited extent, performance can be improved by providing larger buffers in bridges. However, in general, large bridge buffers are not sufficient to overcome congestion problems. 4) Generally, the congestion problem becomes more severe the larger the number of active stations in the network.

From these observations, we concluded that the architecture should be enhanced by a suitable flow-control mechanism. Our proposed solution is to add a dynamic window-size algorithm to the LLC protocol. Simulations demonstrate that the algorithm suggested yields close-to-optimal network performance under both normal traffic load and overload conditions, different traffic patterns, different number of stations, and even relatively small bridge-buffer sizes. Besides its effectiveness in minimizing congestion, the new flow control method has the following attractive properties: i) it is simple to implement; ii) is local to the station sending information frames, hence no additional information exchange is required; iii) is compatible with the fixed window-size protocol; iv) bridges need not be involved in flow control; and v) the medium-access control protocol is not affected.

ACKNOWLEDGEMENT

The authors would like to thank D. W. Andrews, N. A. Bouroudjian, K. Kümmerle, D. A. Pitt and K. K. Sy for many helpful discussions.

REFERENCES

[1] Standard ECMA-89: Local Area Networks Token Ring Technique.

[2] ANSI/IEEE Standard 802.5 – 1985, Token Ring Access Method and Physical Layer Specifications.

[3] K. K. Sy and D. A. Pitt, "An architecture for interconnected token rings," Proposal to IEEE 802.5 Committee, February 1984.

[4] ANSI/IEEE Standard 802.2 – 1985, Logical Link Control.

[5] C. H. Sauer and E. A. MacNair, "Simulation of computer communication systems", Prentice Hall, Englewood Cliffs, N.Y., 1983.

[6] W. Bux, F. Closs, K. Kümmerle, H. Keller, and H. R. Müller, "A reliable token ring for local communications," *IEEE Selected Areas in Commun.*, vol. SAC-1, pp. 756-765, 1983.

[7] J. F. Shoch and J. A. Hupp, "Measured performance of an Ethernet local network," *Commun. ACM*, vol. 23, pp. 711-721, 1980.

[8] M. Gerla and L. Kleinrock, "Flow control: A comparative survey," *IEEE Trans. Commun.*, vol. COM-28, pp. 553-574, 1980.

[9] A. Giessler, A. Jaegemann, E. Maeser, and J. O. Haenle, "Flow control based on buffer classes", *IEEE Trans. Commun.*, vol. COM-29, pp. 436-443, 1981.

[10] S. S. Lam and M. Reiser, "Congestion control of store-and-forward networks by input buffer limits - An analysis," *IEEE Trans. Commun.*, vol. COM-27, pp. 127-134, 1979.

Optimal Interconnection Networks For Parallel Processors: The Importance Of Being Square

Clyde P. Kruskal
Department of Computer Science
University of Maryland
College Park, Maryland 20742

Marc Snir
Institute of Mathematics and Computer Science
The Hebrew University of Jerusalem
Jerusalem, Israel

ABSTRACT

We present a theory that defines the performance (delay and bandwidth) and cost of packet-switching interconnection networks in terms of their geometry. This is used to prove that square banyan networks provide optimal performance versus cost. Some conjectures generalizing the results to nonsquare banyan networks are also given.

1. INTRODUCTION

The current interest in large scale parallel processors has motivated a large amount of research on multistage interconnection networks for parallel processing (see, for example, [DJ2,Fe,KS1,Si]). Most of the literature centers on the analysis of circuit-switching networks.

More recently, packet-switching networks have been considered for MIMD machines, where a large number of independent, asynchronous processors generate requests to shared memory modules. The performance of different network configurations, mostly variants of the

Part of this work was done while the first author was at the University of Illinois and the second author was at New York University. This work was supported in part by a grant from IBM. A preliminary version of this material appeared in the *11th Annual International Symposium on Computer Architecture* [KS3].

"banyan networks" have been analyzed (see, for example, [BA,DJ1,Pa,KJ,KS2]). On the other hand, there has been practically no research on the inverse, *synthesis*, problem: Given a particular performance requirement from a network, find the least cost network fulfilling this requirement. This is, of course, the problem that arises when parallel computers are designed.

The performance of a network depends on many factors. One factor is the traffic pattern, i.e. the statistical properties of the traffic submitted to the network. Other factors include the geometry (i.e. the structure) of the network, the service provided by the network nodes, the global control, if there is such, etc. The first factor mentioned above, the traffic pattern, is the "free variable" that defines the communication problem to be solved. The remaining parameters are coordinates of the solution domain.

In this paper we attempt to establish a theory of the performance of interconnection networks in terms of their geometry. In order to do so, we have to define the cost of a network only in terms of its geometry, and define the performance of a network only in terms of its geometry and the traffic pattern. Informally, networks are modeled in the following way: switches have unbounded capacity, and the cost of a network is the number of connections between switches. This provides a reasonable model of networks composed of switches with large buffers. We do not restrict the type of service provided by the switches, but we show that optimal performance can be obtained with service policies that can be locally implemented. We can now ask the question: What are the optimal network geometries for a given traffic pattern?

We shall consider two performance measures: delay and bandwidth. Inequalities relating these two performance measures to cost are derived for networks with bounded fanin or bounded fanout. The main application given in this paper to this "geometric theory" of network performance will be a proof that "square banyan networks" have optimal bandwidth/cost ratio for symmetric traffic (the same amount of traffic occurrs between each input-output pair). This holds for an extremely general class of distributions of arrivals and of service times. When requests are restricted to being M/M/1 (Poisson arrivals, exponential service times), as is typically assumed in queueing theory, square networks also provide optimal delay. We also give some conjectures generalizing the results to nonsquare banyan networks.

2. DEFINITIONS

We model packet-switching networks as follows: A network consists of switches connected by unidirectional lines; each switch is a store and forward node, with unbounded buffers; and the switches are *non-blocking*, i.e. there is no interference between service of messages outgoing a switch through distinct edges. Thus, a separate server is attached to each edge in the network, which forwards messages on that edge.

Formally, an *(M,N)-network* G consists of a directed graph, with a set I of M distinguished input nodes, and a set O of N distinguished output nodes. The *cost* $C(G)$ *of* G is defined to be the number of edges in G.

We model each server in the network as a G/G/1 queue. The probabilistic assumptions are:

(1) Messages are generated at i for destination o by a random process; intervals between successive messages generated at input i for destination o are independent, identically distributed random variables, with finite expectation. Note that traffic between distinct input-output pairs is not required to be independent.

(2) The service times of messages at edges (i.e. the time required to forward a message on an edge) are identically distributed random variables; distinct service times are independent (even for the same message at different edges). We assume w.l.g. that the average service rate on an edge is one.

We shall prove stability results for such networks, that is, analyze their bandwidth. The results are, in fact, valid under even weaker assumptions: it is only required that average traffic load per edge be defined in the limit.

We cannot give an analysis of delays in such a general framework: no decomposition results are known for networks of G/G/1 queues. A more elaborate analysis can be carried out for an M/M/1 network model. In the M/M/1 model, the assumptions are:

(3) The service time per message at each edge has an exponential distribution, with rate one.

(4) For each (i,o) pair, messages are generated at i for o by a Poisson process.

The service required from a network is characterized by the distribution of messages generated at each input i for each output o. We shall use two parameters to define that distribution:

(1) The *traffic intensity* τ is the average number of messages entering the network per time unit.

(2) The *load balance* $\phi(i,o)$ is the relative frequency of message transmissions from input i to output o.

Thus, $\tau\phi(i,o)$ is the average number of messages sent from i to o per time unit. Note that the probabilistic assumptions we have on the message generating processes imply that these averages are well defined.

The service provided by a network depends on its geometry, and on the *service policy* used. In particular, one has to *route* messages, and assign to each a path in the network. We characterize this routing statistically by a *route distribution* $\rho(p)$, which is the relative frequency of usage of path p. The average number of messages sent from i to o through path p per time unit is equal to $\tau\rho(p)$.

We do not make any assumptions on the mechanism used to assign paths to messages. It may be centralized or distributed; it may be explicit or implicit. We do assume that the service policy is stationary so that ρ is well defined in the limit.

We assume that no path uses the same edge twice (although this restriction can be dropped). Let $\Pi(i,o)$ be the set of (loopless) paths connecting input i to output o. We have

$$\phi(i,o) = \sum_{p \in \Pi(i,o)} \rho(p) .$$

A route distribution ρ *is consistent* with the load balance ϕ if this last equality is fulfilled for each input-output pair (i,o).

A network G, with given traffic distribution ϕ and service policy S, is *stable* if the expected transit time per message through the network is uniformly bounded. We define $B(G)$, the *bandwidth* of a network G, to be the l.u.b. of the traffic intensities for which the network is stable. Formally,

$$B_\phi(G) = \sup\{\tau : G \text{ is stable for some service policy, with traffic defined by } \tau \text{ and } \phi\} .$$

This definition implicitly assumes that stability does not depend on the distribution of the message generating process, but only on the parameters ϕ and τ. We justify this assumption in the next section, where an explicit formula is given for $B_\phi(G)$.

3. BANDWIDTH OF G/G/1 NETWORKS

Consider a network G that supports traffic with intensity τ and load balance ϕ. Let ρ be the route distribution. Let χ_p be the characteristic function of the path p : $\chi_p(e) = 1$ if $e \in p$, $\chi_p(e) = 0$ otherwise. The average number of messages sent through edge e per time unit is equal to

$$\sum_p \tau\rho(p)\chi_p(e) .$$

Since the service rate is equal to one, we must have

$$\tau\sum_p \rho(p)\chi_p(e) \leq 1$$

for any edge e of the network G, in order that the network be stable. Define

$$B_\rho(G) = \min_e \left[\sum_p \rho(p)\chi_p(e)\right]^{-1} .$$

Then traffic intensity in network G, with a routing policy that has distribution ρ, fulfills the inequality

$$\tau \leq B_\rho(G) . \tag{3.1}$$

We proceed to show that any traffic intensity $\tau < B_\rho(G)$ can be supported by G with route distribution ρ. We prove it by defining a suitable service policy. This service policy decouples service on each path, so that each path forms a tandem system that is in equilibrium.

Let $P_e(p)$ is the fraction of time the server on edge e should devote to messages following path p , i.e.

$$P_e(p) = \begin{cases} \dfrac{\rho(p)}{\sum_{p'} \rho(p')\chi_{p'}(e)} & \text{if } e \in p \\ P_e(p) = 0 & \text{otherwise.} \end{cases}$$

Let $P(p)$ be the fraction of messages going from i to o that use path p, i.e.

$$P(p) = \frac{\rho(p)}{\sum_{p' \in \Pi(i,o)} \rho(p')} .$$

We use the following service policy:

a) A message generated at i for o is randomly assigned a path $p \in \Pi(i,o)$, where path p is chosen with probability $P(p)$. This yields a distribution ρ on routes.

b) When a previous service period terminates, the server of edge e randomly picks a path p, where p is picked with probability $P_e(p)$; if there is a message traversing path p waiting to be served, then the earliest arrival is transmitted; otherwise, the server is idle for a random period of time; the length of the idle period is a random variable, with the same distribution as the service periods.

This service policy can be implemented locally, by tagging each message with a label of the path it follows.

Let $e_1, \ldots, e_k$ be the edges on a path e. The interarrival times of messages to the path p are i.i.d. random variables; the arrival rate of messages onto path p is equal to $\tau\phi(i,o)P(p) = \tau\rho(p)$. These messages are served by k successive servers. Queueing policy at each server is First Come First Serve (FCFS).

Consider the service of one server e_j on behalf of path p. Let x_n be the time between the end of the $(n-1)$-th service period and the end of the n-th service period that e_j reserves for path p. Then x_n is the sum of ν independent service periods, where ν is a random variable that has a geometric distribution with parameter $P_{e_j}(p)$. As each service period has expected length one, the expected value of x_n is

$$E(x_n) = E(\nu) = \left(P_{e_j}(p)\right)^{-1}.$$

If a message arrives at e_j when other messages from the same path are there, then its "service time" will be the length of some period x_n; if it arrives when there are no messages from the same path, then its "service time" will be part of such a period (the residual part of the current period x_n); thus, service rate is at least $E(x_n)^{-1} = P_{e_j}(p)$.

Assume now that $\tau < B_\rho$. Then

$$\tau\rho(p) < \rho(p)B_\rho \leq \rho(p)\left[\sum_{e_j \in p'} \rho(p')\right]^{-1} = P_{e_j}(p).$$

The arrival rate to the tandem system is smaller than the service rate at each server. It follows that the system is stable (see [Ha]). We have proven

THEOREM 3.1. Let ρ be a route distribution on network G that is consistent with the load balance ϕ. If the network is stable for a traffic intensity τ, and route distribution ρ, then $\tau < B_\rho(G)$. Conversely, there exists a service policy with route distribution ρ such that the network is stable for any traffic intensity $\tau < B_\rho(G)$ when this policy is used.

COROLLARY 3.2. The bandwidth $B_\phi(G)$ of network G is equal to $\max_\rho B_\rho(G)$, where maximum is taken over all route distributions consistent with the load balance ϕ.

Note that optimal bandwidth is achieved using a very simple service policy that can be implemented with no central control.

4. PERFORMANCE OF M/M/1 NETWORKS

Because the queueing discipline defined in the previous section decouples service on the different paths, it probably yields higher delays, for reasonable distributions, than the FCFS discipline. However, we are not aware of a general stability result that is valid for networks of G/G/1 queues, with the FCFS queueing discipline. We can prove such a result for the M/M/1 model. Moreover, in this model we can give closed form formulas for delay.

Let G be a network, ϕ be the load balance for G, and ρ be a route distribution that is consistent with ϕ. We assume the following service policy:

a) Each message generated at i for o is randomly assigned a path $p \in \Pi(i, o)$, where path p is chosen with probability

$$P(p) = \frac{\rho(p)}{\sum_{p' \in \Pi(i,o)} \rho(p')} .$$

b) Messages are served at each edge according to the FCFS discipline.

The routing policy yields the distribution ρ on routes. Messages sent from i to o via path p form a Poisson process, with rate $\tau\rho(p)$. Thus, we have an open network of M/M/1 queues, where customers of each type enter the network following a Poisson process, routing is determined by customer type, and service requirements at each server are i.i.d. exponential random variables. The equilibrium distribution of such a system has a product form representation [Ke, §3.1].

The average number of messages arriving at edge e per time unit is equal to

$$\lambda_e = \tau \sum_p \rho(p) \chi_p(e) .$$

The equilibrium condition for the network is $\lambda_e < 1$, for every e, i.e.

$$\tau < \min_e \left[\sum_e \rho(p) \chi_p(e) \right]^{-1} = B_\rho(G) .$$

This, together with (3.1), yields

THEOREM 4.1. Assume the M/M/1 model for networks. Let ρ be a route distribution on network G that is consistent with the load balance ϕ. If the network is stable for traffic intensity τ then $\tau < B_\rho(G)$; conversely there exists a simple routing policy such that the network is stable for any traffic intensity $\tau < B_\rho(G)$, when this routing policy and the FCFS queueing discipline are used.

COROLLARY 4.2. Assume the M/M/1 model for networks. The bandwidth $B_\phi(G)$ of network G using the FCFS service policy is equal to $\max_\rho B_\rho(G)$, where maximum is taken over all route distributions consistent with the load balance ϕ.

Assume the M/M/1 network model, and the service policy previously defined. Then the average queueing delay (in the limit) for a message on path p is

$$\overline{\delta}_{G,\rho,p}(\tau) = \sum_e \left[1-\lambda_e\right]^{-1} \chi_p(e)$$

[Ke, §3.1, ex. 4]. The average queueing delay per message is

$$\overline{\delta}_{G,\rho}(\tau) = \sum_p \rho(p)\overline{\delta}_{G,\rho,p}(p) = \sum_e \frac{\lambda_e}{1-\lambda_e} . \tag{4.1}$$

The maximum queueing delay is

$$\delta_{G,\rho}(\tau) = \max_p \overline{\delta}_{G,\rho,p}(\tau) .$$

This is the average queueing delay for a message on the worst path.

We define the average queueing delay for network G and load balance ϕ as

$$\overline{\delta}_{G,\phi}(\tau) = \min_\rho \overline{\delta}_{G,\rho}(\tau) ,$$

where the minimum is taken over all route distributions ρ that are consistent with ϕ. The maximum queueing delay is defined similarly:

$$\delta_{G,\phi}(\tau) = \min_\rho \delta_{G,\rho}(\tau) .$$

5. FUNDAMENTAL INEQUALITY

We derive in this section the fundamental "thermodynamic" inequality for interconnection networks. This inequality captures the following obvious relation: The rate of work done by a network in forwarding messages is bounded from above by the sum of the rate of work of all the servers in the network; or, the efficiency of an interconnection network is never larger than one. This inequality represents the basic physical constraint on the performance of a network.

Let $L(p)$ be the length of path p. For a given route distribution ρ, define the *average path length of G*

$$d_\rho(G) = \sum_p \rho(p) L(p) .$$

It is the average number of service periods needed to forward a message through the network G. If τ is the average number of messages entering the network per time unit, then the network must provide on average $\tau d_\rho(G)$ service periods per time unit; this is the useful rate of work of the network. Recall that the cost $C(G)$ of network G is the number of edges in G. This is also the average number of service periods the network can provide per time unit. We get the fundamental inequality

$$\tau(G) \cdot d_\rho(G) \leq C(G)$$

from which a bound on the network bandwidth follows:

$$B_\rho(G) \cdot d_\rho(G) \leq C(G) .$$

This inequality is proven formally in the next lemma.

LEMMA 5.1.

$$B_\rho(G) \cdot d_\rho(G) \leq C(G) .$$

PROOF: We have

$$\frac{C(G)}{B_\rho(G)} = C(G) \max_e \sum_p \rho(p) \chi_p(e) \geq \sum_e \sum_p \rho(p) \chi_p(e)$$

$$= \sum_p \rho(p) L(p) = d_\rho(G) .$$

□

We may take the ratio $\frac{B_\rho(G) \cdot d_\rho(G)}{C(G)}$ to be a measure of the *efficiency* of the network for a given route distribution. The efficiency is always between zero and one. An efficiency of one is achieved when we have equality in the last lemma. This happens if and only if $\sum_p \rho(p)\chi_p(e)$ is constant for every edge e, i.e. the load on each edge is equal.

Let $d(i,o)$ be the length of the shortest path connecting i to o. For a given load balance ϕ define the *average depth of* G

$$d_\phi(G) = \sum_{i,o} \phi(i,o) d(i,o) .$$

Clearly, $d_\phi(G) = \min_\rho d_\rho(G)$, where the minimum is taken over all route distributions ρ consistent with ϕ: the minimum is obtained for the route distribution that assigns probability $\phi(i,o)$ to a shortest path connecting i to o, and probability zero to all other paths.

We can derive a fundamental inequality for the network G with route distribution ϕ.

LEMMA 5.2.

$$B_\phi(G) \cdot d_\phi(G) \leq C(G) .$$

PROOF: Let $B_\phi(G) = B_\rho(G)$, for some optimal route distribution ρ. Then

$$B_\phi(G) \cdot d_\phi(G) = B_\rho(G) \cdot d_\phi(G) \leq B_\rho(G) \cdot d_\rho(G) \leq C(G) .$$

□

In the next section, we use the last inequality in order to establish bounds on the bandwidth of networks in terms of their cost.

6. APPLICATIONS

From now on we shall assume the *symmetric* load balance: $\phi(i,o)$ is constant. We furthermore assume that nodes have indegree bounded by k (symmetrical results obtain if the outdegree is bounded), input nodes have indegree zero, and output nodes have outdegree zero. Let $\mathbf{G}(M,N,k)$ be the family of such networks with M inputs, N outputs, and indegree bounded by k.

A straightforward fanin argument shows that the shortest path length of a bounded degree network is logarithmic in the number of inputs. More precisely, we have

LEMMA 6.1. Let $G \in \mathbf{G}(M,N,k)$. Then $d(G) \geq \log_k M$.

PROOF: Let T be a tree of shortest paths connecting an output o to each of the M inputs $i \in I$. This tree has indegree bounded by k, and therefore its average path length is at least $\log_k M$. It follows that $\sum_i d(i,o) \geq M \log_k M$ for each output o, so that

$$d(G) = \frac{1}{MN} \sum_{i,o} d(i,o) \geq \frac{1}{MN} \sum_o M \log_k M = \log_k M .$$

□

COROLLARY 6.2. Let $G \in \mathbf{G}(M,N,k)$. Then

$$B(G) \leq \frac{C(G)}{\log_k M} .$$

PROOF: This claim follows immediately from the two last lemmas. □

Equality holds in the last formula if and only if each edge is equally loaded, and each input-output path has length $\log_k M$. Networks with this property have optimal bandwidth/cost ratio. We will investigate the structure of these optimal networks.

There is another constraint on the bandwidth of networks in $\mathbf{G}(M,N,k)$: There are at most kN edges connected to the output nodes, so that the bandwidth is at most kN. Formally, we have

LEMMA 6.3. Let $G \in \mathbf{G}(M,N,k)$. Then

$$B(G) \leq kN .$$

PROOF: Let Γ be the set of edges incoming output nodes of G. Then

$$|\Gamma| \leq k\,|O| = kN .$$

Also

$$\sum_{e \in \Gamma} \sum_p \rho(p) \chi_p(e) \geq \sum_p \rho(p) = 1 .$$

It follows that

$$\sum_p \rho(p) \chi_p(e) \geq \frac{1}{|\Gamma|} \geq \frac{1}{kN}$$

for some edge $e \in \Gamma$. Thus,

$$B_\rho(G) = \min_e \left[\sum_p \rho(p) \chi_p(e) \right]^{-1} \leq kN .$$

□

We recall the following definitions: A network with a unique path from each input to each output is called a *banyan network* [GL]. A banyan network is *layered* if the nodes can be arranged in successive layers, with inputs at the first layer, outputs at the last layer, and edges connecting nodes from one layer to nodes at the next layer. A *square banyan network* is a layered banyan network where all nodes (with the exception of inputs) have indegree exactly k, and all nodes (with the exception of outputs) have outdegree exactly k. A square banyan network has $r+1$ layers, each consisting of k^r nodes. A square banyan network is illustrated in Figure 1.

THEOREM 6.4. Let $G \in \mathbf{G}(k^r, k^r, k)$. Then the following are equivalent:

(i) G is a square banyan network.

(ii) G has maximum bandwidth $B = k^{r+1}$, and achieves this bandwidth with the least possible cost.

(iii) G has the best possible bandwidth/cost ratio.

PROOF: Note that, for each network $G \in \mathbf{G}(k^r, k^r, k)$ we have
(a) $C(G) \geq rB(G)$ (Corollary 6.2), and
(b) $B(G) \leq k^{r+1}$ (Lemma 6.1).

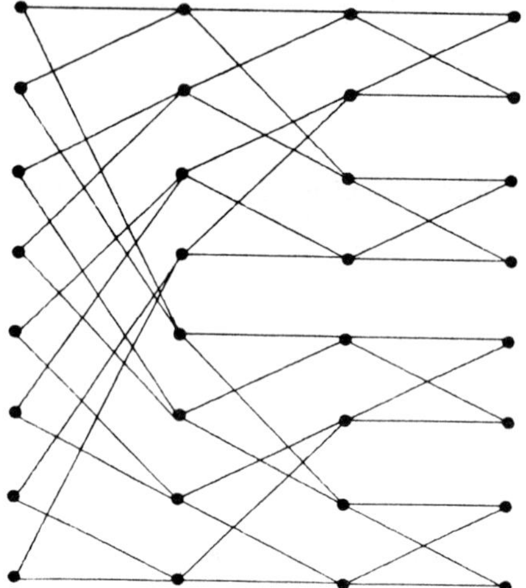

Figure 1. Square banyan network ($r=3$).

Let G be a square banyan network. The number of edges of G is equal to

$$C(G) = rk^{r+1} .$$

Each edge occurs on exactly k^{r-1} paths, so that

$$B(G) = \min_e \sum_p k^{-2r} \chi_p(e) = k^{r+1} .$$

It follows (by (b)) that G has maximum bandwidth, and (by (a)) that this bandwidth is achieved at least possible cost. Thus, (i) $\Longrightarrow$ (ii).

The least cost of a network $G \in \mathbf{G}(k^r, k^r, k)$ with bandwidth k^{r+1} has been shown to be rk^{r+1}. For such networks $B(G)/C(G) = 1/r$, which is optimal, by (a). Thus, (ii) $\Longrightarrow$ (iii).

Let $G \in \mathbf{G}(k^r, k^r, k)$ be a network such that $B(G) = C(G)/r$. Then each input-output path that is used in G has length exactly r, and each edge is shared by an equal number of paths. The last fact implies that if v is a node that is neither input nor output to the network, then the indegree of v equals to its outdegree. If i is an input of G then i is connected to each of the k^r outputs by a path of length at most r. These paths form a tree of degree bounded by k. It follows that this is a complete tree, and each internal node on the tree has outdegree exactly equal to k. The tree therefore contains all paths outgoing i. It follows that there is a unique path from each input to each output. Since the tree of paths is complete, the paths connecting distinct outputs to the same node all have the same length, which means network is layered. The indegree and outdegree of each internal node is exactly equal to k. The network is therefore a square banyan network. Thus, (iii) $\Longrightarrow$ (i). □

Stronger results can be obtained in the M/M/1 model: for their cost, square banyan networks have minimal delays at any traffic intensity.

Assume that traffic and service conform to the M/M/1 model, with the assumptions made in §4: messages are randomly assigned to paths with each path chosen with the probability defined by ρ, and service at each edge is FCFS. By (4.1), the average queueing delay for route distribution ρ is

$$\overline{\delta}_{G,\rho}(\tau) = \sum_e \frac{\lambda_e}{1-\lambda_e} . \tag{6.1}$$

But,

$$\sum_e \lambda_e = \tau \sum_e \sum_p \rho(p) \chi_p(e) = \tau \sum_p \rho(p) L(p) = \tau d_\rho(G) . \tag{6.2}$$

Using Lagrange multipliers, (6.1) is minimized under constraint (6.2) when the λ_e are all equal; thus

$$\overline{\delta}_{G,\rho}(\tau) \geq \sum_e \frac{\tau d_\rho(G)/C(G)}{1-\tau d_\rho(G)/C(G)} = \frac{\tau d_\rho(G)}{1-\tau d_\rho(G)/C(G)} , \tag{6.3}$$

and equality obtains if and only if the λ_e are all equal. The right side of (6.3) is an increasing function of d_ρ. Thus,

$$\frac{\tau d_\rho(G)}{1-\tau d_\rho(G)/C(G)} \geq \frac{\tau d(G)}{1-\tau d(G)/C(G)} ,$$

and equality obtains if and only if $d_\rho(G) = d(G)$. Finally, for any network $G \in \mathbf{G}(k^r, k^r, k)$,

$$d(G) \geq r .$$

A square banyan network with the symmetric load balance has $B(G) = k^r$, $d_\rho(G) = d(G) = r$, and equal load on each edge. Thus, it achieves minimum average queueing delay for any fixed traffic intensity τ and fixed cost $C(G) = rk^{r+1}$. Conversely, we have shown in the first part of this section that a network with the previous three properties must be a square banyan network. We have proven

THEOREM 6.5. Let $G \in \mathbf{G}(k^r, k^r, k)$ be a square banyan network, and let $G' \in \mathbf{G}(k^r, k^r, k)$ be another network, with $C(G') \leq C(G)$. Then, for every $\tau < k^{r+1}$,

$$\bar{\delta}_G(\tau) < \bar{\delta}_{G'}(\tau) .$$

Note that the total delay of a message in a network is the length of the path it traverses plus its queueing delay. The above theorem shows that square networks have minimum queueing delay. Since (independently) they also have minimum average path length (Lemma 6.1), square networks have minimum total delay.

For any network we have

$$\delta_G(\tau) \geq \bar{\delta}_G(\tau) ,$$

and equality holds when G is a square banyan network. Thus, the last theorem is valid, with average delay replaced by maximum delay.

7. EXPANDING AND CONTRACTING NETWORKS

We shall consider in this section networks of higher and lower costs than square banyan networks. We continue to assume the symmetric load balance.

Consider networks in $G(k^r, k^r, k)$. Networks of cost (and bandwidth) less than square banyan networks can be built out of contracting stages of $k \times 1$ nodes, followed by stages of $k \times k$ nodes, followed by expanding stages of $1 \times k$ nodes. Formally, a (k, r, j)-*contracting banyan network* is a layered network with k^r inputs, k^r outputs, and $r+j+1$ stages. The nodes in the first j stages have outdegree 1, and (with the exception of the inputs) indegree k. The nodes in the last j stages have indegree 1, and (with the exception of the output nodes) outdegree k. The nodes in the middle $r-j+1$ stages have indegree and outdegree k; they are connected to form a square banyan network. There is in this network a unique path from each input to each output. A contracting banyan network is illustrated in Figure 2.

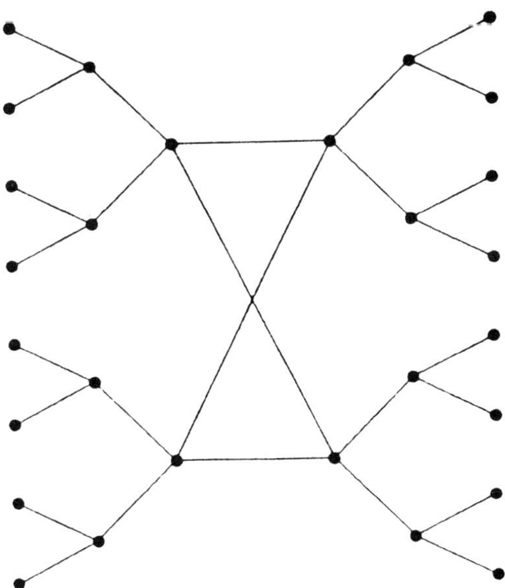

Figure 2. (2,3,2)-contracting banyan network.

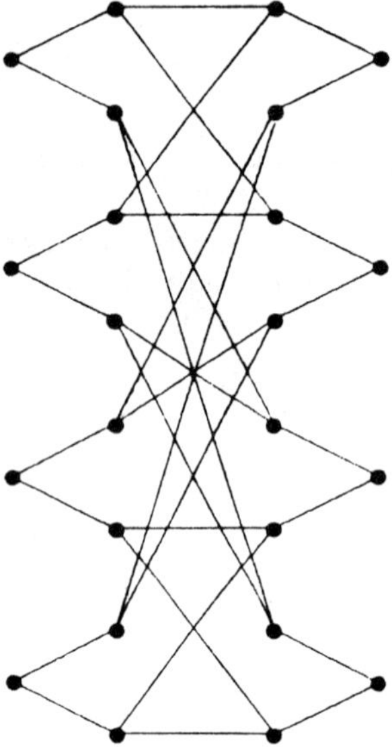

Figure 3. (2,2,1)-expanding banyan network.

Conversely, one can build a network that starts with expanding stages, followed by stages of $k \times k$ nodes, followed by contracting stages. Formally, a (k, r, j)*-expanding banyan network* is a layered network with k^r inputs, k^r outputs, and $r+j+1$ stages. The nodes in the first j stages have outdegree k, and (with the exception of the input nodes) indegree 1. The nodes in the last j stages have indegree k, and (with the exception of the output nodes) outdegree 1. The nodes in the middle $r-j+1$ stages have indegree and outdegree k. They are connected to form k^{2j} disjoint square banyan networks, each with k^{r-j} inputs and outputs. Each input has a path to k^j of these middle banyan networks, and so has each output. The connections are arranged so that for each input-output pair (i, o) there is exactly one middle banyan network connected by paths both to i and o. Thus, there is a unique path connecting each input-output pair. An expanding banyan network is illustrated in Figure 3.

Variants of expanding and contracting banyan networks have been defined and studied [De,KJ]. We have taken the liberty of modifying their definitions to fit our context.

The bandwidth of a (k,r,j)-contracting network is equal to k^{r-j+1}; the bandwidth of a (k,r,j)-expanding network is equal to k^{r+1}.

By (4.1), the average delay, in the M/M/1 model, for a (k,r,j)-expanding network with traffic intensity τ is

$$\tau\left(\frac{2}{1-\tau k^{-(r+1)}}+\cdots+\frac{2}{1-\tau k^{-(r+j)}}+\frac{r-j}{1-\tau k^{-(r+j+1)}}\right).$$

A similar formula may be derived for contracting networks. If $\tau = ck^{r+1}$ for some positive constant $c<1$, i.e. if the load per input is constant, then the average delay, as a function of j is minimized for some $j_0 = \log_k r + O(1)$; it decreases for $j<j_0$, and increases for $j>j_0$. The average delay is an increasing function of j for contracting networks. The cost of an expanding network is an increasing function of j; the cost of a contracting network is a decreasing function of j.

We conjecture that expanding and contracting banyan networks are solutions to the following optimization problems.

Problem 1: Minimize cost for given bandwidth.

Conjecture 1: Let G be a (k,r,j)-contracting banyan network. There is no network in $\mathbf{G}(k^r,k^r,k)$ that has both lower cost and higher bandwidth than G.

Problem 2: Minimize cost for given average delay.

Conjecture 2: Assume the M/M/1 model. Let G be a (k,r,j)-contracting banyan network. For any traffic intensity τ, there is no network in $\mathbf{G}(k^r,k^r,k)$ that has both lower cost and lower average delay than G.

Conjecture 3: Assume the M/M/1 model. For any r, k, and traffic intensity $\tau < k^{r+1}$, there is a number $j_0 \le \log_k r + O(1)$ such that

(i) A (k,r,j_0)-expanding banyan network achieves minimum average delay at traffic intensity τ among all networks in $\mathbf{G}(k^r,k^r,k)$.

(ii) For each $j \leq j_0$, there is no network in $G(k^r, k^r, k)$ that has both lower average delay at traffic intensity τ and lower cost than the (k, r, j)-expanding network.

Furthermore, if $\tau = ck^{r+1}$ for some positive constant $c < 1$ (i.e. traffic intensity per input is constant), then $j_0 = \log_k r + O(1)$.

The first conjecture states that for any given bandwidth some contracting network has least cost. The second and third conjectures state that, in the M/M/1 model, for any given traffic intensity and given average delay either some contracting or some expanding network has least cost. The third conjecture also states that it never helps to expand for more than about $\log_k r$ stages, which for all practical purposes is at most five.

8. CONCLUSION

We have proposed in this paper a performance measure for packet-switching interconnection networks, shown how to compute these measures, and used them prove that square banyan networks are optimal for symmetric traffic. We presented conjectures generalizing these results to nonsquare banyan networks. This work is preliminary, and can be extended in many interesting directions.

We would like to know whether the different results proven are valid under weaker probabilistic assumptions. In particular, does a G/G/1 network achieve maximum bandwidth when a simpler queueing discipline, such as FCFS, is used? Do square banyan networks provide minimum delays if other than the FCFS queueing discipline is allowed, in particular, if messages following distinct paths may be assigned different priorities? Note that performance can be improved by departing from FCFS, even in a symmetric network such as a square banyan: for example, one can decrease the priority of messages destined to switches where the load is already high.

The same analysis can be performed for other types of load distributions. In particular, one may ask for what load distributions are rings, binary trees, or other types of network geometries considered in the literature, optimal.

Other performance measures can be considered — for example reliability. The question then is what network achieves the best performance versus cost, when a certain component failure pattern is allowed?

We believe that similar techniques can be applied to the analysis of circuit-switching networks: Assume a traffic pattern consisting of a random sequence of connection requests submitted by the network inputs; at each cycle the network can satisfy a subset of those. Performance is then measured by the average number of connections supported per cycle. Some related work along these lines has been done by Beneš [Be] and Pippenger [Pi].

Another measure of network quality is how easy it is to route messages (i.e. to determine the path of a message given its destination). For this measure "bidelta networks" are provably optimal [Di] [KS1]. As we have shown in this paper, square banyan networks provide optimal performance versus cost. The only networks that provide both easy routing and optimal performance versus cost are the "multistage shuffle-exchange" networks, which are unique given a network size and a degree for the nodes. We believe that this helps explain why few fundamentally different networks have been proposed. Multistage shuffle-exchange networks are also optimal (but not uniquely so) when cost is measured in terms of layout area [KS3].

ACKNOWLEDGEMENT

The authors thank Marty Reiman for pointing out the publications of Harrison [Ha] and Kelly [Ke].

REFERENCES

[Be] V. E. BENEŠ, Growth, Complexity, and Performance of Telephone Connection Networks, *Bell System Technical Journal,* Vol. 62 (1983), pp. 499-539.

[BA] L. N. BHUYAN and D. P. AGRAWAL, Design and Performance of Generalized Interconnection Networks, *IEEE Trans. on Comput.*, C-32, pp. 1081-1090, Dec. 1983.

[De] D. DEGROOT, Expanding and Contraction SW-Banyan Networks, *1983 Intl. Conf. on Parallel Processing,* Aug. 1983, pp. 19-24.

[Di] D. M. DIAS, Packet Communication in Delta and Related Networks, Ph.D. thesis, 1981, Rice University.

[DJ1] D. M. DIAS and J. R. JUMP, Analysis and Simulation of Buffered Delta Networks, *IEEE Trans. on Comput.* C-30, pp. 273-282, Apr. 1981.

[DJ2] D. M. DIAS and J. R. JUMP, Packet Switching Interconnection Networks for Modular Systems, *Computer* 14, Dec. 1981, pp. 43-54.

[Fe] T-Y. FENG, A Survey of Interconnection Networks, *Computer* 14, Dec. 1981, pp. 12-27.

[GL] G. R. GOKE and G. J. LIPOVSKI, Banyan Networks for Partitioning Multiprocessor Systems, *1st Ann. Symp. on Computer Architecture,* Dec. 1973, pp. 21-28.

[Ha] J. M. HARRISON, The Heavy Traffic Approximation for Single Server Queues in Series, *J. Appl. Prob., 10 (1973), pp. 613-629.*

[Ke] F. P. KELLY, *Reversibility and Stochastic Networks,* Wiley, 1979.

[KS1] C. P. KRUSKAL and M. SNIR, The Structure of Multistage Interconnection Networks for Parallel Processing, manuscript; see also *1982 Conference of Information Sciences and Systems,* Princeton University, pp. 305-310.

[KS2] C. P. KRUSKAL and M. SNIR, The Performance of Multistage Interconnection Networks for Multiprocessors, *IEEE Trans. on Comput.* C-32, pp. 1091-1098, Dec. 1983.

[KS3] C. P. KRUSKAL and M. SNIR, The Importance of Being Square, *11th Annual International Symposium on Computer Architecture,* June 1984, pp. 91-98.

[KJ] M. KUMAR and J. R. JUMP, Generalized Delta Networks, *1983 Intl. Conf. on Parallel Processing,* Aug. 1983, pp. 10-18.

[Pa] J. A. PATEL, Performance of Processor-Memory Interconnections for Multiprocessors, *IEEE Trans. Comput.* C-30 (1981), pp. 771-780.

[Pi] N. PIPPENGER, Complexity of Seldom Blocking Networks, *Proceedings of IEEE Communications Conference,* 1976.

[Si] H. J. SIEGEL, *Interconnection Networks for Large-Scale Parallel Processing: Theory and Case Studies,* Lexington Books, Lexington, MA, 1985.

Allocation and Relocation of Processes in Distributed Computer Systems

Christos Nikolaou and Gautam Kar
IBM T. J. Watson Research Center
Yorktown Heights, N.Y. 10598

Donald F. Ferguson and Gerald Leitner
Department of Computer Science
Columbia University
New York, NY 10027

Abstract

Distributed systems become increasingly attractive as a means to achieve higher throughput for a given level of hardware computational power, and higher availability of the overall system. Applications running on distributed systems are usually organized as collections of communicating sequential processes. This paper examines the problem of allocating processes to processors under workload balancing and optimality constraints, and the problem of relocating groups of processes when one or more processors fail.

1.0 Introduction

Distributed systems become increasingly attractive as a means to achieve higher throughput for a given level of hardware computational power, and higher availability of the overall system. Applications running on distributed systems are usually organized as collections of communicating sequential processes. A task or transaction is normally performed by the collective synchronized activity of a group of processes which, in general, reside in distinct physical processors. During such collective activity, the participating processes coordinate their actions by communicating with each other via messages, shared memory, remote procedure calls, etc. One of the goals of the designer of a distributed system is to minimize the volume of communication occurring across interprocessor boundaries. Such minimization is desirable in order to increase the throughput of the distributed system as a whole. Additionally, the collection of processes that constitute the software of the distributed system has to be assigned to the various physical processors in such a way that the workload distribution is as balanced as possible. This will also ensure higher throughput by exploiting the power of each processor evenly. This paper examines the problem of allocating processes to processors under workload balancing and optimality constraints, and the problem of relocating groups of processes when one or more processors fail. Heuristic techniques are proposed that are suitable for distributed environments.

In 2.0, "Formulation of the problem" we formulate the problem and define terms and symbols used in later sections. We also show how to use clustering algorithms from the literature (6) to organize processes and processors into hierarchical clusters, by trying to minimize the intercluster (process or processor) communication costs. In 3.0, "The allocation algorithm" we present an allocation algorithm that maps a hierarchy of process clusters to a hierarchy of processor clusters. The problem of process relocation is addressed in 4.0, "Process Relocation." Finally in 6.0, "Conclusions," we summarize the results and point out directions of further research.

2.0 Formulation of the problem

In the context of this paper we conceive of a distributed system as composed of a set of *nodes* representing the active processing agents (e.g. host computer complexes in a computer network, individual processors in a multiprocessor system or a local area network, etc.) and an *interconnection* structure providing full connectivity between the nodes (e.g. communication lines in a long-haul computer network, shared memory modules or a bus in a multiprocessor system, a ring or a star topology in a local area network).

Given a set of processes $\Gamma_n = \{p_1, p_2, \ldots, p_n\}$, a set of processors $\Pi_n = \{P_1, P_2, \ldots, P_N\}$ and their logical and physical interconnection structure respectively, we define the *process graph* $\Gamma = (\Gamma_n, \Gamma_l)$, where Γ_l

is a set of links defined as: $\Gamma_l = \{l_{ij} \mid l_{ij}$ denotes logical communication between processes p_i and $p_j\}$. Similarly we define the *processor graph* $\Pi = (\Pi_n, \Pi_l)$, where $\Pi_l = \{l_{ij} \mid l_{ij}$ denotes a physical communication link between processors P_i and $P_j\}$. Consider two processes p_i and p_j possibly residing on two different nodes. The costs incurred by their presence are the following:

- They contribute to the workload of the nodes (processors) to which they are assigned. The workload of a node has to lie between an upper bound (capacity) M_i and a lower bound (low threshold of utilization) m_i. Formally,

$$m_i \leq c_i \leq M_i$$

  for $i = 1, \ldots N$. c_i denotes the currently assigned workload of processor P_i . We call the above set of inequalities the *load balancing constraints*. They model the users requirement that each processor is assigned a fair load of processes, without being unduly overloaded or underutilized. They are clearly alternative ways to model the load balancing requirement. For example, one could let λ represent the "ideal" ratio of the assigned workload over the capacity, and ε represent the tolerance from the ideal ratio. One could then require that the actual ratio of the assigned workload over the capacity is always within ε from the ideal ratio (8). Alternatively, one could require that the sum of the squares of the differences of the actual from the ideal ratios, be minimized. Our approach provides a simple yet realistic model for load balancing.

  If the time complexity of the computations of the individual processes is roughly equal, it is realistic to assume that the workload of a processor is increased by one "workload unit", as a result of a process allocation. In what follows, we assume that each process represents a single workload unit and moreover, that the number of processes exceeds - usually by far - the number of processors.
- There is a communication cost (delay) associated with a message transmission from process p_i to p_j, that is directly proportional to:
  - the number of "connections" (i.e logical communication channels) established between processes p_i and p_j. Although this number may vary with time, we assume that it changes rather infrequently and

that there are long periods of stability during which its value remains constant.

- the average number of messages per unit of time sent from process p_i to p_j. We assume for simplicity that the same number is observed for messages flowing from p_j to p_i.
- the average delay of routing a message through the processors' interconnection network.

Storage constraints are ignored in this paper and are a subject of further research. We assume that the links of the process and processor graphs are labelled with weights. Link *(i, j)* in the process graph carries a weight that is proportional to the communication cost of processes p_i and p_j whenever these two processes are assigned to *different* processors. Link ***(i, j)*** is zero otherwise. Similarly, link *(i, j)* of the processor graph carries a weight that is proportional to the delay of the communication link connecting processors P_i and P_j. The total communication cost to the distributed system with a given assignment of processes to processors is the sum of the communication costs of all pairs of processes (p_i , p_j), such that p_i does not reside on the same processor as p_j. The total communication cost can be used as a yardstick to compare the desirability of two different assignments of processes to processors. We call the minimization of this cost the *optimum allocation* problem. It has been shown that this problem can be formulated as a 0-1 integer linear programming problem and is known to be NP-complete (5).

There is, therefore, a need to develop heuristic algorithms for finding suboptimal feasible solutions for the allocation problem. We propose the following combination of heuristic techniques: making use of known clustering algorithms (6), organize the graphs Γ and Π in hierarchies of clusters using the weights on their links as the clustering (similarity) measure. Call Σ and T the resulting process and processor cluster trees respectively. In the following section we show how to map the nodes of Σ to the nodes of T . This mapping defines an assignment of processes to processors. Hagouel (6) has written a good survey of the hierarchical clustering techniques. The basic idea is to start with a weighted graph where each node represents a lowest-level cluster (a leaf in the associated cluster tree). We then form clusters of the next higher level by grouping pairs of nodes connected with links of maximum weight. These pairs are then considered single nodes for the next iteration of the algorithm. Termination occurs when there is only one node left, the root of the cluster tree.

3.0 The allocation algorithm

The Process Allocation Problem (PAP) can be formulated as an integer programming problem. Branch-and-bound, enumeration techniques can be used to solve it, but they are computationally expensive. Our heuristic techniques achieve suboptimal allocation of processes to processors while maintaining the workload balancing constraint. Stone (12) and Rao et al. (9) have also dealt with the problem. They present efficient algorithms for the two-processor case, which, however, can explode combinatorially in the case of three or more processors. Their model includes storage constraints and computing costs, that may vary from processor to processor. Our model, on the other hand, assumes the computing cost to be uniform and introduces the additional constraint of load balancing. Bannister and Trivedi (1) have proposed approximation algorithms to optimize load balancing but they neglect interprocess communication. They also give an upper bound of the error from optimal. Finally, a number of papers deal with the related File Allocation Problem (FAP) (see e.g. survey paper by Wah, Computer, Jan 84 (13)).

The basic idea of our heuristic is to map the process cluster tree Σ to the processor cluster tree T. The allocation algorithm assigns nodes of the process cluster tree at a given level to nodes of the processor cluster tree at the same level. Ideally, such a mapping would allocate clusters of heavily communicating processes to clusters of densely connected processors. The allocation, however, is complicated because neither of the cluster trees is necessarily balanced and because the number of nodes at some given level may in general be different in the two cluster trees. This difference will necessitate merging and splitting of nodes at the same level of the two cluster trees in order to achieve a one-to-one mapping and load balancing. The suboptimality of the allocation is an open problem to be addressed in the future.

We now introduce terms and symbols that are used in the presentation of the allocation algorithm. Let r be a non-leaf node of the process cluster tree assigned by the allocation algorithm to R, a non-leaf node of the processor cluster tree. The children of r represent clusters of processes. Let w_i be the number of processes represented by child i of node r, and let $\mathbf{P}_r = \{w_1, \ldots, w_{n(r)}\}$, where $n(r)$ is the number of children of node r. M_i (m_i) represents the sum of the workload upper bounds (lower bounds) of all processors belonging to the cluster represented by the i-th child of R.

For every pair of nodes r and R, where r has already been assigned to R, the allocation algorithm uses a heuristic method to allocate the children of r to the children of R, possibly by splitting, and/or merging the children of r. Notice that if the workload balancing constraint is satisfied for the pair of nodes r and R, there is at least one way of partitioning the clusters of processes represented by the children of r among the clusters of processors represented by the children of R, without violating the workload constraints. This conclusion is based on the unit workload assumption and the assumption that all weights are integer numbers.

Let

$$V_i = \frac{m_i - c_i}{m_i}$$

be the *violation* of the i-th cluster of processors (child of R). The value of c_i is zero when the allocation algorithm starts, and grows to a value allowed by the workload constraints. The "violation" of cluster i gives the fraction of unfilled minimum allowed capacity of that cluster and therefore the amount of violation of the workload balancing constraint. The allocation algorithm uses the violation values of the children of R, to select a candidate cluster of processors to be assigned processes. Clusters with higher violations are chosen first. For convenient bookkeeping, call $\mathbf{S}_v = \{ V_i \mid V_i > 0 \}$ the set of positive violation values, and assume that it is ordered by decreasing violation values. Figure 1 shows how the various fractions of the maximum workload capacity of a cluster of processors are defined. Last we define the *auxiliary set* $\mathbf{S}_A$. This set consists of all nonpositive V_i values of the processor clusters with current assignment c_i in the range:

$$\frac{m_i - M_i}{m_i} \leq V_i \leq 0$$

$\mathbf{S}_A$ contains V_i 's that, strictly speaking, do not correspond to violations of the workload balancing constraint. Nevertheless, they are associated with clusters of processors (children of R) that can still be assigned processes, without their workload exceeding M_i . The set $\mathbf{S}_A$ is used by the allocation algorithm, to select candidate clusters of processors, whenever there are

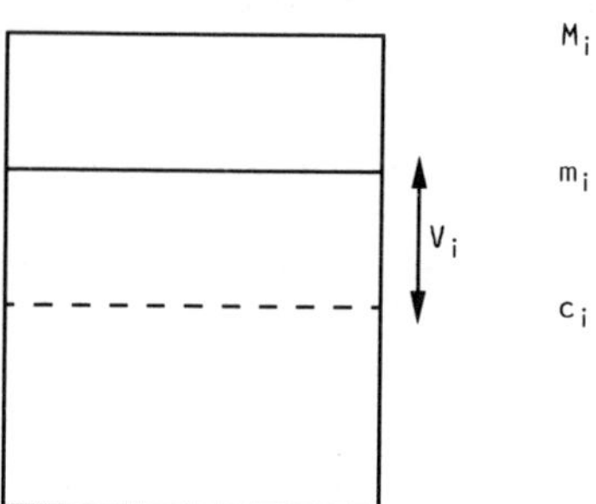

Figure 1. Defining tolerance range and Violation.

clusters of processes left unassigned and there are no clusters of processors violating the workload constraint.

3.1 Description of the allocation algorithm

The allocation algorithm is presented here as a procedure applied on the process and processor cluster trees Σ and T (see Figure 2). We assume that it is executed once at system generation time at one of the processors of the distributed system. The algorithm takes two arguments, r and R, nodes of Σ and T respectively. We assume that at each level, the nodes of Σ and T are numbered from left to right. We now informally present the allocation algorithm. Initially assume that

$$S_V = \{ V_i \mid V_i = 1, i = 1, \ldots, n(R) \},$$

reflecting the fact that initially all children of R are empty.

procedure ***ALLOCATE***(r, R)

1. If r and R are roots of Σ and T respectively, then check the global workload constraint:

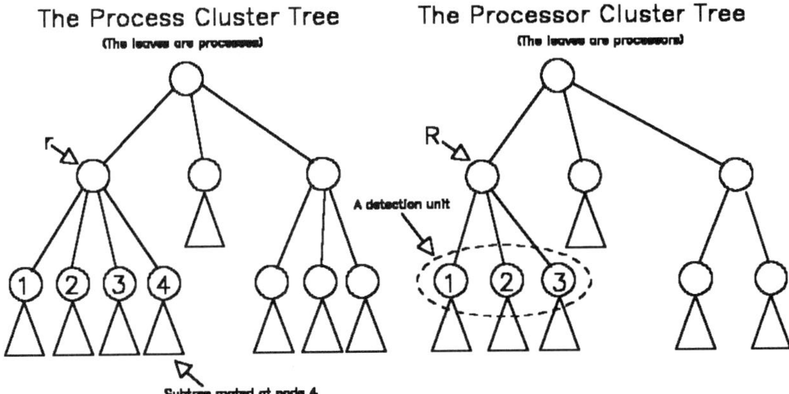

Figure 2. An example of two cluster trees

$$\sum_{i=1}^{i=N} m_i \leq n \leq \sum_{i=1}^{i=N} M_i$$

where n is the total number of processes and each process represents a unit workload. If the above inequality is violated, there is no feasible solution and therefore terminate the algorithm. Otherwise continue.

2. Initialize the sets RA_i , for $i = 1, 2, \ldots, n(R)$, to be empty. The set RA_i will contain the indices of the process clusters (children of r) that have been assigned to the i-th child of R.
3. Repeat until either $\mathbf{P}_r = \{\,\}$, or $\mathbf{S}_v = \{\,\}$:
   a. Let i be the child of R with maximum value of V_i. If there is more than one, break ties by choosing the lowest index. Call function ***SELECT***($\mathbf{P}_r$) to choose a child j of r with weight w_j to assign to i. The function ***SELECT*** is described in the next section.
   b. Perform the following updates:

$$c_i = c_i + w_j , \qquad V_i = \frac{m_i - c_i}{m_i}.$$

If $V_i \le 0$, remove V_i from $\mathbf{S}_v$. If $c_i < M_i$ add V_i to $\mathbf{S}_A$ (intuitively, if V_i is added to $\mathbf{S}_A$ child i of R does not violate the workload constraint any more, but has available capacity to be used if there is a need for it). Insert j in set RA_i.

4. When this step is reached, either one of the following statements is true: a) both $\mathbf{P}_r$ and $\mathbf{S}_A$ are not empty, or b) $\mathbf{P}_r$ is empty. If the first statement is true, repeat the following steps until $\mathbf{P}_r = \{ \}$:
   a. Let i be the child of R, such that the associated value of $| V_i |$ in $\mathbf{S}_A$ is minimum. If there are more than one, break ties by choosing the lowest index. Call function $SELECT(\mathbf{P}_r)$ to choose a child j of r with weight w_j to assign to i.
   b. Perform the following updates:

$$c_i = c_i + w_j, \qquad V_i = \frac{m_i - c_i}{m_i}$$

   If $c_i = M_i$ then delete V_i from $\mathbf{S}_A$ (intuitively, V_i is removed from $\mathbf{S}_A$ if child i of R is filled to the maximum tolerated capacity). Insert j in set RA_i.
5. At this step $\mathbf{P}_r = \{ \}$. For each set RA_i do the following: Create a new node i in the process cluster tree Σ. Make i a child of r and make all nodes contained in RA_i, children of i. See Figure 3 for an example.
6. Recursively call $ALLOCATE(i, i)$ for $i = 1, \ldots, n(R)$ (observe that now $n(r) = n(R)$)

3.2 The Function SELECT

We conclude the presentation of the allocation algorithm by describing function ***SELECT***. In general terms, this function operates on the set $\mathbf{P}_r$ and on the child i of R, that upon invocation of ***SELECT*** has the maximum value of violation. According to some selection criterion, the function chooses a cluster of processes, that may be a child of r or a node inside the subtree of one of r's children; this cluster is then assigned to i and the necessary updates are performed on $\mathbf{P}_r$. We list two possible selection criteria for the choice of a cluster of processes to be assigned to i:

- Select the maximum $w_j \in \mathbf{P}_r$ such that $m_i \le c_i \le M_i$ This criterion would tend to preserve the structure of the process cluster tree intact.
- Calculate the *affinity* of all clusters of processes in $\mathbf{P}_r$ and select the one with the maximum value that satisfies the workload constraint.

The *affinity* of a cluster of processes is defined as follows: Let $\mathbf{P} = \{ p_1, \ldots, p_k \}$ be a set of processes, let $\mathbf{P}_l = \{ l_1, \ldots, l_m \}$ be the set of connecting links in the process graph and let $B_l = \{ \beta_1, \ldots, \beta_m \}$ be the set of weights associated with the links. Then $affinity(\mathbf{P}) = \sum_{i=1}^{i=m} \beta_i$. This criterion would tend to choose densely connected clusters of processes as candidates for assignment.

The two criteria can, of course, be combined in more than one ways. For example, the second criterion may be used to break ties resulting from the first one, or the first may be used to break ties of the second. Observe however, that the selection function may still not be able to come up with a candidate for assignment, since they may all violate the workload constraint. In the following, we show how the selection function resolves this difficulty by splitting the process cluster with the maximum weight (a heuristic decision) and making its children, children of *r*:

Function ***SELECT*** ($\mathbf{P}_r$, i) where i is the child of R with maximum value of violation:

1. Using either one of the selection criteria - or any combination thereof - choose a child j of r; if successful, return j.
2. Otherwise, let $w_j = \max(\mathbf{P}_r)$ based on the selection criteria. Remove j from the process cluster tree and w_j from $\mathbf{P}_r$, make the children of j, children of r, and add them to $\mathbf{P}_r$.
3. Repeat the above two steps until a candidate process cluster for assignment can be successfully identified.

Termination occurs because the total number of processes exceeds the total number of processors and because each process represents a single unit of workload.

3.3 Example Application of the Allocation Algorithm

We conclude this section by illustrating how the allocation algorithm is applied on a simple example. In Figure 3 our objective is to map the process graph to the processor graph. The processes and processors are numbered sequentially as depicted by the numbers within the nodes. The labels on the edges of the process graph denote volume of communication between the adjacent processes (nodes); similarly, the labels on the edges of the processor graph denote communication cost between the associated

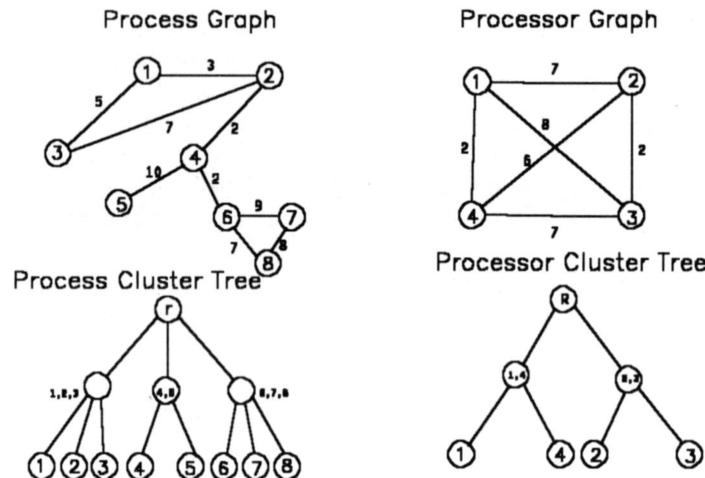

Figure 3. An example application of the algorithm

pair of processors. Using a clustering algorithm, each of the two graphs yields a hierarchical cluster tree. We now apply the allocation algorithm as follows, to map the process cluster tree to the processor cluster tree. For the example $m_1 = m_2 = m_3 = 1,\ m_4 = 2$ and $M_1 = 3,\ M_2 = M_3 = 2,\ M_4 = 4$

1. Call Allocate(r, R).
2. Check global workload constraint: $5 \leq 8 \leq 11$
3. Set $RA_i = \{\ \},\ i = 1,\ 2.$
4. At this point $\mathbf{P}_r = \{3,\ 2,\ 3\}$ and $\mathbf{S}_v = \{V_{1,4},\ V_{2,3}\}$ where $V_{1,4} = V_{2,3} = 1$ and $c_{1,4} = c_{2,3} = 0$.
   a. $i = (1{,}4)$. Call **SELECT**($\mathbf{P}_r$, i)
      function **SELECT**:
         Use first criterion to choose, second to break ties
         Based on this, **SELECT** returns process cluster (6, 7, 8).
   Update $\mathbf{P}_r = \{3,\ 2\}$.

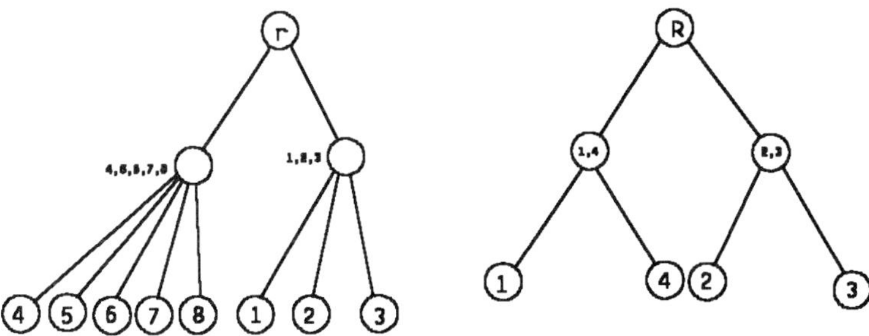

Figure 4. Example. Section 3.3, "Example Application of the Allocation Algorithm"

b. $c_{1,4} = 3$, $V_{1,4} = 0$. , Remove $V_{1,4}$ from S_v and add it to S_A.

5. Next we repeat step 3 of the allocation algorithm two more times to assign process cluster (1, 2, 3) to processor cluster (2, 3) and process cluster (4, 5) to processor cluster (1, 4)

   Note: At this point the process cluster tree has been transformed as shown in Figure 4.

6. Recursively apply the algorithm as follows: ALLOCATE((4,5,6,7,8), (1,4)) and ALLOCATE((1,2,3), (2,3)). This results in the following allocation: processes 4 and 7 are allocated to processor 1, processes 5, 6, 8 to processor 4, processes 1 and 3 to processor 2 and process 2 to processor 3.

4.0 Process Relocation

In this section we present algorithms that cope with the problem of processor failures. These algorithms relocate the workload of failed processors while satisfying the load balancing constraint throughout the network. Various techniques are presented for calculating the new assignment of processes to processors that will result due to a failure. These techniques differ in what they try to optimize: relocation cost, logical communication cost, or load balancing.

Two important assumptions are made in the following discussion. The first is that while recovery from processor failure is taking place, no other processor failure will occur. Adapting the algorithms in this section to handle failures during relocation is a subject for further research.

The second assumption is that some unspecified mechanism exists for relocating processes within the network. The actual mechanisms are not of concern here. This is due to the generality of the techniques presented. We have attempted to develop algorithms that will be useful for multiprocessor systems, local area networks and long haul networks. The actual methods of relocation in these types of networks will be dramatically different.

4.1 Isolating Failures

Before relocation of the workload of a failed processor can take place, the failure must be detected. Considerable work has been done on detecting failures in a distributed system (2, 3, 7, 14). In the following presentation we assume the existence of an algorithm that will detect the failure of a process in a logical group of processors. These logical groups are called **Detection Units**. Each detection unit is a processor cluster (defined by the processor cluster tree) in which the processors monitor each other's status. Each processor in the network is a member of exactly one detection unit.

Let D = $\{P_1, \ldots, P_m\}$ be a detection unit. An ordering is imposed on the set D. We say that $P_i < P_j$ if $i < j$. This ordering is called the **Nomination Order** and is used to select the **Leader** of detection unit D. We are not concerned with how this is determined. Garcia (4) presents an algorithm that can be used to elect a leader in a distributed system. The leader of a detection unit controls the monitoring of the status of the processors in D and coordinates process relocation when a failure occurs. If the leader, P_1, fails, then P_2 becomes the new leader and coordinates the relocation of P_1 's workload. Similarly, if P_1 and P_2 have failed, the new leader will be P_3 . We assume that the detection algorithm can cope with the failure of a leader.

In the coming presentation, the following notation is used:

1. There are K detection units numbered $D_1, \ldots, D_K$.
2. $M(D_i)$ is the total processing capacity of D_i . That is, $M(D_i)$ is the sum of the maximum capacities of the processors in D_i.
3. $m(D_i)$ is the minimum allowed processing capacity of D_i . That is, $m(D_i)$ is the sum of the minimum allowed capacities (m_j for P_j) of the processors in D_i.
4. N_i is the number of processes currently assigned to detection unit D_i . In other words, it is the weight of the root of the process cluster sub-tree assigned to D_i.

If a processor fails in a detection unit D_i , there are two cases to consider. The first is the case when the load balancing constraint is still satisfied in D_i. Formally,

$$m(D_i) - m_j \leq N_i \leq M(D_i) - M_j$$

where m_j and M_j are the minimum and maximum allowed capacities of the failed processor P_j. The second case occurs when this constraint is no longer satisfied. In this case, some process clusters assigned to processors in D_i will have to be relocated to other detection units. We discuss how to handle these two cases in the following sections.

4.2 Relocation Within a Detection Unit

Suppose processor P_j in detection unit D_i fails. The leader of D_i , denoted L_i, will inform all other processors in D_i that P_j is "down." L_i must now determine where to relocate P_j's workload. If the load balancing constraint

$$m(D_i) - m_j \leq N_i \leq M(D_i) - M_j$$

is satisfied where m_j and M_j are the capacities of P_j , then L_i will confine relocation of the workload to processors within D_i.

The relocation algorithm in this case is quite simple. The leader always maintains the following data structures:

1. The set $D_i = \{P_1, \ldots, P_m\}$.
2. R_i, the root of the processor cluster sub-tree corresponding to the processors in D_i.
3. r_i, the root of the process cluster sub-tree assigned to D_i.

To perform relocation, the leader executes the following algorithm:

1. Update R_i to reflect the failure of P_j . This involves deleting the leaf node for P_j and updating the capacities of his ancestor nodes in the processor cluster tree.
2. Call the algorithm **Allocate** (r_i, R_i) .

There are two very good reasons for confining relocation within the detection unit D_i . The first is that failures are isolated from other processor clusters. This lessens the disruption caused to the network by performing the relocation algorithm. This is especially important when processor failures are transient.

The second reason for confining allocation within a detection unit is to minimize the departure from optimality. The processes in the cluster assigned to D_i may have a "strong" affinity for one another. This is indicated by the fact that they were clustered together. For example, assume that we are dealing with the computer network depicted below (Figure 5), and that the measure of affinity between processes is logical communication. Processors are clustered according to the delay required to send data from one to another. If a processor fails in detection unit 1, relocating processes to detection unit 2 could dramatically degrade performance by saturating the link with delay 10.

4.3 Relocating Process Clusters to other Detection Units

In the previous section, we assumed that when a processor failed and its processing capacity was lost, the load balancing constraint was still satisfied in the detection unit. Clearly, this may not always be the case. If P_j is the processor that failed in detection unit D_i and $M(D_i) - M_j < N_i$, then some process clusters will have to be relocated from D_i to other detection units. In this section we present an algorithm that accomplishes

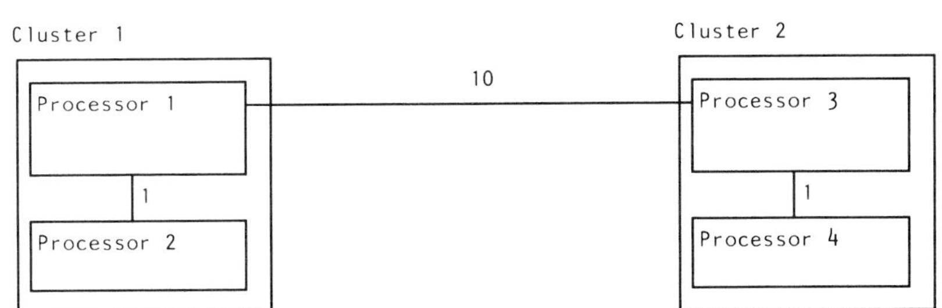

Figure 5. Example. Cluster 1 and Cluster 2 are two detection units. Processors 1 and 2 and Processors 3 and 4 are connected by a link with delay 1. The two Detection Units are connected by a link of delay 10. Relocating processes from one detection unit to another could quickly saturate the slow link.

this task. Basically, the algorithm must make two choices: (1) Which process clusters to relocate? (2) To which detection units are they moved? It is easy to see that these two choices depend upon one another. As in the previous section, the leader L_i maintains the data structures D_i , R_i, and r_i . A leader L_i must also maintain the current values of N_i and $M(D_i)$ and $m(D_i)$. These values may be needed by the leaders of other detection units when they are performing relocation.

If processor P_j in detection unit D_i fails, the leader L_i will perform the following algorithm:

Step 1: Notify all other processors in D_i that P_j has failed.

Step 2: Update R_i to reflect that failure of P_j as in the previous section. L_i will also set $M(D_i) = M(D_i) - M_j$ and $m(D_i) = m(D_i) - m_j$.

Step 3: If $N_i \leq M(D_i)$ then,

1. Call **Allocate**(r_i, R_i)
2. Exit the relocation algorithm.

If the test in step 3 fails, the load balancing constraint at D_i is not satisfied. Some process clusters must be relocated to other detection units. So, L_i must know the status of the other detection units to determine which are capable of receiving processes without exceeding their load balancing constraints. This gives step 4.

Step 4:

1. Send **Query-Status** to all other leaders of detection units, $L_1, \ldots, L_K$.

2. Wait for a response quadruplet $\{j, N_j, M(D_j), m(D_j),\}$ from the leaders. j is the ID of the detection unit. N_j is the currently assigned workload, $M(D_j)$ is the current capacity of the detection unit and $m(D_j)$ is the minimum allowed capacity of the detection unit.

Just as the failure of P_j caused the load balancing constraint within D_i to be violated, the failure may also cause the network wide load balancing constraint to be violated. This constraint must be checked before relocation can be attempted. This yields step 5.

Step 5: If

$$\sum_{i=1}^{K} N_i > \sum_{i=1}^{K} M(D_i)$$

then STOP. Relocation cannot occur.

Since we have assumed that all processes contribute a single unit of weight, if the global load balancing constraint is satisfied it is certain that there is a way to relocate processes from D_i so that no detection unit is in violation.

Once L_i has determined that relocation is possible, it is necessary to decide which process clusters to relocate and where to relocate them. To do so, a **Candidate Set** C is generated. This set contains elements of the form (v,k), where v is a node in r_i and k is the index of some detection unit. If (v,k) is an element of C, then it is feasible to relocate the process cluster rooted at v to detection unit D_k . Generation of the candidate set is step 6.

Step 6:

1. $C = \phi$.[1]
2. For $k = 1$ to K and for every vertex v in r_i do
   If $N_k + W(v) \leq M(D_k)$ and $N_i - W(v) \geq m(D_i)$
   then $C = C + \{(v,k)\}$.

To choose the first cluster to relocate, one has to choose an element of the candidate set C. For this purpose, the elements of C are ranked according to some criteria. The criteria used will depend on what is to be optimized. Some criteria are discussed in the next section. The ranking and choice of a candidate are steps 7 and 8.

Step 7: Rank(C).

Step 8: $(v^{\times}, k^{\times}) =$ Maximum (C) -- Find the element with the highest ranking.

The choice has been made to relocate cluster $v^{\times}$ to detection unit $k^{\times}$. How this is physically performed is not discussed here. It is important to note that the load balancing constraint may still be violated in detection unit D_i . If this is so, it is necessary to choose another process cluster-detection unit pair. Before this choice is made, the relocation of $v^{\times}$ must be reflected by updating r_i and $N_{k^{\times}}$. This yields step 9.

Step 9:

1. $N_i = N_i - W(v^{\times})$.

2. $N_{k^{\times}} = N_{k^{\times}} + W(v^{\times})$.

3. Delete $v^{\times}$ from r_i and update the weights of its ancestors.

4. If $N_i > M(D_i)$, go to step 6.

The relocation algorithm iterates through steps 6, 7, 8 and 9, generating candidates, choosing a pair, relocating and updating until the load balancing constraint is satisfied in D_i . Once this constraint is met by D_i as a whole, it is necessary to verify that it is satisfied by all active nodes in D_i . Since there are still process and processor cluster trees at L_i , calling

---

1 The null set.

Allocate will guarantee satisfaction of these constraints. This gives the final step.

Step 10: **Allocate**(r_i, R_i).

4.4 Receiving Clusters

A failure in one detection unit may cause process clusters to be relocated to other detection units. The question of how these new clusters are accomodated is answered by the following simple algorithm. Assume that $p_1, \ldots, p_s$ are the processes relocated to detection unit D_j and that S is the set of processes already allocated to D_j. L_j performs the following algorithm:

Step 1: $S = S \cup \{p_1, \ldots, p_s\}$.

Step 2: r_j = **Cluster**(S)[2].

Step 3:**Allocate**(r_j, R_j).

Step 4: $N_j = N_j + s$, where s is the cardinality of set S.

There is no need to verify the load balancing constraint. This was done be the leader of the detection unit that assigned the new clusters to D_j . This fact, combined with the correctness of **Allocate** and **Cluster** ensure that this algorithm can accomodate the new clusters.

To perform the clustering in step 2, L_j must know the global process graph. It is not unreasonable to assume that this is so. The process graph is fairly invariant in time and can be distributed to all leaders when initialization occurs and the leaders have been determined.

---

2 We assume there is a procedure that given a set of nodes of a graph, will return an appropriate cluster tree. This algorithm is called Cluster

5.0 The Ranking Function

The leader of detection unit D_i has received a quadruplet $\{j, N_j, M(D_j), m(D_j),\}$ from the leaders of the other detection units. Based on this acquired information and the internal state of D_i, L_i must determine which element of the candidate set should be chosen. The best candidate is that one which incurs the least additional cost when relocated. We now present a heuristic that attempts to measure this cost.

Relocating a cluster rooted at vertex v in r_i to detection unit D_j will cause increased logical communication between detection units D_i and D_j. This increase can be measured by calculating the **Affinity** of the process cluster v for the other process clusters which will remain at D_i. Informally, the affinity of v for the other clusters in r_i is the sum of the logical communication cost between processes which are descendants of v and those which are not. We will denote this affinity as *A(v)* and define it as follows:

If v is a leaf, i.e. - a process p_k, then

$$A(v) = \sum_{j=1}^{m} \beta_{ij}$$

If v is not a leaf,

$$A(v) = \sum_{i} \sum_{j} \beta_{ij}$$

where p_i is a descendant of v, and p_j is not, and β_{ij} is the communication cost between processes p_i and p_j.

To compute *A(v)*, the tree r_i must be traversed to generate the descendant relationships. The values *A(v)* can then be derived from these relationships and from the process graph G_p. The candidate of C with the "best" rank will be a pair *(v,k)* with minimal *A(v)*.

5.1 Load Balancing

Communication cost is not the only metric by which elements of C can be rated. Relocating process cluster v to detection unit D_j will affect load balancing as well as communication cost. Performing this relocation (cluster v to detection unit D_j) will affect the utilization of processors in D_i. We assume that the ideal utilization of a detection unit D_i is the midpoint of the interval defined by the allowed utilizations. We denote this value as λ_i and defined it as

$$\lambda_i = \frac{M(D_i) + m(D_i)}{2}$$

The relative deviation of the resulting utilization from the ideal (λ_i) can be measured by the formula:

$$\frac{|N_i - W(v) - \lambda_i|}{\lambda_i}$$

Relocating v to D_j will also affect the utilization of the processors in D_j. Since this adds $W(v)$ units of work, instead of subtracting, the relative deviation from optimal at D_j is measured by:

$$\frac{|N_j + W(v) - \lambda_j|}{\lambda_j}$$

The function that rates a candidate (v,j) in terms of load balancing, denoted $B(v,j)$, is defined as:

$$B(v,j) = C_i \times \frac{|N_i - W(v) - \lambda_i|}{\lambda_i} + C_j \times \frac{|N_j + W(v) - \lambda_j|}{\lambda_j}$$

N_i and N_j are two constants that measure the relative importance of balancing the load in D_i to balancing the load in D_j. Two reasonable choices of C_k for D_k, $k = i, j$, are: (1) $C_k = 1$ that gives equal importance to all detection units and (2) $C_k = \#(D_k)^3$ that gives more importance to larger detection units. The "best" candidate is the pair *(v,k)* that minimizes *B(v,k)*.

5.2 Combining Heuristics

Rating a candidate in terms of communication cost or in terms of load balancing are not mutually exclusive. A ranking function that combines these two measures is denoted *R(v,k)* and defined:

$$R(v,k) = C_1 \times A(v) + C_2 \times B(v,k).$$

C_1 and C_2 are constants that reflect the ratio of communication cost to deviation from optimal load balancing. Determining C_1 and C_2 depends on the type of distributed system used. In a long haul network, for example, C_1 will be much greater than C_2. In a multiprocessor system with shared memory or high speed interconnection, this may no longer be true.

It is important to note that *R(v,k)* is a heuristic, and using it as a basis for selecting clusters to relocate will not guarantee a minimum cost relocation. To compute such a minimum cost relocation, it is necessary to choose a subset $S = \{(v_1, k_1), \ldots, (v_n, k_n)\}$ of the candidate set C that minimizes the function:

$$R^{\times}(S) = \sum_{i=1}^{n} R(v_i, k_i)$$

subject to the constraints:

1. The load balancing constraint is satisfied in $D_1, \ldots D_k$.
2. There are no elements (v_1, k_1) and (v_2, k_2) in S such that v_2 is an ancestor of v_1 in r_i.

Formulated in this terminology, it is clear that obtaining a minimum cost relocation is equivalent to 0-1 Integer Programming and is NP-Complete.

---

3 The cardinality of the detection unit.

So, the use of heuristics is justified. The error of this heuristic has not yet been determined. This is a subject for future research.

5.3 Relocation Cost

In the preceeding section, we have ignored the cost that will be incurred when a cluster v is relocated to D_k from D_i. Performing this relocation may be a very expensive operation, and could be the dominant factor in deciding which clusters are to be relocated. This is especially true if processor failures are transient, and the clusters will be returned to D_i when the failed processor returns to an active state. In this section, we show how to reflect the cost of relocation in the ranking function.

We model the cost of relocating a process cluster v to detection unit D_k as a function $M(v,k)$ defined as:

$$M(v,k) = C \times W(v) + D,$$

where C and D are constants.

The constant C reflects the cost of relocating a single process to another detection unit. This cost could include transmitting the process' code and current state to another detection unit. Since we have assumed that all processes contribute approximately one unit of work, it is not unreasonable to assume that relocation cost is independent of the process being relocated.

The second constant D is independent of the number of leaf nodes in the cluster, $W(v)$. It accounts for the cost of relocating data sets, library procedure and operating system utilities that are shared by the processes in the cluster v. The ratio of C to D will depend on the type of applications being performed by the processes.

The ranking function $R(v,k)$ that accounts for the relocation cost, in addition to the previous costs is:

$$R(v,k) = C_1 \times A(v) + C_2 \times B(v,k) + C_3 \times M(v,k).$$

5.4 Bidding

The main shortcomming of the ranking heuristic *R(v,k)* is that little information about the current state of D_k is used. Only the current values of $m(D_k)$, $M(D_k)$ and N_k are available to L_i. This information is all that is used by the heuristic *R(v,k)*. In addition to the affinity of *v* for the clusters in D_i, it is important to know the afffinity of *v* for the processes currently assigned to D_k. It is unreasonable to assume that L_i is knowledgeable about which processes are currently assigned to another detection unit D_k. This information will be changing due to failures and relocation. So, L_i will have to receive some additional information from L_k if the affinity of *v* for the processes at D_k is to be considered. Smith (11) has suggested the awarding of contracts as a paradigm for work allocation in a distributed system. This paradigm is easily modified to fit the problem we are examining.

L_i ranks *C* according to the function *R(v,k)*. The elements with the best (smallest) ranking are deleted from *C* and combined to form a set *S*. These are the candidates for which the leaders of other detection units will submit bids. For each element *(v,k)* in S, L_i sends the message **Submit__Bid**(*k, v, Leaves(v)*). The semantics of this message is that L_k is to bid on the cluster of r_i rooted at *v*. *Leaves* is a function that returns a list of the process IDs of processes that are leaf nodes of the process cluster subtree rooted at *v*.

A leader L_k that receives a **Submit__Bid**(*v, k, Leaves(v)*) (L_k may receive more than one) will submit a corresponding bid. To do so, L_k computes the affinity of the processes in *Leaves(v)* with the processes currently assigned to D_k. L_k will respond with the **My__Bid**(*i, v, X_v, k*), where X_v is the affinity of cluster *v* for the processes assigned to D_k.

L_i now updates the ranking of the elements of S by the formula:

$$R^+(v,k) = A \times R(v,k) + B \times X_v$$

The fact that "good" values of *R(v,k)* are small while the "good" values of X_v are large can be handled by properly adjusting the signs of *A* and *B*. The "best" candidate is the element of *S* with the smallest R^+, if we have $A > 0$ and $B < 0$.

6.0 Conclusions

This paper has addressed the problem of process allocation in a distributed system and the subsequent dynamic relocation of workload under conditions of processor failure to achieve high availability. The approach presented in this paper is novel in that it presents a heuristic algorithm that seeks to partition the total workload evenly between a group of processors and, at the same time, minimize communication cost. The result is a suboptimal solution. Further work needs to be done in quantifying the degree of departure from optimality and generating a formal correctness proof for the algorithm.

Detection Units give a distributed system designer flexibility in defining subnetworks within a large network. This arrangement requires smaller network view tables to be maintained at each site and reduces the number of fault detection messages. Further work needs to be done on defining criteria in choosing detection units. The results of this work can then be applied to network design.

7.0 Acknowledgements

Early versions of the allocation algorithm benefited from discussions with John Reif. John Pershing was very helpful with his comments and editing of the paper.

References

1 Bannister J.A., Trivedi K.S., *Task Allocation in Fault-Tolerant Distributed Systems*, Acta Informatica, Vol. 20, 1983

2 Barigazzi G., Ciuffoletti A., Strigini L., *Reconfiguration Procedure in a Distributed Multiprocessor System*, Proc. of FTCS-12, 1982, pp. 73-80

3 Corsini P., Simoncini L., Strigini L., *MuTEAM: A Multimicroprocessor Architecture with Decentralized Fault Treatment*, unpublished manuscript.

4 Garcia-Molina H., *Elections in a Distributed Computing System*, IEEE Trans. on Computers, vol. c-31, no. 1, January 1982.

5 Garey M. R., Johnson D. S., *Computers and Intractability: A guide to the Theory of NP-completeness*, W. H. Freeman & Co. 1979.

6 Hagouel J., *Issues in Routing for Large and Dynamic Networks*, Ph.D. dissertation, Columbia Univ., 1983.

7 Hammer M., Shipman D., *Reliability Mechanisms for SDD-1: A System for Distributed Databases*, ACM Trans. on Database Systems, Vol. 5, No. 4, December 1980, pp. 431-466.

8 Kar G., Nikolaou C., Reif J., *Assigning Processes to Processors: a Fault-Tolerant Approach* Proc. of FTCS-14, June 1984.

9 Rao G. S., Stone H. S., Hu T. C., *Assignment of Tasks in a Distributed Processor System with Limited Memory*, IEEE Trans. on Computers, Vol. C-28, No. 4, April 1979.

10 Smith R.G., Davis R., *The Contract Net Protocol: High Level Communication and Control in a Distributed Problem Solver*, IEEE Trans. on Computers, vol. C-29, December 1980, pp. 1104-1113.

11 Smith R.G., Davis R., *Frameworks for Cooperation in Distributed Problem Solving* IEEE Trans. on Systems, Man and Cybernetics, vol. SMC-11, no. 1, January 1981, pp. 61-70.

12 Stone H. S., *Multiprocessor Scheduling with the Aid of Network Flow Algorithms*, IEEE Trans. on Software Eng., Vol. SE-3, No. 1, January 1977

13 Wah B.W., *File Placement on Distributed Computer Systems*, Computer, January 1984

14 Walter B., *A Robust and Efficient Protocol for Checking the Availability of Remote Sites*, Computer Networks 6(1982), pp. 173-188.

The Canonical Approximation in the Performance Analysis of Packet Radio Networks

Eugene Pinsky and Yechiam Yemini
Department of Computer Science
Columbia University
New York, N.Y. 10027

Moshe Sidi
Department of Electrical Engineering
Technion-Israel Institute of Technology
Haifa 32000, Israel

ABSTRACT

The purpose of this paper is to present the applications of the canonical approximation technique to performance analysis of multihop packet radio networks. The canonical approximation gives a *closed – form* approximation of global performance measures. The computational complexity of the method is *independent* of the size of the network, whereas the precision increases exponentially with the size of the system. The method is applied to analyze some packet radio networks operating under CSMA with perfect capture and C-BTMA protocols.

This research was supported in part by the Department of Defense Advanced Research Project Agency, under contract N00039-84-C-0165, New York State Center for Advanced Technology, under contract CAT(83)-8 and the IBM Research Fellowship.

1. INTRODUCTION

In this paper we apply the method of canonical approximation to the performance analysis of multihop packet radio networks. The method is used to analyze some packet radio networks operating under CSMA with perfect capture and C-BTMA protocols.

A packet radio network (PRNET) consists of geographically distributed radio units broadcasting data packets over a limited range. A key design problem of a PRNET is to resolve interference which occurs whenever two or more nodes try to transmit over the shared channel within the same neighborhood. This is accomplished by means of a multiple access protocol - a set of rules which define the process by which a node proceeds to transmit.

Given an access protocol and a packet radio network, one would like to compute a number of important performance measures. The primary performance measure is the throughput - the average number of packets delivered successfully per unit time. Other measures of interest include steady-state probability distribution of the number of transmissions, the fraction of the channel capacity used for successful transmission, the probability that a scheduled transmission is successful and average number of packets in the system.

Most of the work on multiple access protocols has been confined to the single hop case: a transmission of each node may interfere with transmissions of all other nodes. The work on the performance analysis of protocols in multihop environment, where spatial reuse of the shared channel is possible, is still in progress ([Boor80, Braz85, Toba80, Toba83, Silv83]). In practice, different schemes can be analyzed only numerically or through simulation and only for very small and simple networks. In this paper we present a new method to approximate performance measures of interest. The computational complexity of the method is independent of the size of the network, whereas the precision increases exponentially with the size of the system. The method is applied to analyze some packet radio networks operating under CSMA with perfect capture and C-BTMA protocols.

2. THE MODEL

The model of multihop packet radio networks that is used here is the one introduced by Boorstyn and Kerschenbaum ([Boor80]). In this model the network consists of N nodes† with a specified "hearing matrix". For any two nodes i and j the hearing matrix specifies whether or not i can hear j. The points in time when new and retransmitted packets are scheduled for transmission are called scheduling points. Packets are retransmitted either because at some scheduling point they were inhibited from transmission or because their transmission has been interfered. The process of scheduling points from a node is assumed to be Poisson with parameter λ. In general, one need not to assume the same rate of λ for all the nodes. The lengths of packets are assumed to be distributed exponentially with parameter μ. For notational convenience, we assume $\mu = 1$. The model assumes negligible propagation delay.

Two protocols are considered - Carrier Sense Multiple Access (CSMA) with perfect capture and Conservative Busy Tone Multiple Access (C-BTMA).

Under CSMA, a node wishing to transmit senses the channel. If the channel is sensed idle, the node starts transmitting, else it waits for the next scheduled point in time and repeats the above procedure. Under the perfect capture assumption†, the transmission of a packet from i to j may not be successful only if any of the "hidden nodes" k (neighbors of j but not of i) are transmitting to j at the time i starts its transmission.

Under the C-BTMA, any node that senses carrier emits a busy tone. If a node i transmits a packet to node j, all the other neighbors of i transmit busy tone, thus blocking all nodes in a region within twice the "hearing radius" of node i. Note that under C-BTMA, once a node starts transmitting, it is guaranteed of success.

For these protocols with the above assumptions of Poisson arrivals and exponential service time, it can be shown ([Boor80, Toba83]) that the equilibrium probability distribution $\pi(i)$ of having i simultaneous transmissions in the system is given by

†N will be used to indicate both the set of nodes and network size as long as no confusion arises.

†The capture assumption is defined as the ability of the receiver to correctly receive a packet despite the presence of other time overlapping transmissions. Perfect capture is the ability of receiving correctly the first packet regardless of future overlapping packets, whereas zero capture means the complete destruction of the first packet by any overlapping transmission. We will consider only perfect capture in this paper.

$$\pi(i) = \frac{\rho^i}{Z_N} \tag{1}$$

where $\rho = \lambda/\mu$ and Z_N, the "partition" function of the system is given by:

$$Z_N = \sum_{i=0}^{N} \alpha_N^i \rho^i \tag{2}$$

where α_N^i denotes the number of ways to have i concurrent active nodes. The partition function is a generating function for the concurrency levels of the system.

A number of important measures can be obtained once the partition function is computed. The most important performance measure in a packet radio network is the nodal throughput S_i which is defined as the average number of successful transmissions processed by node i per unit time. Note that it is not just the average number of concurrent transmissions, since some of these will not be received by their destinations. The maximum node throughput is called the node capacity.

To calculate the node throughput, let us first calculate the link throughput $S_{i,j}$, the average number of successful transmissions over i-to-j link per unit time. Let $A_{i,j}$ denotes the set of nodes that must be silent at the initiation of the i-to-j transmission. The probability of success of i-to-j transmission is then

$$P_{i,j} = P(A_{i,j} \text{ idle}) = \frac{\sum_{S \subseteq N \setminus A_{i,j}} \rho^{|S|}}{Z_N} = \frac{Z_{N \setminus A_{i,j}}}{Z_N} \tag{3}$$

Note that if the set of nodes N can be represented as $N = N_1 \cup N_2$ where N_1 and N_2 do not interfere with each other, then

$$Z_N = Z_{N_1} Z_{N_2} \tag{4}$$

If ρ_{ij} denotes the traffic intensity for the packets from node i to node j, then from (1) one obtains

$$S_{i,j} = \rho_{ij} P_{i,j} = \rho_{ij} \frac{Z_{N \setminus A_{i,j}}}{Z_N} \tag{5}$$

And therefore, the nodal throughput is given by

$$S_i = \sum_j S_{i,j} \tag{6}$$

3. CANONICAL APPROXIMATION

From the above discussion it is clear that the main difficulty in analyzing networks operating under CSMA with perfect capture and C-BTMA is the computation of the partition function. Usually, the partition function is difficult to express in a closed form. To overcome this problem, we propose the method of **Canonical Approximation**. The term canonical is borrowed from statistical physics where a similar method is used to show the equivalence of canonical and grand canonical ensembles ([Path84]).

To apply the method, one first computes the generating function of Z_N,

$$Z_G(t) = \sum_{N=0}^{\infty} Z_N t^N \tag{7}$$

By analogy with physics, one calls $Z_G(t)$ the grand partition function. This function is usually much easier to compute than Z_N. By Cauchy's theorem

$$Z_N = \frac{1}{2\pi i} \oint \frac{Z_G(t)}{t^{N+1}} dt \tag{8}$$

Assuming that $Z_G(t)$ is a meromorphic function whose smallest (in magnitude) pole t_0 is real, positive and of order 1, one can approximate the partition function as follows ([Henr77]):

$$Z_N \approx \frac{-Res[Z_G(t_0)]}{t_0^{N+1}} \tag{9}$$

where $Res[Z_G(t_0)]$ denotes the residue of $Z_G(t)$ at t_0. In Appendix 1 we prove the correctness of the above approximation and show that its (relative) error is decreasing exponentially when N increases.

4. APPLICATIONS

4.1. TANDEM NETWORKS: CSMA

Consider a tandem of N packet radios operating under the Carrier Sense Multiple Access (CSMA) scheme ([Boor 80]). In such a system all nodes share the same bandwidth and each node (except for the end nodes) can communicate with two neighbors. To calculate the partition function Z_N one applies the canonical approximation as follows.

Step 1. To calculate the grand partition function, derive a recursive relation for α_N^i, the number of configurations involving i transmissions. To that end, suppose one more node is added to a tandem of size N. Let us examine a configuration involving i transmissions. There are clearly two cases to consider:

Case 1: the $(N+1)$-st radio is not transmitting. There are α_N^i such configurations.

Case 2: the $(N+1)$-st radio is involved in a transmission. There are α_{N-1}^{i-1} such configurations.

Therefore

$$\begin{aligned} \alpha_{N+1}^i &= \alpha_{N-1}^{i-1} + \alpha_N^i \qquad \text{for } N \geq 1, 1 \leq i \leq N \\ \alpha_0^0 &= \alpha_N^0 = 1 \end{aligned} \tag{10}$$

This implies the following recursive relation

$$Z_{N+1} = Z_N + \rho Z_{N-1}, \qquad Z_0 = 1, Z_1 = 1 + \rho \tag{11}$$

Therefore, the grand partition function is

$$Z_G(t) = \sum_{N=0}^{\infty} Z_N t^N = \frac{1 + t\rho}{1 - t - \rho t^2} \tag{12}$$

Step 2. Find the smallest positive pole of the grand partition function.

$$t_0 = \frac{2}{1 + \sqrt{1 + 4\rho}} \tag{13}$$

Step 3. Compute the residue of the grand partition function at t_0

$$Res[Z_G(t_0)] = -\frac{1+\rho t_0}{2\rho t_0 + 1} = -\frac{1+\sqrt{1+4\rho}}{2\sqrt{1+4\rho}} \tag{14}$$

Step 4. The partition function is given by

$$Z_N \approx -\frac{Res[Z_G(t_0)]}{t_0^{N+1}} = \frac{1}{\sqrt{1+4\rho}}\left(\frac{1+\sqrt{1+4\rho}}{2}\right)^{N+2} \tag{15}$$

For this particular example, one can solve the simple recurrence equation (11) to get an exact expression for the partition function

$$Z_N = \frac{1}{\sqrt{1+4\rho}}\left[\left(\frac{1+\sqrt{1+4\rho}}{2}\right)^{N+2} - \left(\frac{1-\sqrt{1+4\rho}}{2}\right)^{N+2}\right]$$

The relative error of the approximation is therefore

$$\text{Error} = \frac{1}{\sqrt{1+4\rho}}\left(\frac{\sqrt{1+4\rho}-1}{\sqrt{1+4\rho}+1}\right)^{N+2} \mapsto 0 \tag{16}$$

and it decreases exponentially with N.

To calculate the link throughput $S_{i,i+1}$ under the perfect capture assumption, consider a typical node i. The transmission of i to node $i+1$ will be successful, if at the start of the transmission, all of the nodes in $A_{i,j} = \{i-1, i, i+1, i+2\}$ are silent. The sets of activities generated by the subsets of nodes $N_1 = \{1, \ldots, i-2\}$ and $N_2 = \{i+3, \ldots, N\}$ are mutually non-interfering and correspond to two tandems of sizes $i-2$ and $N-i-2$ respectively. Therefore, using equations (3) and (7) one finds the probability of successful transmission from node i to node $i+1$ is

$$P_{i,i+1} = \frac{Z_{i-2}Z_{N-i-2}}{Z_N} \approx \frac{1}{\sqrt{1+4\rho}}\left(\frac{2}{1+\sqrt{1+4\rho}}\right)^2 \tag{17}$$

Assuming that node i is equally likely to transmit to node $i+1$ as to node $i-1$, (that is $\rho_{i,i+1} = \rho/2$) the link throughput is given by

$$S_{i,i+1} = \frac{\rho}{2}P_{i,i+1} \approx \frac{\rho}{2\sqrt{1+4\rho}}\left(\frac{2}{1+\sqrt{1+4\rho}}\right)^2 \tag{18}$$

The nodal throughput is obviously $S_i = 2S_{i,i+1}$. Figure 1 gives the graph for the throughput as a function of the load. The link capacity (maximal link throughput) of $S_{i,i+1} = 0.0857$ is achieved at $\rho = 1.2$. For $\rho = 1$ the throughput is 0.085 as has been shown in [Boor80, Toba83] by using numerical methods and simulation. However, one gains a slight improvement in the throughput if packet retransmission attempts are generated faster than the average transmission duration time ($\rho = 1.2$).

4.2. TANDEM NETWORKS: C-BTMA

Let's consider the tandem of N packet radios as before, but assume that it operates under the C-BTMA protocol. This means that a node can transmit only if its immediate neighbors as well as the neighbors of the immediate neighbors are silent. As before, one can derive a recurrence relation for the partition function by adding one more node to the tandem and examining the number of configurations having i transmissions. One would get

$$\begin{aligned} &\alpha_{N+1}^{i} = \alpha_N^{i} + \alpha_{N-2}^{i-1} \qquad N \geq 2 \\ &\alpha_0^0 = \alpha_1^0 = \alpha_N^0 = 1 \end{aligned} \tag{19}$$

The partition function then satisfies

$$\begin{aligned} &Z_{N+1} = Z_N + \rho Z_{N-2} \qquad N \geq 2 \\ &Z_0 = 1, Z_1 = 1 + \rho, Z_2 = 1 + 2\rho \end{aligned} \tag{20}$$

From the above, the grand partition function satisfies:

$$Z_G(t) = \frac{1 + \rho t + \rho t^2}{1 - t - \rho t^3} \tag{21}$$

Let t_0 be the smallest (positive) pole of $Z_G(t)$ (See Appendix 1 for the existence and uniqueness of this pole). In Appendix 1 we show that the residue of $Z_G(t)$ at t_0 is given by

$$Res[Z_G(t_0)] = -\frac{1 + \rho t_0 + \rho t_0^2}{3\rho t_0^2 + 1} \tag{22}$$

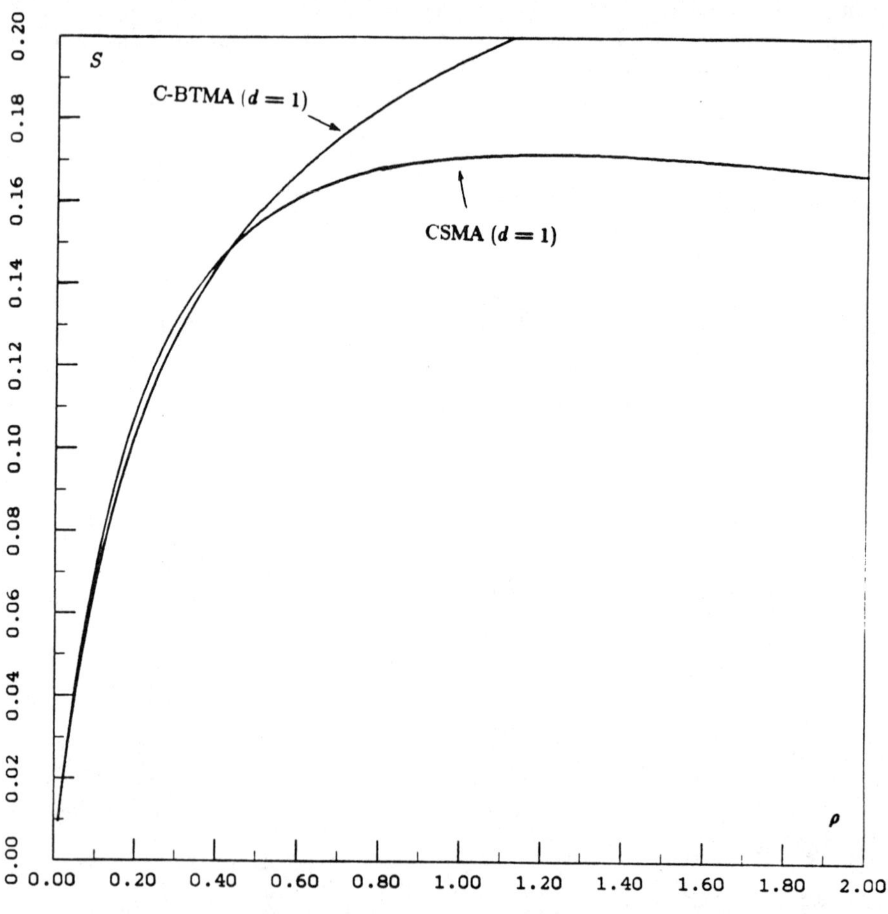

Figure 1: Nodal Throughput: CSMA and C-BTMA (d=1)

Applying the canonical approximation, one gets the following expression for the partition function

$$Z_N \approx -\frac{Res[Z_G(t_0)]}{t_0^{N+1}} = \frac{1+\rho t_0+\rho t_0^2}{(3\rho t_0^2+1)t_0^{N+1}} \tag{23}$$

To calculate the throughput, consider a typical node i in a tandem. This node will be successful in a transmission to node $i+1$ if the set of nodes one and two hops away $A_{i,i+1} = \{i-2, i-1, i, i+1, i+2\}$ are silent. The sets of activities generated by the subsets of nodes $N_1 = \{1, 2, \ldots, i-3\}$ and $N_2 = \{i+3, \ldots, N\}$ are mutually independent and correspond to two tandems of sizes $i-3$ and $N-i-2$, respectively. Therefore, the probability of success

$$P_{i,i+1} = \frac{Z_{i-3}Z_{N-i-2}}{Z_N} \approx \frac{1+\rho t_0+\rho t_0^2}{(3\rho t_0^2+1)} t_0^4 \tag{24}$$

Assuming that a node is equally likely to talk to any two of its neighbors, the link throughput $S_{i,i+1}$ is given by

$$S_{i,i+1} = \frac{\rho}{2} P_{i,i+1} \approx \frac{\rho}{2} \frac{1+\rho t_0+\rho t_0^2}{(3\rho t_0^2+1)} t_0^4 \tag{25}$$

The nodal throughput is

$$S_i = 2S_{i,i+1} = \rho \frac{1+\rho t_0+\rho t_0^2}{(3\rho t_0^2+1)} t_0^4 \tag{26}$$

To calculate the capacity, note that once a node is permitted to start a transmission, the success of transmission is guaranteed. Therefore, the capacity is achieved at $\rho \mapsto \infty$. For large ρ the pole can be approximated by $t_0 \approx \rho^{-\frac{1}{3}}$. With this approximation

$$S_i = \frac{\rho(1+\rho^{\frac{2}{3}}+\rho^{\frac{1}{3}})}{3\rho^{\frac{1}{3}}+1} \rho^{-\frac{4}{3}} \mapsto \frac{1}{3} \tag{27}$$

The throughput per node is $\frac{1}{3}$. This is what one expects: as $\rho \mapsto \infty$ the tandem will be densely packed with transmissions. One would expect every 3-rd node to be active.

It is interesting to compare the above results to the simulation studies on ring networks reported in [Toba83]. The link throughput for a ring under C-BTMA exhibits a quasi-periodicity of period 3: all rings with a number of nodes which is a multiple of 3 have a little higher throughput than those which are not multiples of 3. The difference decreases as the number of nodes increases. This can be explained using the canonical approximation. First, note that tandem and ring exhibit similar behavior, especially for large N. The grand partition function has three roots - one is t_0 (real, positive and smallest in magnitude) and two are complex conjugates. If one considers the exact expression of the partition function, it is dominated by the smallest root. However, for small N, the contributions from the complex roots are not negligible. These contributions are the largest when N is a multiple of 3. As N increases, the contributions from these complex roots become smaller as the partition function is increasingly dominated by t_0. For large N, the partition function is insensitive to the divisibility of N by 3. The simulation results were reported for relatively small size ($N < 20$) rings.

Figure 1 gives the the nodal throughput and compares it to the one using CSMA with perfect capture. For $\rho < 0.43$, CSMA outperforms C-BTMA. This says that for lighter loads, there is no need to be overly restrictive ("conservative"). For heavier loads when there is a lot of interference, being restrictive helps.

4.3. LINEAR ARRAY: CSMA

Consider a packet radio network of N nodes placed on a linear array of degree $2d$ - nodes can transmit up to d nodes in either direction. To calculate the partition function Z_N one can derive a recursive relation for α_N^i.

Suppose one more node is added to the network. Let's examine a configuration involving i transmissions. There are clearly two cases to consider:

Case 1: the $N+1$-st radio is not transmitting. There are α_N^i such configurations.

Case 2: the $N+1$-st radio is involved in a transmission. There are α_{N-d}^{i-1} such configurations.

Therefore,

$$\begin{aligned} \alpha^i_{N+1} &= \alpha^{i-1}_{N-d} + \alpha^i_N && N \geq d \\ \alpha^i_N &= 1 && N \leq d \end{aligned} \tag{28}$$

The above relation implies the following

$$\begin{aligned} Z_{N+1} &= Z_N + \rho Z_{N-d} && \text{for } N \geq d \\ Z_N &= 1 + \rho N && \text{for } 0 \leq N < d \end{aligned} \tag{29}$$

It follows then

$$Z_G(t) - \sum_{k=0}^{d} Z_k t^k = t\left[Z_G(t) - \sum_{i=0}^{d-1} Z_i t^i\right] + \rho t^{d+1} Z_G(t)$$

which after some algebraic manipulations reduces to

$$Z_G(t) = \frac{t - 1 + \rho t^{d+1} - \rho t}{(t-1)(1 - t - \rho t^{d+1})} \tag{30}$$

The residue of the grand partition function at its smallest pole t_0 (see Appendix 1 for the existence and uniqueness of this pole)

$$Res[Z_G(t_0)] = -\frac{-\rho t_0^2}{(1-t_0)[1 + d(1-t_0)]} \tag{31}$$

Applying the canonical approximation, one obtains the following expression for the partition function:

$$Z_N \approx -\frac{Res[Z_G(t_0)]}{t_0^{N+1}} = \frac{\rho t_0^2}{(1-t_0)[1 + d(1-t_0)]t_0^{N+1}} \tag{32}$$

To calculate the throughput, consider a typical node i and let $S_{i,i+k}$ $(0 < k \leq d)$ be the throughput of a link connecting nodes i and $i+k$ which are k hops apart. Since node i can communicate with up to d successive nodes in either direction, under the perfect capture assumption, the transmission to node $i+k$ $(0 < k \leq d)$ will be successful if the set of nodes $A_{i,i+k} = \{i-d, i-d+1, \ldots, i-1, i, i+1, \ldots, i+k+d\}$ are silent at the initiation of that transmission. The probability of success is therefore

$$P_{i,i+k} = P(A_{i,i+k} \text{ idle}) = \frac{Z_{N \setminus A_{i,i+k}}}{Z_N} =$$

$$= \frac{Z_{i-d-1} Z_{N-i-k-d}}{Z_N} \approx -Res[Z_G(t_0)] t_0^{2d+k} \tag{33}$$

Let us consider the case when the traffic is equally distributed among $2d$ outgoing links from node i, that is $\rho_{i,i+k} = \rho/2d$. In such a case, the link throughput

$$S_{i,i+k} = \frac{\rho}{2d} P_{i,i+k} \approx \frac{\rho^2 t_0^{2d+k+2}}{2d(1-t_0)[1+d(1-t_0)]} \tag{34}$$

The nodal throughput of i,

$$S = 2\sum_{k=1}^{d} S_{i,i+k} \approx \frac{\rho^2 t_0^{2d+3}}{d(1-t_0)[1+d(1-t_0)]} \frac{1-t_0^d}{1-t_0} =$$

$$= \frac{t_0(1-t_0^d)}{d[1+d(1-t_0)]} \tag{35}$$

Figure 2 gives the curves of the nodal throughput as a function of load for $d = 3$, $d = 5$ and $d = 10$. The corresponding capacities are $S_i = 0.0826$ at $\rho = 0.735$, $S_i = 0.0544$ at $\rho = 0.525$ and $S_i = 0.0293$ at $\rho = 0.31$.

Let us calculate the capacity for large d. From equation (35) one differentiates the nodal throughput S_i with respect to t_0 and solves the equation $S'(t_0) = 0$.

One would obtain

$$d^2 t_0^{d+1} - (d+1)^2 t_0^d + d + 1 = 0 \tag{36}$$

For large d, the pole t_0 is very close to 1. Therefore, writing $t_0 = 1 - \alpha$ and using the approximation $(1-\alpha)^d \approx 1 - d\alpha$ one gets that the

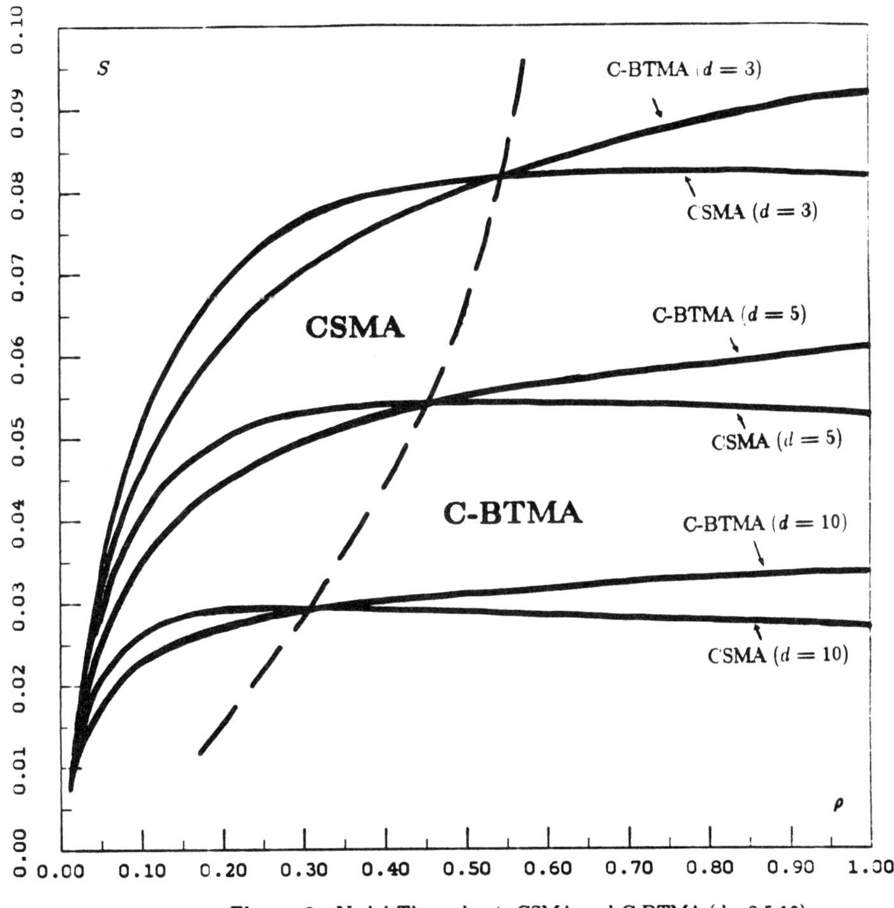

Figure 2: Nodal Throughput: CSMA and C-BTMA (d=3,5,10)

capacity is achieved at

$$t_0 \approx 1 - \frac{1}{d+1} \tag{37}$$

From equation (35) one gets that the capacity is

$$S_i \approx \frac{\frac{d}{d+1}\left[1 - \left(1 - \frac{1}{d+1}\right)^d\right]}{d\left(1 + \frac{d}{d+1}\right)} \approx \frac{1 - \frac{1}{e}}{2d} = \frac{0.318}{d} \tag{38}$$

The corresponding load

$$\rho = \frac{1 - t_0}{t_0^{d+1}} \approx \frac{e}{d} \tag{39}$$

4.4. LINEAR ARRAY: C-BTMA

Consider the same linear array of packet radio nodes but now operating under the C-BTMA scheme. As before, one can derive a recurrence relation for the partition function by adding one more node and considering the corresponding two cases. Because of the C-BTMA the recurrence relation becomes $\alpha_{N+1}^i = \alpha_N^i + \alpha_{N-2d}^{i-1}$ for $N \geq 2d$ with initial conditions $\alpha_N^1 = N$ for $N \leq 2d$

This gives

$$\begin{array}{ll} Z_{N+1} = Z_N + \rho Z_{N-2d} & \text{for } N \geq 2d \\ Z_N = 1 + \rho N & \text{for } 0 \leq N < 2d \end{array} \tag{40}$$

The grand partition function $Z_G(t)$ can be shown to satisfy

$$Z_G(t) = \frac{t - 1 + \rho t^{2d+1} - \rho t}{(t-1)(1 - t - \rho t^{2d+1})} \tag{41}$$

Let t_0 be the smallest positive pole. (See Appendix for the existence and uniqueness of this pole.) The residue is then

$$Res[Z_G(t_0)] = -\frac{t_0 - 1 + \rho t_0^{2d+1} - \rho t_0}{(t_0 - 1)(1 + \rho(2d+1)t_0^{2d})} =$$

$$= -\frac{\rho t_0^2}{(1-t_0)[1+2d(1-t_0)]} \tag{42}$$

The partition function is given by

$$Z_N \approx -\frac{Res[Z_G(t_0)]}{t_0^{N+1}} = \frac{\rho t_0^2}{(1-t_0)[1+2d(1-t_0)]t_0^{N+1}} \tag{43}$$

As in the previous case, define $S_{i,i+k}$ $(0 < k \leq d)$ to be the link throughput between nodes i and $i+k$ that are k hops apart. Because of the C-BTMA, the node i it will be successful at every transmission to $i+k$. It can initiate a transmission if the set of nodes $A = \{i-2d, i-2d+1, \ldots, i+2d\}$ is silent. The probability of that is

$$P_{i,i+k} = \frac{Z_{i-2d-1} Z_{N-i-2d}}{Z_N} \approx Res[Z_G(t_0)]t_0^{4d} =$$

$$= \frac{\rho t_0^{4d+2}}{(1-t_0)[1+2d(1-t_0)]} \tag{44}$$

Assuming that node i is equally likely to talk to any of its $2d$ neighbors, the link throughput is given by

$$S_{i,i+k} = \frac{\rho}{2d} P_{i,i+k} \approx \frac{\rho^2 t_0^{4d+2}}{2d(1-t_0)[1+2d(1-t_0)]} \tag{45}$$

The nodal throughput

$$S_i = 2\sum_{i=1}^{d} S_{i,i+k} \approx \frac{\rho^2 t_0^{4d+2}}{(1-t_0)[1+2d(1-t_0)]} \tag{46}$$

Since every transmission results in success, the capacity is achieved at $\rho \mapsto \infty$. For large ρ the pole can be approximated as follows

$$t_0 \approx \rho^{-\frac{1}{2d+1}} \tag{47}$$

The asymptotic nodal throughput is easily seen to be $S_i = 1/(2d+1)$. This is what one would intuitively expect - for very large ρ the linear array will be packed with transmissions. Since every i-to-j transmissions blocks $2d+1$ nodes and the system is densely packed, one would expect that the throughput per node is $1/(2d+1)$.

It is interesting to compare the capacity S_i^{max} for CSMA with perfect capture and C-BTMA for large d. For CSMA we obtained that

$$S_i^{max} \approx \frac{0.318}{d} \tag{48}$$

For C-BTMA

$$S_i^{max} \approx \frac{0.5}{d} \tag{49}$$

This says that for the same (large) d the capacity under CSMA is 36% worse than under C-BTMA.

Figure 2 gives the nodal throughput and compares it with CSMA with perfect capture for $d=3, d=5$ and $d=10$. Just as in the case of $d=1$, for lighter loads CSMA outperforms C-BTMA. However, we note that as the level of interference increases (d increases), the range of the loads for which CSMA is better decreases. The reason is that one should be more and more restrictive as the interference increases.

5. CONCLUSION

This paper presented an application of the new method of canonical approximation to analyze CSMA and C-BTMA protocols with perfect capture for a number of network topologies. The method allows to analyze a number of network topologies with relative ease. Further work will extend the application of the new method to study other multiple access protocols and network topologies.

APPENDIX 1

Theorem 1. Let t_0 be the smallest pole of the grand partition function. Then for large N one has ([Henr77])

$$Z_N \approx \frac{-Res[Z_G(t_0)]}{t_0^{N+1}}$$

Proof. Let $t_0, t_1, ...t_k$ be the singularities of $Z_G(t)$. Assume that there are a finite number of poles and all poles are of order 1. For more general case, the proof proceeds along similar lines and is given in [Pins85].

$$0 < |t_0| < |t_1| < ... < |t_k|$$

Let C be the circle around the origin excluding all the poles and let C' be the circle around the origin surrounding all the poles of $Z_G(t)$.

Then by residue theorem ([Alfh66])

$$Z_N = \frac{1}{2\pi i}\oint_C \frac{Z_G(t)}{t^{N+1}}dt = -\sum_{i=0}^{k} \frac{Res[Z_G(t_i)]}{t_i^{N+1}} + \frac{1}{2\pi i}\oint_{C'} \frac{Z_G(t)}{t^{N+1}}dt =$$

$$= -\frac{Res[Z_G(t_0)]}{t_0^{N+1}}\left[1 + \sum_{i=1}^{k} \frac{Res[Z_G(t_i)]}{Res[Z_G(t_0)]}\left(\frac{t_0}{t_i}\right)^{N+1}\right] + \frac{1}{2\pi i}\oint_{C'} \frac{Z_G(t)}{t^{N+1}}dt$$

But since

$$\left|\frac{1}{2\pi i}\oint_{C'} \frac{Z_G(t)}{t^{N+1}}dt\right| \leq \frac{\max_{t\in C'}[Z_G(t)]}{|t|^N}$$

and $|\frac{t_0}{t_i}| < 1$ one obtains that for large N

$$Z_N = \frac{-Res[Z_G(t_0)]}{t_0^{N+1}}[1 + \mathrm{E}]$$

With the (relative) error of the approximation

$$\mathrm{E} \leq \left[\sum_{i=1}^{k} \frac{Res[Z_G(t_i)]}{Res[Z_G(t_0)]}\left(\frac{t_0}{t_i}\right)^{N+1}\right] + \frac{\max_{t\in C'}[Z_G(t)]}{Res[Z_G(t_0)]}\left(\frac{t_0}{|t|}\right)^{N+1} \mapsto 0$$

Therefore, for large N

$$Z_N \approx \frac{-Res[Z_G(t_0)]}{t_0^{N+1}} \tag{50}$$

The partition function is asymptotically determined by the smallest pole of its grand partition function. ∎

To use the above approximation, one must be able to compute residues fast. The calculation of residues becomes very easy with the help of the following theorem ([Alhf66]):

Theorem 2. Suppose $f(t)$ has a pole of order m at $t = t_0$ and put $g(t) = (t - t_0)f(t)$. Then the residue of $f(t)$ at point t_0 is given by

$$Res[f(t_0)] = \frac{1}{(m-1)!} g^{(m-1)}(t_0) \tag{51}$$

In particular, if $Z_G(t)$ is of the form

$$Z_G(t) = \frac{F(t)}{1 - t - \rho t^{n+1}}$$

and t_0 is a simple pole of $Z_G(t)$ then

$$Res[Z_G(t_0)] = -\frac{F(t_0)}{(n+1)\rho t_0^n + 1} \tag{52}$$

∎

Theorem 3. The function $f(t) = 1 - t - \rho t^n = 0$ has only one positive root t_0. This root is of order 1 and is the smallest in magnitude among all other roots.

Proof. Since $f(0) = 1 > 0$ and $f(1) = -\rho < 0$ the function has a root t_0 satisfying $0 < t_0 < 1$. Moreover, since $f'(t) < 0$ for $t > 0$ it follows that $f(t)$ is a decreasing function for positive t and hence, the root is unique and of order 1.

For any other root t_1 one can write $t_1 = R\cos\theta + iR\sin\theta$ where $\theta \neq 0$. Since t_1 satisfies $1 - t_1 - \rho t_1^n = 0$ one obtains

$$g(R,\theta) = 1 - R\cos\theta - \rho R^n \cos n\theta = 0 \tag{53}$$

But $g(R,\theta) > 1 - R - \rho R^n = f(R)$. The function $f(R)$ has only one positive real root $R = t_0$. Moreover, the function $f(R)$ is decreasing for larger R. Therefore, $g(R,\theta)$ is bounded below by a decreasing function intersecting the X-axis at t_0. But this implies $t_1 > t_0$. ∎

REFERENCES

[Alfh66] L.V. Alfhors, "Complex Analysis", *McGraw-Hill*, New York, 1966.

[Boor80] R.R. Boorstyn, A. Kershenbaum, "Throughput Analysis of Multihop Packet Radio", *Proc. International Conference on Communications*, Seattle, Wa, June 1980.

[Braz84] J.M. Brazio, F.A. Tobagi, "Theoretical results in Throughput Analysis of Multihop Packet Radio Networks", *Proc. IEEE International Conference on Communications*, Amsterdam, May 1984, pp. 448-455.

[Henr77] P. Henrici, "Applied and Computational Complex Analysis", *J. Wiley and Sons*, New York, 1977.

[Kell80] F.P. Kelly, "Reversibility and Stochastic Networks", *J. Wiley and Sons*, New York, 1980.

[Klei75] L. Kleinrock, "Queueing Systems, Volume I: Theory", *J. Wiley and Sons*, New York, 1975.

[Path84] R.K. Pathria, "Statistical Mechanics", *Pergamon Press*, New York, 1984.

[Pins84] E. Pinsky, Y. Yemini, "A Statistical Mechanics of Interconnection Networks", *Proc. Performance'84*, E. Gelenbe (editor), North-Holland 1984.

[Pins85] E. Pinsky, "Canonical Approximation in the Performance Analysis of Distributed Systems", *Ph.D. Thesis*, Computer Science Department, Columbia University, 1985

[Silv83] J.A. Silvester, L. Kleinrock, "On the Capacity of Multi-Hop Slotted ALOHA Networks with Regular Structure", *IEEE Trans. on Communications*, **COM-31**, 8, August 1983, pp. 974-982.

[Toba83] F.A. Tobagi, J.M. Brazio, "Throughput Analysis of Multihop Packet Radio Networks under Various Channel Access Schemes", *Proc. INFOCOM 1983*, San Diego, California, April 1983, pp. 381-389.

[Yemi83] Y. Yemini, "A Statistical Mechanics of Distributed Resource Sharing Mechanisms", *Proc. INFOCOM 1983*, San Diego, California, April 1983, pp. 531-540.

Part Two

Protocols

Automated Protocol Validation in *Argos*, Assertion Proving and Scatter Searching

Gerard J. Holzmann
AT&T Bell Laboratories
Murray Hill, New Jersey 07974

ABSTRACT

Argos is a validation language for data communication protocols. To validate a protocol a model in *Argos* is constructed consisting of a control flow specification and a formal description of the correctness requirements. This model can be compiled into a minimized lower level description that is based on a formal model of communicating finite state machines. An automated protocol validator *trace* uses these minimized descriptions to perform a partial symbolic execution of the protocol to establish its correctness for the given requirements.

1. Introduction

In the last few years some experience has been gained with the capabilities and the restrictions of automated protocol validators [2,3,4,8,10,11,12,13]. The first validation methods required considerable effort from the user to translate an abstract protocol specification into the formal code used in the validation process. The analyses were often run in batch mode and the interpretation of the results again required considerable human ingenuity. It was soon found that the time and space complexity of even the best known exhaustive search techniques prohibits their application to larger protocols. Similarly, an apparent conflict between the need for *general* validation tools, applicable to a wide range of protocols, and the need to test protocols on more *specific* protocol-dependent properties prohibited the development of tools that could be used effectively in a design environment.

We will describe a protocol validation methodology that overcomes most of these problems. A protocol is specified in a high level language *Argos*, which is compiled into the code accepted by the analyzer. The output of the analyzer is presented in interpreted form, as execution histories that either violate user-specified *specific* requirements or *general* correctness criteria such as completeness and absence of deadlock.

The analyzer was written in C and is portable across Unix† systems with virtual memory. In exhaustive searches the new validator can be several orders of

† Unix is a trademark of AT&T Bell Laboratories.

magnitude faster than the earlier tools that were non-portable and required custom-coded input. For protocols that are beyond the scope of exhaustive searches the validator can perform *scatter* searches: fast scans over the state space in an effort to localize design errors in seconds where a full search would take days.

2. The Problem

Consider a protocol for two processes, each having one hundred states and each accessing five local variables. Message buffers are restricted to five slots each, and the effective range of the local variables is assumed to be limited to ten values. The number of distinct messages exchanged is ten.

Intuitively the simplest way to analyze the working of this protocol is to perform an exhaustive search of all reachable system states. Let us consider the worst case. There are $10^{5 \cdot 2}$ possible states of the protocol variables. Each process can be in one of 10^2 different states, so two processes can generate 10^4 states. Finally, each buffer can hold between zero and five messages, where each message can be one out of ten possible messages. The total number of system states in the worst case then is:

$$10^{10} \cdot 10^4 \cdot \left(\sum_{i=0}^{5} 10^i \right)^2$$

or in the order of 10^{24} different states. If we assume, quite unrealistically, that each state can be encoded in 1 byte of memory and can be analyzed in 10^{-6} sec of CPU time we would still need a machine with at least 10^{15} times as much memory as currently available, and would need roughly 10^{11} *years* of CPU time to perform the analysis. By any standard, this can be called an inadequate strategy. To improve it we will either have to abstract from protocol specifics or restrict the scope of the analysis.

One method to abstract from protocol specifics is to use *assertions* in a formal logic, such as Floyd-Hoare logic or temporal logic. We then annotate the specification with suppositions that can establish the observance of the protocol requirements in which we are interested. The key phrase here is clearly 'in which we are interested.' It allows us to abstract from the details in which we are not interested. To automate this approach, however, is a challenging but open problem.

Another method is to construct a partial model of the protocol, leaving out as many details as we can get away with, and then analyze the model instead of the original protocol. A few models have proven to be useful for these experiments. Well known are the Petri Net model and its derivatives, and the Finite State Machine model. There is, however, an unfortunate tradeoff between the descriptive clarity and flexibility of a model on the one hand and its analytical power on the other hand.

Traditionally, this tradeoff has been interpreted to mean that we can either choose a restrictive model that allows us to validate trivial properties with polynomial time algorithms, or a more powerful model that would allow us to validate more interesting properties with nonpolynomial time algorithms.

This interpretation is based on the assumption that the protocol to be validated is error free. If the protocol has bugs, the assumption is further that the validation should produce an exhaustive listing of *all* the errors present. This leads to a validation strategy where one tries to establish *conformance* to the correctness criteria by exhaustive analysis. If exhaustive analysis within the finite amount of time that we are willing to spend on it becomes infeasible, the strategy fails to produce an answer on the correctness of the protocol.

In practice, and especially in a design process, however, neither of the above assumptions is true. If we do assume that the protocol submitted to a validator has errors and that a designer is interested in seeing any nonempty subset these we can improve the validation strategy substantially. The validator can scan the state space with a heuristic searching algorithm in an effort to find a typical *violation* of the requirements in as short a time as possible. The objective of such a partial analysis, or *scattersearch*, is then to establish the presence rather than the absence of errors. If it fails to locate an error it fails to produce an answer on the correctness of the protocol.

For a protocol that generates a state space of 10^8 reachable states we would need in the order of 10^6 seconds, or at least 12 days of CPU time for an exhaustive analysis. In the design phase, knowing or assuming that our first protocol design has errors, it is unlikely that we would be willing to spend more than a few minutes, say 10^3 seconds, on an analysis.

- The most commonly used *breadth first* search method [4,8,12,13] would generate the top 10^{-3}% of the state space tree, which is unlikely to contain errors or a single complete execution sequence.
- The *depth first* search method, used in [10,11], would generate the first 10^{-3}% of all complete execution histories. The detection of an error sequence among the first few generated is still unpredictable since we have no control over the choice of the sequences that are tested.
- The *scatter searching* method, described below, would attempt to select those 10^{-3}% of all execution histories that are most likely to lead to errors. Unlike in the *depth first* method the sequences to be analyzed would be selected from different parts of the tree and not be taken systematically from the one part of the tree that happens to be generated first.

Scatter searching, then, can be a worth-while addition to our range of tools for testing protocol designs. As such, however, it is a bug-finding tool, not a 'validation' tool in the true sense of the word.

It is, of course, important that we be able to verify the reliability of partial searches. We will return to this at the end of section 5, after a more detailed overview of the various searching strategies and a discussion of the different variants of scatter searching that have been implemented.

In the next two sections we will first describe a general language that allows for the specification of both protocols and of protocol correctness requirements. We then describe the extended finite state machine model that can be used for analyzing protocols, and we discuss a compiler that can translate from the language to the machines. The compiler performs static checks for the syntactical correctness and completeness of the specification. The code it produces is targeted to efficient symbolic execution, for instance by precomputing state information that is relevant in the analysis.

In protocol analysis by symbolic execution it is hardly ever necessary to exhaustively search all possible executions to perform a complete analysis. We show that only a subset of the number of feasible process interleavings is relevant to the analysis. Then we describe a modified depth first search algorithm that is used for both complete searches through the state space and for heuristic searches.

3. A Protocol Validation Language

Argos is a simple nondeterministic guarded command language [7,9] that can be used for protocol specification and protocol analysis. Perhaps the most important feature of the language is that there is no difference between a condition and a statement. A condition can appear wherever a statement can appear and vice versa. A statement is said to be *executable* if it evaluates to *true* when it is interpreted as a condition.

The behavior of a distributed system is described by a collection of *process* specifications, where each *process* is an asynchronous agent that can perform *internal* actions and/or synchronize with its environment by performing *external* actions. A process can wait for an event to happen by simply waiting for a statement to become executable. For instance, instead of writing a busy wait loop:

```
while (a ≠ b)
        skip;
```

we can write in *Argos*:

```
(a ≠ b);
```

The boolean test is equivalent to a statement, but it is only executable when the test will return *true*. When it happens to be false execution blocks until it becomes true. To specify control-flow *Argos* has the standard set of structuring tools: case selection, repetition, function call, and macros. In the above case, for instance, we could write:

```
if
:: (a ≠ b) → option1
:: (a == b) → option2
fi;
```

to use the relative values of a and b to choose between two options. Since $(a \neq b)$ is an internal action it is usually embedded in these larger control flow structures.

Internal actions can be boolean tests of or assignments to local variables. External actions are used to communicate messages and values between processes.

The assignment

$$v = e$$

where v is a variable and e an expression, is an internal action which always returns *true* and is therefore always executable†. On the other hand, the boolean test

† Note that the assignment does not return the value of expression e.

(e)

where e is an expression without side effects, is an internal action which returns *false* when expression e returns zero and is therefore only executable if expression e evaluates to a nonzero value. Other types of internal actions are a *jump*, a *call* to a procedure, and a *return* from a procedure. These three actions are always executable and have no side effects. To guarantee this, procedures cannot return values.

The send statement

$c!m(e)$

specifies an external action that returns *true* when channel c can accept message m, i.e. whenever channel c is nonfull. When executed, expression e is evaluated and the value returned is attached to the message m. Similarly, the receive statement

$c?m(v)$

specifies an external action that returns *true* when channel c can deliver message m, i.e. whenever channel c is nonempty and the oldest message in c is m. When executed, the value attached to message m, if any, is assigned to variable v. As with the *send* statement, the specification of a value transfer is optional. The shorthand forms for sending and receiving are $c!m$ and $c?m$.

Control flow is specified by using *concatenation*, *case selection*, *repetition*, and *jumps*.

The statement separators for specifying concatenations are the traditional semicolon ';' and the arrow '→', which may be used interchangeably. Case selection is specified in an if statement with one or more options:

```
if
:: option1
:: option2
...
fi
```

The first statement of an option determines whether the option is executable. Such an option *guard* can be any legal statement: a boolean test, and assignment, a procedure call, a send or a receive, a jump or even another control flow specifier. The repetitive construct

```
do
:: option1
:: option2
...
od
```

also specifies a selection from a list of options, but this time the construct is repeatedly executed until either an explicit *break* statement is encountered or a *jump* transfers control to another part of the program. Note that the repetitive construct is not implicitly terminated when all guards are false, unlike in CSP [9].

The following example specifies a simple filter that receives messages from channel *in* and divides them into two streams named *large* and *small* depending on the values attached.

```
#define N    128
#define size  16

channel in[size], large[size], small[size];

proc split
{           var cargo;

            do
            :: in?mesg(cargo) →
                        if
                        :: (cargo ≥ N) → large!mesg(cargo)
                        :: (cargo <  N) → small!mesg(cargo)
                        fi
            od

}
```

A process that merges the two streams back into one, most likely in a different order, and writes it back into channel *in* could be specified as follows.

```
proc merge
{           var cargo;

            do
            ::          if
                        :: large?mesg(cargo)
                        :: small?mesg(cargo)
                        fi;
                        in!mesg(cargo)
            od
}
```

So, with an initial contents for channel *in*, specified as

```
channel in[size] = { mesg(256), mesg(13), mesg(4555) };
```

the split and merge filters could busily perform their task forever on. To break a loop on a negative input it is valid, though redundant, to write

```
            do
            :: in?mesg(cargo) →
                              if
                              :: (cargo <  0) → break
                              :: (cargo <  0) → goto out
                              :: (cargo ≥ 0) → skip
                              fi
            od;
out:        skip
```

In this case the *break* and the *goto* have precisely the same effect and one of the two corresponding options could be deleted. The last option in the if statement above is necessary to avoid the other two options from blocking the control flow when *cargo* is nonnegative.

There is no restriction on the type of statements that can appear as guards in options. If more than one guard turns out to be executable one of them will be selected nondeterministically. If all guards are false the process will block until at least one of them becomes true. In a simple concatenation, therefore, it is valid to write:

```
in?mesg(cargo); cargo = N; (cargo ≠ N) → larger!mesg(cargo)
```

Execution can block at three different places in this sequence: at the two external actions, and at the boolean test

```
(cargo ≠ N) .
```

In this case the executing process is certain to hang in that test as a result of the assignment that precedes it. The variable is necessarily local, so the execution of no other process could ever reset *cargo*'s value.

Assertions

By default the protocol analyzer that will be discussed in more detail in a later section will check a protocol for the observance of general correctness requirements such as absence of deadlock, and completeness. Assertions are used to test for more specific aspects of a protocol's behavior, The assertions specify global behavior in terms of external actions. For example, the specification

```
assert
{       do
        :: large!mesg; small!mesg
        od
}
```

is a requirement on the order in which messages of the type *mesg* are sent to the two channels *large* and *small*. The assertion is that in each execution sequence a message on channel *large* must precede a message on channel *small*, and that these two actions will always be executed in alternation.

The main restriction to assertion specifications is that they can only refer to external actions, i.e. sends and receives. The control flow constructs, however, are the same as those for process specifications: concatenations, selections, iterations, jumps, procedure calls, and macros. The scope of the assertion, that is the set of external actions that is traced to verify or to violate it, is implicitly defined by the set of external actions specified within the assertion. If an external action occurs at least once in an assertion body all its occurrences in an execution of the protocol are required to comply with it. The appendix gives an example of the use of assertions in the validation process.

Implementation

The version of the validation language that has been implemented for the protocol analyzer has a number of restrictions, some of which were made to simplify the compiler and some to simplify the analyzer. Perhaps the main restriction to the language as implemented is that it requires all processes and all channel names for a protocol to be defined at compile time: there is no facility for the dynamic creation of processes or channels. Another main restriction, that was made to alleviate the memory requirements for the protocol analyzer, is that the specification language has only one type of data element: the short integer. There are no arrays or record structures. Further, though the language allows for procedures to call other procedures, it rules out direct or indirect recursive calls, and provides no means for procedures to return values to a caller.

4. Finite State Machines

Having a protocol validation language, as described above, it is relatively straightforward to develop an interpreter to perform a simple exhaustive search for protocol errors. As indicated in section 2, however, that strategy inherently limits the class of protocols that can effectively be analyzed to a small subset of what is feasible. The alternative we will explore is to translate the description into a form that is targeted at efficient state space searching methods. In this section a formalism for finite state machines is defined that is used to optimize state space searches.

A finite state machine is usually defined as an abstract demon that can accept input signals, generate output signals and change its inner state in accordance with some predefined plan. In the definitions given below, we will extend this basic model with variables and with channels that map the output signals of one machine upon the input signals of another. We will also replace the conventional notion of the finite state machine as an automaton that can only perform input, output and state transitions with a more general notion of an automaton performing internal or external *actions* that may or may not have a *side effect* on its environment.

A protocol, then, is a collection of processes, channels and variables.

> A *protocol* is a tuple (P, B, V, M_b, M_v), where:
> - P is a finite set of *processes*,
> - B is a finite set of *channels*,
> - V is a finite set of *variables*,
> - M_b is a mapping of P onto B. and
> - M_v is a mapping of P onto V.

Mapping M_b defines via which channels a process can receive input, and similarly M_v defines which variables a process can access. Each process must be able to send to all channels and to receive input from a subset of the channels. No channel, however, need be read by more than one process. The mapping M_b therefore defines a partitioning of set B into a number of disjoint subsets, where each subset contains the input channels of a single process in P. Process interactions are restricted to message passing, so the same rules can be enforced for the access to variables: each process should be able to access zero or more variables, but no more than one process may access any single variable. M_v therefore also partitions set V into disjoint subsets, each set containing the local variables of a single process.

The choice not to include the definition of variables and channels in the definition of processes is important. It allows us to divide a protocol model into automata representing process behavior and a single *context* automaton representing the environment. The context automaton is defined by the state of variables and channels and in turn defines the executability of actions in the process automata. As a result, the size of a finite state machine description for a given protocol, measured in numbers of states, can be smaller. In the extreme case the improvement can be the difference between the size of a Cartesian product and a sum of two sets of states.

As part of the definition of a channel, we use the notion of a *channel sort*: the set of all messages that can be sent to a given channel.

A *channel* is a triple (S, C, N), where:

> S is the *channel sort*,
> C is the *channel contents*, an ordered set of elements from S, and
> N is the number of messages the channel can maximally hold.

Note that a channel can be in only a finite number of states

$$\sum_{i=0}^{N} |S|^i$$

where $|S|$ is the cardinal number of set S.

Similarly, a variable can be defined to have both a value and a finite *range* of possible values. Each variable then can only be in a finite number of different states.†

A *process* is defined as a tuple (Q, q_s, q_e, A, T), where:

> Q is a finite, non-empty set of states,
> q_s is the *startstate*, and q_e is the *endstate*, elements of Q,
> A is a set of *actions*, and
> T is the state transition relation: a mapping of $Q \times A$ into the powerset of Q.

Since the language to be represented is nondeterministic the state transition relation T can define a subset of Q for every element of $Q \times A$. This nondeterminism is illustrated by the following valid protocol fragment in *Argos*

† In the validation language the range of the variables is 2^{15}.

```
state1: if
        :: a?m → goto state2
        :: a?m → goto state3
        fi;
state2: ...
```

which gives us

$$T(state\,1, a\,?m) = \{state\,2, state\,3\}.$$

Executability

For each state-action pair (q,a) in $Q \times A$, a fixed set of rules determines whether the action a is executable or not. The execution rules, discussed below, define a mapping E of $Q \times A$ onto the set *true*, *false*. If a is executable in state q we define $E(q,a) = true$; If a turns out to be non-executable $E(q,a) = false$ and we will set $T(q,a) = \emptyset$.
Performing an action will in general change the *environment* of a process. Receiving a message, for instance, will change the state of a channel. The execution of an action can also affect the executability of other actions, both in the executing process and in other processes. By sending a message we can enable another process to execute the matching receive action, and by changing the value of a variable we can enable other actions within the same process to pass a boolean test. We distinguish between actions that do, and actions that do not change the state of the environment of other processes. The first class corresponds to the *external* actions of the validation language, such as *send* and *receive*. The second class corresponds to the *internal* actions, including assignments to and testing of local variables.

A receive action *qname?ack* is only executable when the message *ack* is the first message in channel *qname*. Similarly, a send action *qname!data* is executable whenever the channel *qname* is not full. We could define an assignment to a variable to be unexecutable if it attempts to assign a value outside the variable's range. Such a definition would make it easy to model, for instance, semaphores that synchronize parallel processes executing in a shared memory system. However, since we are modeling distributed systems, we instead define a modulo arithmetic on variables. An attempt to assign a value outside its range will result in an assignment *modulo* its range.

The null action *skip* and assignments to variables, then, are always executable. With the guarded command language that we use for protocol specification in mind, however, we define a *condition* to be executable when it is true and unexecutable when it is false. Though it seems odd that we will have to evaluate a condition to find out if it can be 'executed,' this definition will guarantee that a condition can not be passed unless it holds, and thus that conditions that are used as 'guards' in selection and loop structures can be modeled with the same ease as send and receive actions.

Symbolic Execution

Given an initial state q for a process, it can be 'executed' by nondeterministically selecting an executable action a, executing it, and changing the process state to an element of $T(q,a)$. Similarly, the execution of a protocol system is a three-step process: (1) selecting an action from any process, (2) executing the action, and (3) changing the state of the executing process. The explicit *selection* of a candidate action (step 1) allows us to perform the partial searches referred to in section 2.

Optimization

A simple way to translate a description in the validation language into a finite state machine specification is to assign a *state* in set Q to every single statement in the process specification. Statements that start an option in an 'if' or in a 'do' structure (guards), however, are to be treated specially. The guards are part of the 'if' or 'do' statement and do not get a separate entry in set Q. The transition relation T can then be defined in the obvious way to reproduce the control flow of the original specification. Unfortunately, the finite state machines produced in this manner are far from minimal. For one thing, they contain many *transit states* that merely connect two other states with the null action *skip*, e.g. to connect the end of a loop 'od' to its start 'do'. Suppressing the transit-states during compilation saves many useless transitions in the analysis, where every execution step counts. To suppress all transit states we can use a simple one-pass scan of the states in the transition table:

```
for (all action-state pairs (q,a))
for (all states s in T(a,q))
{       t = s;
        while (transitstate(t))
                t = T(skip,t);
        replace s by t in T(a,q);
}
```

The number of states can be reduced still further by combining equivalent states. The definition of an appropriate equivalence relation, however, has to be chosen with some care. Consider the following protocol fragment.

```
if
:: a?m → b?m
:: a?m → skip
fi;
more...
```

Under a standard notion of *language* equivalence, it can be reduced to:

```
a?m; if :: b?m :: skip fi; more...
```

But, this reduction has changed the behavior of the protocol. In particular, for an input sequence "*a* !*m*; *b* !*d*" the original version can deadlock but the reduced version cannot. A stronger notion of equivalence, that avoids this problem, can be defined recursively as follows.

- Two states q_1 and q_2 are (1)*equivalent* if $E(q_1,a)=E(q_2,a)$ for all a.

- Two states q_1 and q_2 are (k)*equivalent* if they are (1)*equivalent* and for each immediate successor state of either state q_1 or q_2 there is a $(k-1)$*equivalent* immediate successor of the other state q_2 or q_1.
- Two states are *strongly equivalent* if they are (k)*equivalent* for all $k \geq 1$.

Using a standard algorithm [1] to partition the set of states under this equivalence relation we can reduce each finite state machine to a strongly equivalent one with a minimal number of states. With this definition we can reduce the redundant:

```
do
::      do
        :: receiver?msg1 → channel!ack1; break
        :: receiver?msg0 → channel!ack0
        od;
        do
        :: receiver?msg0 → channel!ack0; break
        :: receiver?msg1 → channel!ack1
        od
od
```

corresponding to a finite state machine of seven states, to the strongly equivalent:

```
do
:: receiver?msg1 → channel!ack1
:: receiver?msg0 → channel!ack0
od
```

corresponding to a reduced machine of four states, with the same deadlock behavior.

Assertions

We have defined assertions as restricted processes. This means that the assertion primitives can be compiled into a restricted class of state machines and minimized as such, with the same algorithm that is used for the compilation of the protocol processes. The protocol validator can use the assertion state machines to *monitor* the external actions on which they are defined, and perhaps even to try and select those executions in a partial search that have the best chance of violating the correctness requirements they express. The assertion defines a constraint on the execution of the protocol system. This simplest way to use this constraint is to verify that no protocol execution can violate the assertions (see also section 5 below). An alternative could be to constrain a symbolic execution to the sequences covered by the assertion, for instance, to verify the capability of a protocol to perform a given service. This option, however, remains to be explored.

5. State Space Searching

The most commonly used method to perform protocol analysis is to attempt to search the complete *system state space* with an iterative *breadth first* algorithm:

```
breadthfirst()
{       R = { initial state, };        /* set of reachable states */
        A = { };                       /* set of analyzed states  */
        do {
                analyze();
        } while (set R nonempty);
}
analyze()
{       while (R is non-empty)
        {       select an arbitrary state q from R;

                if (q is an errorstate)
                        reporterror();

                delete q from R;
                add q to A;

                for (all executable actions a)
                for (all states s in T(a,q))
                {
                        if (s is not in A or R)
                                add s to R;
}       }       }
```

We know that the state space generation process must terminate since the size of all channels, the range of all variables, and the number of process states is restricted. As illustrated in the introduction, however, their cross product could well be unmanageably large.

If we succeed in sufficiently bounding the depth of each execution sequence, we can replace the *breadth first* algorithm, with a simpler recursive *depth first* method:

```
depthfirst()
{       q = initial state;
        analyze(q);
}
analyze(q)
{       if (q is an errorstate)
                reporterror();
        else
                for (all executable actions a)
                for (all states s in T(a,q))
                        analyze(s);
}
```

The recursion depth of this algorithm is not necessarily bounded, since even finite systems can have infinite executions. By guaranteeing that the same state is never analyzed twice, however, we can bound the search depth straightforwardly:

```
boundeddepthfirst()
{       P = { }; /* set of states in one execution sequence */
        q = initial state;
        analyze(q);
}
analyze(q)
{       add q to P;

        if (q is an errorstate)
                reporterror();
        else
                for (all executable actions a)
                for (all states s in T(a,q))
                        if (s is not in P)
                                analyze(s);

        delete q from P;
}
```

The maximum size of set P is determined by only the *depth* of the state space tree, while the combined size of set R and set A from the *breadth first* algorithm is determined by its *volume*. At each execution step, set P only contains those states that lead from initial state to the current state. The memory requirements can be reduced even further by observing that not every system state can be found at the start of an execution loop, and therefore it is not necessary to remember every state in set P. The validation language strictly defines which states can start a loop. The state of the protocol consists of the states of variables, channels and processes. The state of the processes in this set of sets is defined by a tuple $(q_1, q_2, \ldots, q_n)$ with n is the number of processes. Now, a system state that includes $(q_1, q_2, \ldots, q_n)$ can only be found at the start of an execution loop through the system state space if for at least one $1 \le i \le n$ q_i corresponds to a 'labeled' state in the language specification of process q_i, where a 'labeled' state is either a state that is prefixed with a true label (i.e. the target of a goto jump) or the start of a 'do' loop. We can therefore upgrade our algorithm still further:

```
analyze(q)
{       if (q is labeled)
                add q to P;
        if (q is an errorstate)
                reporterror();
        else
                for (all executable actions a)
                for (all states s in T(a,q))
                        if (s is not in P)
                                analyze(s);
        if (q is labeled)
                delete q from P;
}
```

The 'labeled' states in each process can be precomputed by the protocol compiler.

Assertion Checking by Symbolic Execution

For assertion checking we have to perform a controlled execution of the finite state machine generated for the assertion primitives. If an action is within the scope of an assertion, the state of the corresponding state machine is to be updated as a side effect of the execution of that action, as if the assertion machine itself generated the action. Since the assertion primitives do not themselves access variables or channels the 'state' of an assertion machine is uniquely defined by its control-flow state. The 'execution' of an assertion machine then costs very little in the search algorithm. Wherever the behavior of a normal finite state machine, modeling the behavior of a process, is non-deterministic, the search algorithm described above will inspect every possible execution in turn, one after the other in arbitrary order. With the assertion machines, however, we can define the current state to be a true *set* of legal states. If the next-state function T defines two possible successors for state q under external action a, we replace q by *both* successors in the current state set. When the protocol system reaches an endstate, compliance with the assertion can be established by verifying that the current state set of the assertion machine includes its endstate. If this is not true the assertion is violated and the current execution sequence can be listed as a counterexample. Similarly, if, before the protocol has reached an endstate, the assertion machine can not be executed for an action that is within its scope, the assertion has been violated and a counter example can be produced. With little overhead or added complexity, we can thus exploit the finite state machine model to combine the depth-first search with assertion checking capabilities.

Running the bounded *depth first* algorithm to completion, achieves an exhaustive exploration of the system state space, equal to the one obtained with the *breadth first* search method, but using less space to store intermediate results.

Apart from the space complexity of the exhaustive search algorithm, however, we have another problem: time complexity. In the next section we will explore methods we can use to overcome that problem.

Reducing Run Time

Let us first note that, no matter how fast or how sophisticated our search algorithm will be, there will always be cases where exhaustive analysis is no longer feasible. The limits can be moved, but not removed [4,5,6]. Reduction strategies that preserve the scope of an exhaustive analysis are necessary and precious but can never be sufficient. For large protocols an exhaustive analysis generally requires not only unacceptable but also unpredictable amounts of time. Below we will discuss some strategies that can be used to optimize symbolic executions. Then, we will discuss a *scatter* search strategy that can be used to analyze state spaces of which the size precludes analysis by traditional means.

The State Space Cache

We have seen above that the depth first search method can be executed with a state space that only contains states encountered along a single execution path. If an execution path joins a previously analyzed sequence, though, this search strategy will do double work. To avoid it, we can store all states encountered along each execution sequence and create a complete state space, as in the *breadth first* search strategy, while maintaining the *depth first* search discipline. The problem, however, remains that such a 'complete' state space may well be too large to store. Fortunately, with the depth first search we can be selective about the states that are stored: the state space does not have to be complete as long as it contains at least the minimal subset of states that specifies the current execution sequence. We can therefore create a restricted *cache* of selected system states that are likely to return in different parts of the tree. Initially, we can simply store all system states encountered into the cache. When the cache fills up, however, we may have to delete old states to accommodate new ones. The revised search algorithm now looks as follows:

```
modified_depthfirst()
{       A = { }; /* subset of the previously analyzed states */
        P = { }; /* set of states in one execution sequence  */
        q = initial state;
        analyze(q);
}

analyze(q)
{
        if (q is labeled)
                add q to P;

        if (q is an errorstate)
                reporterror();
        else
                for (all executable actions a)
                for (all states s in T(a,q))
                        if (s is not in P or A)
                                analyze(s);

        if (q is labeled)
        {       delete q from P;
                if (size of A is maximum)
                {       select a state s from A
                        delete s from A;
                }
                add q to A;
}       }
```

The size of the cache itself is irrelevant to the scope of the analysis. But extending the size of the cache to the maximum that can fit in main memory can avoid double work and thereby decrease the runtime of an analysis.

The question remains what the selection criterion should be for determining which states can be deleted when the cache overflows. One readily available piece of information on the probability that a state will be revisited in a different part of the state space tree is the number of times that it was visited before. Figure 1 shows the results of measurements on two medium size protocols.

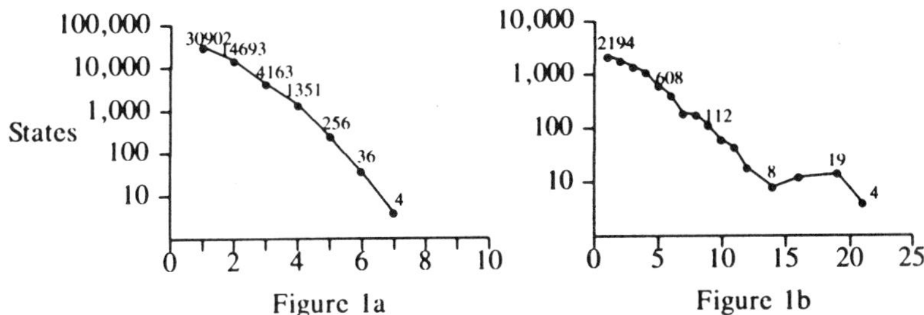

Figure 1a Figure 1b

Frequency of Occurrence in State Space
Figure 1

The probabilities that a given states are revisited, given that they were visited N times before, for these two protocols, is shown in figure 2.

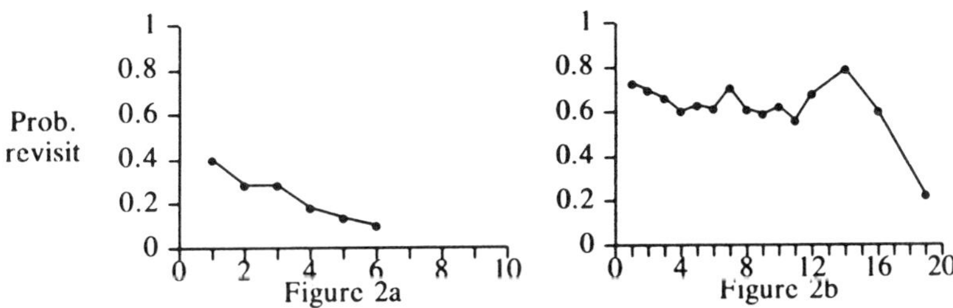

Figure 2a Figure 2b

Number of previous visits
Figure 2

For the protocol in Figure 2a the best strategy seems to be to replace those states that were visited most frequently before, since these have the least chance of being visited again later in a search. It must, however, be noted that the absolute number of states that are visited more than twice is relatively small. This strategy can therefore result in the elimination of *all* states visited more than once, thereby invalidating the assumptions we made for a replacement strategy. For the protocol in Figure 2b, the probability of a return to a previous state is largely indepedent of the number of previous visits to that state.

The performance of five different replacement strategies where measured for a range of medium sized protocols. The first two strategies required a complete scan of the state space cache to select a state that was either visited

(a) most frequently, or
(b) least frequently

before.
In the third strategy the states were divided dynamically in classes according to the number of times they had been visited before in the search. To replace a state the state space cache was scanned round-robin until a state was found that belonged to the currently

(c) largest class

of states under this criterion. In the fourth strategy the number of previous visits to a state was ignored entirely. The cache is viewed as a circular buffer. To replace a state with this strategy we blindly picked the one at the pointer and advanced the pointer to the next one in the circle to make sure that the oldest states in the cache are selected first:

(d) blind, round-robin selection.

In the last strategy we used the depth in the state space tree at which a state was last encountered. It is based on the observation that states near the root of the tree are also roots of the largest subtrees. To replace a state, therefore, it should be advantageous to select a victim as deep in the tree as possible, having the

(e) smallest subtree.

To avoid having to make a complete scan of the state space to find the deepest state in the tree, this strategy was implemented by a round-robin search for a state that was at least in the bottom half of the current tree.

The results of two of the tests are summarized in Figure 3. In the first test we used a protocol that generated a state space of 4523 unique states, and analyzed it with a cache of 1000 states. The protocol from the second test generated 8139 unique states and was analyzed with a cache of 6000 states.

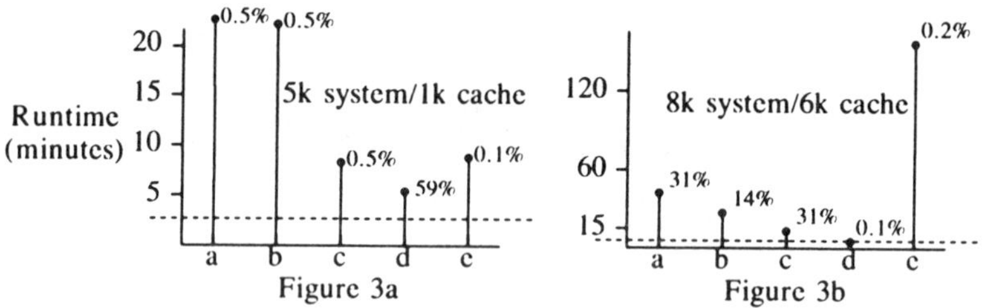

Replacement Strategy
Figure 3

The amount of double work incurred with each strategy is shown as percentages in the dot charts. The runtime of strategies **(a)** and **(b)** is dominated by the frequently recurring scan of the state space (88% of the runtime in strategy **(a)**). Strategy **(c)** requires only partial scans of the state space, which makes it faster than **(b)** even though it is not always quite as succesful in avoiding double work (Figure 3b). The worst performance in Figure 3b, is obtained with strategy **(e)**. For this protocol it turns out that the states that are revisited most frequently are all in the bottom half of the state space tree. Remarkably, the simplest strategy **(d)** is consistently the fastest, independent of its quality.

The dashed lines in Figure 3 give the runtime for the algorithm when a cache size is used that can accommodate all unique states. The penalty for reducing the cache by 80% in Figure 3a, or by 25% in Figure 3b is negligible. The effect of larger reductions depends largely on the structure of the state space tree, which is protocol dependent. For the protocol in Figure 3b, reducing the cache to 3000 states increases the runtime more than 100 times, which invalidates it as a useful strategy. In the next section we will therefore consider other, more succesful, strategies to restrict the size of the state space.

Scatter Searching

If we drop the requirement that reductions must maintain the scope of analysis, we will need criteria for deciding which sequences are to be analyzed and which ignored. It is relatively straightforward to give preference to the shortest complete execution sequences and to defer analysis for longer sequences corresponding too, for instance, ten-fold overlapping executions of processes. In the protocol validator that was implemented for specifications written in *Argos* an optional depth-bound is used that sets an upper limit the depth of recursion in the search algorithm. The depth bound is by default the sum of the number of states in all state machines, multiplied with a constant factor ten, but it can be set to any value as a parameter of an analysis run.

An obvious candidate to restrict the amount of work to be done in a search further is to trim the number of options in the inner loop. Our basic tool for this is to add a selection *criterion* that determines which executions will, and which will not, be analyzed:

```
for (all executable actions a)
for (all states s in T(a,q))
        if (criterion is met ∩ s is not in P or A)
                analyze(s);
```

In some cases we can still skip analyzing an option without restricting the scope of the analysis. Consider the case where the combined set of action state pairs of all processes contains just two executable actions: and internal action a in machine A and an external action b in machine B. There are two possible orders in which these two actions could be executed, corresponding to the two sequences

$$a\,;\,b \text{ and } b\,;\,a.$$

The two sequences each lead into a new states that form the root of two subtrees in the state space graph. But it is easy to see that these two states must be equal. The execution of the internal action a did not change the environment for the remote machine B, so neither the executability nor the result of b can be any different when a is executed first or last. Similarly, the execution of a is independent of the environment affected by B and also its executability and result is independent of whether b preceded it or not. In this case then, it suffices to search one of the two possible interleavings and to ignore the other. The more vigorous restrictions to be discussed below, however, do pay a penalty in the scope of an analysis for limiting the runtime of the analysis. We discuss them in order of severity.

Channel Limits

The capacity of a communication channel for holding messages can have an important effect on the size of a state space. Reducing the capacity of a channel N by one can reduce the size of the state space, and speed up the analysis, by a factor of maximally

$$\sum_{i=0}^{N} |S|^i \;-\; \sum_{i=0}^{N-1} |S|^i \;=\; |S|^N$$

(cf. section 4). If the complexity of the analysis precludes it from running to completion a relatively painless method is therefore to analyze the protocol with reduced channel sizes. The analysis will not be complete, but produces results faster. Fortunately, many, if not all, protocol design errors of interest manifest themselves independently of the absolute size of message channels.

Noninterleaved Actions

The size of the state space tree is determined by the branching factor at each node in the tree. By restricting the branching factor uniformly for all nodes we can select executions from all parts of the state space tree, touching upon every part of the protocol in a short scan, hopefully catching most of the more fundamental flaws in a design. The basic tool for restricting the branching factor of the tree is to extend the set of noninterleaved actions. Above we have discussed a case where one specific interleaving of actions could be ignored since it would predictably lead into sequences that were analyzed before. By relaxing the conditions under which actions need to be interleaved for a complete analysis we can obtain major reductions in search time for a relatively small penalty in scope. Below we give three specific examples that were used in the protocol validator *trace*.

The first example concerns the treatment of *timeouts*. The purpose of an exhaustive analysis is, of course, to examine even unlikely sequences of events to spot the errors that a protocol designer could miss. For timeouts this means that we would like to perform an analysis that is independent of timing considerations. In such an analysis, only the possibility of a timeout will be taken into account, but not it's probability [13]. In practice, validating a protocol for all feasible timings causes valuable reports on the logical inconsistencies of a protocol to be lost in a plethora of reports on errors that may result from choosing inappropriate timeout values. To filter out the errors that are not caused by timing problems *trace* therefore allows the user to require that timeout options be only used to resolve locks, never to generate traffic. The scope of the analysis is restricted, but in a controlled way that, under the assumption of a proper choice for the timeout values, maintains the characteristic behavior of the protocol.

Another particularly interesting method, that succeeds surprisingly well in identifying errors in larger state spaces in seconds where complete searches takes hours, is to restrict the branching factor for each process to one. The branching factor is then maximally equal to the number of state machines in the protocol. The single option that can maximally be explored in each state should then of course be chosen with some care to optimize our chances of finding errors. Since deadlocks are the most common type of protocol errors searched for, the program *trace* will give preference to those actions that can bring the system closer to a deadlock state. This condition is satisfied, for instance, for the execution of a receive action, since it will reduce the number of messages queued in the channels and moves closer to a state where all channels are empty and all state machines are waiting for input.

A third method that is faster still, but not quite as successful in finding nontrivial protocol errors is to set the branching factor for each system state to one. The result will be the analysis of a single complete execution sequence. Only if a protocol is desperately wrong will this be helpful as an analysis tool. It is however a useful mode to start an analysis session that is performed by slowly extending the scope of an analysis, while repeating the analysis runs up to the point where either an exhaustive analysis is completed or proves to be infeasible within a reasonable amount of time.

Foldings

A final method to restrict the run time of an analysis is to define equivalence relations, or *foldings*, on the set of system states. The user could for instance decide that the state of one specific process, message channel, or set of variables is less relevant to the proper execution of the protocol. By defining a folding of the state space that maps all states that only differ in the state of an irrelevant protocol part onto the same class we can reduce the complexity of the analysis. The option was implemented in the protocol validator *trace* but has proven to be a less useful tool. Unlike the methods discussed above, the effect of a folding on an analysis is less predictable, and its usefulness quickly deteriorates.

The Scope of a Partial Analysis

The objective of a partial search is to use a small fraction of the runtime of an exhaustive search to find a large fraction of the errors. There is a minimal fraction of the runtime that has to be spent to find at least the first error in a protocol. Above that threshold, the fraction of all errors found should quickly approach unity. The rate at which the number of errors found approaches the number of errors present, then, can be used to measure the quality of a partial search.

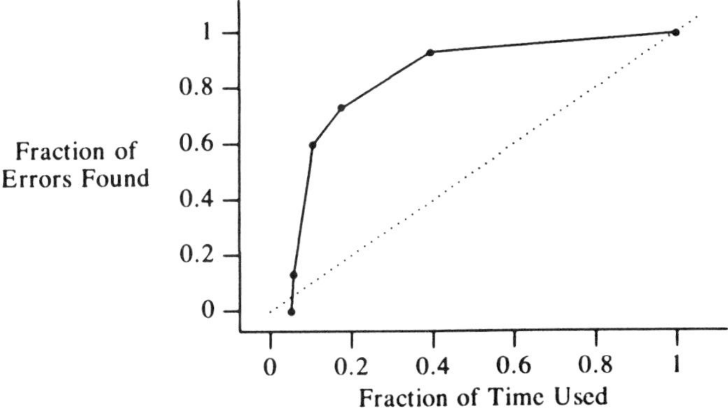

Figure 4

The curve in Figure 4 was compiled from a series of tests on a small protocol with a well-known set of errors (X.21). In these tests we experimented with depth bounds and with restrictions on the branching factors in the state space tree in a limited size cache, and compared the number of errors found in each test to the class of errors traced by an exhaustive search. As yet, there is insufficient data to conclude that the performance from Figure 4 can consistently be achieved, or is perhaps too pessimistic. From these first tests, however, we have every indication that the scatter search technique can be effective.

6. Conclusions

Protocol validation by symbolic execution is inherently a time- and space-consuming problem. So far, however, most protocol validation tools are based on symbolic execution algorithms. We have discussed strategies for expanding the capabilities of symbolic execution tools by reducing the time and space requirements. For reducing space complexity we have discussed a modified depth-first search algorithm, state space foldings, and the storage of subsets of the state space in a limited size cache. For reducing time complexity we have discussed a range of scatter search techniques, such as search depth bounding, restricting channel capacities, and the restriction of branching factors in the state space tree.

The protocol validation language *Argos* allows us to specify both protocol specifications and correctness requirements in a single higher level specification format that can be checked for syntactic correctness and optimized for analysis by a compiler. The analyzer we have described was written in C and is portable across Unix systems with virtual memory. Small to medium sized protocols can be specified with these tools in a few minutes. Compilation and analysis of these specifications take rarely more than a few minutes of CPU times. The largest protocol analyzed with these tools so far is the control protocol for a dataswitch consisting of four processes and six message channels, specified in an *Argos* description of 270 lines. An exhaustive analysis was performed, with a state space cache of 150,000 states (6.5 Mbyte). With the search depth restricted to 230 steps the analysis completed in 9 hours of CPU time, analyzing a state space 16% larger than the cache (175748 states of which 172402 were unique states). The first deadlock (out of a series of hundreds) was found after 20 minutes of CPU time. A scatter search, with the same depth bound completes in less than 3 minutes of CPU time, and produces an equivalent listing of the main types of protocol errors, by inspecting 4523 or 2.5% of the states. The first deadlock with the scatter search is reported in 3 seconds of CPU time.

The typical use of the validation tools described in this paper then is as follows. We start by building a restricted model of a protocol and its correctness requirements in the language *Argos*. The specification is checked for syntactical correctness, and for a small range of completeness criteria that can be verified at compile time. If the description passes these tests it is minimized and compiled into finite state machines of the type discussed in section 4. The protocol validator *trace* is then invoked, in a first run with the most restrictive setting for all analysis parameters, for instance with channel capacities restricted to one slot, with a large class of noninterleaved actions, and with a depth bound equal to the sum of the states in all automata generated by the compiler. Largely independent of the complexity of the protocol analyzed, this first analysis run will complete in a few seconds of CPU time. If no errors were found in this first restrictive scatter search the restrictions are weakened and the run is repeated, taking slightly longer while analyzing a slightly larger fraction of the state space. This iterative search process can continue until either the first error is found, or until an exhaustive search is completed. The third case is, of course, to find no errors and still be unable to complete an exhaustive search. In that case, our only hope would be to return to the first step of this validation process and to try and define a more restricted, but functionally equivalent, version of the protocol itself, by changing the model built in *Argos*.

Acknowledgement

Many people have contributed ideas to the protocol validation methodology explored in this paper. I am grateful to Rob Pike and Tom Cargill for their help in speeding up the algorithms, and to Doug McIlroy, Mike Merritt, and Bob Kurshan for inspiring discussions.

7. References

1. Aho, A.V., Hopcroft, J.E., Ullman, J.D., "The design and analysis of computer algorithms," Addison-Wesley Publishing Co., 1974.

2. Bochmann, G., & Sunshine, C.A., "Formal methods in communication protocol design," IEEE Trans. on Communications, Vol. COM-28, No. 4, April 1980, pp. 624-631.

3. Brand, D., and Joyner, W.H. Jr., Verification of protocols using symbolic execution. Computer Networks, Vol. 2 (1978), pp. 351-360.

4. Brand, D., & Zafiropulo, P., "Synthesis of protocols for an unlimited number of processes," Proc. Computer Network Protocols Conf., IEEE 1980, pp. 29-40.

5. Cunha, P.R.F., & Maibaum, T.S.E., "A synchronization calculus for message oriented programming," Proc. Int. Conf. on Distributed Systems, IEEE 1981, pp. 433-445.

6. DeTreville, J., "On finding deadlocks in protocols," March 22, 1982, unpublished technical memorandum, Bell Laboratories.

7. Dijkstra, E.W., "Guarded commands, nondeterminacy and formal derivation of programs," Comm. ACM, Vol. 18, No. 8, Aug. 1975, pp. 453-457.

8. Hajek, J., "Automatically verified data transfer protocols," Proc. 4th ICCC, Kyoto, Sept. 1978, pp. 749-756.

9. Hoare, C.A.R., "Communicating sequential processes," Comm. ACM, Vol. 21, No. 8, August 1978, pp. 666-677.

10. Holzmann, G.J., "A Theory for protocol validation," August 1982, IEEE Trans. on Computers, Vol. C-31, No.8, pp. 730-738.

11. Holzmann, G.J., "The Pandora system — an interactive system for the design of data communication protocols," Computer Networks, Vol. 8, No. 2, pp 71-81.

12. West, C., "Applications and limitations of automated protocol validation," Proc. 2nd IFIP WG 6.1 Int. Workshop on Protocol Specification, Testing, and Verification, USC/ISI, Idyllwild, CA. May 1982, pp 361-373.

13. Zafiropulo, P., West, C.H., Rudin, H., Cowan, D.D., and Brand, D., Toward analyzing and synthesizing protocols, IEEE Trans. Commun. COM-28, No. 4, (1980), pp. 651-661.

APPENDIX

The following is an example of a simple alternating bit protocol specified in *Argos*. The specification consists of four different processes: a sender, a receiver, a processes modeling the behavior of a communication link that can lose messages, and a user process that stores the messages that the receiver claimed to have received correctly from the sender process.

```
channel sender[1], receiver[1], link[1], user[1];

proc sender
{       do
        ::      link!msg1;
                do
                :: sender?ack1 → break
                :: sender?ack0 → skip
                :: sender?timeout → link!msg1
                od;
                link!msg0;
                do
                :: sender?ack0 → break
                :: sender?ack1 → skip
                :: sender?timeout → link!msg0
                od
        od
}


proc receiver
{       do
        ::      do
                :: receiver?msg1 → link!ack1; user!msg1; break /* accept */
                :: receiver?msg0 → link!ack0           /* reject */
                od;
                do
                :: receiver?msg0 → link!ack0; user!msg0; break /* accept */
                :: receiver?msg1 → link!ack1 /* reject */
                od
        od
}


proc user
{       do
        :: user?default → skip /* receive any message and store it */
        od
}
```

```
proc link
{       do
        :: link?msg0 → if :: receiver!msg0 :: skip fi  /* transfer or lose */
        :: link?msg1 → if :: receiver!msg1 :: skip fi
        :: link?ack0 → if :: sender!ack0 :: skip fi
        :: link?ack1 → if :: sender!ack1 :: skip fi
        od
}
```

When analyzing this protocol we would like to establish that the link processes will correctly see messages with alternating sequence numbers. A first attempt to express this in an assertion in *Argos* could be:

```
assert
{       link!msg1;
        link!msg0
}
```

Submitting this specification to the analyzer produces a violation of the assertion in 1.2 of CPU time. The error report produced by *trace* looks as follows:

queue:	channel	sender	receiver
event:			
1	msg1,		
2		tau,	
3	[msg1],		

Every column corresponds to a message channel. A message in a column represents a message sent to the corresponding channel. A bracketed name represents a message sent but not received. The counter example to the assertion produced by *trace* shows that the sender can timeout and retransmit a message with the same sequence number as the last message sent to the link process. We can try again by stating that at least the receiver should see messages with an alternating sequence number:

```
assert
{       receiver!msg1;
        receiver!msg0
}
```

But, again *trace* produces a counter example, this time in 1.4 sec.:

queue:	receiver	sender	channel	user
event:				
1			msg1,	
2	msg1,			
3			ack1,	
4				msg1,
5		tau,		
6			msg1,	
7	[msg1],			

We try again.

```
assert
{       user!msg1;
        user!msg0
}
```

and after 1.6 seconds *trace* reports:

queue:	user	sender	channel	receiver
event:				
1			msg1,	
2				msg1,
3			ack1,	
4	msg1,			
5		tau,		
6			msg1,	
7				msg1,
8			ack1,	
9		ack1,		
10			msg0,	
11				msg0,
12			ack0,	
13	msg0,			
14		tau,		
15			msg0,	
16				msg0,
17			ack0,	
18		ack0,		
19			msg1,	
20				msg1,
21			ack1,	
22	[msg1],			

Note that the sender and receiver can loop through their specifications, while the assertion stated that the sequence could occur only once in any given execution sequence. The counter example showed that this is not true. Finally, we can try specifying what we meant to say all along:

```
assert
{       do
        :: user!msg1; user!msg0
        od
}
```

An exhaustive validation by *trace* now completes in 1.7 sec. announcing that it was unable to violate the assertions or to find deadlocks or an incompleteness in the specification.

Tracing Protocols

Gerard J. Holzmann
AT&T Bell Laboratories
Murray Hill, New Jersey 07974

ABSTRACT

Automated protocol validation tools are by necessity often based on some form of symbolic execution. The complexity of the analysis problem however imposes restrictions on the scope of these tools. The paper studies the nature of these restrictions and explicitly addresses the problem of finding errors in data communication protocols of which the size precludes analysis by traditional means. The protocol tracing method described here allows one to locate design errors in protocols relatively quickly by probing a partial state space. This *scatter searching* method was implemented in a portable program called *trace*. Specifications for the tracer are written in a higher level language and are compiled into a minimized finite state machine model which is then used to perform either partial or exhaustive symbolic executions. The user of the tracer can control the scope of each search. The tracer can be used as a fast debugging tool but also, depending on the complexity of the protocol being analyzed, as a slower and rather naive correctness prover. The specifications define the control flow of the protocol and may formalize correctness criteria in assertion primitives.

1. Introduction

Protocol validation by symbolic execution is inherently a time and space consuming task. For lack of better methods, though, many automated protocol validation tools do use symbolic execution algorithms [1,2,7,16,17], and even methods based on validation algebras such as CCS [14] or PVA [9,10] still implicitly formalize symbolic executions[1]. Unfortunately, the assumption that a computer will always be able to take over when the complexity of a complete analysis surpasses our ability to perform algebraic expansions by hand is decidedly wrong [3,5].

A protocol of a realistic size can generate a state space of in the order of 10^9 system states and up. As little as adding one single message type, one protocol variable, or one slot to the message queues can further expand the number of

1) Cf. the expansion theorem in CCS and the shuffle operator in PVA.

reachable system states by orders of magnitude. For a protocol of this size a symbolic execution algorithm can at best analyze in the order of 10 to 100 system states per second of CPU time, if the state space is built in core [12]. To analyze 10^9 states exhaustively would then take at least 115 days of computation. Furthermore, assuming that each state can be encoded in no more than 10 to 100 bytes, storing a state space of this size would still require a machine with several gigabytes of main memory.

So, if this appears to be infeasible, what is the best that can be done? In the design phase one would like to have tools that can trace the most glaring bugs in a protocol in no more than a few seconds of real time. The completeness of an analysis is not really at issue here; *speed* is. To find more subtle design errors of a completed protocol one may be willing to spent more time, but not much more than perhaps 10 hours or in the order of 10^5 seconds of CPU time. For symbolic execution algorithms, this requirement sets an upper limit to the number of states that can be searched at roughly 10^7 states. At 10 to 100 bytes per state, however, we cannot expect to do anything useful with a state space of more than in the order of 10^6 states. The tracer should therefore preferably be able to perform complete analyses in small state spaces holding just a fraction of the total number of states. In the remainder of this paper we will concentrate on these two issues: the effectiveness of partial searches and the possibility of performing complete searches in partial state spaces.

Overview

In the following we will assume that the protocol submitted to a tracer is likely to contain errors and that a designer is interested to see any nonempty subset of these. A protocol tracer may, for instance, scan the state space in an effort to quickly discover typical violations of user specified correctness requirements. It is important to note that the objective of such a partial analysis, or *scatter search* as we shall call it, is to establish the presence rather than the absence of errors.

What we are aiming for is a protocol tracing method that allows us to spent a small fraction of the time required by an exhaustive analysis to find a substantial portion of all design errors. The emphasis is on speed, not on completeness. If a protocol contains an error an exhaustive search would meticulously report every possible circumstance under which the error could make the protocol fail. For our purposes, tracing a single variant of the error in a partial search will suffice.

Section 2 explains how a general symbolic execution algorithm based on depth first search can be organized. It discusses a variant of symbolic execution called scatter searching and compares its performance with exhaustive searching. Section 3 discusses in more detail heuristics that can be used to perform a partial search, and section 4 shows how depth first searches can be organized in incomplete state spaces. Section 5 shows how protocol specific correctness criteria can be verified with a standard symbolic execution algorithm. Section 6 gives a small example of the use of correctness assertions in tracing bugs in a protocol. A larger example is presented in the appendix. Section 7 summarizes the main results.

2. Scatter Searching

Below we will discuss some experiments with a program called *trace* that performs a simple depth-first search in a partial state space generated by a set of interacting finite state machines, where the state space is maintained as a tree of system states. To determine the effectiveness of partial searches the performance of exhaustive searches and scatter searches was compared, using a search depth restriction as a parameter. But, first let us consider the working of the tracer in a little more detail.

With the exhaustive tracing method a state space tree is searched starting from the initial system state, exploring every possible execution path until an endstate, a previous state or an error state is reached, or until the search depth limit is encountered. A return to a previously analyzed state terminates the search under two conditions:

- if the previously analyzed state is in the execution path that leads from the root of the state space tree to the current state, or
- if the previously analyzed state was encountered elsewhere in the state space tree either at the same depth or closer to the root of the tree than the current state.

In the first case the tracer has discovered an execution loop in the protocol. The loop could be checked further on liveness, but to save time the program *trace* simply checks that its repetition does not violate the user specified correctness criteria and continues. In the second case the subtree that would be explored by continuing the search down to the search depth restriction would be contained in the subtree of the previously analyzed state, and cannot lead to new results. The tracer can therefore ignore the subtree and continue exploring new leaves in the tree.

Though the state matching method is more general than the one described in for instance [1], the design of the experimental tracer so far is fairly standard. The exhaustive trace method, however, can be considered to be a special case of the *scatter search*. In a scatter search not every possible execution sequence is necessarily explored. The tracer makes an estimate of the likelihood that exploring a new sequence can lead to the discovery of a new error, and will search only those sequences that optimize its chances of finding the largest set of unique errors in the smallest amount of time. The tracer's estimate will be based on a heuristic that should be general enough to work on any type of protocol. One straightforward way to do this, for instance, is to restrict the amount of nondeterminism that will be taken into account by the tracer. These and other techniques will be discussed in more detail in section 3.

Test Results

To test the performance of a partial search we want to compare its coverage or 'scope' with that of an exhaustive search. The test protocol chosen for these comparisons was large enough to show the necessity of partial searches and also to give some room for experimenting with different flavors of partial searches. The size of the testcase however precluded, by the nature of the problem, the compilation of a definitive list of 'all' errors for reference. As a measure of the scope of the scatter search we will therefore take the number of errors traced and compare it with the number of errors traced by an exhaustive search method.

Figure 1 shows results of tracing an experimental data switch control protocol, generating a state space in the order of 10^9 system states [12]. The protocol was analyzed several times, both for the exhaustive search and the scatter search, with a search depth restriction that was incremented in steps of 10 levels for each new analysis run.

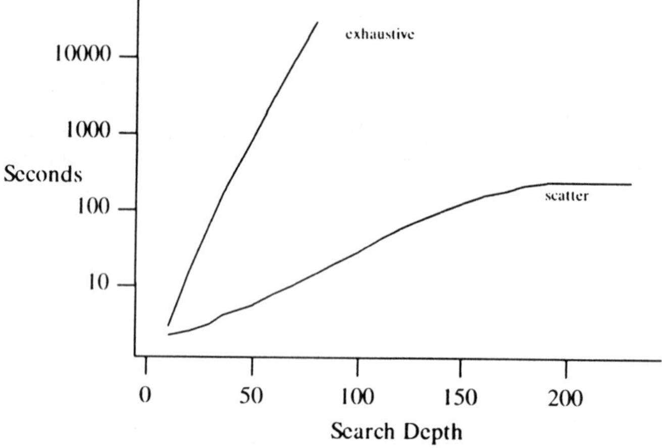

Figure 1 — Runtime

An exhaustive search for this protocol became unfeasible beyond a depth of 80 levels, i.e. numbers of states down from the root of the state space tree. The tree scanned by the scatter search method had a maximum depth of 189 steps. Setting the search depth restriction beyond 189 therefore no longer affects the scope of the analysis. To illustrate this, the curve for the scatter search was continued in Figure 1 up to a depth of 230. The longest scatter search required less than 4 minutes of CPU time to complete. The runtime of the exhaustive search tends to be exponential in the search depth. Using Figure 1 it can be estimated that searching the state space tree down to the same depth (189 steps) with the exhaustive search would take some 3000 years of CPU time.

Fortunately, the test protocol analyzed contained a generous number of design errors. No attempt was made to classify them. In Figure 2a the number of deadlocks reported by the tracer is shown as a function of the search depth, and in Figure 2b the number of deadlocks versus the time it took to find them is plotted on logarithmic scales.

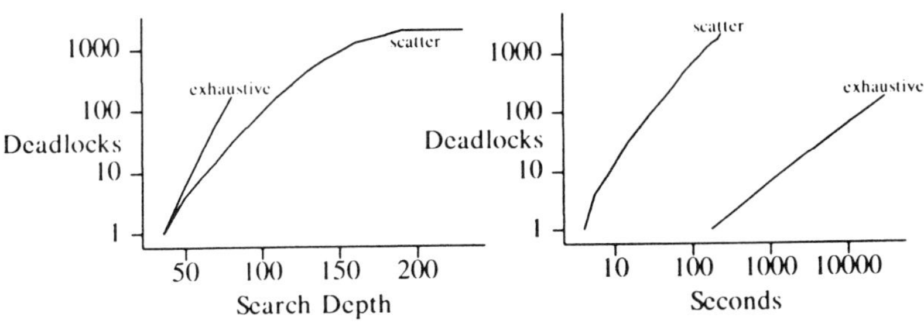

Figure 2 — Deadlocks

No deadlocks are found at search depths 10, 20, and 30. The first error is reported with the scatter search for a search depth of 40 steps, requiring 4 seconds of CPU time. For the same search depth restriction the exhaustive search reports the first 3 errors in 6 minutes. By repeating the analyses for intermediate levels between 30 and 40 we found that the first error is reported both in the scatter and the exhaustive search mode at level 35, requiring 4 seconds for the former and 3 minutes for the latter search. The two intermediate tests were included in the results shown in Figure 2.

Very probably, no protocol designer would be interested in tracing this protocol beyond the first 100 error sequences generated. For the given testcase this would mean that with an exhaustive search the first 70 steps in state space can be searched requiring roughly 3 hours of CPU time. Alternatively, the first 100 steps can be traced with a scatter search in only 30 seconds of CPU time.

Note that the time required to find the first error, the minimum search depth required to trace it and the relation between search depth and the number of errors reported are favorable for the scatter search method.

State Space

The protocol used for these tests requires roughly 40 bytes in the state space per system state. A total of 332,527 system states is generated in the longest exhaustive search analysis performed. As a result, for every new state generated, in the exhaustive search a data base of up to 15 Megabyte must be probed for a state match. Even with the best hashing methods this is bound to slow down the analysis noticeably. In the scatter search the largest number of states seen is 172,402 at a depth of 189 in the tree, corresponding to a data base of 8 Megabyte. The scatter search therefore should slow down less rapidly. This effect is illustrated in Figure 3. The time efficiency is expressed in the average number of states analyzed per second for each analysis run.

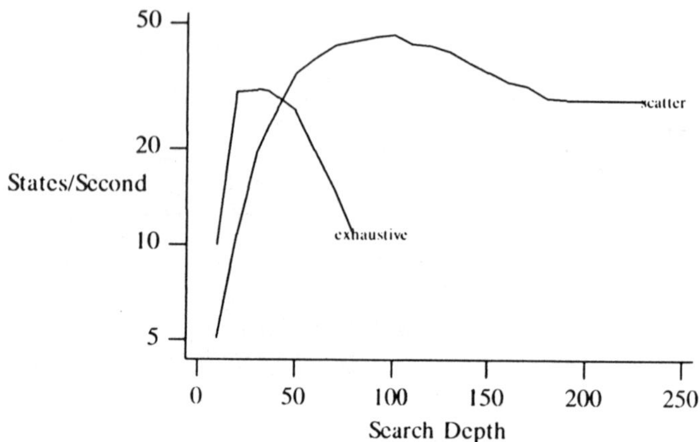

Figure 3 – Time Efficiency

The steep left hand side of the curves can be attributed to the overhead involved in the setup of a state space, which is felt more if the number of states explored is small. With the current tracer, the optimum speed for both search methods is reached when the state space contains roughly 1000 states.

3. Search Heuristics

It is relatively straightforward to give preference to the shortest complete execution sequences and to defer analysis for longer sequences. We have already used this method in the preparation of the figures above by bounding the depth of the tree explored during a search. In this section we consider some other partial search heuristics.

3.1. Fewer Interleavings

A method for reducing the run time of an analysis effectively is to restrict the amount of nondeterminism in the protocol model. In an exhaustive search each node in the state space tree is root to one subtree for each executable option in each finite state machine in the protocol. Not all interleavings of these actions is necessarily relevant. Consider two executable actions: one action a local to machine $M1$, e.g. an assignment to a local variable, and the other an external action b in machine $M2$, e.g. a send or a receive. There are two possible orders in which these two actions could be executed, corresponding to the two sequences

$$a\,;\,b \text{ and } b\,;\,a.$$

Each of the two sequences leads into a new state that forms the root of an entire subtree in the state space. The question is of whether or not the two subtrees are equivalent with respect to the errors to be traced. Note that the execution of internal action a will not change the environment for the remote machine $M2$, so neither the executability nor the result of b can be any different when a is executed first or last. Similarly, the execution of a is independent of the environment affected by $M2$ and also its executability and result is independent of whether b preceded it or not. In this case then, it suffices to search one of the two possible interleavings and to ignore the other. Unfortunately, there are not many cases where a complete subtree can be ignored without restricting the scope of an analysis. In some cases, though, we can predict in what way the scope will be affected. It would be unwise to restrict the nondeterminism that is local to a finite state machine, as shown in the following *Argos* [11] fragment:

```
if
:: A?one -> P()
:: B?two -> Q()
fi
```

Argos is a CSP-like [8] guarded command language [6] defined on buffered message channels. A detailed discussion of the language itself can be found in [11]. In the above example A and B are channel names (bounded buffers declared elsewhere), *one* and *two* are message names, and P and Q are procedure names. If message *one* is the first message in A and message *two* is the first message in B both input statements are executable and the process executing the above fragment can make a nondeterministic choice between the two alternatives, and then proceed with the execution of either $P()$ or $Q()$. The protocol tracer cannot foresee which of the two alternatives may produce an error without executing them. Note that ignoring one of the two alternatives in an analysis implies ignoring a potentially important code fragment, i.e. either $P()$ or $Q()$, without having reason to assume that this code would be error free. In this case then both alternatives will have to be explored. The situation is different for the nondeterminism that results from concurrency, as illustrated by the following *Argos* fragment:

```
proc P1 { A?one -> P() }
proc P2 { B!two -> Q() }
```

It defines two processes $P1$ and $P2$. Assuming that both initial actions are executable, it must be decided in what order they will be executed by the tracer. This time it may, but it will not always make a difference in what order these two i/o statements are executed. In an exhaustive search both orders are always analyzed. Ignoring one of the two possible orders, however, can half the amount of work to be done for this node in return for the chance that it will cause the tracer to miss error sequences. No code fragments are ignored here, only a potentially erroneous timing of executions. Fortunately, not all orderings have the same probability of leading into error states. For instance, if we are primarily interested in finding deadlocks states, that is states in which all message channels are empty and not all processes have reached their endstates, we may choose to explore the sequence starting with a receive action and ignore the other. In practice this heuristic performs remarkably well, as illustrated by the results discussed earlier.

3.2. Tracing Priorities

If at some node in the state space tree there are N concurrent processes, all executable, the tracer can decide to ignore any $M \leq N$ of the processes to reduce the search. In the tests reported in Figures 1 to 3 we set $M = 1$ for the scatter search and $M = N$ for the exhaustive search. In the case where $M = 1$ the search heuristic is implemented as a priority scheme that determines which process should be executed next. Highest priority is given to internal actions. At the next level we place receive actions, since these tend to bring the system closer to a deadlock state with empty channels. A lower priority is given to send actions, and a lower priority still to channel timeouts. Timeouts are given lowest priority in the partial searches since they tend to create many spurious error reports. In partial search mode the correct working of the timeout mechanism is assumed, that is, a timeout is only considered to be enabled when there is no other option to continue the protocol. Though this definitely reduces the scope of an analysis, it does allow us to trace for another class of errors first and defer the costly tracing of timing errors.

3.3. Queue Sizes

The capacity of a communication channel for holding messages can also have an important effect on the size of a state space. In the specification language *Argos* the channels are modeled by finite queues. A channel then can be in only a finite number of states

$$\sum_{i=0}^{N} |S|^i$$

where N is the number of slots in the channel (i.e. the queue size), and S is the size of the channel *sort*, i.e. the set of all messages that can be recognized by the channel. Reducing the number of slots N by one can reduce the size of the state space, and speed up the analysis, by a factor of up to

$$\sum_{i=0}^{N} |S|^i \ - \ \sum_{i=0}^{N-1} |S|^i \ = \ |S|^N$$

In the scatter searches of Figures 1 to 3 the queue sizes were restricted to two slots. To study the effect of a variation of the queue size the tests were repeated for a small range of sizes.

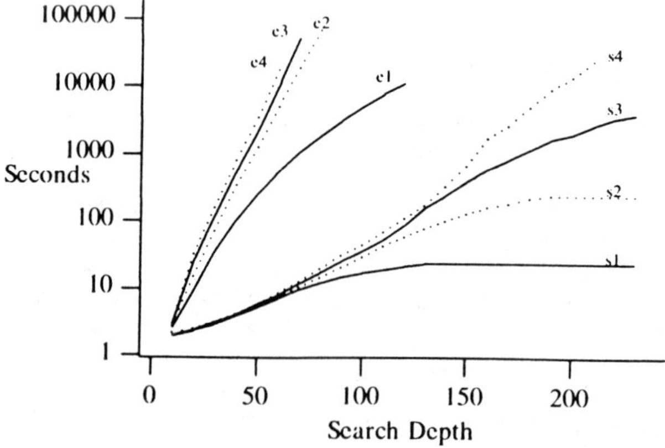

Figure 4 — Effect of Queue Sizes on Runtime
s — scatter search; e — exhaustive search; 1,2,3,4 — queue sizes

Figure 4 shows the effect of a variation in the number of slots between one and four for both the exhaustive and the scatter search.

4. Restricting The State Space

In the introduction we mentioned that the tracer should be able to perform searches in even incomplete state spaces since the size of a complete state space generally precludes its storage or even its usage during the search. In this section we will see how this can be accomplished.

First it should be noted that in a depth first search, at each execution step only those states that lead from initial state to the current state are indispensable in the state space. The presence of these states is necessary for the detection of system execution loops. Not every system state, though, can be found at the start of such an execution loop, and therefore it is not necessary to remember each state along a single execution path. The only states that must be remembered are those in which at least one of the interacting finite state machines is at the start of a local execution loop. Figure 5a shows a small but consistent reduction in the numbers of states if we restrict the state space to such 'loop states.'

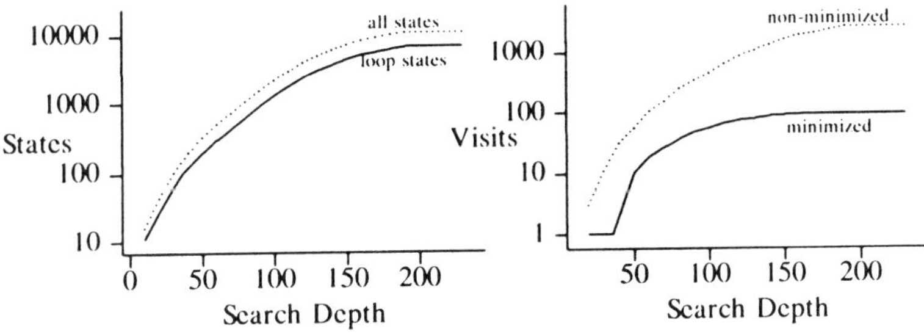

Figure 5 – Reducing Numbers of States Stored (scatter searches)

4.1. Minimization

Since the analysis is performed on finite state machines we can try to minimize the machines in an effort to reduce time or space complexity without affecting the scope of an analysis. The machines can not be reduced under the standard notion of language equivalence, since that will change the behavior or the protocol. A stronger notion of state equivalence [11], similar to that defined in CCS [14] can be used.

Figure 5b compares the analyses of minimized state machines and non-minimized state machines. The protocol tested defines 4 processes, 34 message types, 6 message channels, and 3 local variables. The state machines generated for the processes contain 69, 47, 7, and 5 states respectively. The strongly equivalent minimized machines contain 35, 31, 7, and 5 states. As it turns out, the number of states generated in the state space is roughly the same in both cases. The connectivity of the state space tree, however, is different, causing the same states to be visited more frequently for the non-minimized machines, resulting in a small increase in runtimes.

The effort to minimize the amount of work to be done in the search algorithm is concentrated on minimizing the theoretical maximum number of states in the product space of the individual finite state machines. We can do this by reducing the number of states per state machine (eg by masking a variable or a message queue) or, less straightforwardly, by reducing the number of state machines as such. The last thing we would like to do is of course to extend the number of state machines that we begin an analysis with.

Somewhat paradoxically, this approach seems to conflict with the more conventional structured approach to program design that tells us to identify functions and to separate these in a relatively large number of logical entities. For protocol design this approach was most recently suggested in [13], describing a method where each logical entity is formalized in a small finite state machine that interacts with the others. Dividing a single automaton of 16 states into two state machines of 8 states each, however, quadruples the number of states in the product space. Similarly, dividing it into 4 even simpler state machines of 4 states each expands the product state space to 16 times its original size. In general, increasing the number of state machines leads to an exponential growth of the product state space and is counterproductive in analyses.

4.2. Cache Size

We noted above that, unlike the more commonly used *breadth* first search (e.g. [3,13,17]), the state space in a *depth* first search need only contain the states in a single execution path from the root to the current state. Storing other states can avoid double work, but does not affect the scope of the analysis. This property of the depth first search method gives us greater flexibility in controlling the state space size during analysis runs. If more states can be stored, though, the search will be more time efficient. Figure 6 shows the effect of the size of the state space on the time and space requirements of a search, for a state space cache of 150,000 states that is reduced in steps of 1,000 to a cache of 50,000 states. 'Double work' is measured here as the total number of states created or recreated while searching. Note that the number of states stored in the cache could roughly be halfed without noticeable effect on the runtime or the total number of states created.

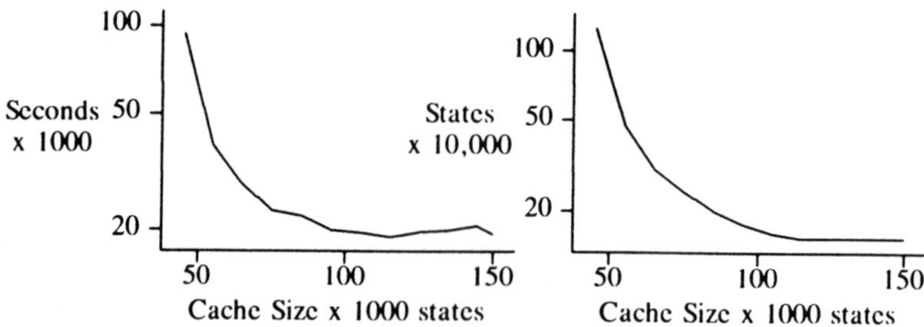

Figure 6 — Size of State Space Cache

With a partial state space cache it has to be decided which state will be deleted from a full cache when a new state must be created. A simple blind round robin selection of states was found to outperform a series of other, more subtle, schemes

[11,12]. It is the strategy used in the test of Figure 6.

5. Assertion Checking by Symbolic Execution

By default a protocol tracer can check a protocol for the observance of general correctness requirements such as absence of deadlock and completeness. The validation language *Argos* allows for the specification of assertions to check on the observance of other correctness requirements. Assertions are defined as a restricted class of processes. They specify global system behavior in terms of external actions. For example, the specification

```
assert
{       do
        :: large!mesg; small!mesg
        od
}
```

is a requirement on the order in which messages of the type *mesg* are sent to the two channels *large* and *small*. The assertion is that in each execution sequence a message on channel *large* must precede a message on channel *small*, and that these two actions will be executed repeatedly (the are enclosed in a *do* loop) in precisely this order.

The main restriction to assertion specifications is that they can only refer to external actions, i.e. sends and receives, and not to variables. Assigments and boolean conditions are only allowed in process definitions, not in assertions. The control flow constructs are the same as those for process specifications: concatenations, selections, iterations, jumps, procedure calls, and macros. In other words: the assertions specify *global* constraints on the execution of the system as a whole in terms of message exchanges only. The scope of the assertion, that is the set of external actions that is traced to verify or to violate an assertion, is implicitly defined by the set of external actions it refers to. If an external action occurs at least once in an assertion body all its occurrences in an execution of the protocol are required to comply with it. Compliance with the assertion then means that the execution of these actions should match the context specified in the assertion.

Since we define assertions as restricted processes, the assertion primitives can be compiled into a restricted class of state machines and minimized with the same algorithm that is used for the compilation of the protocol processes. The protocol tracer uses the assertion state machines to *monitor* the external actions on which they are defined. Alternatively, though our tracer does not exploit this possibility, it may be possible to develop a heuristic that allows the tracer to select those executions in a partial search that have the best chance of violating the correctness requirements expressed in the assertions.

If an action is within the scope of an assertion, the state of the corresponding state machine will be updated as a side effect of the execution of that action, as if the assertion machine itself generated it. Since the assertion primitives cannot access variables or channels the 'state' of an assertion machine is uniquely defined by its control-flow state. The 'execution' of an assertion machine then costs very little in the tracing algorithm. When the protocol system reaches an endstate, compliance with the assertion can be established by verifying that the assertion machine can reach an endstate too. If this is not true the assertion is violated and the current execution sequence can be listed as a counter example. Similarly, if the assertion machine can not be executed for an action that is within its scope, the assertion has been violated and a counter example can be produced. With little overhead or added complexity, the finite state machine model can thus be exploited to combine the depth-first search with assertion checking capabilities.

6. An Example

A small example can illustrate how the experimental protocol tracer described in this paper is typically used. More elaborate examples can be found in the appendix and in [11]. A protocol is defined in the language *Argos*. The example below shows three processes *a*, *b*, and *c*, three message queues of one slot each named *A*, *B*, and *C*, and one assertion labeled *assert* (a keyword in the language).

```
assert { C!a; C!b }

proc a
{           queue A[1];

            C!a; A?c
}

proc b
{           queue B[1];

            C!b; B?c
}

proc c
{           queue C[1];

            if
            :: C?a -> A!c; C?b -> B!c
            :: C?b -> A!c; C?a -> B!c
            fi
}
```

The assertion states that the two messages *a* and *b* will be appended precisely once to queue *C* when the three processes are executed, and that they can be sent in that order only. Process *a* starts by sending message *a* to queue *C* and then waits for a response *a* to arrive in queue *A*. Similarly, process *b* first sends *b* to queue *C* and then waits for a message *c*. The third process waits for a message to arrive in queue *C*, which is assumed to be either an *a* or a *b*, anything else would be an error. Process *c* then responds by sending a *c* message to queue *C* and waits for a second message to arrive: a *b* is the first received message was an *a*, or an *a* if the first message was a *b*. It will complete by sending a *c* into queue *B*.

The protocol is compiled into four finite state machines of three states each for *a* and *b*, three states for the *assert* primitive, and seven states for process *c*. The protocol tracer then takes over and completes an exhaustive search in 1.35 seconds, reporting the obvious assertion violation for the execution sequence that starts with C!b. The violation is reported by the tracer in the following format.

```
queue:   A   B   C
event:
  1              b
  2      c
  3              a
  4          c
```

Each column corresponds to a queue and each line to a time step. The first event is the sending of message *b* to queue *C*, which already violates the assertion. Then message *c* is sent to *A* by process *c*, message *a* is sent to *C* by process *a*, and finally a *c* message is sent to queue *B* by process *c*.

Changing the assertion to a more reasonable statement such as "assert { A!c; B!c }" will avoid the problem. The exhaustive search for this assertion completes in 1.32 seconds. Omitting the assertion completely will trigger a default search for deadlocks and incompleteness (eg. unspecified receptions), which completes in 1.18 seconds. Note that it is relatively straightforward to formalize liveness criteria in assert statements. In this case, as for many protocols generating up to 10^5 system states, exhaustive analyses are quite feasible. The real problems of partial searching only occur for the larger protocols comparable in size to the experimental protocol used for the tests reported earlier in this paper.

7. Conclusions

The main assumption we make in this paper is that in a design phase a protocol is typically known to contain errors and there is a need for a protocol tracing tool that can quickly find a representative subset of these errors. The user of such a protocol tracer is not so much interested in completeness but is very much interested in speed. With these assumptions important reductions in the time and space requirements of a tracer become feasible.

The protocol tracer described here consumes only a small fraction of the time and space required by an exhaustive analysis algorithm to find a relatively large fraction of the errors present. The run time of a state space search is reduced by several orders of magnitude by restricting the number of interleavings, by using search depth and queue size restrictions and compile time minimizations (Figures 1, 2, 4, and 5b). A more general method of reducing runtime would be the definition of equivalence classes, or *state space foldings*, as described in e.g. [10]. The experimental protocol debugger *trace* does allow for the definition of such foldings, but too little experience with this technique has yet been gained to report any results.

The number of states stored in a state space can be reduced by carefully selecting the states that may be revisited (Figure 5a). More importantly, though, the depth first search technique used allows one to perform searches with an incomplete state space cache. For the protocol tested the cache could be reduced to less than 50% of the state space size (Figure 6).

Acknowledgement

The experiments with assert primitives and the statespace cache were inspired by discussions with Bob Kurshan and Sudhir Aggerwal. I am also grateful to Doug McIlroy, Lee McMahon, Rob Pike, Ed Sitar and Ken Thompson for discussions, support and inspiration during the development of the protocol tracer.

8. References

1. T.P. Blumer, and R.L. Tenney, "A formal specification technique and implementation method for protocols," Computer Networks, **6**, (1982), No. 3, pp. 201-219.

2. D. Brand and W.H. Joyner Jr., "Verification of protocols using symbolic execution," Computer Networks, **2**, (1978), pp. 351-360.

3. D. Brand and P. Zafiropulo, "Synthesis of protocols for an unlimited number of processes," Proc. Computer Network Protocols Conf., IEEE 1980, pp. 29-40.

4. C.S. Crall and D.P. Sidhu, "Executable logic specifications for protocol service interfaces," unpublished report, Iowa State University, May 8, 1985, 52 pgs.

5. P.R.F. Cunha and T.S.E. Maibaum, "A synchronization calculus for message oriented programming," Proc. Int. Conf. on Distributed Systems, IEEE 1981, pp. 433-445.

6. E.W. Dijkstra, "Guarded commands, nondeterminacy and formal derivation of programs," Comm. ACM, **18**, No. 8, (Aug. 1975), pp. 453-457.

7. J. Hajek, "Automatically verified data transfer protocols," Proc. 4th ICCC, Kyoto, Sept. 1978, pp. 749-756.

8. C.A.R. Hoare, "Communicating sequential processes," Comm. ACM, **21**, No. 8, (August 1978), pp. 666-677.

9. G.J. Holzmann, "A Theory for protocol validation," IEEE Trans. on Computers, **C-31**, No.8, (August 1982), pp. 730-738.

10. G.J. Holzmann, "The Pandora system — an interactive system for the design of data communication protocols," Computer Networks, **8**, No. 2, (1984), pp 71-81.

11. G.J. Holzmann, "Automated protocol validation in 'Argos,' assertion proving and scatter searching," 1984, submitted for publication, available from the author, 23 pgs.

12. G.J. Holzmann, "Trace — performance measurements," AT&T Bell Laboratories, unpublished internal report, Jan. 1, 1985, 29 pgs.

13. R.P. Kurshan, "Proposed specification of BX.25 link layer protocol," AT&T Technical Journal, **64**, No. 2, (Feb. 1985), pp. 559-596.

14. R. Milner, "A Calculus for Communicating Systems," Lecture Notes in Computer Science, **92**, (1980).

15. National Bureau of Standards, Specification of a transport protocol for computer communications, **4**, "Service Specifications," June 1984.

16. C. West, "Applications and limitations of automated protocol validation," Proc. 2nd IFIP WG 6.1 Int. Workshop on Protocol Specification, Testing, and Verification, USC/ISI, Idyllwild, CA. May 1982, pp 361-373.

17. P. Zafiropulo, C.H. West, H. Rudin, D.D. Cowan and D. Brand, "Toward analyzing and synthesizing protocols," IEEE Trans. Commun., **COM-28**, No. 4, (1980), pp. 651-661.

APPENDIX

The following specification describes a transport protocol defined by the National Bureau of Standards [15]. The specification is based on the model given in [4]. Four processes are defined: a local user process *AU* connected to a server process *A*, and a remote user *BU* connected to server process *B*. The control flow constructs and the I/O statements in *Argos* are based on CSP, using buffered message channels instead of rendez-vous. Process *A*, for instance, receives messages via two channels: one is named *ua* and is used by the user process to request services, the other is named *ca* and is used here to receive control messages from the remote server. Messages from server to user are sent through channel *UA*. The communication between the two servers is modeled with control messages *m*1 to *m*7, as defined in [4]. The analysis discussed here uses no *assert* primitives and is thus a general one for completeness and absence of deadlocks. The arrow and the semicolon are syntactically equivalent statement separators. A double colon flags the start of an option in a repetitive construct (*do* · · · *od*) or in an alternative construct (if · · · *fi*). In this case, the state transition diagram defining the protocol is most conveniently, though not most elegantly, modeled by assigning a label to every state and including a goto-jump for every transition. Processes *A* and *B* are symmetrical. Null transitions from the original protocol were deleted from the model.

```
proc A
{       queue ca[8], ua[8];

closed:
        do
        :: ca?m1 → UA!conn_ind → goto rcvd
        :: ua?conn_req → cb!m1 → goto crsent
        :: ua?abort  → cb!m4
        :: ca?m4 → UA!d
        od;
crsent:
        if
        :: ca?m2 → UA!conn_conf → goto estab
        :: ca?m7 → UA!disconn → goto closed
        :: ua?abort  → cb!m4 → goto closed
        :: ca?m4 → UA!d  → goto closed
        fi;
rcvd:
        if
        :: ua?conn_resp → cb!m2 → goto estab
        :: ca?m7 → UA!disconn → goto closed
        :: ua?abort  → cb!m4 → goto closed
        :: ca?m4 → UA!d  → goto closed
        fi;
estab:
        do
```

```
		:: ua?close_req → cb!m3 → goto Aclose
		:: ca?m3 → UA!close_ind → goto Pclose
		:: ua?data_req → cb!m5
		:: ca?m5 → UA!data_ind
		:: ua?expid_req → cb!m6
		:: ca?m6 → UA!expid_ind
		:: ca?m7 → UA!disconn → goto closed
		:: ua?abort  → cb!m4 → goto closed
		:: ca?m4 → UA!d  → goto closed
		od;
	Aclose:
		do
		:: ca?m3 → UA!close_ind → goto closed
		:: ca?m5 → UA!data_ind
		:: ca?m6 → UA!expid_ind
		:: ca?m7 → UA!disconn → goto closed
		:: ua?abort  → cb!m4 → goto closed
		:: ca?m4 → UA!d  → goto closed
		od;
	Pclose:
		do
		:: ua?data_req → cb!m5
		:: ua?expid_req → cb!m6
		:: ua?abort  → cb!m4 → goto closed
		:: ca?m4 → UA!d  → goto closed
		:: ua?close_req → cb!m3 → goto closed
		:: ca?m7 → UA!disconn → goto closed
		od
}

proc B
{	queue cb[8], ub[8];

closed:
		do
		:: cb?m1 → UB!conn_ind → goto rcvd
		:: ub?conn_req → ca!m1 → goto crsent
		:: ub?abort  → ca!m4
		:: cb?m4 → UB!d
		od;
crsent:
		if
		:: cb?m2 → UB!conn_conf → goto estab
		:: cb?m7 → UB!disconn → goto closed
		:: ub?abort  → ca!m4 → goto closed
		:: cb?m4 → UB!d  → goto closed
		fi;
rcvd:
		if
```

```
        :: ub?conn_resp → ca!m2 → goto estab
        :: cb?m7 → UB!disconn → goto closed
        :: ub?abort  → ca!m4 → goto closed
        :: cb?m4 → UB!d  → goto closed
        fi;
estab:
        do
        :: ub?close_req → ca!m3 → goto Aclose
        :: cb?m3 → UB!close_ind → goto Pclose
        :: ub?data_req → ca!m5
        :: cb?m5 → UB!data_ind
        :: ub?expid_req → ca!m6
        :: cb?m6 → UB!expid_ind
        :: cb?m7 → UB!disconn → goto closed
        :: ub?abort  → ca!m4 → goto closed
        :: cb?m4 → UB!d  → goto closed
        od;
Aclose:
        do
        :: cb?m3 → UB!close_ind → goto closed
        :: cb?m5 → UB!data_ind
        :: cb?m6 → UB!expid_ind
        :: cb?m7 → UB!disconn → goto closed
        :: ub?abort  → ca!m4 → goto closed
        :: cb?m4 → UB!d  → goto closed
        od;
Pclose:
        do
        :: ub?data_req → ca!m5
        :: ub?expid_req → ca!m6
        :: ub?abort  → ca!m4 → goto closed
        :: cb?m4 → UB!d  → goto closed
        :: ub?close_req → ca!m3 → goto closed
        :: cb?m7 → UB!disconn → goto closed
        od
}

proc AU
{       queue UA[8];
        pvar m = 0;

        do
        :: UA?conn_conf → ua!close_req; UA?close_ind
        :: UA?close_ind → ua!close_req
        :: UA?conn_ind → ua!conn_resp
        :: (m == 0) → m = 1; ua!conn_req
        :: (m == 1) → m = 2; ua!abort
        :: UA?default
        od
```

```
}

proc BU
{       queue UB[8];

        do
        :: UB?conn_conf → ub!close_req; UB?close_ind
        :: UB?close_ind → ub!close_req
        :: UB?conn_ind → ub!conn_resp
        :: UB?default
        od
}
```

The queue sizes were arbitrarily set to 8 slots per channel. The protocol tested is defined by the behavior of the two server machines, as visible to the users. The user behavior is no part of the formal protocol. An arbitrary set of user processes was defined specifically for the test. The local user *AU* will open the connection by sending a *conn_req* message to *ua* and some arbitrary time later it will close it with an *abort* message. The remote user *BU* is considered to be passive, responding only to close messages and accepting, but ignoring all others. *Default* is a keyword for receptions that match any input from the queue specified.
The protocol as specified above is compiled, in 23 seconds of CPU time on a VAX-750, into four finite state machines of 27, 27, 10 and 6 states respectively. The compiler flags a series of incompleteness errors, noting for instance that control message $m7$ can be received but is never sent. Ignoring those warnings, an exhaustive analysis with *trace* takes just under 3 seconds of CPU time and reports 4 error sequences that reduce to two types of errors. The first one is an unspecified reception of the message *conn_resp* in state *closed*, for instance, after the following message exchange:

queue:	ca	ua	UA	cb	ub	UB
event:						
1		conn_req,				
2				m1,		
3						conn_ind,
4		abort,				
5				m4,		
6						d,
7					[conn_resp],	

Each column corresponds to a queue and each line to a time step. The first event recorded is the sending of a message *conn_req* into queue *ua*, followed by an $m1$ into queue *cb*, etc. The last message sent is enclosed in square brackets to indicate that it was sent but could not be received. Comparing the event sequence with the program shows that server process *B* is in state *closed* at the time.
The second problem is an unspecified reception of $m2$ also in state *closed*:

queue:	ca	ua	UA	cb	ub	UB
event:						
1		conn_req,				
2				m1,		
3						conn_ind,
4		abort,				
5					conn_resp,	
6				m4,		
7	[m2],					
8						d,

It is now straightforward to study the behavior of the protocol for different user behaviors, which can reveal, for instance the possibility of the unspecified reception of a message *conn_resp* in state *Pclose*, or the more obvious deadlock after a simultaneous *conn_req* message from both users.

Recent Results in the Static Analysis of Communicating Finite State Processes

Scott A. Smolka†
Department of Computer Science
SUNY at Stony Brook
Zip + 4 = 4400
Stony Brook, NY 11794

Paris C. Kanellakis†
Department of Computer Science
Brown University
Box 1910
Providence, RI 02912

1. Introduction

The Finite State Process (FSP) is a modelling technique for concurrent programs and network protocols stemming from several recent algebraic treatments of concurrency [Mil, Br, BHR, Hol]. We examine the FSP in the context of two problems of static analysis: (1) FSP equivalence, and (2) cooperation vs. antagonism in networks of FSPs.

Regarding (1), we analyze two equivalence notions from Milner's CCS [Mil], observation equivalence and congruence. We also consider failure equivalence from the [BHR] failure model. We show that observation equivalence ($\approx$) and congruence can be tested in cubic time. Observation equivalence is the limit of a sequence of successively finer equivalence relations, $\approx_k$, where $\approx_1$ is NFA equivalence. We show that, for each fixed k, $\approx_k$ is PSPACE-complete. We also provide an $O(n \log n)$ test for congruence of n-state processes of bounded fanout by extending Hopcroft's algorithm for minimizing the states of a DFA [Hop].

†Supported by NSF grant DCR-8505873.

‡Supported by NSF grants MCS-8210830 and DCR-8302391, ONR-DARPA grant N00014-83-K-0146, and by the Office of Army Research under Contract DAAG29-84-K-0058.

Finally, we show that testing for failure equivalence is PSPACE-complete, even for a very restricted type of process.

Concerning (2), we characterize the familiar problems of potential blocking, lockout [La], and termination in terms of cooperative and antagonistic processes. Using this approach, we show that all three problems can be decided efficiently for loosely connected networks of tree FSPs. If not all acyclic FSPs are trees, then the cooperative properties become NP-complete and the antagonistic ones PSPACE-complete. For the considerably harder cyclic case, we provide a natural extension of the method as well as a subcase reducible to integer programming with a constant number of variables.

The rest of this paper is organized as follows. Section 2 is devoted to the equivalence problem and summarizes our results from [KS1]. Section 3 considers cooperative vs. antagonistic processes and summarizes our results from [KS2]. Section 4 concludes.

2. The Equivalence Problem

We consider several recently proposed notions of equivalence of processes, namely *observation equivalence*, *congruence*, and *failure equivalence*. In particular, we analyze the complexity of testing FSPs under these equivalences and, whenever possible, provide corresponding efficient decision procedures. These decision procedures can be used to verify that an implementation in the form of a network of FSPs meets a finite state specification. For example, in [SFD] we use our decision procedure for observation equivalence to prove that the AUY protocols [AUY] satisfy the quintessential safety property for communication protocols: messages are delivered in transmitted order.

Intuitively, two processes are said to be "observation-equivalent" [Mil] if they cannot be discerned by an external observer no matter what experiment (sequence of actions) he chooses to perform. Observation equivalence was one of the original equivalence notions proposed by Milner in connection with his CCS [Mil].

Congruence [Mi2], defined recursively, identifies FSPs that reach congruent states after one action, for each possible action. Importantly, if process P is congruent to process Q, than the result of replacing P with Q in any program context yields congruent programs (this is not necessarily true of observation equivalence). An iterative definition of congruence, termed "strong congruence", was given in [Mil]. This definition will serve as the basis of our decision procedure for congruence.

Finally, failure equivalence [BHR] captures the ways in which a process can refuse to interact with its environment, thus bringing on deadlock. Failure equivalence is a weaker notion than observation equivalence (see Proposition 4), i.e. it distinguishes fewer processes, and is sometimes more appropriate than observation equivalence [Da]. This is true of the next section where we use a variant of failure equivalence as the basis of a divide-and-conquer algorithm for analyzing cooperation and antagonism in networks of FSPs.

2.1. Finite State Processes

The basic building block of our model for distributed computation is the Finite State Process (FSP), which very much resembles the Nondeterministic Finite state Automaton (NFA) of the classical theory of computation.

Definition 1: For a set of symbols Σ (called *actions*), and a special symbol τ not in Σ (called the *unobservable action*), and a set of symbols V (called *variables*), we define a *Finite State Process* (FSP) as a quadruple $<K, p_0, \Delta, E>$, where:

1) K is a finite set of ***states***.

2) $p_0 \in K$ is the ***start state***.

3) $\Delta : K \times (\Sigma \cup \{\tau\}) \rightarrow 2^K$ is a function called the ***transition function***.

4) $E : K \rightarrow 2^V$ is a function called the ***extension function***. ∎

An FSP can be represented, in the obvious fashion, as a directed graph with labels on the arcs (i.e. transitions) from $\Sigma \cup \{\tau\}$ and labels on the nodes from 2^V. The various extensions (i.e. the labels on the nodes) represent different flavors of acceptance and are used in [Mi3]. These extensions are the only difference from the classical notion of a NFA with empty transitions.

We call this the *general* model of FSPs. If no τ–transitions are present we have the ***observable model*** [Mi3], and if in this case there is exactly one transition for each symbol in Σ we have the *deterministic* model. On the other hand, for $|V| = 1$, we have the classical NFA with empty transitions which we call the ***standard*** model. If in the standard model, for all states p, $E(p) = V = \{X\}$ (i.e. all states are accepting states, but there could be some missing transitions), we have the ***restricted*** model. Nontrivial subsets of the restricted model are the ***restricted observable*** model (called ***r.o.u.*** when $|\Sigma| = 1$), and the model where the FSP is a ***finite tree*** rooted at p_0. The hierarchy of models is depicted in Figure 1a. Every one of the these models corresponds to some nontrivial case in our exposition. Examples of such FSPs are presented in Figure 1b (we use standard notation from [HU] for the standard model).

We will always deal with ***states of FSPs*** (e.g. equivalent states) and the processes to which these states belong will be clearly defined from the context. We will use capital letters P, Q, $\cdots$ to denote FSPs and small letters p, q, $\cdots$ to denote states.

Let $s \in \Sigma^*$ and p, p' be states of a FSP. If $s = \epsilon$, we say that $p \overset{s}{\Longrightarrow} p'$ when there is a path of length k in the FSP from

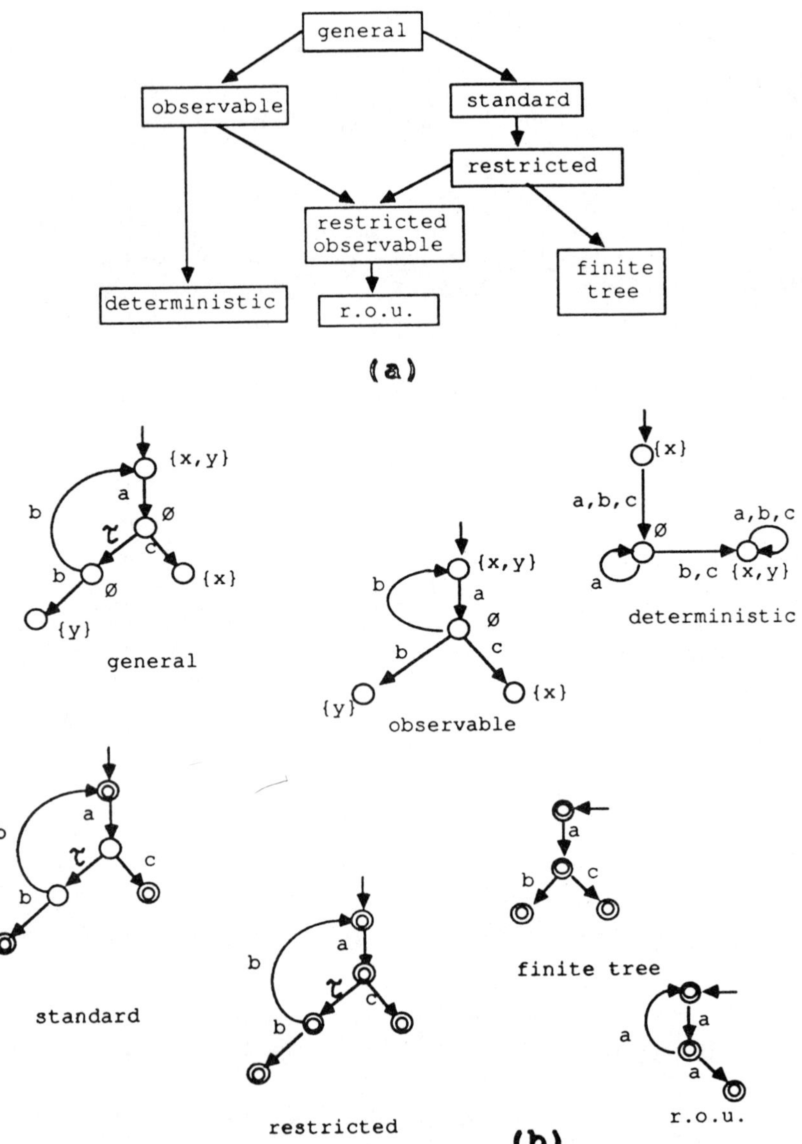

Figure 1. Hierarchy of models of FSPs with examples.

p to p' labeled by τ^k, $k \geq 0$. (Obviously always $p \overset{\epsilon}{\Rightarrow} p$.) If $s = s_1 s_2 \cdots s_n$, $s_i \in \Sigma$, $1 \leq i \leq n$, we say that $p \overset{s}{\Rightarrow} p'$ when there is a path of length $k_0 + k_1 + \cdots + k_n + n$ in the graph of the FSP from p to p' labeled by $\tau^{k_0} s_1 \tau^{k_1} s_2 \cdots s_n \tau^{k_n}$, $k_0, k_1, \cdots, k_n \geq 0$. We use a different symbol for τ and the empty string ϵ because of the particular role of τ as the unobservable action in distributed computation [Mi1]. We write $p \overset{s}{\rightarrow} p'$ when $k_i = 0, 0 \leq i \leq n$.

In the *restricted* model of FSPs, the only feature that distinguishes states is the absence of certain transitions. This concept is formalized in [BHR] as the *failures* of an FSP state, defined as follows for state p in the restricted case: Let p be a state and $s \in \Sigma^*$. We say that $p \overset{s}{\Rightarrow} dead$, when there is no p' such that $p \overset{s}{\Rightarrow} p'$. Then:

$$failures(p) = \{(s,Z) \mid s \in \Sigma^*, Z \subseteq \Sigma \text{ such that}$$

$$\exists p' \in K : p \overset{s}{\Rightarrow} p' \text{ and } \forall z \in Z : p' \overset{z}{\Rightarrow} dead\}.$$

For example, assuming $\Sigma = \{a, b, c\}$, the failures for the start state of the finite tree process of Figure 1b are:

$$\{\epsilon\} \times 2^{\{b,c\}} \cup \{a\} \times 2^{\{a\}} \cup \{ab\} \times 2^{\Sigma} \cup \{ac\} \times 2^{\Sigma}.$$

2.2. Equivalence of FSP States

A number of "candidates" for the correct notion of equivalence between states of FSPs have been proposed and investigated [Mi1, Mi2, Mi3, BHR, Br]. We will deal with three such notions: *observation equivalence, congruence,* and *failure equivalence.* The expositions of [Mi1, BHR] are, to a great extent, devoted to establishing the practical relevance of such choices in the context of distributed computation.

In general, for two FSP states p, q to be "equivalent" it is not enough to say that they represent start states of NFAs accepting the same language (as in the classical case). In particular:

Definition 2: Two FSP states p, q in the general model are *k-observation equivalent* ($p \approx_k q$) iff (if and only if):

1. $E(p) = E(q)$. when $k = 0$
2. For every $s \in \Sigma^*$ when $k > 0$

   (i) $p \overset{s}{\Rightarrow} p' \supset (\exists q' : q \overset{s}{\Rightarrow} q' \wedge p' \approx_{k-1} q')$,

   (ii) $q \overset{s}{\Rightarrow} q' \supset (\exists p' : p \overset{s}{\Rightarrow} p' \wedge q' \approx_{k-1} p')$.

Note that p', q' in (i) may be different from p', q' in (ii). States p, q are *observation equivalent* [Mil] ($p \approx q$) iff $p \approx_k q$ for all $k \geq 0$. ▮

Limited observation equivalence is similar to observation equivalence except that only strings of length zero or one are considered.

Definition 3: Two FSP states p, q in the general model are *k-limited observation equivalent* ($p \simeq_k q$) iff:

1. $E(p) = E(q)$. when $k = 0$
2. For every $\sigma \in \Sigma \cup \{\epsilon\}$ when $k > 0$

   (i) $p \overset{\sigma}{\Rightarrow} p' \supset (\exists q' : q \overset{\sigma}{\Rightarrow} q' \wedge p' \simeq_{k-1} q')$,

   (ii) $q \overset{\sigma}{\Rightarrow} q' \supset (\exists p' : p \overset{\sigma}{\Rightarrow} p' \wedge q' \simeq_{k-1} p')$.

States p, q are *limited-observation equivalent* ($p \simeq q$) iff $p \simeq_k q$ for all $k \geq 0$. Brookes and Rounds have defined a similar equivalence, weak observation equivalence [BR]. In the observable model, we denote $p \simeq q$ as $p \sim q$ and call p, q *congruent* [Mi2]. ▮

Failure equivalence identifies states having the same failure set.

Definition 4: Two FSP states p, q in the restricted model are *failure equivalent* ($p \equiv q$) [BHR] iff:

$$failures(p) = failures(q).$$ ▮

Intuitively, an **R**–fixpoint is a relation that, for all strings, takes **R**–equivalent states to **R**–equivalent states.

Definition 5: Let $\Lambda \subseteq \Sigma^*$ be a set of strings. We call a relation **R** between FSP states a Λ-*fixpoint* when
p **R** q iff
1. $E(p) = E(q)$
2. For every $s \in \Lambda$

$$p \stackrel{s}{\Longrightarrow} p' \supset (\exists q' : q \stackrel{s}{\Longrightarrow} q' \wedge p' \; \mathbf{R} \; q')$$
$$q \stackrel{s}{\Longrightarrow} q' \supset (\exists p' : p \stackrel{s}{\Longrightarrow} p' \wedge p' \; \mathbf{R} \; q')$$

▌

Lemma 1: In the general model of FSPs:
(a) $\simeq$ is a $\Sigma \cup \{\epsilon\}$-fixpoint. (b) $\simeq$ is a Σ^*-fixpoint. (c) $\approx$ is a Σ^*-fixpoint. ▌

Based on this lemma and the state of the art of CCS, we have a number of interesting propositions that relate the various notions of equivalence. Also, in the standard model whenever p, q denote start states of finite state automata accepting the same language, we will say $L(p)=L(q)$.

Proposition 1: For FSP states p, q in the *general* model,

$$p \approx q \text{ iff } p \simeq q. \quad ▌$$

Proposition 2: For FSP states p, q in the *standard* model, (i.e. p, q represent start states of NFAs)

$$p \approx_1 q \text{ iff } L(p)=L(q). \quad ▌$$

Proposition 3: For FSP states p, q in the *deterministic* model, the following are equivalent:

(a) $p \approx q$ (or $p \simeq q$, or $p \sim q$).

(b) for some $k \geq 1$, $p \approx_k q$.

(c) When the model is also standard, (i.e., p, q represent DFA start states), $L(p)=L(q)$

(d) When the model is also restricted, $p \equiv q$. ▌

Proposition 4 [Br]: For FSP states p, q in the *restricted* model, $p \approx_2 q$ implies $p \equiv q$ which implies $p \approx_1 q$. ∎

2.3. Efficient Algorithms for Testing Congruence

The problem of language equivalence of two finite state automata of size n (i.e. whether they accept the same language) has received a great deal of attention in the literature. For DFAs there is a $O(n\ G(n))$ algorithm that uses UNION–FIND [AHU, §4.8], and for NFAs the problem has been shown to be PSPACE–complete [StM]. Also, the problem of minimizing the states of a DFA of size n has an elegant $O(n \log n)$ solution, and is related to a combinatorial partitioning problem [AHU §4.13, Hop].

For testing congruence of states of deterministic FSPs, the above techniques for DFAs are directly applicable (see also Proposition 3). For the larger class of observable FSPs, congruence of states can still be tested efficiently! This is one more justification for choosing congruence as the appropriate notion of equivalence in CCS. In this case, unfortunately, the UNION–FIND technique does not lead to an efficient algorithm because of possible multiple transitions for one symbol of the alphabet. However, we can show that congruence of states can be tested by solving the following partitioning problem, which is also of independent interest. A *partition* of a set S consists of disjoint nonempty subsets of S called *blocks*, whose union is S.

PARTITIONING

Input: A set S, a partition of S into disjoint blocks $\pi = \{B_1, B_2, \cdots, B_p\}$, and a function $f : S \rightarrow 2^S$.

Output: A partition of S into disjoint blocks $\pi' = \{E_1, E_2, \cdots, E_q\}$, such that:

1. π' is *consistent* with π (i.e. each E_i is a subset of some B_j).
2. For a, b in block E_i and any block E_j: $f(a) \cap E_j \neq \emptyset$ iff $f(b) \cap E_j \neq \emptyset$.
3. π' is the coarsest such partition (i.e. has the fewest blocks).

Obviously, f can be represented as a directed graph with node set S and arcs (i, j) iff j is in $f(i)$. The size of an instance of PARTITIONING is (n, m), where we denote $|S|$ as n and the number of arcs in the corresponding graph as m. In the deterministic case, we have $f: S \rightarrow S$ and $m = n$.

Intuitively, the initial partition π is refined into the final partition π' (in the coarsest fashion possible) so that f induces a mapping from blocks of π' to sets of blocks of π'.

Lemma 2: Let p, q be the start states of two observable FSPs over the fixed sets of actions Σ and variables V. Let these FSPs have a total of n states and a total of m transitions. We can test whether $p \sim q$ by linear-time reducing it to a PARTITIONING problem of size at most (n, m). ∎

Note that the PARTITIONING problem is *different* from that of minimizing the states of a DFA because having more than one symbol in Σ is different from having many transitions for each symbol; we therefore have to generalize [Hop].

An obvious solution to the PARTITIONING problem is, starting from π, refine the blocks of the partition by the following method. Let B_i be a block. Examine $f(a) \subseteq S$, for each a in B_i. We can think of $f(a)$ as denoting a set of blocks (those blocks such that each one contains some element of $f(a)$). Now we partition B_i so that two elements a and b are put in the same block if and only if $f(a)$ and $f(b)$ denote the same set of blocks. We will refer to this method as the *naive method.*

Lemma 3: The *naive method* solves an instance of the PARTITIONING problem of size n and m, and can be implemented in $O(nm)$ time. ∎

For the important case of bounded fanout, we can improve upon the naive method by generalizing the divide-and-conquer method of [AHU]. We say that we have *bounded fanout* if for all a in S, $|f(a)| \leq c$, for some constant c. This case corresponds to FSPs that have at most c transitions out of any state for each symbol of the action alphabet. In [AHU], an $O(n \log n)$ algorithm was presented for the deterministic version of this problem, i.e. $|f(a)| = 1$, for all a in S.

Theorem 1: The bounded fanout PARTITIONING problem (i.e. for all a in S, $|f(a)| \leq c$) can be solved in time $O(c^2 n \log n)$. ❙

Our algorithm for this problem can be found in [KS1]. As a result of Lemmas 2 and 3, and Theorem 1 we have:

Corollary 1: Let p, q be two states of observable FSPs, where the FSPs have n states and m transitions. Then $p \sim q$ can be decided in $O(nm)$ time and, in the case of FSPs with at most c transitions out of every state on any action, in $O(c^2 \cdot n \log n)$ time. ❙

2.4. The Complexity of Observation and Failure Equivalence

As shown by the following theorem, deciding $\approx_k$ is a problem that has a polynomial-time solution as $k \to \infty$, but is otherwise intractable for (almost) any fixed k.

Theorem 2: Let p, q be FSP states and assume that the FSPs to which these states belong have a total of n states.

a) In the general model, whether $p \approx q$ can be decided in $O(n^3)$ time.

b) In the restricted and observable model, whether $p \approx_k q$ for any fixed $k \geq 1$ is PSPACE-complete.

c) In the r.o.u. model, whether $p \approx_k q$ for some fixed $k \geq 2$ is NP-complete, and decidable in linear time for $k = 1$. ❙

Result a) is obtained by noticing that observation equivalence is a problem very similar to congruence except for the presence of τ-moves. A suitable modification to the naive algorithm for congruence (Lemma 3) gives us the upper bound.

For result b), we polynomially reduce the problem of testing $p \approx_1 q$ (i.e. $L(p) = L(q)$ - see Proposition 2) to $p \approx_k q$ $k \geq 2$. This is sufficient for showing PSPACE-hardness since it is known [StM] that $\approx_1$ is PSPACE-complete to decide in the standard, observable model. Also, as was recently shown [CS], deciding $\approx_1$ is PSPACE-complete even in the restricted, observable case. For membership in PSPACE, we can reduce $\approx_k$ to $\approx_1$.

The NP-completeness results of c) are obtained in a manner analogous to b). Finally note that it is easy to decide $p \approx_1 q$ in the r.o.u. model since the languages $L(p)$ and $L(q)$ are closed under prefix.

Switching to failure equivalence, recall (Section 2.2) for states p, q in the restricted model:

$$failures(p) = \{(s,Z) \mid s \in \Sigma^*, Z \subseteq \Sigma \text{ such that } \exists p' \in K: p \stackrel{s}{\Longrightarrow} p' \text{ and } \forall z \in Z: p' \stackrel{z}{\not\Longrightarrow} dead\}.$$

Moreover:

$$p \equiv q \text{ iff } failures(p) = failures(q).$$

Theorem 3: Let p, q be states of restricted observable FSPs. Then, deciding whether $p \equiv q$ is PSPACE-complete and NP-complete in the r.o.u. model. |

Using the definition of failure equivalence, we can reduce the problem of deciding $p \equiv q$ to $L(p) = L(q)$. Thus in both the restricted observable and the r.o.u models we can show membership in PSPACE and NP, respectively. PSPACE-hardness and NP-hardness are proven by reducing $L(p) = L(q)$ to $p \equiv q$ in the respective models.

3. Cooperation and Antagonism

In this section we consider networks of FSPs and their concurrent composition. In particular, we analyze the complexity of the problems of potential blocking, lockout, and termination of FSPs. These problems, which may be viewed in terms of the notions of cooperation and antagonism among processes, are hard to solve for general networks. However, we present a new algebraic technique for efficiently deciding several interesting special cases, including loosely connected networks of tree FSPs.

3.1. Networks of Processes

The FSP was defined in Section 2.1, Definition 1. Throughout this section, we need only consider restricted FSPs, i.e. those in which every state is an "accept" state. We thus omit the extension function from an FSP specification. However, it is now essential that we explicitly specify an FSP's communication alphabet, since FSPs in a network of processes typically will have distinct alphabets (see Definition 6). An FSP is thus a quadruple $<K, p, \Sigma, \Delta>$, where K is the state set, p is the start state, Σ is the communication alphabet, and Δ is the transition function.

An FSP can be represented by a directed graph G. If G is a path we have a *linear* FSP; if it is a tree (rooted at p) we have a *tree* FSP; and if it is a directed acyclic graph with single root p, we have an *acyclic* FSP. A state of an FSP with no transitions leaving it is called a *leaf.*

The meaning of the actions of an FSP is messages exchanged with other FSPs. For example, if $x \in \Sigma_1 \cap \Sigma_2$ then x is a message that FSP_1 could exchange with FSP_2. As will be clear from the definition of composition (given in the following subsection), the message exchange is in the form of a "handshake" between the two processes. Intuitively, no distinction is made between *send* and *receive.* A message can only be exchanged between two processes, i.e. communication is *point-to-point.* The meaning of a τ (the unobservable action) is a step inside the FSP invisible to the outside world.

Definition 6: A *network N of processes* is a set of m FSPs, $N = \{P_1, P_2, \cdots, P_m\}$, where we let P_i denote $<K_i, p_i, \Sigma_i, \Delta_i>$, and

1) the K_i's are disjoint sets of states, $1 \le i \le m$;
2) each $x \in \bigcup_i \Sigma_i$ belongs to *exactly two* process sets of actions. ∎

Therefore a network N is a closed system of communicating processes. Since each action symbol belongs to exactly two processes, we can describe the potential to communicate using a labeled undirected graph C_N. The nodes of C_N correspond to the processes in N and there is an edge $\{i, j\}$ between nodes i and j iff $\Sigma_i \cap \Sigma_j \neq \emptyset$. The label of the edge $\{i, j\}$ is $\Sigma_i \cap \Sigma_j$ (i.e. process P_i can communicate with process P_j using any number of x's, where $x \in \Sigma_i \cap \Sigma_j$). If C_N is a tree (ring), we say that *network N is a tree (ring).*

In Figure 2a we have an example of a ring network of three processes; P_1 is a tree process, P_2 is an acyclic process, and P_3 is a cyclic process. C_N is given in Figure 2b.

Let N be a network of processes with $C_N = (V, E)$, and π a *given* partition $(V_1, V_2, \cdots, V_l)$ of V into disjoint sets. We will call N a k*-tree* if:

(a) $|V_i| \le k, (i = 1,2, \cdots, l)$
(b) the graph with node set $\{1, 2, \cdots, l\}$ and edge set $\{(i, j) \mid$ where E contains an edge with endpoints in V_i and $V_j\}$ is a tree.

Note that a tree network is a 1-tree, a ring network a 2-tree, and if the largest biconnected component of C_N has size k we have a k-tree.

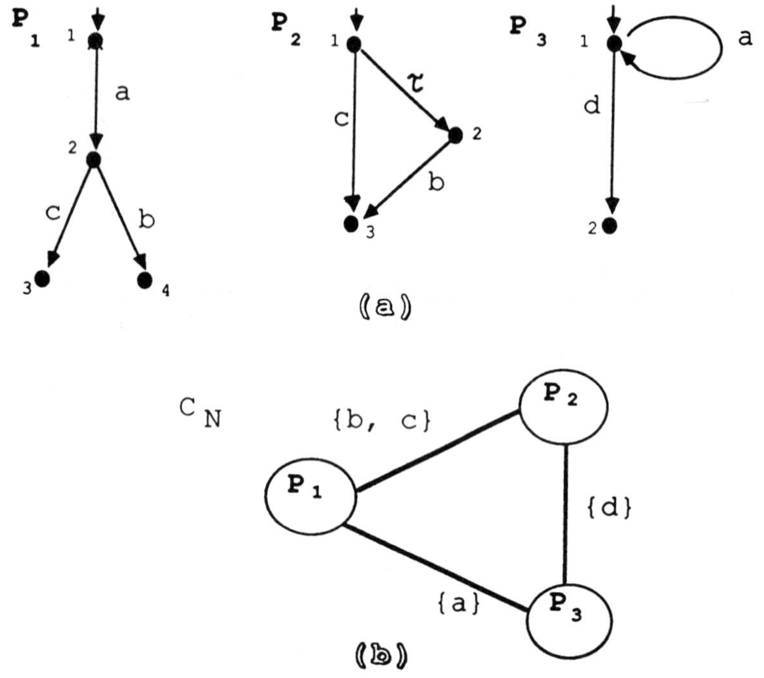

Figure 2. Example of a network of FSPs.

3.2. Process Composition: Algebraic Properties

We can now describe the interaction of processes in a network using the algebraic operation of *composition* (||).

Definition 7: Let N be a network of FSPs and $P_1 = <K_1, p_1, \Sigma_1, \Delta_1>$, $P_2 = <K_2, p_2, \Sigma_2, \Delta_2>$ two distinct processes in N. The *composition* of these two processes is a new FSP:

$$P_1 || P_2 \quad = \quad <K_1 \times K_2, (p_1, p_2), (\Sigma_1 \cup \Sigma_2) - (\Sigma_1 \cap \Sigma_2), \Delta>$$

where the new transition function Δ is defined as follows:

if $r_1 \in \Delta_1(q_1, \lambda)$ and $r_2 \in \Delta_2(q_2, \mu)$ then

if $\lambda \in (\Sigma_1 \cup \{\tau\}) - \Sigma_2$ then $(r_1, q_2) \in \Delta((q_1, q_2), \lambda)$

if $\mu \in (\Sigma_2 \cup \{\tau\}) - \Sigma_1$ then $(q_1, r_2) \in \Delta((q_1, q_2), \mu)$

if $\lambda = \mu \in \Sigma_1 \cap \Sigma_2$ then $(r_1, r_2) \in \Delta((q_1, q_2), \tau)$

∎

In Figure 3a we illustrate composition on the FSPs P_1 and P_2 from Figure 2. Note that we restrict $P_1 || P_2$ to states reachable from the start state (p_1, p_2). Composing these two processes can be viewed as transforming C_N into $C_{N'}$ (Figure 3b).

The composition of two processes $P_1 || P_2$ with $|K_1| = n_1$ and $|K_2| = n_2$ produces, in general, a process of size $n_1 \cdot n_2$. This algebraic operation describes the possible interleavings of the actions of the two processes as viewed from outside these processes. At the same time, it hides from the outside world their internal communication. In the CCS language of [Mil], our composition is a combination of interleaving and restriction. The transitions of $P_1 || P_2$ are either moves of P_1 with respect to $P_3, \cdots, P_m$, moves of P_2 with respect to $P_3, \cdots, P_m$, or simultaneous moves occurring whenever P_1 and P_2 can "handshake".

The composition operator is associative and commutative [KS2]. Therefore, given a network $N = \{P_1, P_2, \cdots, P_m\}$, the *global* process $P_1 || P_2 || \cdots || P_m$ having only τ-moves is well-defined. The states of this process are n-tuples of local states from $P_1, P_2, \cdots, P_m$ and represent the reachable *global* states of N. Analysis of the reachability properties of the global process is a standard, albeit inefficient, way of studying the behavior of a network of FSPs.

The operation of composition ($||$) in a network of processes has a number of interesting properties. In particular it matches well with the notion of *possibilities*, which will be a powerful tool in analyzing FSPs.

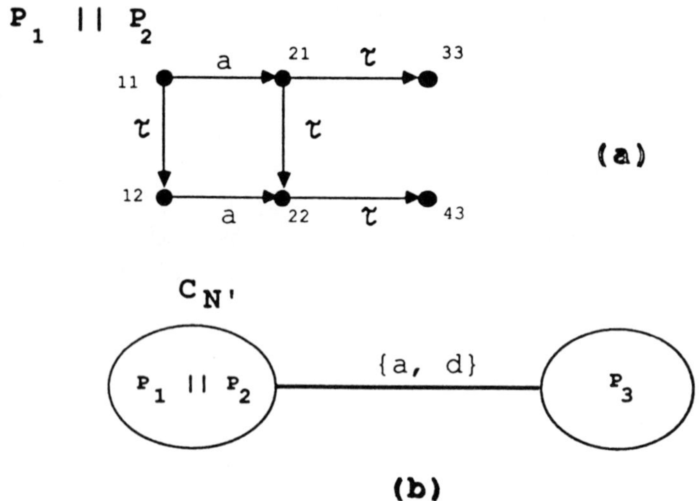

Figure 3. Example of composition.

Definition 8: Let $P = <K, p, \Sigma, \Delta)$ be an *acyclic* FSP. The *possibilities* of P are given as:

$Poss(p) = \{(s, Z) \mid s \in \Sigma^*, Z \subseteq \Sigma$, such that:
$\exists q, p \overset{s}{\Longrightarrow} q$ and
(q has no outgoing τ-moves) and
(q has outgoing set of actions exactly Z) $\}$.

∎

A possibility (s, Z) is a pair consisting of a string s and a set Z of actions. The string s takes the process from the start state p to a state q with no outgoing τ's and with exactly the set of actions in Z as outgoing actions. Two acyclic FSPs are ***possibility equivalent*** if they have identical possibility sets. Possibility equivalence is a refinement of the [BHR] failure equivalence, and, like failure equivalence, is a congruence with respect to composition.

3.3. Acyclic Processes

Let $N = \{P_1, P_2, \cdots, P_m\}$ be a network of FSPs, let $P = P_1$ be the *distinguished* process, and let Q be its *context* $P_2 || P_3 || \cdots || P_m$. The *global* FSP $G = P_1 || P_2 || \cdots || P_m$, which has only τ-moves, captures all possible state changes in the system.

During execution, P may encounter nondeterministic choices, due either to multiple enabled communications or to τ-moves. We consider P "successful" if the choices it makes leads it to one of its leaves. We will investigate the complexity of three notions of success for P, each posed as a predicate involving P and Q. $S_u(P, Q)$ (**unavoidable success**) means that P has to reach one of its leaves no matter what choices it makes. $S_a(P, Q)$ (**success in adversity**) means that P can reach one of its leaves even if Q is antagonistic. Finally, $S_c(P, Q)$ (**success with collaboration**) means that P can reach one of its leaves if Q is collaborative.

More formally:

$S_u(P, Q) = true$ (**unavoidable success**) when, $\forall p', q' . [(p', q')\ leaf\_of\ G] => [p'\ leaf\_of\ P]$.

$S_a(P, Q) = true$ (**success in adversity**) when, P has a winning strategy in $Game(P, Q)$ (see Figure 4).

$S_c(P, Q) = true$ (**success with collaboration**) when, $\exists p', q' . [(p', q')\ leaf\_of\ G] \wedge [p'\ leaf\_of\ P]$.

Obviously, $S_u(P, Q) => S_a(P, Q) => S_c(P, Q)$. However, even in very simple cases, $S_c(P, Q) \not=> S_u(P, Q)$.

We will use the term *potential blocking* for $\neg S_u(P, Q) = true$, *no-lockout* for $S_a(P, Q) = true$, and *potential termination* for $S_c(P, Q) = true$.

Game(P, Q)

Initial Position: Network of FSPs $\{P, Q\}$, Σ is common alphabet.

$p_1 \leftarrow start\_state\_of\ \ P$

$q_1 \leftarrow start\_state\_of\ \ Q$.

Round i $(i = 1, 2, \cdots, n)$:

Player-Q: Sets $a_i \leftarrow a$, $q_{i+1} \leftarrow q$, where $a \in \Sigma$, $q_i \overset{a}{\Longrightarrow} q$, and $\exists p' \,.\, p_i \overset{a}{\Longrightarrow} p'$.

Player-P: Sets $p_{i+1} \leftarrow p$, where $p_i \overset{a_i}{\Longrightarrow} p$.

Information: Q knows everything. P knows initial position and sequence of a_i's.

Goal: Player-P wins iff p_i is $leaf\_of\ P$.

Assumptions: Players have to play if they can.
The FSP P has no τ-moves.

Figure 4.

For success in adversity we assume that P, the distinguished process, has no τ-moves. This is to simplify the rules of the *Game* of Figure 4, which captures the evolution of the system. Player Q has a strong adverse role since it knows the global state and selects the next legal action. Player P knows only it local state and can estimate the global state from messages received and Q's structure. Whereas player Q chooses q_{i+1} and a_i (its next local state and the next action), player P only chooses p_{i+1} (its next local state). This is a ***game of partial information*** for P and ***total information*** for Q [Re]. Since the FSPs are acyclic, the game is a finite one.

For arbitrarily connected networks of linear FSPs there are no significant choices to be made and we have a computationally simple problem.

Proposition 5: If all processes in N are linear, then:
$S_u(P, Q) = S_a(P, Q) = S_c(P\ Q)$ and can be decided in $O(n)$ time. ▮

For the case of acyclic FSPs, even simple choices can lead to a combinatorial explosion.

Theorem 4: Let the processes in N be acyclic and such that $|\Sigma_i \cap \Sigma_j| \leq 1$ for $1 \leq i \neq j \leq m$. $S_c(P, Q)$ and $\neg S_u(P, Q)$ are NP-complete even if either

(1) C_N is a tree and all FSPs but one are $O(1)$ linear FSPs, or

(2) each P_i, $1 \leq i \leq m$, is an $O(1)$ tree FSP. ▮

In case (1), the result holds both if P is the only acyclic but non-linear FSP, or if P is linear. Note that communication between any two processes in Theorem 4 is restricted to repetitions of just one symbol.

The reductions are from 3SAT, where each variable is restricted to appear once negated and once or twice unnegated, a well-known NP-complete problem. Both $S_c(P, Q)$ and $\neg S_u(P, Q)$ are in NP since the desired "witness", which we use to verify success with collaboration and potential blocking respectively, is an $O(m \cdot n)$ sequence of moves from the initial global state (i.e. the length of the maximum path in the global machine G).

Theorem 5: Let the processes in N be acyclic. Even if C_N is a tree and all processes except P are tree FSPs,

$S_a(P, Q)$ is PSPACE-complete. ▮

The reduction is from QBF [GJ]. $S_a(P, Q)$ is in PSPACE since we have a finite game of linear-time bounded alternation (i.e. the length of the maximum path in the distinguished machine P). Thus $S_a(P, Q)$ is in PSPACE.

Theorems 4 and 5 show that we have intractable problems when either high connectivity is present in the network topology, or when there exists an FSP that can encode an exponential number of strings. Fortunately, for k-tree networks of tree FSPs we have the following result.

Theorem 6: Let N be a network of *tree* processes of size n and let C_N be a k-tree. Then,

$S_u(P, Q)$, $S_a(P, Q)$, $S_c(P, Q)$ can be decided in $O(n^k)$ time.

∎

Our $O(n^k)$-time algorithm [KS2] rests on the fact that we are able to express each of the success predicates in terms of the possibilities of P and the possibilities of Q. Letting P be the root of the k-tree, we use $||$ to combine processes from the leaves, always making sure that possibilities are preserved. Upon completion, the possibilities of Q will have been computed and the success predicates can be straightforwardly answered. The fact that we are dealing with tree FSPs allows us to maintain the possibilities of Q efficiently.

3.4. Cyclic Processes

In this section we analyze the complexity of the three success problems in the case of FSP that may have cycles in their underlying graphs. We will assume throughout that $N = \{P_1, P_2, \cdots, P_m\}$ is the given network of processes of size n, $P = P_1$ is the distinguished process, and $Q = P_2 || P_3 || \cdots || P_m$ its context. We will also assume that each P_i in N has no τ-moves and no leaves. These assumptions simplify our arguments, without loss of generality. Note that even if $P_2, \cdots, P_m$ have no leaves and no τ-moves, Q very well could have such features.

Informally, the success predicates for the distinguished process P in context Q become:

(a) $S_u(P, Q)$: P cannot stop moving;

(b) $S_a(P, Q)$: P can keep moving forever even if Q is antagonistic;

(c) $S_c(P, Q)$: P can keep moving forever if Q collaborates with it.

As for acyclic processes, S_u and S_c can be defined formally using the *leaf-of* predicate if process P is thought of as an infinite tree whose leaves are at infinity. Also, S_a can be expressed as *Game* (P, Q) having the same rules as the game in Figure 4. The only difference is that if *the game stops* Q is the winner. P wins if it can force *the game to go on forever.*

Proposition 6: $S_u(P, Q)$ and $S_c(P, Q)$ are PSPACE-complete, even if N consists strictly of constant size cyclic processes and C_N is a tree. $S_a(P, Q)$ can be decided in deterministic time d^n for some $d > 1$, and cannot be solved in deterministic time $c^{n/\log n}$ for some $c > 1$. ▌

The reductions are from LBA acceptance [GJ] and alternating linear space Turing machine acceptance. We use techniques similar to [RT] and [La]. Binary communication alphabets are needed. These worst case bounds are not surprising, however, in the case of unary alphabets we can show that:

Theorem 7: Let $N = \{P_1, P_2, \cdots, P_m\}$ be a network of $O(1)$ size cyclic processes such that C_N is a k-tree. Also let $|\Sigma_i \cap \Sigma_j| \leq 1$ for $1 \leq i \neq j \leq m$. Then:

$S_c(P, Q)$ can be decided in $O(m^k)$ time for some constant k. ▌

Our $O(m^k)$ algorithm is similar to the one we used for k-trees of tree FSPs in the previous subsection. It also makes use of the powerful combinatorial result in [Le] for integer programming with a fixed number of variables.

4. Conclusions

We presented the FSP model of communicating processes. In Section 2 we examined the complexity of deciding FSP equivalence. Theorem 1 showed that congruence can be tested in $O(n^3)$ time. If the FSPs are of bounded fanout c, then congruence can be tested in $O(c^2 n \log n)$ time using an extension of Hopcroft's algorithm [Hop]. In Theorem 2 we showed that observation equivalence can be tested in $O(n^3)$ time, even though k-observation equivalence is PSPACE-complete for any fixed $k \geq 1$. If we have r.o.u. FSPs, then k-observation equivalence is NP-complete, $k \geq 2$. Finally, we showed (Theorem 3) that testing for failure equivalence is PSPACE-complete even for restricted and observable FSPs, and NP-complete for r.o.u. FSPs.

In Section 3 we introduced composition into our model and examined the complexity of deciding potential blocking, lockout, and termination. For acyclic processes, we showed (Theorem 4) that potential blocking and termination are NP-complete even if (1) C_N is a tree and all FSPs but one are $O(1)$ linear FSPs, or (2) each FSP is an $O(1)$ tree FSP. Theorem 5 showed the no-lockout problem for acyclic processes to be PSPACE-complete. For tree FSPs and C_N a k-tree, we showed (Theorem 6) that all three problems can be decided efficiently in $O(n^k)$ time. This result uses a new algebraic technique based on possibility equivalence. Moving to cyclic processes, potential blocking and termination become PSPACE-complete, even for constant size FSPs and C_N a tree, and no-lockout requires exponential time (Proposition 2). Theorem 7 presented a subcase of potential termination reducible to integer programming with a constant number of variables.

Our algebraic technique for tree processes can be extended to cyclic processes through a slight modification of the definition of composition [KS2]. We believe that this approach will yield a practical heuristic, a claim we intend to validate empirically through the construction of a static analysis system. The front-end (an FSP editor) is near completion, and coding of the back-end has begun. The system will run on the Sun workstation or Macintosh personal computer.

Acknowledgements: Many thanks to Wrolf Courtney for his help in MacDrawing the figures, and to Dick Solo for the use of his lazer writer.

5. References

[AUY] A.V. Aho, J.D. Ullman, M. Yannakakis, "Modeling Communication Protocols by Automata", *Proceedings of the 20th Foundations of Computer Science,* San Juan, PR, pp. 267-273 (Oct. 1979).

[Br] S.D. Brookes, "On the Relationship of CCS and CSP", *Proceedings of the 10th ICALP,* Springer Verlag *LNCS 164,* pp. 85-96 (July 1983).

[BHR] S.D. Brookes, C.A.R. Hoare, A.W. Roscoe, "A Theory of Communicating Sequential Processes", *JACM 31,* pp. 560-569. (1984).

[BR] S.D. Brookes, W.C. Rounds, "Behavioural Equivalence Relations Induced by Programming Logics", *Proceedings of the 10th ICALP,* Springer Verlag *LNCS 164,* pp. 97-108 (1983).

[CS] A.K. Chandra, L.J. Stockmeyer, private communication (July 1982).

[Da] P. Darondeau, "An Enlarged Definition and Complete Axiomatization of Observational Congruence of Finite Processes", INRIA, Technical Report No. 140, Rocquencourt, France (June 1982).

[GJ] M.R. Garey, D.S. Johnson, *Computers and Intractability: A Guide to the Theory of NP-Completeness,* W.H. Freeman and Company, San Francisco (1979).

[Hol] G.J. Holzmann, "A Theory for Protocol Validation", *IEEE Transactions on Computers,* Vol. C-31, No. 8, pp. 730-738 (Aug. 1982).

[Hop] J. Hopcroft, "An n log n Algorithm for Minimizing States in a Finite Automaton", in *Theory of Machines and Computations*, pp. 189-196, Eds. Z. Kohavi and A. Paz, Academic Press, New York (1971).

[HU] J.E. Hopcroft, J.D. Ullman, *Introduction to Automata Theory, Languages, and Computation*, Addison-Wesley (1979).

[KS1] P.C. Kanellakis, S.A. Smolka, "CCS Expressions, Finite State Processes, and Three Problems of Equivalence", *Proceedings of 2nd ACM Symposium on the Principles of Distributed Computing*, Montreal, Canada, pp. 228-240 (Aug. 1983).

[KS2] P.C. Kanellakis, S.A. Smolka, "On the Analysis of Cooperation and Antagonism in Networks of Communicating Processes", *Proceedings of 4th ACM Symposium on the Principles of Distributed Computing*, Minaki, Ontario, Canada, pp. 23-38 (Aug. 1985).

[La] R. Ladner, "The Complexity of Problems in Systems of Communicating Sequential Processes", *Journal of Comput. Systems Science 21*, No. 2, pp. 179-194 (1980).

[Le] H.W. Lenstra, Jr., "Integer Programming with a Fixed Number of Variables", Mathematics Department Report 81-03, University of Amsterdam (1981).

[Mi1] R. Milner, "A Calculus of Communicating Systems", *Lecture Notes in Computer Science 92*, Springer-Verlag (1980).

[Mi2] R. Milner, "Calculi for Synchrony and Asynchrony", Department of Computer Science, University of Edinburgh, Internal Report CSR-104-82 (Feb. 1982).

[Mi3] R. Milner, "A Complete Inference System for a Class of Regular Behaviors", Department of Computer Science, University of Edinburgh, Internal Report CSR-111-82 (April 1982).

[Re] J.H. Reif, "Universal Games of Incomplete Information", *Proceedings of 11th ACM Symp. on Theory of Computing*, pp. 288-308 (1979).

[RT] T. Raeuchle, S. Toueg, "Exposure to Deadlock for Communicating Processes is Hard to Detect", Department of Computer Science, Technical Report No. TR 83-555, Cornell University, Ithaca, NY (May 1983).

[SFD] S.A. Smolka A.J. Frank, S. Debray, "Testing Protocol Robustness the CCS Way", in *Protocol Specification, Testing, and Verification, IV*, Y. Yemini, R. Strom, and S. Yemini (eds.), North Holland, pp. 93-108 (1985).

[StM] L.J. Stockmeyer, A.R. Meyer, "Word Problems Requiring Exponential Time", *Proceedings of the 5th ACM Symposium on Theory of Computing*, pp. 1-9, Austin, TX (April 1973).

Synthesizing Distributed and Parallel Programs Through Optimistic Transformations

Rob Strom and Shaula Yemini
IBM T. J. Watson Research Center
P.O. Box 218
Yorktown Heights, NY, 10598

Abstract

We propose a programming methodology for distributed systems, based upon writing programs in a high-level, implementation-independent programming language in which distribution and physical parallelism are hidden, and where the programmer sees only a "single systems image". A distributed implementation of the program is then obtained by translating the program into a lower level language, in which distribution and parallelism, as well as other implementation-dependent and performance-related details are exposed. The translation is further optimized by applying correctness-preserving program transformations.

We introduce one particular family of such program transformations called *optimistic transformations.* Optimistic transformations allow a logically serial sequence of computations C1; C2 to be executed in parallel whenever C1's effect on C2 can be guessed in advance with high probability. If the guess is wrong, C2 will have to be undone, but if the probability of a correct guess is sufficiently high, the losses due to undoing computations will be compensated by performance gains due to increased parallelism.

We give three examples of "guesses" which lead to optimistic transformations of practical value: (a) the guess that multiple iterations of a loop will not conflict, (b) the guess that exceptional program conditions will not occur, and (c) the guess that machine failures will not occur.

We demonstrate our approach by applying transformations to a particular serial program – a database "transaction-processing" program. The original program has only local data (the data of the database), no communication, and is completely serial, while the transformed program, implemented on a network of computers, has both shared and distributed data, internal parallelism, and a communication protocol between sites very similar to the classical "two-phase commit" protocol, but with improved response time.

1.0 Synthesizing Distributed and Parallel Programs through Optimistic Transformations

1.1 Introduction

A programming language presents programmers with a certain computation model. The simpler and more abstract the computation model, the easier it is for programmers to develop correct algorithms and demonstrate that they meet their specifications.

Distributed data, concurrent computations on shared data, and the possibility of hardware failures are all factors which complicate the computation model. As a result, to invent a distributed algorithm and prove it correct is still a difficult art.

We suggest that distributed programs can be designed more effectively by using a more abstract model of computation which presents a "single-system-image". Details of the underlying architecture, such as the number of physical processors, the means of communication between them, the degree of physical concurrency, and the existence of failures, are all hidden.

In order to realize such an abstract model, it is necessary to first *map* the abstract model onto the available physical hardware, and then to *optimize* the resulting implementation by transforming it into a behaviorally equivalent one which takes better advantage of the hardware.

Typical mappings include allocating logical processes to physical processors, implementing inter-process communication over shared memory or over physical links, masking processor failures by checkpointing onto stable storage, etc.

Typical optimizations relevant for distributed systems include: replicating data to reduce communication delays, retaining copies of stable storage data in main memory, performing subactions of a serial program in parallel, etc.

Individual mappings and optimizations can be tailored to particular hardware, particular performance objectives, and particular usage patterns. These mappings can be analyzed for both correctness and performance properties independent of programs to which they may eventually be applied.

1.2 Optimistic Program Transformations

1.2.1 Computation model

Our starting point will be a high-level programming language such as NIL [STR 83], which composes large systems from *modules*. Each module executes a serial program, has only local (private) data, and communicates with other modules only by message passing. There is no data sharing. Module boundaries are determined solely on the basis of software engineering principles such as low inter-module coupling, abstraction and information hiding. The language does not allow specifying any performance-related or implementation-dependent decisions since these decisions typically restrict the ability to apply program transformations.

The low-level computation model into which we map our programs includes multiple processor sites, multi-programming at each site, physical links connecting between sites, and stable storage to backup the volatile storage at each site.

1.2.2 Optimistic schedules

Optimistic program transformations convert a set of serially scheduled computations into an equivalent computation in which computations are scheduled in parallel.

Given a sequence of computations, *an optimistic schedule* allows several logically serial computations to execute *in parallel.* The increased parallelism is obtained by scheduling a computation C_n even before computations C_k, $(k < n)$ *preceding* it in the serial sequence have terminated, whenever it is possible to "guess" the effect of the preceding computations (e.g. their results or the values that they write) with a high probability of correctness.

Provided we maintain the ability to undo the effects of optimistically scheduled computations whenever the corresponding guesses prove incorrect, C_n can be executed in parallel with the preceding computations, by assuming they will have the guessed effect, and undoing when guesses prove incorrect. The optimistic schedule thus preserves the serial semantics, but allows computations which normally could not be scheduled until later to be executed earlier, thus eliminating the synchronization involved in waiting for the earlier computations to terminate before scheduling the later computations.

Whether or not optimistic scheduling is an improvement depends upon the probability of successful guessing, the savings when the guess is successful, the costs of undoing computations when the guess is unsuccessful, and the fixed costs of making computations undoable.

1.2.3 Examples of useful guesses

The following are examples of situations in which we can guess the effect of computations with a high probability of correctness, and therefore optimistic scheduling is likely to improve performance.

1. most likely value: consider the following statement:

   ```
   if p(x) then f(y) end if;
   ```

   If we know that p(x) is almost always true, we may start to execute f(y) even before the computation of p(x) has completed.

2. no-conflict guess: consider the following two statement sequences:

   ```
   Sequence A:              Sequence B:
   A1: a[i] := f(x);        B1: a[i] := f(x);
   A2: a[j] := g(y);        B2: z := f(a[j])
   ```

   When i does not equal j, either of these sequences could be executed concurrently without conflict. Therefore, if we know that the probability of i being equal to j is low, we may choose to execute the two statements of a sequence concurrently.

3. no failures: consider the following statement:

   ```
   y := f(x);
   ```

   If x is in volatile storage (storage lost upon a crash) and y is in stable storage (storage that survives crashes), a crash would cause y to become invalid (*orphaned*) since the value of x from which it was computed would be lost. One way to make sure this does not happen is to *log* (copy onto stable storage) the value of x *before* computing y. However, if crashes are very infrequent, and logging progresses asynchronously we may guess that the value of x will be logged before the next crash, and thus use the volatile value to compute y, without waiting for logging.

1.2.4 Implementing optimistic schedules

Optimistic schedules involve associating predicates called *commit guards* with computations executed on the basis of guesses. A predicate P is called a *commit guard* of an optimistically scheduled *guarded computation* C if whenever is true, C will produce the same effect as it would had it been scheduled in its proper sequence. Intuitively, P implies that the guess was successful. Commit guards must be monotonic, i.e., once a commit guard becomes true it must stay true.

If P is eventually found out to be true, then C will never need to be undone, and is said to be *committable*. If, on the other hand, P is found to be false, it is necessary to *undo* C. Until P's truth is known, C is *in doubt*. As long as a computation is in doubt, it must be possible to undo *all* its effects. Therefore any of a computation's irreversible side-effects, (e.g. printing a result, opening a cash-drawer) must be delayed by being buffered.

A computation C_2 is a *causal descendent* of C_1 if it depends on the effects of C_1, (e.g. C_2 reads variables written by C_1) or C_2 depends on the effect of any other computation which is a causal descendent of C_1. If C_2 is a causal descendent of C_1, and C_1 is guarded by P, C_2 *inherits* the commit guard P. A computation inherits the conjunction of the commit guards of *all* its causal antecedents.

When P's truth is eventually determined, it is communicated via a *commit message*. Once the commit message is received, C is by discarding the information needed to undo it, and by releasing the buffered side-effects, or *aborted* by undoing its effects and discarding the buffered side-effects.

A number of algorithms in the literature can be viewed as optimistic with suitable choices of guesses, e.g. Time Warp, [JEF 85], Optimistic Recovery [STR 84b], and concurrency control methods including time-stamping and two-phase locking, as well as so-called "optimistic" concurrency control[KUN 81].

1.3 Example: A Transaction System

A transaction processing system can be specified as a single module – the *transaction manager* – whose local data includes the database. Users of the system are independent modules which request the processing of individual *transactions* by *calling* the transaction manager, passing it a transaction request. The transaction manager continuously repeats the following sequence: (1) remove a transaction request from the queue, (2) service the request, possibly updating the database, and (3) return a response to the requestor. The order in which transactions requested by *different* users are dequeued is non-deterministic, but a new transaction is not begun until the previous one has completed. This specification reflects the usual requirement of *serializability* of transactions.

Figure 1 shows the logical process modules in such a system. These are the user processes and the transaction manager process.

Figure 2 is an example of such a transaction program, written in NIL [STR 84a]

Rq is a transaction request, which is a record consisting of a password, identification of the source account for the transfer, identification of the target account for the transfer and the transfer amount. Each iteration of the loop processes a single transaction: a funds transfer between bank accounts. Each transfer consists of first checking the validity of the password, and then performing the updates associated with the transfer. To simplify the code, we assume accounts can be overdrawn without limit.

Figure 3 shows the messages exchanged between a user requesting a transaction and the transaction manager. Message 0 is the request to perform the transaction, and r(0) is the response.

Although the serial specification of the transaction manager is simple and correct, a direct implementation as a serial process would perform very poorly because of I/O delays in reading and writing the database.

We assume that the target environment onto which we are mapping the transaction system has the following properties: 1) There are several processor sites interconnected by a communications network; 2) The database (passwords and account data) is distributed among the processor sites; 3) Both high throughput and low response time are desired. Therefore it is important not only to overlap execution of independent transactions, but also to schedule computations of a single transaction (*subactions*) in parallel wherever possible. 4) Individual sites may fail. Stable storage exists for storing recovery information. After a failure, a "live" processor will be able to promptly load the stable storage data of the failed site, perform recovery actions and resume processing.

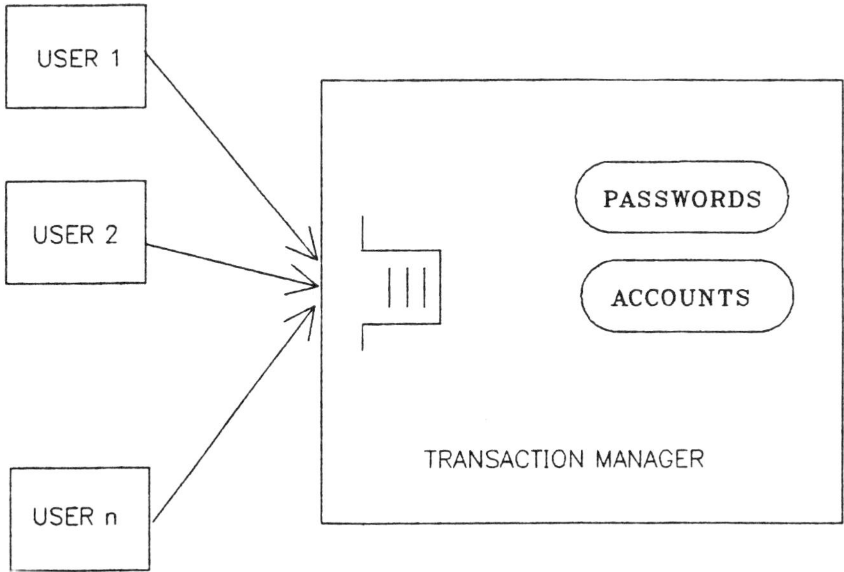

Figure 1. The processes in a NIL transaction system.

```
TransactionManager:
 declare
  Accounts: AccountRelation;
  Passwords: AuthorizationRelation(Accounts);
  . . .
 begin
  loop: forever repeat

   Receive Rq from Queue;

    if Valid ( Passwords, Rq.Password, Rq.Acctno1, Rq.Acctno2)

    then
     find FromAcct in Accounts key (Rq.Acctno1) update;
     FromAcct.Balance = FromAcct.Balance - Rq.Amount;
     find ToAcct in Accounts key (Rq.Acctno2) update;
     ToAcct.Balance = ToAcct.Balance + Rq.Amount;
     return Rq;

    else
     return Rq exception (InvalidPassword);
    end if

   end loop;

end TransactionManager;
```

Figure 2. A transaction manager written as a non-distributed, serial process.

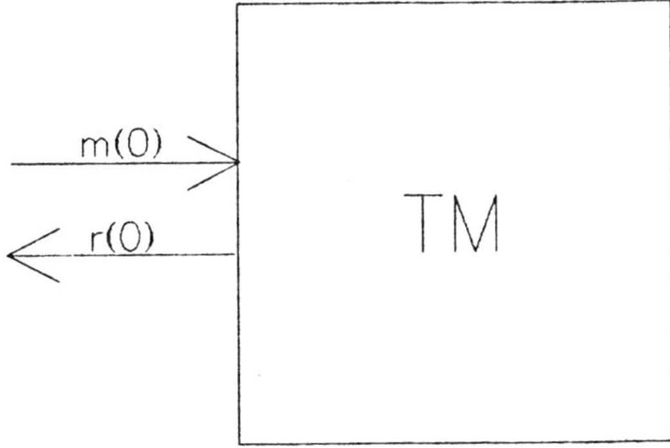

Figure 3. Messages associated with a single transaction in a non-distributed transaction system

Our implementation strategy is to first split the original single process into several processes, each running at a different site, and each managing program transformations to the resulting distributed processes to increase the degree of concurrency in the system and yield an efficient distributed implementation.

1.3.1 Transformation 1: Distributing the database

We distribute the transaction manager over three sites by partitioning its state and its computations among the sites. The state of the transaction manager consists of: the queue of requests, the passwords relation, the accounts relation and the program counter. In the particular partitioning we choose, site A holds the program counter and the queue, i.e. the control part of the original process, and will be called the *coordinator*. Site B holds the passwords, and site C holds the accounts. Sites B and C will be called *subordinates*. The computations to check passwords and update the accounts will be performed on the sites owning the respective data, and will be called the *subactions*.

Figure 4 shows the resulting distributed system. For each subaction, a pair of messages is introduced between the coordinator and the appropriate subordinate: one from the coordinator to the subordinate to initiate the subaction and pass parameters, and one from the subordinate to the coordinator to notify that the subaction is complete and to return results. In this case message 1 initiates the password validity check, and message 2 is the response from site B. Message 3 initiates the funds transfer, and message 4 is the response from site C.

1.3.2 Optimistic Transformations

The program of Figure 4 is serial, even though it has been distributed over multiple sites. We will now apply optimistic transformations to reduce synchronization and introduce concurrency into the above system in order to make it more efficient.

In each transformation, one or more sites will be performing computations guarded by a commit guard, while other sites will be asynchronously

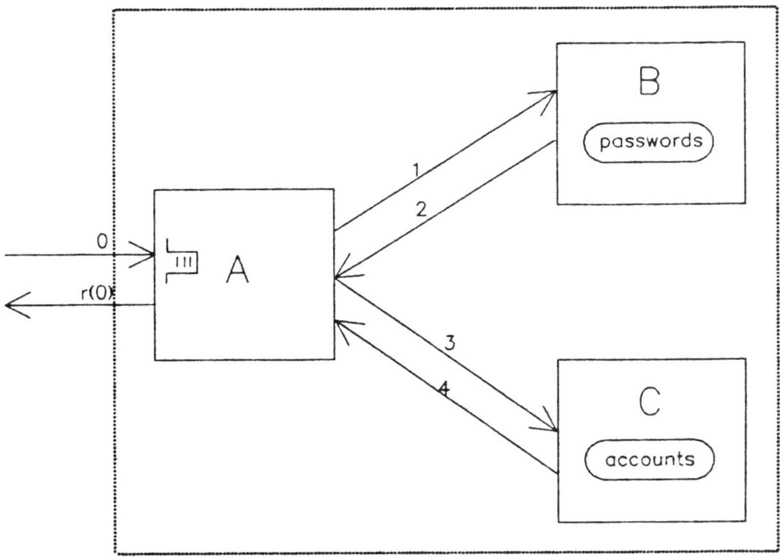

Figure 4. messages associated with a single distributed transaction:

computing whether the commit guard is true or false. The commit messages will be shown as dotted lines in the diagrams.

1.3.2.1 Transformation 2: concurrency within a single loop iteration

Our first optimistic transformation will be based on the guess that the predicate Valid will usually evaluate to true – i.e., that customers will most often supply valid passwords. If this is so, we are likely to improve response time by performing the funds transfer *concurrently* with checking the validity of the password, provided we maintain the ability to undo the transfer if the password check fails. This is the transformation associated with the first type of guess discussed earlier in "Examples of useful guesses" on page 3.

The result of applying this transformation to the transaction implementation is a new implementation in which A initiates both subactions concurrently, i.e., it sends message 3 without first waiting for message 2. Since the validity of the transfer depends on the outcome of the password check, the transfer in C must be guarded by a commit guard encoding the optimistic assumption "the password is valid": CG_{valid}. The truth of CG_{valid} implies that the password check and the account update *as executed* have an effect equivalent to the effect produced under the normal serial schedule. Since message 4 is caused by message 3, message 4 inherits the commit guard of message 3, i.e., message 4 too is guarded by CG_{valid}.

Figure 5 shows the messages in the resulting transformed implementation together with their corresponding commit guards. Once the password check has completed, A must send C a message announcing its outcome. This introduces a commit message from A to C, which appears as message 5.

The response to the transaction associated with message 0, i.e., r(0), is causally dependent on both messages 2 and 4. As a result, r(0) inherits the conjunction of their commit guards. Since 2 is unguarded, the conjunction yields CG_{valid} . Since the destination of the response is to outside our system, sending r(0) is irreversible and therefore r(0) must be buffered until the outcome of evaluating CG_{valid} is known.

1.3.2.2 Transformation 3: Concurrent Loop Iterations

The second category of useful assumption is based upon the non-conflict of successive accesses to a database. More precisely, we are guessing that

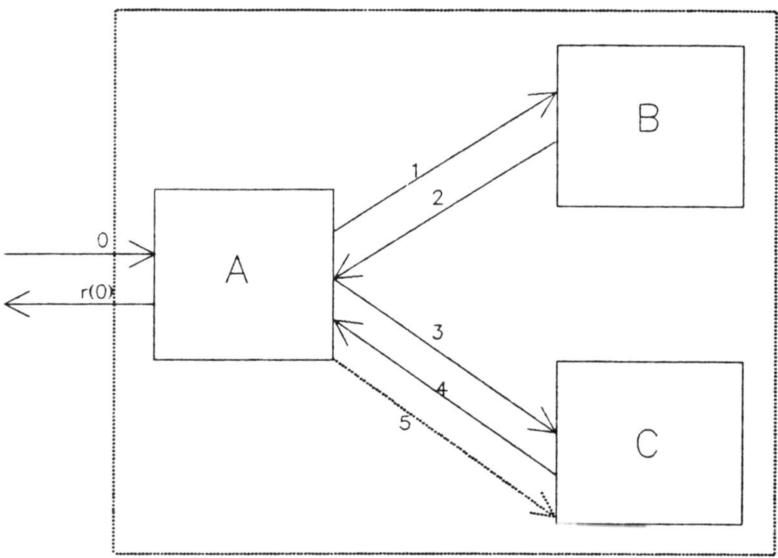

message	*commit guards*	*comments*
0	–	original request
1	–	rq check password
2	–	password valid
3	CG_{valid}	rq update accounts
4	CG_{valid}	update done
5	–	CG_{valid} true
r(0)	CG_{valid}	response to request

Figure 5. Messages associated with a single transaction after applying the internal concurrency translation: (in this and other figures, commit messages are shown with dotted lines)

the reads and writes of iteration $i + 1$ of the loop will yield the same result whether they are scheduled before or after the completion of iteration i. The optimistic schedule based upon this guess is one in which the servicing of a transaction is initiated as soon as the transaction is received by the coordinator, the computations possibly being interleaved with those of other transactions arriving at around the same time.

This is of course the transformation performed by traditional database systems using concurrency control ([BER 80], [BER 81], [KUN 81], [PAP 79], and others). For our transformed program, we may choose an arbitrary concurrency control algorithm.

We denote the concurrency control commit guard by $CG_{certified}$ which guards the initial request for performing the transaction, message 0. All computations of the transaction are causal descendents of message 0, and thus inherit its commit guard. Thus, once we apply the concurrency control transformation all of messages 0-5 and r(0) are guarded by $CG_{certified}$.

Figure 6 shows the messages in the implementation resulting from applying only the concurrency control transformation, together with their commit guards. Since we do not wish to restrict the example to a particular concurrency control algorithm we represent the concurrency control commit message as an explicit message (message 6) from an unspecified sender to the coordinator of the transaction. The coordinator then relays this message to the subordinate sites using commit messages 7 to site B and 8 to site C. In the case in which two-phase locking is the concurrency control mechanism, no message is needed at all in the case in which the transaction commits, since a transaction which successfully completes without blocking is automatically certified.

1.3.2.3 Transformation 4: Recovery From Site Failures

Up to now, we have assumed that sites are perfectly reliable. In reality, sites may crash, in which case the volatile storage used for high speed data access is lost, and only stable storage survives. Our third optimistic transformation is Optimistic Recovery ([STR 84b]).

In optimistic recovery, computation at each site proceeds independently of saving the site's volatile state onto stable storage. Since all computations are message-driven, the state after processing the nth message can always be reconstructed by loading a prior full state, and then re-executing

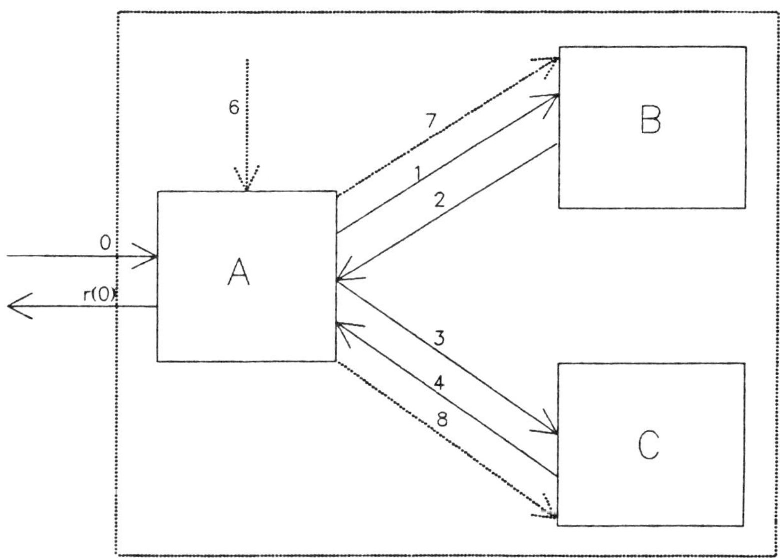

message	*commit guards*	*comments*
0	$CG_{certified}$	original rq
1	$CG_{certified}$	rq check password
2	$CG_{certified}$	password valid
3	$CG_{certified}$	rq update accounts
4	$CG_{certified}$	update done
6	–	$CG_{certified}$ true
7	–	$CG_{certified}$ true
8	–	$CG_{certified}$ true
r(0)	$CG_{certified}$	response to rq

Figure 6. Messages associated with applying concurrency control: Since there exist many possible algorithms for evaluating $CG_{certified}$, we leave the choice open, and therefore do not show a specific origin for message 6.

the program with saved (*logged*) copies of subsequent messages through message *n*. Each site periodically saves full-state checkpoints, and also logs its input messages in the order received. The "optimism" results from the fact that computation and communication with other sites occur without waiting for the messages which caused these computations to be logged.

Computations causally dependent on unlogged messages have a commit guard predicate which asserts that these messages will eventually be logged. Each site *S* encodes this commit guard as a *dependency vector* containing the number of the latest message from each other site on which *S*'s current computation depends.

As sites log input messages, they broadcast commit messages. By accumulating commit messages, a site can construct a *log vector*, which records how many messages each site in the system has logged. The log vector enables each site to determine which of its computations have true recovery commit guards. These are the computations whose dependency vector is pointwise less than or equal to the current log vector, i.e., all their causal antecedents are already known to be logged.

If a site fails, and the failure has occurred before the site has made all of its input messages recoverable, and if other sites have executed computations which causally depend on the lost messages, the commit guards of these dependent computations will be false, and they will therefore be aborted. On the other hand, if a computation depends upon input messages of other sites, and if these have all been made recoverable, then that computation may be committed. [The full paper will provide more details of how this information is determined].

We note the following causal dependencies of the messages exchanged in our distributed system:

Message r(0), the response to the user, is causally dependent on messages 0, 2 and 4 received by A, 1 received by B (since 2 is causally dependent upon 1) and 3 received by C (since 4 is causally dependent upon 3). R(0) is thus known to be recoverable as soon as it can be determined that A has logged all of 0, 2 and 4, B has logged 1 and C has logged 3. Thus, r(0) is guarded by the commit guard $CG_{(0,1,2,3,4)}$*recoverable* denoting that all of messages 0-4 have been logged. R(0) can thus be sent out to the initiator of the transaction as soon as these messages are known to have been logged by their respective receivers.

Figure 7 shows the messages resulting from applying optimistic recovery to the distributed transaction system, together with their commit guards. Since A knows when it has logged its own messages, the additional messages introduced by applying an optimistic recovery transformation to our distributed transaction system, are message 9 from B to A notifying that 1 is logged, and message 10 from C to A notifying that 3 is logged.

1.3.3 Composing All 3 Transformations vs. Classical 2 Phase Commit

We have taken a serial implementation of the example of Figure 2 on page 17 and applied one translation partitioning the data, and three optimistic transformations. We can now compose all these transformations to yield a distributed implementation (transformation 1), supporting parallel subactions (transformation 2), concurrency control (transformation 3), and recovery (transformation 4).

Figure 8 shows the messages in an implementation derived by applying all four transformations in combination. Note that commit messages can be "piggybacked", i.e., combined into a single message. (For example, 5 and 8 have been combined into a single message) There are several interesting points to note about this example:

First, the resulting protocol is similar to classical "two-phase commit" ([GRA 78]) for distributed databases, using the same number of messages, except that the version we have synthesized has better response time than does classical two-phase commit. In standard two-phase commit, subordinates send the "prepared" message only after having completed their respective subactions, *and* after having completed logging their results to stable storage. Using our protocol subordinates can send the results of subactions early, before logging them to stable storage. The response to the user can be released as soon as subordinates have logged the messages assigning them their respective subactions, (messages 1 and 3), and the coordinator has logged the initial transaction and the results of the subactions (messages 0, 2 and 4). The subordinates could have logged messages 1 and 3 and communicated that fact to the coordinator long before the subactions have completed. Recall however that in the optimistic recovery transformation, we are assuming that there will be no long-term network partitioning. While this assumption is easy to satisfy for a local area network, it may

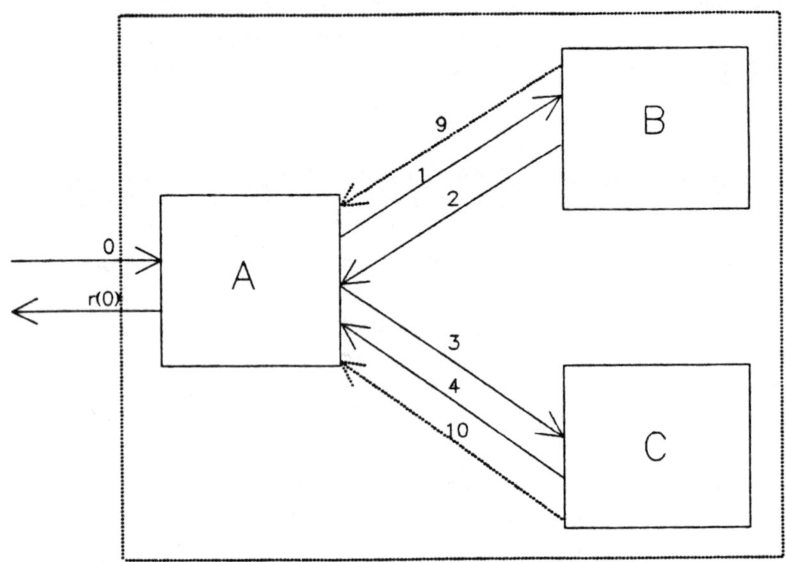

message	*commit guards*	comments
0	–	original rq
1	$CG_{(0)recoverable}$	check password
2	$CG_{(0,1)recoverable}$	password valid
3	$CG_{(0)recoverable}$	update accounts
4	$CG_{(0,3)recoverable}$	update done
9	–	$CG_{(1)recoverable}$ true
10	–	$CG_{(3)recoverable}$ true
r(0)	$CG_{(0,1,2,3,4)recoverable}$	response to user

Figure 7. Messages in protocol after applying optimistic recovery transformation

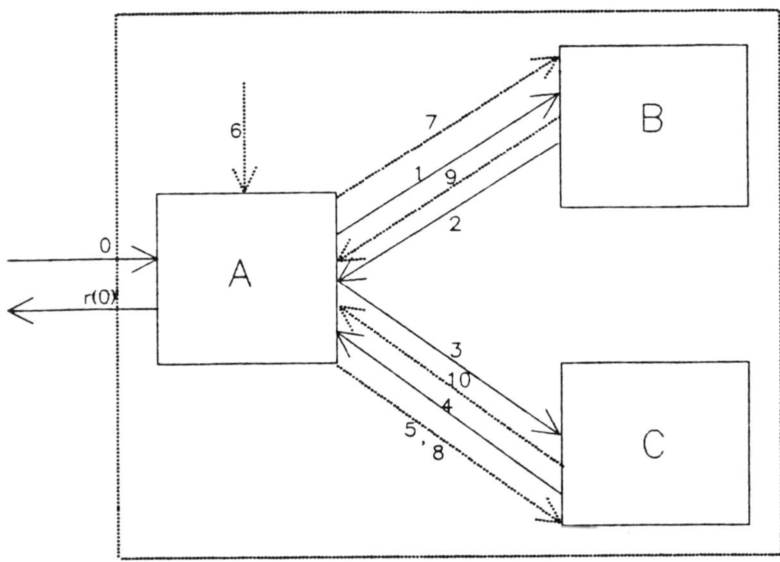

message	***commit guards***
0	$CG_{certified}$
1	$CG_{certified}$ & $CG_{(0)recoverable}$
2	$CG_{certified}$ & $CG_{(0,1)recoverable}$
3	CG_{valid} & $CG_{certified}$ & $CG_{(0)recoverable}$
4	CG_{valid} & $CG_{certified}$ & $CG_{(0,3)recoverable}$
5	$CG_{certified}$ & $CG_{(0,1,2)recoverable}$
6	$CG_{(0,1,2,3,4)recoverable}$
7	$CG_{(0,1,2,3,4,6)recoverable}$
8	$CG_{(0,1,2,3,4,6)recoverable}$
9, 10	/
r(0)	CG_{valid} & $CG_{certified}$ & $CG_{(0,1,2,3,4,6)recoverable}$

Figure 8. Messages in the protocol obtained by applying all three optimistic transformations.

be hard to satisfy for a network that is geographically dispersed.

Secondly, our synthesized protocol has the advantage of being decomposable. For instance, for certain environments we may wish to have concurrency control without recovery, or recovery without concurrency control. The latter, enables us to make arbitrary distributed systems reliable, without having to redesign them as transaction systems.

1.4 Acknowledgements

We would like to acknowledge the helpful comments of C. Mohan and Fred Schneider who reviewed earlier drafts of this paper. R. Bernstein assisted in the formatting of this paper.

1.5 References

[BAR 78] Bartlett, J. F., "A 'NonStop' Operating System", *Eleventh Hawaii International Conference on System Sciences*, 1978.

[BER 80] Bernstein, P. A., and Goodman, N. "Timestamp based algorithms for concurrency control in distributed database systems", *Proc 6th Int. Conf. Very Large Data Bases*, Oct. 1980

[BER 81] Bernstein, P. A., and Goodman, N. "Concurrency Control in Distributed Database Systems", *Computing Surveys*, Vol. 13, No. 2., June 1981.

[BER 83] Bernstein, P. A., and Goodman, N. "The Failure and Recovery Problem for Replicated Databases", *Proc. 2nd ACM SIGACT/SIGOPS Symposium on Principles of Distributed Computing*, Montreal, Canada, August 1983.

[BOR 83] "A Message System Supporting Fault Tolerance", *9th ACM Symp. on Operating Systems Principles*, October 1983.

[GRA 78] Gray, J. "Notes on Data Base Operating Systems", *Operating Systems: An Advanced Course*, in *Lecture Notes in Computer Science*, v. 60, Springer-Verlag, 1978.

[GRA 81] Gray, J., et al., "The Recovery Manager of the System R Database Manager", *Computing Surveys*, Vol. 13, No. 2, June 1981.

[HOA 78] Hoare, C. A. R., "Communicating Sequential Processes", CACM 21:8, August 1978.

[KUN 81] Kung, H. T., and Robinson, J. T., "On Optimistic Methods for Concurrency Control", *ACM Transactions on Database Systems*, v. 6, no. 2, June 1981.

[JEF 85] Jefferson, D. "Virtual Time", *ACM Transactions on Programming Languages and Systems*, July 1985.

[LAM 78] Lamport, L. "Time clocks, and the ordering of events in a distributed system", *CACM*, vol. 21, July 1978.

[LAM 79] Lampson, B. and Sturgis, H. "Crash recovery in a distributed storage system", Xerox PARC, Palo Alto Ca, April 1979.

[MOH 83] Mohan, C., Lindsay, B., "Efficient Commit Protocols for the Tree of Processes Model of Distributed Transactions", *Proc. 2nd ACM SIGACT/SIGOPS Symposium on Principles of Distributed Computing*, Montreal, Canada, August 1983.

[PAP 79] Papadimitriou, C. H., "Serializability of concurrent updates", JACM 26, 4, October 1979.

[RUS 80] Russell, D. L., "State Restoration in Systems of Communicating Processes", *IEEE Transactions on Software Engineering*, SE-6(2), pp. 193-194 (March 1980).

[STR 84b] Strom, R. E., and Yemini, S. "Optimistic Recovery: An Asynchronous Approach to Fault Tolerance in Distributed Systems" to appear in proc. FTCS-14, June 1984, also available as IBM Research Report RC 10353.

Development Tools For Communication Protocols*

Nihal Nounou and Yechiam Yemini
Computer Science Department
Columbia University
New York, New York 10027

ABSTRACT

The past decade has witnessed a surge in research efforts aimed at developing tools to aid the designer of communication protocols. Most of these efforts have been directed towards designing individual tools. Recently, however, there has been a growing interest in building development environments that support an integrated set of such tools. This paper presents a survey of commonly used protocol development tools. Two categories of protocol development tools are examined: construction tools to successively refine communication protocols from specifications to working systems and validation tools to assess whether the refinements meet functional and performance protocol objectives. Construction tools surveyed include tools for specification, synthesis, and implementation. Validation tools surveyed include tools for formal verification, performance analysis and testing. A simple send-and-wait protocol is used as an example throughout the paper.

*This research was supported in part by the Defense Advanced Research Projects Agency under contract N00039-84-C-0165, the New York State Center for Advanced Technology in Computers and Information Systems under NYSSTF CAT(83)-8, and a grant from AT&T.

Revised February 1986.

1 Introduction

In a *computer network*, distributed processes can communicate and share information through message-exchange. Such communication involves a rather complex set of problems since the distributed processes are allowed to concurrently access shared resources and to proceed asynchronously. Moreover, they may be executed by heterogeneous processors, and their communication channels are often unreliable -- they might lose, duplicate, reorder, and/or corrupt messages. *Communication protocols* are thus required to regulate the communication between distributed processes in a computer network. They constitute a set of rules and a set of message formats. The reader is referred to [Tane 81] for a tutorial on protocols.

The International Standards Organization (ISO) has proposed a reference model of protocol architecture for Open Systems Interconnection (OSI) (described in [Zimm 80]). The model has seven hierarchical layers illustrated in Fig. 1; protocols at layers 1 through 4 are referred to as *low-level protocols* and those at layers 5 through 7 as *high-level protocols*. The purpose of each protocol layer is to provide *services* to the layers above while concealing the details of the layers below. A description of these services including the service interaction primitives, their possible orders and their possible parameter values, is referred to as the layer's *service specification*. A protocol designer is also concerned with the internal structure and operation of the layer's black box which is illustrated in Fig. 2.

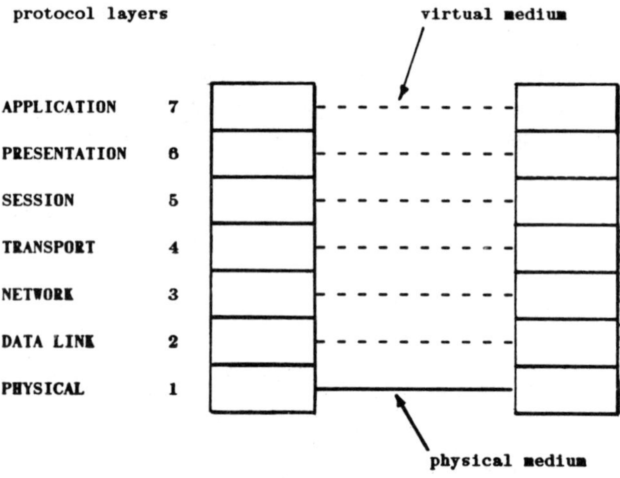

Figure 1: Illustration of protocol layers

In this figure each protocol process (also referred to in the literature as component, module, entity, and party) resides typically at a different site and communicates with other *peer* (i.e., neighboring) processes according to the protocol rules. These rules describe how the processes respond to commands from the upper layer, messages from other peer processes (through the lower layer), and internally initiated actions (e.g., time-outs); they are referred to as the *protocol specification*. Finally, the protocol specification refined into actual code describing aspects of internal behavior related to inter-process communication and detailed external behavior of each protocol process is referred to as *protocol implementation*.

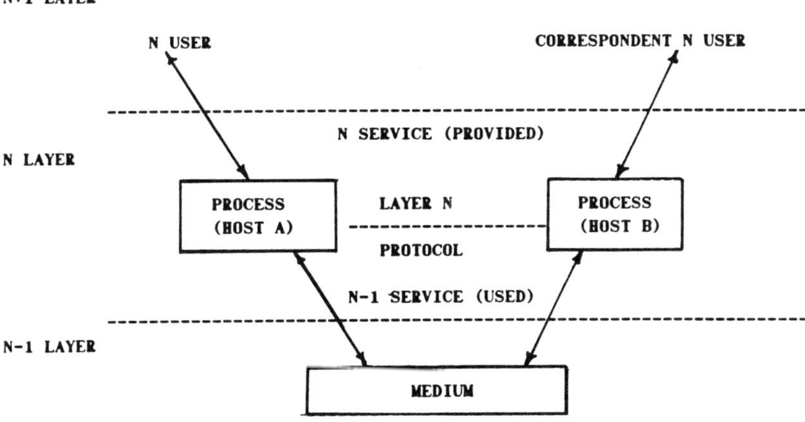

Figure 2: A local view of a protocol layer

This successive refinement of protocols indicates a phased approach to their development. In such a framework of phased development (for details see in particular [Boeh 76, Lehm 80, Oste 80]) there are three main phases: *service statement*, *protocol design*, and *implementation*. *Development tools* are required to support the evolution of protocols from specifications into working systems. This survey covers two kinds of protocol development tools: *construction tools* for developing and refining protocol specifications and *validation tools* to assess how a specification meets its functional (e.g., deadlock freedom) and performance (e.g., maximizing throughput) design objectives. Although development tools for general software systems have been studied extensively (see for instance [Lond 80, Ridd 80, Wass 81], their application to protocols is not straightforward. Protocols involve processes that are distributed, concurrent, asynchronous, communicating through unreliable transmission mediums, and whose behavior is often time-dependent. These features affect protocol development tools in various ways. First, the communication nature of protocols becomes the prime concern underlying the tools. The basic objective of protocol validation tools, for example, is to assure robustness and efficiency of the communication between the protocol processes. Second, timing requirements as well as functional requirements of protocol behavior should be considered in the various tools. This integration provides a more realistic and relatively simpler description of protocol behavior than when only functional requirements are considered. Third, tools used for general software systems might have varied importance for protocols. One example of a tool that is rarely used for general software, but that is becoming highly desirable for protocols is *certification* of independently developed protocol implementations to ensure that they comply with a standard, and thus will be able to internetwork.

Recently there has been a growing interest in building protocol development environments that integrate the various development tools required throughout the entire protocol development. An ideal protocol development environments should encompass a comprehensive set of tools and a methodology for their use. Therefore, a prime objective of this survey is to examine the **complete** set of commonly used protocol development tools. Other surveys concerned with only subsets of the tools examined in this paper can be found in [Boch 80a, Dant 80, Hail 81, Suns 81, Diaz 82, Schw 82, Suns 83].

The paper is organized as follows: in sections 2 through 4 we survey the *construction tools* including specification, synthesis, and implementation, respectively. Sections 5 through 7 are surveys of *validation tools* including formal verification, performance analysis, and testing respectively. Finally, in section 8 we present some conclusions and remarks on possible directions for future research.

2 Specification Tools

Specification tools are construction tools required to describe a protocol at each of its three development phases as a service specification, protocol specification, and protocol implementation. High-level languages are used for describing implementation specifications. These will not be discussed here; throughout the rest of the paper we limit our discussion to specification tools required for the service statement and protocol design phases.

Experience has shown that protocols specified informally are error-prone even when augmented with some graphical illustrations. For example, 21 errors have been found [West 78a] in the informal specification of the X.21 protocol [X.21 76] (a protocol at layer 2 in Fig. 1); they are generally due to the ambiguity and incompleteness of the informal specifications. Formal specifications, on the other hand, are concise, clear, complete, unambiguous, and often used as the basis for other protocol development tools. Protocol development tools are indeed highly dependent on the specification tool used. For example, a different verification tool might be required if the specification tool used in the protocol environment is changed.

Throughout this section and subsequent sections, a simple send-and-wait protocol will be used as an example. The basic function of the protocol is to provide robust message transfer between a source process C and a destination process D over an unreliable transmission medium. There are three distributed processes involved in the protocol: a sender S, a receiver R, and a transmission medium M. The operation of the protocol is as follows. If the sender is idle and receives a new message m from a source C, it sends it to the receiver through the medium which either delivers or loses it. The sender waits for an acknowledgment a to arrive, upon which it again waits for a new message from the source. A new message arriving at the sender that is busy waiting for the acknowledgment of the previous message, is buffered. To recover from cases of message and acknowledgment loss, if the sender does not receive an acknowledgment after a time-out period T, it retransmits the same message and then waits again for either an acknowledgment or a time-out. The receiver process waits for the new message *m* to arrive from the medium, after which it delivers it to a destination D and then sends an acknowledgment *a* to the sender through the medium. For the sake of simplicity, it is assumed that the medium does not lose acknowledgments, and that the time-out period is ideally set such that the probability that a time-out occurs only after a message is lost is equal to 1. If the sender and receiver processes are at one protocol layer N, then the source and destination processes would be at the next higher layer N+1 representing the user of the services of the layer N, and the medium process represents the next lower layer N-1.

It should be noted that this is not the most efficient data transfer protocol. For example, in order to make full use of the medium's bandwidth, a more sophisticated protocol would send several messages successively instead of one at a time. In this case it is necessary to assign sequence numbers to messages in order to differentiate between them.

In the following section, requirements of specification tools for protocols are outlined, the various specification tools are surveyed in section 2.2, and a taxonomy of the these tools is proposed in section 2.3.

2.1 Requirements of Specification Tools for Protocols

The key requirements of a specification tool to adequately express protocols include the following.

1. Supporting abstract descriptions such that implementation-dependent parts can be left unspecified.

2. Supporting modeling of concurrency.

3. Supporting modeling of nondeterminism, which is a behavior exhibited typically by protocols (e.g., the sender is waiting for either the arrival of an acknowledgment or time-out in the send-and-wait protocol example).

4. Supporting the description of the two categories of functions involved in protocols: *control functions* involving connection initialization and inter-process synchronization, and *data transfer* functions involving processing of messages texts and related issues such as message sequence numbering.

5. Supporting modular descriptions to facilitate readability and ease of use of specifications.

Since specification tools often are the basis of other development tools, they must also include the following features to facilitate their application:

1. Executability of the specification to facilitate its direct simulation, and the automation of the implementation process.

2. Providing constructs for expressing functional properties of protocols, thus facilitating their automated formal verification.

3. Supporting the specification of the timing requirements of protocols. Since the behavior of protocol is often time-dependent, their correct

functioning might depend on certain timing requirements. For example, the specification of the value of the time-out period in a protocol with such a feature greatly affects its function. If the the time-out period is too short, the network would be flooded with duplicate messages and the protocol would enter an infinite cycle of time-outs.

4. Providing constructs for expressing performance properties of protocols (including properties of transmission mediums such as bit error probability and desired performance such as bounds on throughput and delay measures), thus facilitating automated performance analysis.

5. Supporting the clear definition of the interfaces between the protocol layer concerned and the layers above and below to allow for separate testing of the implementation of each protocol layer.

The extent to which a specification tool exhibits the first set of requirements is examined in section 2.2. In section 2.3 we examine the extent with which the various classes of specification tools based on the proposed taxonomy in that section support the second set of requirements.

2.2 Survey of Specification Tools

2.2.1 Finite State Machines

A finite state machine (FSM) consists of the following components: 1) finite set of states, 2) finite set of input commands, 3) transition functions (command×state→state), and 4) an initial state. A FSM is a natural choice for describing protocol processes whose behavior consist primarily of simple processing in response to commands to or from peer processes in the same layer, and/or the upper and lower protocol layers. A FSM responds to an command according to the input and its current state representing the history of past commands. FSM's were used in early work on specification of protocols [Bart 69, Suns 75].

Consider using FSM's to describe a protocol specification. Each local process involved in the protocol can then be modeled as a FSM. The behavior resulting from the concurrent execution of these local processes can be obtained by considering all possible interleaving of the executions of these processes. It is in effect a global description of the operation of the protocol layer. To describe the mode of communication between the distributed processes, three approaches are possible. The simplest assumes that the distributed processes communicate synchronously through *rendezvous interactions* (also referred to as *direct coupling* by Bochmann [Boch 78]). That is, the process issuing a send event should wait for the destination process to issue a corresponding receive event (and vice versa) at which time a rendezvous is said to occur and message exchange takes place. Since messages are not buffered in this approach, no modeling of channels between the processes is required. This approach is too restrictive for protocols in which the communicating processes operate asynchronously, or for protocols in which the behavior of the transmission channel is integral to its operation. In the second approach, channels are modeled *implicitly* by specifying their characteristics such as queueing policy (e.g., FIFO) and bound on the number of messages allowed in transit at any one time. Protocols with a number of messages in transit can thus be modeled using this approach. The FSM's specifications in this approach are referred to as *communicating finite state machines* [West 78a, Goud

84a]. In the third approach, channels behavior are specified explicitly as FSM's in which case only channels with a low bound on the number of messages can be feasible assumed. Even then their FSM specifications are considerably more complex than in the second approach.

Following the latter approach, specifications of the three communicating processes in the send-and-wait protocol are shown in Fig. 3. In this figure, states are represented by circles, transitions by directed arcs, the initial state is the state labeled 1, and input commands are either events with an overbar denoting send events or events with an underbar denoting receive events. Events' subscripts are used such that for event $e_{i,j}$ the flow of data is from process i to process j. Non-deterministic behavior at a state, for example the choice between receiving a time-out or an acknowledgment at state 3 of the sender, is modeled by multiple output arcs from that state. A service specification for the same protocol is shown in Fig. 4 in which the service primitive events GET and DELIVER between the protocol system and its users (source and destination processes) and their order, are described.

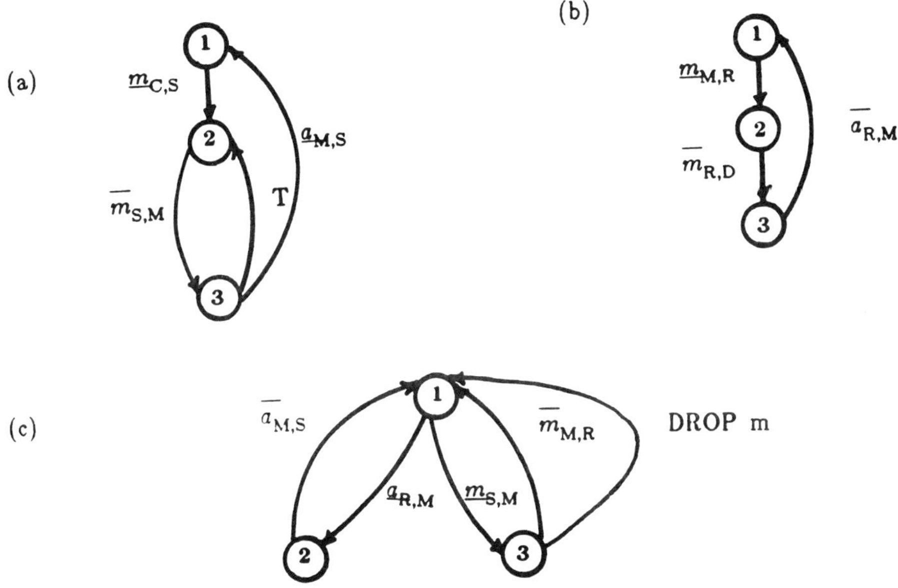

Figure 3: A protocol specification for the send-and-wait protocol using FSM's (a) Sender (b) Receiver (c) Medium

In specifying this simple protocol, and control functions of more complex real-life protocols, e.g., the X.21 interface [West 78b], FSM specifications have proven adequate. They are simple, easy to understand and analyze. They fail, however, to describe data transfer functions that include decision (e.g., priority of messages) or timing considerations (e.g., specification of a time-out period). This is because no mechanisms

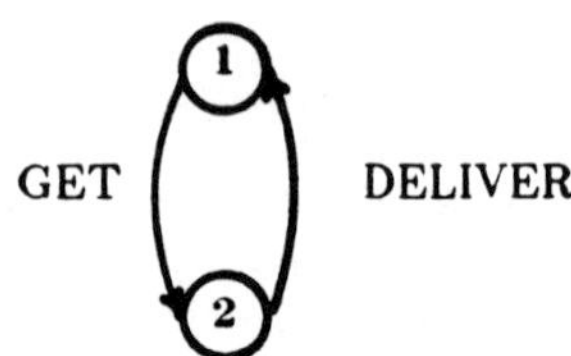

Figure 4: A service specification for the send-and-wait protocol using FSM's

are provided for expressing such features. Moreover, in order to specify messages with sequence numbers using this approach, a state is required for each possible value of a pending message and/or sequence number. This leads to an explosion in the number of states; a phenomena known as the *state explosion problem*. Extensions of the model, as described in the following section, alleviate most of these limitations.

2.2.2 State Machine Models

State machines are FSM's augmented with variables and high-level language statements. These statements are associated with transitions and can refer to the variables and input commands. They are either predicates representing conditions for the transition to occur, or actions to be performed upon its occurrence. The state of the machine is represented either by the values of all the variables, or by one of the variables. Consider, for example, extending the send-and-wait protocol with a binary sequence number mechanism for messages so that the receiver can distinguish between messages and their duplicates. A partial state machine specification (whose constructs are adapted from [Boch 83a]) of the sender process of this extended protocol, is given in Fig. 5. In this specification a variable representing the current message sequence number should be defined at the sender and the receiver. The transition out of a sender's state in which it is waiting for an acknowledgment could have a predicate stating that it should be not corrupted and its sequence number is the one expected; and an action that increments the sequence number of the next message to send.

Bochmann and Gesci [Boch 77a] first used this specification model to specify a simple data transfer protocol and later to specify the HDLC [Boch 77b] and X.25 [Boch 79] protocols. Various other specification systems based on this model have been also developed. They differ essentially in the way they structure the protocol system into subprocesses which are then specified as state machines.

A state machine model proposed by the ISO TC97/SC16/WG1 subgroup B on formal description techniques (FDT) [Iso 83a, Boch 84] employs Pascal-like constructs in extending FSM's. Channels are specified separately from the protocol processes using abstract data types [Gutt 78]. Certain queuing mechanisms can be modeled and time delays before transitions can be specified.

A Specification and Description Language (SDL) [Rock 81] which is primarily represented graphically has been proposed by another standard body, the International

```
module Sender

var
  state : (state1, state2, state3);
       (* same states labels as in Fig. 3(a) *)


  corrupted : boolean;

  next-message-to-send : integer;

  ack-received : integer;
  .
  .

trans    (*  transitions are described in the
             general form of a predicate given by
             when <input command> provided
             <boolean expression> from
             <current state>, followed by an
             action given by to <next state>
             begin <statement> end; *)
     .
     .
     .
     when RECEIVE-A
     provided {not(corrupted)
     and ack-received = next-message-to-send}
     from state3
     begin
          next-message-to-send :=
             (next-message-to-send + 1) mod 2;
     end;
     to state1
     .
     .
     .
  end module Sender
```

Figure 5: A partial state machine specification of the sender process of a modified send-and-wait protocol with binary sequence numbers

Consultative Committee for Telephones and Telegraphs (CCITT). Specifications of channels and timing are not supported. Dickson [Dick 80a], [Dick 80b] has used SDL to specify the packet level of the X.25 interface [X.25 80].

Examples of other works based on the state machine model for specification were reported by Schwabe [Schw 81a], Divito [Divi 82] and Shankar and Lam [Shan 84]. These efforts are distinguished in the following. Schwabe differentiates between the specification of the topology describing the connectivity of the processes from the specification of the protocol processes. This feature could be especially desirable in the specification of high level protocols. Divito uses buffer histories to record process interactions. This facilitates the specification of certain desirable protocol properties such as the number of messages sent is the same as those received whereas other properties involving order of messages in the histories, for example, are not as naturally expressed. Shankar and Lam allow time variables to be included and time operations to age them. This facilitates the specification of certain protocol real-time requirements such as an upper bound on the time a message can occupy a transmission channel; a requirement that is needed for the correct functioning of many network layer protocols (those at layer 3 in Fig. 1).

Combining the two formalisms of FSM's and high-level languages provides a rich specification tool in which one can express the syntax and the semantics of protocols. On the other hand, such a combination is informal and there is no rule of how much of each to use.

2.2.3 Formal Grammars and Sequence Expressions

A formal grammar is defined by a set of *terminal symbols*, a set of *nonterminal symbols*, a *start symbol* and a set of *production rules*. The nonterminal symbols are defined recursively in terms of each other and terminal symbols using the production rules. The start symbol belongs to the set of nonterminal symbols and denotes the language generated by the grammar. In a formal grammar specification of a protocol, nonterminal symbols denote states, terminal symbols denote transitions and operations (e.g., nondeterministic composition), the start symbol denotes protocol behaviors generated by the grammar, and production rules define *how* the various protocol behaviors are generated. A formal grammar specification of the sender process of the send-and-wait protocol is given in Fig. 6. It is a direct translation of its FSM in Fig. 3(a) with terminal symbols (represented by upper-case letters) denoting input commands and non-terminal symbols (represented by lower-case letters) denoting states.

```
G = {V,T,S,P},

where the set of nonterminal symbols
V = {state1,state2,state3},
the set of terminal symbols
T = {GET-M,SEND-M,T,RECEIVE-A},
the start symbol S is state1, and
the set of production rules P is given by

state1 ::= GET-M state2

state2 ::= SEND-M state3

state3 ::= T state2
         ! RECEIVE-A state1

  ''!'' denotes nondeterministic composition.
```

Figure 6: A formal grammar specification for the sender process of the send-and-wait protocol

Since regular grammars and FSM's are equivalent, they share the same limitations. The state explosion problem is manifested here as an explosion in the number of production rules. To overcome this problem, Harangozo [Hara 77] used a regular grammar in which indices are added to terminals and nonterminals to allow the representation of sequence numbers. A formal grammar specification of HDLC can be found in [Hara 77]. Teng and Liu [Teng 78] used a context-free grammar, which provides more expressive power than regular grammars. They also uses a shuffle operation to integrate grammars defining processes in the same protocol layer by computing all possible interleaving of their behavior, and a substitution operation to integrate grammars defining different protocol layers by substituting terminal symbols in the grammar of the high-level protocol by nonterminal symbols in the grammar of the low-level protocol to form a new integrated grammar.

These two approaches to formal grammar specification for protocols do not support the specification of any predicates or actions associated with protocol behavior. This limitation is overcome by Anderson and Landweber [Ande 84] by using context-free attribute grammars, which are formal grammars in which terminal and nonterminal symbols have attributes associated with them. The terminal symbol SEND-M in the send-and-wait protocol can have the attribute *address* associated with it to determine the address of the addressee. The semantics of protocol operation can then be specified in terms of attribute assignment statements associated with production rules.

In contrast to formal languages, sequence expressions define directly the valid sequences resulting from protocol execution and not how they are generated. A protocol behavior is described in one expression where no nonterminal symbols are used. The sender process of the send-and-wait protocol can be specified as a sequence expression given by

$$\text{SENDER} = \{\text{GET-M} \rightarrow \text{SEND-M} \rightarrow \{\text{T} \rightarrow \text{SEND-M}\}^{*} \rightarrow \text{RECEIVE-A}\}$$

where operations "*", "→" , and "+" denote the Kleene star, sequential composition, and nondeterministic choice operations, respectively.

Sequence expressions have been used by Bochmann for service specification [Boch 80b]. Other examples include work done by Schindler, et al. [Schi 80, Schi 81] to specify the X.25 layer 3 protocol.

2.2.4 Petri Net-Based Models

A Petri Net (PN) (see [Pete 77] for a comprehensive survey) graph contains two kinds of nodes: *places* and *transitions*. Directed arcs connect places and transitions. Arcs from places to transitions are called input arcs, and arcs from transitions to places are called output arcs. The execution of the net is controlled by the position and movement of *tokens* which reside in the places. The distribution of tokens in the net at any certain time, known as a *marking*, specifies the state of the net at that time. A PN specification includes a PN graph and an initial marking. A transition in the graph is *enabled* if there are tokens residing in all the input places (i.e., places connected with the transition through input arcs). It can fire any time after it is enabled, upon which tokens are removed from input places and deposited into output places of the transition. PN's are in many ways similar to FSM's, with places in a PN corresponding to states or inputs in a FSM and transitions in a PN corresponding to transitions in a FSM. However unlike FSM's, PN's can directly model interactions between the concurrent processes by merging output arcs from one process to an input arc of another process. Also the concurrent execution of the distributed processes is naturally captured by the presence of more than one token in the net -- a token for each distributed process.

In a protocol modeled as a petri net, the presence of a token in a place typically represents that the protocol is waiting for a certain condition to be satisfied, and the firing of a transition represents the occurrence of an event enabled by the condition. Examples of using PN's to model protocols can be found in [Post 76, Azem 78, Dant 80]. A PN specification of the send-and-wait protocol is given in Fig. 7. Places are represented as circles, transitions as bars and tokens as filled circles. It should be noted that this PN specification follows the assumption that time-out is ideally set such that a time-out occurs only after a loss of a message or an acknowledgment and the assumption that acknowledgments are not lost.

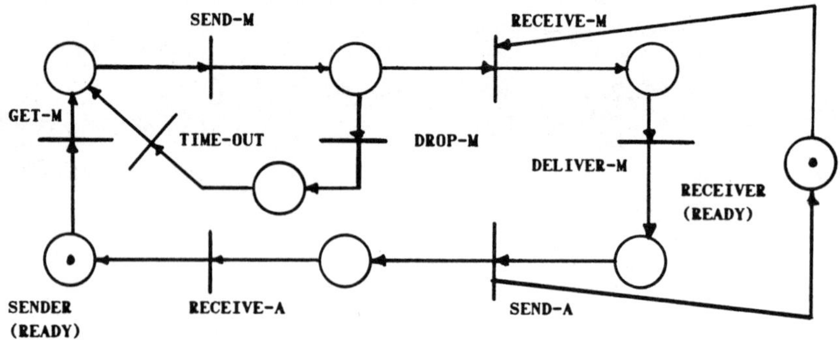

Figure 7: A send-and-wait protocol specification using petri nets

Similar to FSM's, PN's cannot adequately model complex data transfer of protocol without suffering from explosion of the net size, or timing considerations such as time-out. Two major extensions to PN's that add to their power in modeling protocols lead to *hybrid PN's* and *timed PN's*. The price for these extensions is more complex validation.

Hybrid Petri Nets

Hybrid petri nets are extended PN's in which tokens can have identities and transitions can have predicates and actions associated to them. Adding predicates to PN's produces *predicate/transition* nets formalized by Genrich and Lautenbach [Genr 79], where transitions fire only after they are enabled and their associated predicate (i.e., some condition in terms of tokens values) is true. Berthelot and Terrat [Bert 82] used predicate/transition nets to model the ECMA (European Computer Manufacturer Association) [Ecma 80] transport protocol.

Adding actions to predicate/transition nets produces *predicate/action* nets. Actions are associated with transitions such that when a transition fires, the action is executed and new tokens are put in the output places. For example, data transfer protocols can be modeled as predicate/action nets such that the receiving of a message *m* with certain parameters is described in a predicate, and the sending of *m* is described in the action [Diaz 82].

Keller's model for parallel programs [Kell 76] and numerical PN (NPN) [Symo 80] belong to this category. Keller divides systems into a control part and a data part, with places representing control states and transitions representing the changes between states. Variations of this model were used in modeling protocols [Boch 77a, Azem 78, Baue 82]. NPN's introduced by Symons are similar to Keller's model with the variation of allowing tokens to have any identity not just integer values, and associating read and write memory with the net. Billington used NPN to model a Transport service [Bill 82].

Timed Petri Nets

A Timed PN is a PN extended to support some description of time. Timed PN's that have been used for protocols include *time PN's* (TPN's) introduced by Merlin [Merl 76] and *stochastic PN's* (SPN's) introduced by Molloy [Moll 81]. In a TPN a pair of deterministic time values (t_{min}, t_{max}) is added to each transition of a PN. The pair defines the interval of time in which the transition must fire after it is enabled. This extension allows the modeling of time-out actions of protocols by specifying the t_{min} of the retransmission transition to be equal to the time-out value. Danthine [Dant 80] used a combination of TPN's and Nutt's evaluation nets [Nutt 72] (a kind of abbreviated PN) to model the Transport protocol of the Cyclade network.

SPN's are PN's extended by assigning to each transition a random variable representing the firing delay of that transition. State changes occur in the SPN model with some probability rather than arbitrarily as in a PN. Distributions of the transition delays are restricted to exponential in the continuous case, or geometric in the discrete case. This is because a markov model is extracted from the PN graph describing the global protocol behavior; in a markov model all transitions should be either exponentially or geometrically distributed. The random representation of time involved in protocol events is used in SPN's to allow for quantitative performance analysis.

2.2.5 Algebraic Methods

Algebraic specification derives its name from its relationship to universal algebra [Grat 68]. An algebra consists of a nonempty set of *objects* and a set of *operations*. Each operation takes a finite number of objects and produces an object. The meaning of operations is defined in terms of *equational-axioms*. The interpretation of objects and operations when specifying protocols depends on the specific algebraic approach used. We examine next two examples of algebraic systems used for specification of protocols.

In the calculus of communicating systems (CCS) introduced by Milner [Miln 80], objects are protocol behavior expressions generated from a set of send and receive events exchanged between the communicating processes. Operations include "•" denoting sequential composition, "+" denoting nondeterministic composition, "|" denoting concurrent composition, and "NIL" (a nullary operation) denoting deadlock. The concurrent composition of interacting processes produces a new composite process whose behavior includes rendezvous interactions for corresponding send and receive events and shuffling of all other events generated by the interacting processes.

A CCS specification of the sender process of the send-and-wait protocol is given next. Let τ denote a rendezvous event produced from a previous concurrent composition of the sender with a timer process (for time-out). Also, let m represent a send port for messages and $\bar{a}$ represent a receive port for acknowledgments on the channel between S and M. In addition, let $\bar{d}$ represent a receive port for message incoming from the source. The sender specification S is described recursively as follows.

$$S = \bar{d} \bullet m \bullet S_1 \qquad\qquad S_1 = \tau \bullet m \bullet S_1 + \bar{a} \bullet S$$

Capabilities for value passing and high-level language statements are also provided. To overcome the imposed synchronous mode of inter-process communication in CCS, one has to explicitly model transmission mediums between any two processes communicating asynchronously.

Many concepts from CCS are employed in the specification language proposed by the ISO TC97/SC16/WG1 subgroup C [Iso 83b, Brin 84]. Holzmann [Holz 82] also introduced a CCS-variant algebraic model with a division operation used to represent send events and message buffers used to allow for asynchronous inter-process communication. Another CCS-variant model introduced by Nounou [Noun 84] associates probability and time attributes with protocol behavior expressions to allow for the specification of protocol timing behaviors as well as their functional behaviors. This allows protocol timing requirements to be specified as will be described in section 6.1.

In the AFFIRM system [Muss 80, Suns 82a], the objects of the algebraic model are *abstract data types* [Gutt 78]. The system can be used to specify protocols modeled conceptually as state transition machines as follows: each protocol model is defined as an abstract machine data type, with its variables as *selectors* of the type, and its state transition as *constructors* of the type. A set of axioms defines the effects of each transition on the variables. Abstract data types can also be used in specifying protocol message formats. Desired properties of the protocol are expressed as theorems that refer to the elements of the given specifications. An advantage of this system is its use of abstract data types which provide only abstract description of the systems under consideration. Experience with modeling several protocols in AFFIRM [Suns 82b] has shown the following system limitations: no support for true modeling of concurrency; difficulty in dealing with exception handling, separate specification of local protocol processes, and specification of protocols with more than two processes.

One advantage of algebraic specifications is their rigorous formal base from algebra. Elements of other development tools in a protocol environment can be viewed as an algebra that is homomorphic to the specification algebra [Yemi 82]. One basic limitation of algebraic specifications is the difficulty in dealing with exception handling (for more information on this see [Berg 82]).

2.2.6 Temporal Logic Models

Temporal logic [Pnue 77] is an extension of predicate calculus to support the specification of temporal properties of systems (i.e., properties that change during the system execution). Invariant properties that must hold throughout the execution could be stated using predicate calculus. Within the temporal logic framework, the meaning of a computation is considered to be either the sequence of states (state-based approach) or the sequence of events (event-based approach) resulting from the system's execution. The two basic temporal operations in temporal logic besides predicate calculus operations are *henceforth* "$\Box$" and *eventually* "$\Diamond$". Let P be any predicate, then $\Box P$ is true at time i (representing the i-th instance of the execution sequence) if and only if P is true at *all* times j, where $j \geq i$, and $\Diamond P$ is true at time i if and only if P is true at *some* time j, where $j \geq i$. A specification in temporal logic consists of a set of axioms that assert properties which must be true of all sequences resulting from a system's execution [Lamp 80, Mann 81].

Temporal logic specifications can be classified into state-based and event-based approaches according to the underlying model of the execution of the protocol. Three different approaches to the state-based temporal logic method have been pursued by Lamport [Lamp 83], Schwartz and Melliar-Smith [Schw 81b], and Hailpern and Owicki [Hail 80]. The three approaches differ essentially in how close they are to the state machine model with the first being the closest followed by the second and then the third.

Schwartz and Melliar-Smith use a model in which state variables are introduced in the specification only when it is more convenient to express temporal properties in terms of finite history of the past rather than using temporal formulas. The variables used are assumed to be bounded. A specification of the Sender process of the send-and-wait protocol in this approach is given in Fig. 8 (adapted from [Schw 82]).

A1. $S_o=p$ **implies** ($S_o=q \neq p$
Latches-Until-After after RECEIVE-A and
$S_o=q \neq p$ **Latches-Until-After**
$S_i=q$)

A2. $\Box\Diamond$ ($S_i=S_o=p$) **implies**
{$\Diamond \sim$ *empty*(**InQ**) **implies** $\Diamond$($S_o \neq p$ **and**
at SEND-M)}

A3. $S_o=p$ **and** $\Diamond$ $S_o=q \neq p$ **implies**
$\Diamond$($S_o=q \neq p$
and at SEND-M) **Until** ($S_i=q \neq p$)

A4. $\Diamond$ **at SEND-M Until** $\Box$ *empty*(**InQ**)

Where S_o and S_i are two variables of the underlying state transition model used to record the last message value transmitted by the Sender, and the last acknowledgment value received from the medium, respectively. InQ is a sequence variable representing the queue of message ready at the source. Labels for events are the same as those used in Fig. 3(a).

Figure 8: A state-based temporal logic specification for the sender process of the send-and-wait protocol

Besides the temporal operations eventually and henceforth, the following constructs have also been used in the specification: **Until** and **Latches-Until-After**. *P* **Until** *Q* is interpreted as *P* must remain true until *Q* becomes true if ever, and *P* **Latches-Until-After** *Q* is interpreted as *P* when becoming true, remains true until after *Q* becomes true if ever. Also the predicates **at**, **in**, and **after**, have been used to reason about the currently active control point of each process. The interpretation of **at** *S*, **in** *S*, or **after** *S* is true if control is at the beginning, within, or at the end of the execution of statement *S* respectively. The axioms in Fig. 8 have the following interpretations. Axiom A1 states that a message value remains in S_o until both its successful acknowledgment has been received and a new message has been fetched from the source. Axiom A2 states that whenever the sender gets a message from the source while it is not busy, it eventually sends that message. Axiom A3 states that whenever a new message is placed in S_o, it is infinitely often transmitted until its successful acknowledgment is received. Axiom A4 ensures that message transmission continues until all messages available in InQ are serviced.

The above described approach to temporal logic specifications does not consider the complete set of a system's state space; some of the states are excluded if temporal axioms can be used to reason about them. This sometimes leads to complex specifications requiring several additional constructs (such as **Until** and **Latches-Until-After**) and thus rendering specifications complex and difficult to understand. In subsequent work [Schw 83] another approach has been followed in which the protocol required properties are stated on *intervals* of the protocol's execution sequences. It is claimed that this allows higher level temporal logic specifications.

Lamport considers the complete set of system's variables, and all state transitions are specified in terms of the changes they are allowed to affect the variables. This is done by using an "allowed changes" construct in addition to the other basic temporal operations. Although specifications based on this approach are easier to transform into implementations, they are lenghtier than those based on the former approach. Hailpern and Owicki use unbounded history variables, without employing any states, to record the sequences of messages that are inputs or outputs of the systems. Protocol properties such as number of messages sent equals number of messages received could be stated quite naturally with this approach, but it would be difficult to state properties that depend on the ordering of a sequence in a history. Moreover, the introduced history variables are actually "auxiliary" variables; that is, they are not variables that are required to describe the protocol implementation and thus can not be used to reason about its correctness.

The state-based temporal logic approach has been used to specify and verify a multidestination protocol [Sabn 82a], and in [Kuro 82] both history variables and internal states were used in specifying and verifying the three way handshake connection protocol. Shankar and Lam [Shan 84] use a variant of the eventually operator in stating temporal properties of a bounded length of the global state sequence resulting from a systems' execution.

In the event-based approach, protocol desirable properties are specified using temporal assertions that define constraints on the possible sequences of interaction events. No variables are considered in this approach. Establishing context, meaning a record of the history of previous events, in event-based specifications is much more difficult than in state-based specifications, where states naturally provide the required context. This leads to specifications that are somewhat complicated and lengthy. Vogt [Vogt 82] uses a history variable to represent the sequence of past events and thus establish the required context. In another event-based approach, Wolper [Wolp 82] introduced extended propositional temporal logic, in which temporal logic is extended with operators corresponding to properties definable by a right linear grammar. This allows the specification of some properties that otherwise could not be expressed in temporal logic such as stating a proposition that is to hold in every other state in a sequence.

2.2.7 Procedural Languages

In a procedural language, the unit of specification is a procedure containing type declarations and statements describing detailed computational steps of the system under consideration. Much of the early work done on protocol or service specifications used this method. Examples of such works can be found in [Sten 76, Haje 78, Krog 78].

The Gypsy programming language [Good 78, Good 82], is a procedural language that includes most of the basic facilities of a Concurrent PASCAL, and has the unique feature of supporting the specification of protocols at any of the three design phases using the same language. Descriptions of service or protocol specifications make use of *buffer histories* to record all send and receive operations executed on a system's buffer. One limitation of specifications employing buffer histories, is the difficulty in modeling unreliable communication mediums [Divi 82] since processes communicate through message buffers that do not model loss or corruption of messages. Another limitation is the difficulty of stating properties on a history if the properties depend on the ordering of messages in the buffer.

While procedural languages are a natural choice for coding implementation specifications, there has been much controversy regarding their use for specification in early design phases. The shortcoming of using procedural languages for specification lies in their detailed descriptions of a systems' operation. This makes it rather difficult to specify the abstract requirements of protocols without getting into the details. There is also a biasing effect to implement the protocol in the same language used for specification. The other side of the controversy, though, could argue that such languages, with their rich expressive power, support the specification of both control and data transfer functions of protocols.

2.3 A Taxonomy for Specification Tools

As a summary of this section, we propose a taxonomy of specification tools that will be helpful in judging the extent by which a specification tool meets the second set of requirements given in section 2.1. The first three are requirements of specification tools to be executable, to support the specification of desired properties of protocols, and to support the specification of performance parameters of protocol behavior. The fourth requirement of providing clear descriptions of interfaces between protocol layers can be met by a service specification that describes both the service used and the service provided by the protocol layer concerned.

We classify specification tools along two axis. Based on the first classification, they are either *state-based* or *event-based*. The underlying model of a protocol in state-based tools is concerned with the states through which the protocol passes during its operation and with the events that cause changes in its state. States can be either explicitly represented or described by variables. On the other hand, the underlying model in event-based tools is only concerned with the events generated by a protocol without any mention of its state. They include sequence expressions and event-based temporal logic specifications whereas the remaining specification tools covered in this section belong to the state-based class. Since state-based specifications describe the actions and responses of protocol operation, they can be directly executable. Event-based tools can at best be first transformed into an executable form (as will be explained in section 4). However, they seem to be more abstract than state-based tools since they are not concerned with the internal state of the protocol model.

Alternatively, specification tools can be classified into *behavioral* and *assertional* tools. Specifications belonging to the former class describe the flow of execution of protocols and how it proceeds after each event. They constitute a description of the cause and effect of all modeled protocol events. Assertional specification tools, on the other hand, state the requirements of protocol behavior in terms of desired properties of its possible execution sequences. As will become clear in the following sections, the more a specification tool is behavioral the more it is executable, and the more a specification tool is assertional the better support it provides for formal verification.

Most specification tools actually exhibit features belonging to both the behavioral and assertional classes. Also, each of these classes constitute a spectrum of specification tools. The extent to which a specification tool is behavioral depends on how much support it provides for the specification of protocol semantics besides its syntax. The extent to which a specification tool is assertional depends on how much support it provides for the statement of functional properties including liveness and safety, and timing properties. Furthermore, specification tools belonging to any of these classes can be either state-based or event-based. Therefore, we illustrate in Fig. 9 the relative positions of the various specification tools covered in this section.

3 Protocol Synthesis Tools

The job of composing a specification for an entire protocol system is quite complex. Furthermore, given such a protocol, the problem of formally verifying that it is free from certain design errors has shown to be generally undecidable (see [Bran 83]). Towards simplifying the complexity of specifying entire protocol systems, some research has been directed towards synthesizing complete specifications of protocols, which are specifications that include all the communicating processes involved, from incomplete ones. In some of these efforts the produced specifications are also guaranteed to be free from certain design errors and thus avoid the possibly undecidable formal verification problem. The various synthesis approaches vary primarily in the kinds of design errors considered, the maximum number of communicating processes in a protocol that are supported, and the features of the transmission channel that are assumed. However, they all take advantage of the duality inherent in the interactions among protocol processes where a message sent by one process should be received at another communicating process.

Zafiropulo, et al. [Zafi 80] have proposed an interactive and incremental synthesis technique. in which the protocol local processes are modeled as communicating FSM's with error-free FIFO channels. In each increment of interaction between the protocol designer and the synthesis program, the designer provides a sending interaction of one of the communicating processes. The program uses the already synthesized, partially constructed FSM's and a set of rules to find the state at which the receiving process can accept the sent interaction. It then prompts the designer for the state which the receiving process would enter upon receiving the found reception. The synthesis algorithm uses a set of three production rules that find the receive interactions in such a manner as to prevent the designer from creating *unspecified receptions* and *nonexecutable interactions*. An unspecified reception indicates that a message reception that can take place is missing in the specification. A nonexecutable interaction is a reception or a transmission interaction that is included in the specification but that cannot be exercised under normal operating conditions. The designer is also notified of the presence of *state deadlocks* and *state ambiguities*. A state deadlock occurs when each and every process has no possible transition out of its current state. A state ambiguity occurs when one process can coexist in a certain state with more than one state in any other process provided that all channels are empty.

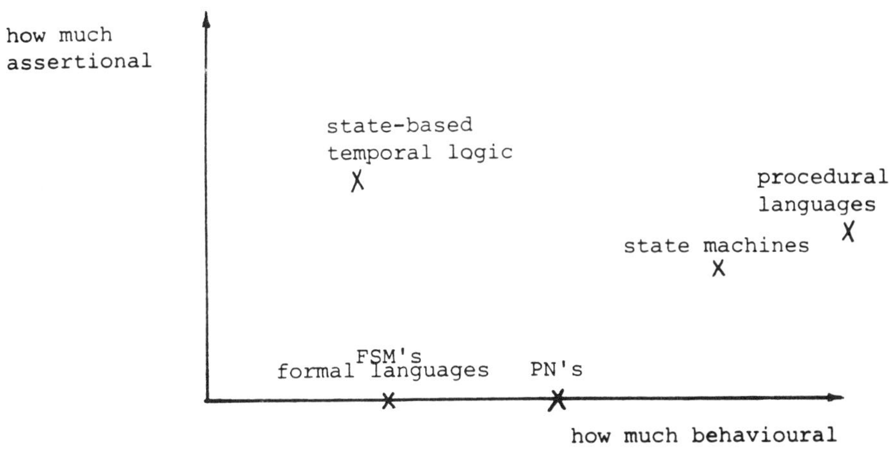

(a) State-based specification tools

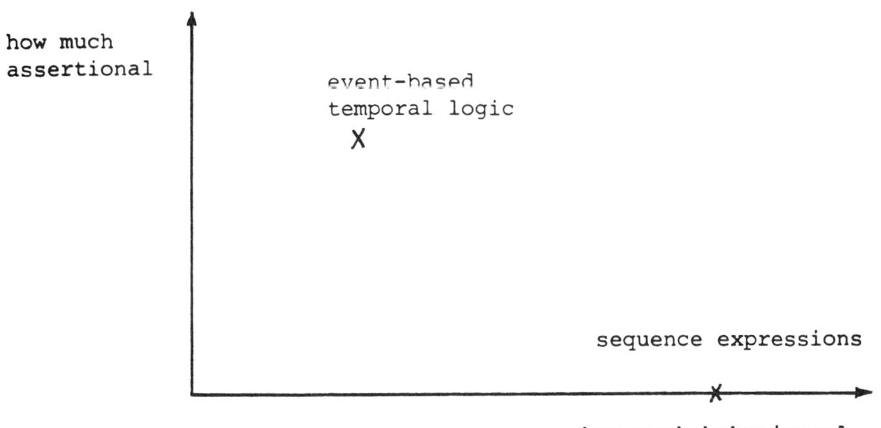

(b) Event-based specification tools

Figure 9: An illustration of the proposed taxonomy of specification tools

The synthesis algorithm accepts information from the designer and uses it in incrementally building trees that trace all possible executions of each process' FSM. The algorithm is in control of the incremental construction of the protocol. It must decide at which point to stop the growth of the execution trees; that is, when continuation cannot reveal any new information about the protocol. If all channel capacities are finite, or if there are only two processes with not more than one unbounded channel, then the termination of the algorithm is guaranteed [Bran 80]. Otherwise the trees can grow indefinitely and heuristics must be used to decide when to terminate their growth. For example, if channels were unbounded and there was a transmission loop in one of the FSM's, then the execution tree corresponding to this FSM can grow indefinitely. The complexity of the termination problem is the major limitation of this approach. The initial work done on the synthesis algorithm has been limited to only two communicating processes. In an attempt to generalize the algorithm for more than two processes [Bran 80], it was found that a different set of rules (still three rules) should be used. However, a proof of the production rules being necessary and sufficient only exists for the case of two processes.

Gouda and Yu [Goud 84a] proposed another synthesis methodology that accepts the complete specification of one process and produces a mirror-like specification of its communicating process. Similar to the work of Zafiropulo, et al. specifications are given as communicating FSM's, and the synthesized specifications are guaranteed to be free from the same design errors. It also computes the smallest bound on the number of messages in transit in the channels at any one time. The synthesis methodology consists of two algorithms. The first algorithm takes as input one process specification P_1 and produces two processes Q_1 and Q_2. Q_1 is computed from P_1 by adding some receiving transitions to it. Q_2 is then computed such that the communication between Q_1 and Q_2 is deadlock-free, bounded, with no unspecified receptions, no nonexecutable receptions, and no state ambiguities. The first step of this algorithm constructs a process Q_2 whose behavior mirrors that of input processes specification P_1. That is, they have the same states and transitions with the conversion of each sending (receiving) transition in P_1 to a receiving (sending) transition in Q_2 with the same label. A loss of synchronization leading to deadlock, though, might happen if some of the states in P_1 have outgoing transitions which are both sending and receiving since both P_1 and Q_2 might traverse sending transitions. To resolve this synchronization problem, correction transitions are added to P_1 to produce Q_1, and also included in Q_2. This restricts the communication pattern of the synthesized specification to a pattern of the communicating processes proceeding until a loss of synchronization is detected upon which they backup by following their correcting transitions.

The second algorithm takes, as an input, Q_1 and Q_2 and computes the smallest size for each of the two channels between Q_1 and Q_2. The communication channels are assumed to be error-free and FIFO, and the number of processes supported by the algorithms is limited to two. An advantage of this synthesis approach is that each of the two algorithms takes a deterministic time of $O(st)$, where s is the size of the state space and t is the number of transitions in the input process specification.

Bochmann and Merlin [Boch 83b] describe a synthesis approach that in contrast to the two described above, does not produce error-free specifications. It has, though, the unique feature of employing the service specification of the protocol in the synthesis procedure. Both the duality principle of communication between processes and the fact that the combined communication of a protocol layer process should provide its service are used in the synthesis procedure. The synthesis algorithm takes as input the service specification as well as the specifications of the protocol layer (n-1) communicating processes and determines the specification of the remaining process (provided one is possible). The process specifications are given as sequence expressions and inter-process communication is modeled by direct coupling.

A formula is used in generating the specification of the remaining process. The specification produced is maximal in the sense that it includes the largest number of execution sequences possible, and thus corresponds to the most general process (including possibly redundant transitions). Also, it might reach deadlock when interacting with the other processes. The approach does not guarantee that all execution sequences specified for the system will be produced by the interaction of the n subprocesses. If this is the case, then there exists no process that together with the given (n-1) process can provide the required system service. The communication channel is modeled as process in the layer, and the approach could support any number of interacting processes.

This synthesis approach can be applied to the send-and-wait protocol as follows. Given the specifications of the Service to be provided, the Medium, and the Sender of the protocol, the approach can produce the specification of the receiver process.

4 Implementation Tools

An implementation tool is a construction tool (a compiler in effect) that transforms a protocol specification into code. While low-level protocols in the ISO hierarchy are often implemented in firmware, high-level protocols are implemented in software. For an example of the former, the reader is referred to [Goud 76]. In this section we will limit our discussion to software implementations of protocols.

Clearly, one would like protocol implementation tools to be automated in order to minimize both the effort involved and the probability of errors. This depends not only on the protocol specification tool used but also on the programming language used for implementation, and on the complexity of the protocol. Subsequently, we first examine the extent to which the various specification tools facilitate the automation of the implementation process and the general approaches employed. We then examine some implementation choices encountered when translating protocols given in any specification tool.

In our proposed taxonomy in section 2.3, we classified specification tools into behavioral and assertional tools along one axis and into state-based and event-based tools along another. Behavioral specifications, such as state machines and petri net-based tools, lend themselves more easily to direct translations into implementation than assertional specifications, such as temporal logic. This is because the former describe how the execution of a protocol proceeds, while the latter are concerned with requirements of protocol operation and not with how the requirements are achieved. Furthermore, event-based specification are more difficult to translate into implementations than state-based specification because they are concerned with the outcomes of the protocol operation and not with how the outcomes are produced. In summary, state-based, behavioral specifications are the most suitable for direct translations into implementations.

Let us next discuss some works on implementing protocols specified in the various specification tools. Procedural specifications are clearly the easiest to be transformed into code because they are the richest in terms of expressing both the syntax and detailed semantics of protocol operation. The resulting implementation would probably be in the same language used for specification, with the addition of implementation specifics such as buffer management functions.

The typical approach for implementing a FSM specification, as described in [Boch 82], is to translate it to a looping program, with each cycle of the loop executing a transition. The loop would consist of a set of conditional statements with each testing for one kind of input interaction. Note that this construct is basically Dijkastra's guarded command [Dijk 75]. For each of these cases another set of conditional statements would test the major state of the module and compute the next state accordingly. State machine specifications and hybrid petri net specifications, which combine state transition specifications with high-level language statements, can be translated into code by simply transforming the state transition parts as described above and using the high-level statements as they are or with minor variations in the implementation. Bochmann, et al. [Boch 79] transformed manually a state machine specification of the X.25 protocol into an implementation in a Concurrent Pascal. Blumer and Tenney [Blum 82] in translating a state machine specification of the National Bureau of Standards' (NBS) transport protocol into C implementations, were able to produce 40% of the implementation automatically.

Sequence expressions, which belong to the event-based specification class, can not directly be directly translated into implementation, but need to be first transformed into a behavioral specification. This is similar to the derivation of a FSM that would generate a given regular expression. In implementing sequence expressions, which have much in common with regular expressions, Schindler, et al. [Schi 81] uses a two pass compiler to derive a Flow Control Graph (FCG) from the specification and then checks whether this graph is equivalent to some extended finite state machine (EFSM). If so, a PASCAL implementation of this EFSM is generated in the second pass.

Yelowitz, et al. [Yelo 82] describe an experiment of manually implementing AFFIRM algebraic specifications with its underlying abstract data types and state machine models in the Ada programming language. Abstract data types, state variables, and events in AFFIRM are mapped into types, objects, and tasks in Ada, respectively. In order to describe concurrency of the implementation of local processes, a feature not supported by AFFIRM, a special synchronization task that does not correspond to any AFFIRM event is added to the Ada implementation. Any task corresponding to an AFFIRM event has to get permission before proceeding with its actions, and upon completion thereof, notifies the synchronization task. Then, the synchronization task can be used to implement any desired imitation of, or even true, concurrency.

Finally, there are issues underlying any implementation tool, which preclude completely automated implementations. Human intervention in protocol implementations is required for two purposes. First, to add the implementation dependent parts, and message coding. Second, the implementor often has to make certain choices based on the specific protocol being implemented. For example, whether to implement the protocol modules as part of the operating system or as cooperating user processes, and how will the different modules interact: using shared memory, or using some kind of interrupt mechanism, are two possible choices.

5 Verification Tools

Protocol verification consists of logical proofs of the *correctness* of each of the specifications of the protocol, and the *mapping* between the service and the protocol specifications and between the protocol and implementation specifications. Proof of correctness of a specification constitutes proving the validity of certain desirable properties that would assure its correct operation under all conditions. Proof of mapping constitutes proving that a specification of a protocol refined at a certain development phase correctly implements the specification input to that phase. Proof of mapping between the service statement phase and the protocol design phase is referred to as *design verification*, and between the design phase and implementation phase is referred to as *implementation verification* [Boch 80a].

To prove that a specification is correct, one has to prove that it satisfies protocol *safety* and *liveness* properties [Lamp 77]. Safety properties state the design objectives that a specification must meet if the protocol ever achieves its goals. Liveness properties state that the specification is guaranteed to *eventually* achieve these goals. For example, an informal description of a safety property S and a liveness property L for the send-and-wait protocol specification could be

S : `the order of messages received is the same`
`as the order of the messages sent.`

L : `having received a new message, then`
`retransmission must continue until an`
`acknowledgment is received at the sender.`

Safety and liveness properties such as those listed above are highly dependent on the protocol under consideration. However, there are some general properties that are common to any protocol such as include freedom from unspecified receptions, nonexecutable interactions, and state deadlocks (as defined in section 3). Other general properties include *progress* and *absence of medium overflow*. Progress means absence of cyclic behavior (also called tempo-blocking) where the protocol enters an infinite cycle accomplishing no useful work. Absence of medium overflow means that the number of messages in transit in the medium is always less than a specified upper bound.

The approach used in proving a mapping between a specification output from a protocol development phase and the specification input to the phase, depends on the specification tool used. Consider the design verification problem. If behavioral specifications are used to describe the protocol service, proof of mapping would be equivalent to proving that the components of the service specification are correctly implemented by those of the protocol specification. On the other hand, if assertional specifications are used, then the service specification constitutes safety and liveness assertions of protocol specification; and design verification coincides with proving the correctness of protocol specification. That is, since proving the correctness of protocol specification in this case constitutes proving that the protocol specification meets its service assertions, it proves at the same time that the protocol specification is a correct implementation of the service specification.

Since protocol implementations are specified using high-level languages, they can be verified using traditional program verification tools. We will limit our discussion throughout the rest of this section to surveying tools for the verification of service and protocol specifications, and the problem of design verification.

5.1 State Exploration

State exploration examines all possible behaviors of a protocol. It is used in verifying specifications belonging to the state-based and behavioral class of Fig 9(a). State exploration of the concurrent behavior of the processes local to a protocol layer produces a *reachability graph*. In this graph, each node represents the combined states of all the local processes, and each arc represents a local transition. Starting from the initial state of the graph, interactions of the processes are examined by exploring all possible ways in which the initial states and all subsequent states can be reached. Each node the protocol can reach is checked for deadlock and unspecified receptions. The whole graph can be then checked for general desirable properties of the protocol such as progress, absence of tempo-blocking and medium overflow [Suns 75, West 78a]. In the case of petri nets specifications, each state in the reachability graph corresponds to a marking of the net [Ayac 81, Diaz 82, Jurg 84].

The reachability graph for the send-and-wait protocol is depicted in Fig. 10. All send events in the graph are followed by the corresponding receive event indicates absence of unspecified receptions, and all the transitions in the FSM specification of the communicating processes in Fig. 3 have corresponding links in the reachability graph indicates absence from nonexecutable interactions. Also, there is no tempo-blocking because the only cycle in the graph which involves time-out (other than the repetition of the entire protocol behavior) performs useful work each time a message is lost. In addition, since all nodes in the reachability graph have outgoing links, then there is no deadlock in the global behavior of the protocol. To see how a deadlock behavior would be detected by this approach, consider removing the time-out transition from the Sender process in Fig. 3. The system would then deadlock at state 5 in Fig. 10 if the medium loses a message. Note that in producing the graph of Fig. 10, we followed the idealistic assumption that time-outs only occur after a message loss. However, if one assumes that the time-out period can have any time duration, then one would get another reachability graph that differs from that in Fig. 10 in that there would be a time-out transition from each of states 4, and 7 through 12 back to state 2. There would be then a possibility of tempo-blocking due to any of these time-out loops. This illustrates how the behavior of protocols can be time-dependent and the importance of integrating the verification of timing requirements with functional verification, as will be discussed in more detail in section 6.

Using this verification tool, design verification consists of demonstrating how the protocol's reachability graph can be mapped to its service specification. Such a mapping for the send-and-wait protocol is defined as follows: in Fig. 4 states 1 and 2 are implemented by states 1 and 8 in Fig. 10. respectively, and events GET and DELIVER in Fig. 3 correspond to $\underline{m}_{C,S}$ and $\overline{m}_{R,D}$ in Fig. 10 respectively.

The principal advantage of state exploration is that it could be readily automated. Automated state exploration tools have been used successfully in discovering errors in several protocols; see for example [West 78c, Boch 79]. An automated and interactive verification tool called OGIVE [Prad 79] has been used successfully in proving certain general properties of petri nets [Jurg 84].

A principal limitation of the state exploration is the explosion in the number of states as the the complexity of the protocol analyzed increases. Note that the number of states in the reachability graph is equal to the product of the number of states in the FSM specifications of each of the communicating processes. In fact, Brand and Zafiropulo proved that the problem of verifying the general properties of communicating FSM's, is generally undecidable [Bran 83] except for a restricted class of communicating FSM's [Bran 83, Goud 84b]. The state explosion problem can be partially overcome by verifying each protocol process separately and then the protocol as a whole [Goud 84b], limiting the number of messages in the medium [West 82, Noun 84], assuming direct coupling between corresponding send and receive transitions such that there concurrent composition involves just one rendezvous interaction instead of two possibilities due to the shuffling of the two transitions, using some equivalence relation to minimize the reachability graph [Rubi 82]. In addition, instead of verifying

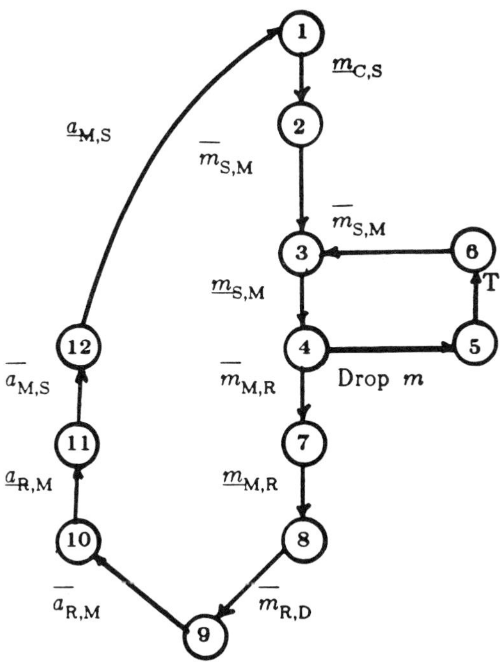

Figure 10: A reachability graph for the send-and-wait protocol

the complete global behavior of a protocol, considerable simplification could be achieved by verifying projections of that behavior according to the various distinct functions of the protocol (for example separate connection establishment from data transfer functions of data link protocols) [Lam 82]. *Symbolic execution* in which states are grouped into classes that are specified by assertions [Bran 78, Haje 78, Bran 82] is another approach to alleviate the state exploration problem. Various reduction techniques have been also used in verifying petri net specifications [Diaz 82].

Although state exploration is usually adequate in verifying general properties of protocols, it can not be used for the verification of specific protocol safety and liveness properties such as properties S and L given above for the send-and-wait protocol. These are addressed by the verification tool discussed next.

5.2 Assertion Proof

Assertion proof follows the Floyd/Hoare [Floy 67, Hoar 69] technique for program verification. Safety and liveness properties of a protocol can be expressed as assertions, which are attached to different control points of a specification. To verify an assertion means to demonstrate that it will always be true whenever the control point it is attached to is reached, regardless of the execution path taken to reach that point.

When a protocol specification is decomposed into a number of local process specifications, local invariants are first verified for each process directly from their specifications. Global service invariants can be then verified using the already proven local assertions. Invariants of a specification are special assertions which describe properties that are true at every control point in the specification. To prove assertions of a local process, the introduction of auxiliary variables, which are variables not required in implementing the protocol, is often required. For example, arrays of data sent and received are required in a data transfer protocol employing sequence numbers, in order to make precise statements about the order in which messages are sent and received [Sten 76].

Assertion proof is related to the class of assertional specification tools described in the taxonomy of section 2.3. In particular, it is used in verifying assertions associated with specification using procedural languages [Krog 78, Sten 76], state machines [Boch 77a], hybrid petri nets [Diaz 82], and temporal logic [Hail 80, Schw 82, Sabn 82a, Schw 83]. In the case of procedural languages, inference rules (i.e. rules that define the effect of each statement type on the assertions preceding it) for each type of statement are used in proving local assertions. This also applies to the high-level statements in a state machine specification. In the case of petri net-based models, net invariants deduced directly from the net structure, are used in proving local assertions. Within the temporal logic framework, temporal axioms, which constitute a temporal logic specification, are used in specifying and verifying safety and liveness assertions. Temporal logic has the unique feature of supporting the specification and verification of liveness properties.

Formulating assertions and proving them require a great deal of user ingenuity. This difficulty could be partially alleviated by using some proof strategy such as induction on the structure of specifications [Suns 81] and by automation as is provided by several verification systems; examples of verification systems that have been applied to protocols are described in [Good 82, Suns 82a, Divi 82]. It should be noted though that automating assertion proof is considerably more complex than automating state exploration. For a detailed comparison of verification systems used for protocols, the reader is referred to [Suns 82b, Suns 83].

6 Performance Analysis Tools

Performance analysis of protocols includes *specification and analysis of timing requirements*, and *performance measures*. Protocol behavior is typically time-dependent, and their efficient performance hence depend on certain timing requirements. Performance measures are used as indications of how well a protocol performs. The combination of these two performance analysis problems is natural since both problems are concerned with the timing behavior of protocols. This allows the protocol designer to study the effect of various performance parameters on their timing behavior. We first examine some issues common to the two performance analysis problems and then survey approaches to each of them.

In order to analyze protocol performance, it is necessary to establish a model of the communication medium and the timing behavior of the protocol. The former is provided in the form of data specifying the medium's characteristics. For example, in the case of data link protocols (at layer 2 of Fig. 1), the following medium characteristics should be specified: bandwidth, bit error probability, topology, medium configuration (i.e., half or full duplex), and the upper bound on the number of messages in transit at any one time.

A model of the timing behavior of a protocol can be either formulated directly from first principles, or extracted from a formal specification of the protocol. We will refer to the former approach as *direct* and to the latter as *specification-based*. In both approaches, the model should specify the global view of protocol operation. It should also include the specifications of the following features. First, since a protocol's timing behavior is often non-deterministic, the probabilities of all possible protocol events at the various instants of its behavior should be specified. Second, a representation of the times involved in each of the events is also required. Typically, they are represented by their *bounds* or *distributions*. Bounds on an event time specify the minimum and maximum time before its occurrence. This time representation has been used in [Merl 76, Sabn 82b, Krit 84, Shan 84]. Distributions of event times provide more complete description of their random nature. This time representation is often used especially in evaluating protocol performance measures; see for example [Suns 75, Moll 81, Rudi 84, Noun 84]. Using this random representation of event times, Nounou and Yemini [Noun 86] model protocol timing behavior as marked point processes, while Molloy [Moll 81] models it as markov processes. Both follow a specification-based approach using an algebraic method in the former and petri nets in the latter. The event times are assumed to be exponentially distributed. Third, some statistics for message lengths should be provided. These are typically considered as constants or represented by their distributions.

6.1 Timing Requirements

Protocol timing requirements are conditions on the protocol's timing behavior to ensure its efficient performance. Consider, for example, a retransmission on time-out protocol such as the send-and-wait protocol. The efficient performance of the protocol depends on the requirement that time-out would occur after a message loss only with a very small probability and that the time between a loss and a time-out is minimized. Another example of a protocol timing requirement is to restrict the lifetime of messages occupying the protocol system [Sloa 83]. A third example of a timing requirement that underlies the behavior of many protocols is that if they do not achieve progress within a specified amount of time, then they either reset or abort. Such a requirement is crucial to prevent protocols from being stalled due to exceptional situations such as when one of the protocol process has crashed, or when the transmission links are heavily loaded.

Specification and analysis of protocol timing requirements can also affect the verification of protocol functional properties. In particular, if timing requirements are ignored, then verification of safety might be unnecessarily expensive and verification liveness might be not enough. Verification of safety properties might be complicated by the consideration of unrealistic protocol behaviors that do not satisfy the given protocol timing requirements. Also, proving that the protocol's goals will be eventually achieved is not enough if these goals are achieved after a very long time. In fact, a timing error was found in the alternating bit protocol [Bart 69], which has been proven safe and live [Yemi 82]. It was shown that the protocol would never achieve its eventual goal if the time-out rate is not properly set. By specifying and analyzing protocol timing requirements, performance parameters of the protocol (such as the time-out rate in the send-and-wait protocol) can be properly set. The resulting timing behavior would thus be (time-wise) realistic and estimates of its duration can be computed.

Early work on the specification of timing requirements was done by Merlin [Merl 76] using time PN's (see section 2.2.4). A bounds representation of time was used to describe minimum and maximum firing times for a time-out transition in the alternating bit protocol. Similar time representation has been used by Sabnani [Sabn 82b] but for FSM specifications. Note that in both of these cases, the state exploration of the concurrent behavior of the local processes resulting in a description of the protocol global behavior, should be modified. Consider a state in the global state description where n possible transitions are possible. Let $t_{i,min}$ and $t_{i,max}$ denote the minimum and maximum time for transition i, respectively. The corresponding transition in the global description has the bounds of $(Min[t_{i,min}], Min[t_{i,min}])$, where Min is an n-ary operation to compute the minimum. A transition in one of the local processes with t_{min} greater than the upper bound on the corresponding transition in the global behavior, would be then time-wise unrealizable. The limitation of these two efforts stems from the state explosion problem associated with the specification tools used.

Shankar and Lam [Shan 84] assume a constant time representation and use time variables to refer to the occurrence times of events. By including time variables in the enabling condition of an event e, time constraints of the form "event e can only occur after a given time interval". Time constraints of the form "event e will occur within a certain elapsed time interval" are stated as safety properties and verified accordingly.

Nounou and Yemini express timing requirements as mathematical statements or inequalities in terms of probability, mean-time, and variance-time attributes of protocol timing behavior. Consider the example of the send-and-wait protocol without the assumption that time-out occurs only after message loss. Let the global behavior of the protocol that terminates after delivery of an acknowledgment to the sender be denoted by C. This behavior consists of event sequences in which time-out occurs before a loss in the medium (which would be represented by an internal event), and other event sequences in which time-out occurs after a loss. The latter sequences can be isolated using *Restrict* function on C to get C_R. The timing requirement of the protocol can be then specified as *minimize* $\mathbf{M}_C(C)$ *and maximize* $\mathbf{P}_C(C_R)$, where $\mathbf{M}_C(C)$ denotes the mean-time of behavior C and $\mathbf{P}_C(C_R)$ denotes the mean-time of behavior C_R relative to C. Given the algebraic specification of the protocol and the exponential rates of the event times involved in it, a set of rules were proposed for evaluating probability and mean-time attributes. The timing requirement can be thus analyzed and an optimal setting of the time-out period can be computed.

6.2 Performance Measures

Key protocol performance measures include *execution time, delay,* and *throughput.* The execution time is the time required by the protocol to reach one of its final states, starting from the initial state. It would be a valuable performance measure for terminating protocols such as a connection establishment protocol where it represents the time required for the distributed processes involved in the protocol to get connected. Throughput is the transmission rate of useful data between processors, excluding any control information or retransmission required by the protocol. It indicates how efficiently the transmission channel is utilized. Delay is the time from starting a message transmission at the sender to the time of successful message arrival at the receiver. It is useful in indicating the degree of service that the protocol provides.

Two tools are typically used in evaluating protocol performance measures: *analytic tools,* and *simulation tools.*

6.2.1 Analytic Methods

Various instances of resource contention and the related queueing delays are often witnessed in the operation of communication protocols. For example, in the send-and-wait protocol a new message arriving at the sender has to be queued if the sender is busy waiting for the successful acknowledgment of a previously sent message. Therefore, queueing theory provides a convenient mathematical framework for formulating and solving protocol performance models [Klei 75, Koba 78, Reis 82]. In such a queueing model, the server denotes the protocol system under consideration which is typically modeled as a stochastic process.

Let us demonstrate how the delay of the send-and-wait protocol can be computed using basic probability laws and the protocol's FSM specification. Assume that the time involved in each transition of the reachability graph in Fig. 10 is an exponentially distributed random variable. Also, assume that a negligible delay is involved at both the sender and receiver ends of the medium. Based on these assumptions and considering a single cycle operation of the protocol, a modified reachability graph is shown in Fig. 11. The problem can be stated as follows: given a medium bandwidth of 9600 bits/sec (for terrestrial links), mean message and acknowledgment lengths l of 1024 bits (therefore the mean transmission time t_s is 0.017sec/message), bit error probability p_b of 10^{-5}, mean propagation delay t_d of 0.013 sec/message, and mean time-out t_T of 1 sec/message, evaluate the mean value of delay d between state 2 to 8 in Fig. 11.

Recall from section 1 our assumption that time-out only occurs after the medium has lost a message, this indicates that the probability of time-out is the same as the probability of a lost message. Therefore, the probability of the time-out loop denoted by p is given by

$$p = 1 - (1 - p_b)^l \qquad (6.1)$$

which is approximately $1 - e^{-lp_b}$ if $lp_b << 1$

The mean delay is given by

$$\begin{aligned} E[d] &= p/(1-p)\,(t_T + t_s) + 3t_s + 2t_d \qquad (6.2) \\ &= 0.357 \text{ sec/message} \end{aligned}$$

and the second moment of d is

$$\begin{aligned} E[d^2] &= p/(1-p)\,(2t_T^2 + 2t_s^2) \\ &\quad + 2p^2/(1-p)^2\,(t_T + t_s)^2 + 6t_s^2 + 4t_d^2 \qquad 6.3 \\ &= 0.09 \end{aligned}$$

Derivations of equations 6.2 and 6.3 are given in appendix I. Assume that messages arrive at state 2 in Fig. 11 with rate λ, then the protocol's *mean transfer time* T which is the sum of delay and a waiting time is given by the Pollaczek-Khinchine formula [Klei 75]:

$$T = E[d] + (\lambda\, E[d^2])/(2[1-\lambda\, E[d]]) \qquad (6.4)$$

In Fig. 12, we plot T versus λ for various message lengths. As expected, T increases as λ increases and the system becomes saturated when λ approaches $1/E[d]$. Also, as l increases T increases due to the increases in transmission times and p.

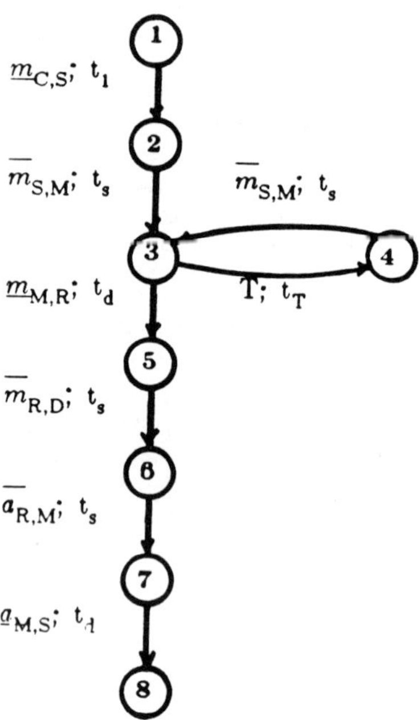

Figure 11: A modified reachability graph for the send-and-wait protocol

Examples of specification-based performance evaluation tools include works by Molloy [Moll 81] and Nounou and Yemini [Noun 84]. Molloy introduced stochastic petri nets (SPN) which are petri nets extended by assigning a random firing delay to each transition in the net. The reachability set of the net is first generated and analyzed for logical correctness, then a Markov process, that is isomorphic to the set, is generated. The steady-state probabilities of the Markov process can be calculated and used in modeling and computing throughput and delay. This approach is limited only to exponentially (in the case of continuous representation of transition firing times) or geometrically (in the discrete case) distributed firing delays. Nounou and Yemini use devised rules for evaluating probability, mean-time, and variance-time attributes of protocol timing behavior in evaluating any performance measure specified in terms of these attributes. Examples of performance measures that can be evaluated are throughput and delay. Other specification-based approaches to protocol performance evaluation can be found in [Bolo 84, Krit 84, Razo 84, Rudi 84].

The specification-based approach has the advantage of allowing performance evaluation tools to be automated. This would also facilitate its integration with other development tools in a protocol development environment. However, the approach largely depends on devising a mapping between protocol specification and the performance model. This mapping might be in some cases too restrictive as is the case, for example, with the markovian property of the resulting performance model of SPN's.

Examples of works based on the direct approach can be found in [Gele 78, Tows 79, Yu 79, Bux 80]. In this approach, all possible behaviors of the protocol under study has to be directly determined from a human understanding of its operation.

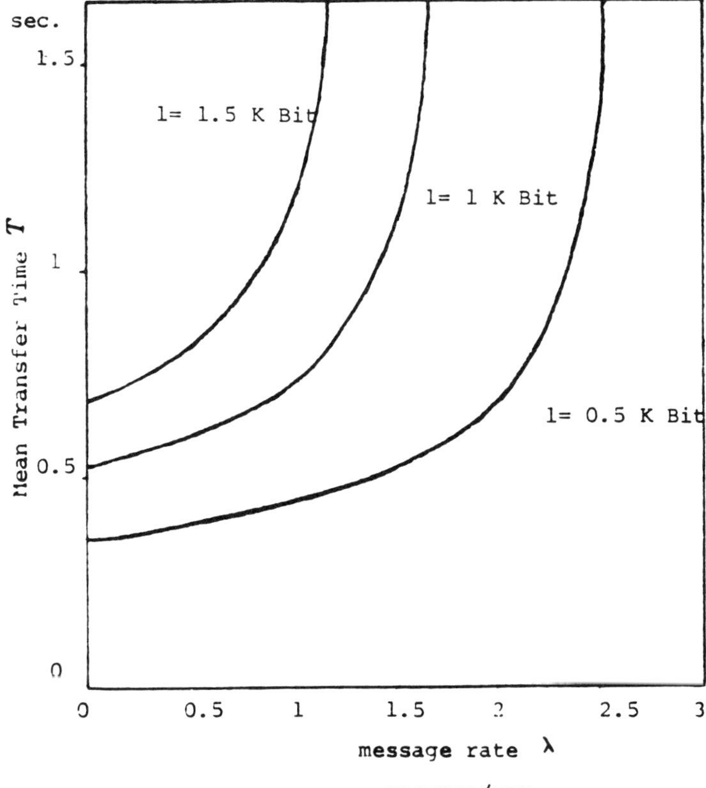

Figure 12: Transfer time vs. arrival rate of the send-and-wait protocol

6.2.2 Simulation

Analytic performance models of real-life protocols are usually intractable. In this case, simulation is used in evaluating protocol performance. Even when an approximate model of the system is sought, simulation could be a valuable tool in validating the modeling approximations and assumptions.

In the case of specification-based simulations, the protocol specification used should be executable. Referring to our taxonomy of Fig. 9, a method that is easily executed is one that could also be easily transformed into an implementation. Therefore, the same discussion in section 4 on the ease of implementing a protocol specification also applies here. An example on specification-based simulation of protocol can be found in [Regh 82]. Direct protocol simulations, on the other hand, are based on a protocol implementation. A direct simulation of the HDLC procedures was carried out by Bux, et al. [Bux 82].

The shortcomings of simulation are clearly its high cost in terms of time and effort, and the little understanding of the system gained. The second problem could be alleviated through a large number of simulation runs.

7 Testing Tools

Testing is a validation tool that can be used to examine whether a protocol implementation satisfies the functional requirements set by its standard, measure its performance and assess its robustness in recovering from exceptional conditions. Exhaustive testing basically aims at exercising all possible behaviors of the protocol under consideration. This, however, is not realistic for most real-life protocols which typically exhibit a large set of possible behaviors. Therefore, part of the protocol testing problem is to find a way of identifying the most probable protocol behaviors and thus produce testing results which are within a certain range of accuracy. Consequently, testing as a validation tool is weaker than formal verification because it does not guarantee correctness and is less rigorous than analytic methods of performance analysis because it can only provide measurements for specific performance parameters. Nevertheless, testing is a valuable validation tool required to confirm that the implementation under test (IUT) satisfies the standard implementation of the protocol and thus ensure that different implementations of the protocol will be able to internetwork.

In the context of the ISO hierarchically layered architecture, a protocol module at layer N has two interfaces: the N interface through which service requests to layer N are provided, and the N-1 interface through which layer N requests services from layer N-1. In order to test an implementation of such a protocol, one must test its response to erroneous as well as correct requests across each of these two interfaces. An incorrect request at the N interface indicates an incorrect service request, but an incorrect response at the N-1 interface could result from either an incorrect response from the remote peer module or an error in the transmission of a correct response through the communication medium. All these possibilities must be covered in testing an IUT.

Testing of protocols can be either *direct* or *remote*. In direct testing the IUT is tested in a simulated environment where correct and faulty responses from the lower protocol layer are simulated, and the results compared with those of a standard reference implementation. In remote testing, an IUT is tested in its normal operating environment, where it is at one end of the network and some reference implementation of the protocol is at the other end. The reference implementation is driven by the protocol tester and the operation of the implementation under test is observed remotely. Note that testing in the second approach is probably more complete and more detailed than the first approach. This is at the cost of increased complexity however.

Several groups around the world are currently involved in proposals for testing centers that would be responsible for carrying out the remote tests and accordingly provide certificates describing the performance of a client's (an implementor of a protocol implementation) IUT on them. The groups include the National Physics Laboratory (NPL) group in England [Bart 80, Rayn 82], the Agency de l'Informatique (ADI) in France [Ansa 81, Ansa 82], the Gesellschaft fuer Mathematik und Datenverarbeitung (GMD) in Germany [Falt 83], and the National Bureau of Standards (NBS) in the USA [Nigh 82]. Other specialized protocol testing architectures for certain network architectures have been proposed. For example, the X.25 testing facilities for the Datapac network [Weir 78], an architecture for testing IBM's systems network architecture (SNA) protocols [Cork 83], and a BX.25 (an X.25 compatible protocol developed at Bell Labs) certification facility [Meli 82]. We will restrict our discussion to general testing architectures.

We examine next the two main issues pertinent to testing: logical architectures for testing and techniques for selecting test sequences.

7.1 Logical Architectures for Testing

Within the framework of the ISO model, a common logical testing architecture is given in Fig. 13. In this architecture the peer protocol implementation (PPI) of the IUT is a combination of a reference implementation and a protocol-data-units generator (see Fig. 13). The PPI at layer N together with reference implementations for layers 4,5,...,N-1 are located at the test center, while the IUT is at the implementor's site. Both ends are connected to an X.25 network which provides the first three network layers* . The protocol-data-units generator is responsible for generating correct N level service requests, requests for the generation of N-th level protocol errors, indications of undetected N-th level protocol errors, and acts as an encoder and decoder of both valid and invalid (N-1) service. The PPI and the protocol-data-units generator are driven by a test driver (TD) at the testing center. The test responder (TR) is the software module which acts as the user of the N service, and whose operation is totally predictable so that the results of the tests depend only on the behavior of the IUT. The TD and TR communicate through a non-standard protocol.

Based on this architecture, the various groups mentioned above differ in the following respects. At GMD, the TR function is performed manually thus making testing inexpensive for the implementor but slow and error-prone. At NBS, the TR is the same as the TD except that all send (receive) requests are changed to receive (send) requests. In this case no special TD-TR protocol is required. At both ADI and NPL, the full architecture is supported with the difference that the TR at ADI can handle multiple connections through the IUT which is necessary in testing protocols with multiplexing functions, whereas at NPL the TR handles only one connection at a time which has the advantage of a simpler TR. Multiple connections at NPL are handled by parallel instantiations of the same TR design.

In order to assess the IUT, it is necessary to test its response to erroneous and correct requests across both the N and N-1 interfaces. However, if the N-1 service of the protocol being tested is not end-to-end (as in the case of the packet-level of the X.25), then it is not possible to control it remotely. Therefore, a portable box is introduced between the communication medium and the implementor's system (see Fig. 14) in the testing architectures established at NPL and ADI. It is used to detect any errors introduced by the sub-network and introduce errors in it upon request from the testing center.

Clearly, making testing independent of the protocol being tested as much as possible is highly desirable so that only minimum variations need to be made when a protocol at another network layer is tested. This can be achieved by minimizing the protocol dependent parts of the architecture, and automating the process of test sequences selection. The only part of the testing architecture that needs be protocol dependent is the protocol-data-units generator, especially the part for testing normal and faulty N service. This dependency could be minimized by automating that part of the generator such that it is derived from some specification of the protocol.

*Only end-to-end protocols above X.25 are tested in such architectures

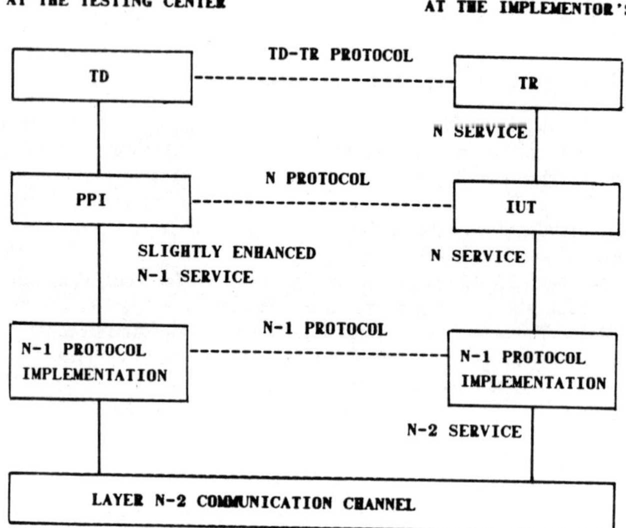

Figure 13: Logical architecture for testing

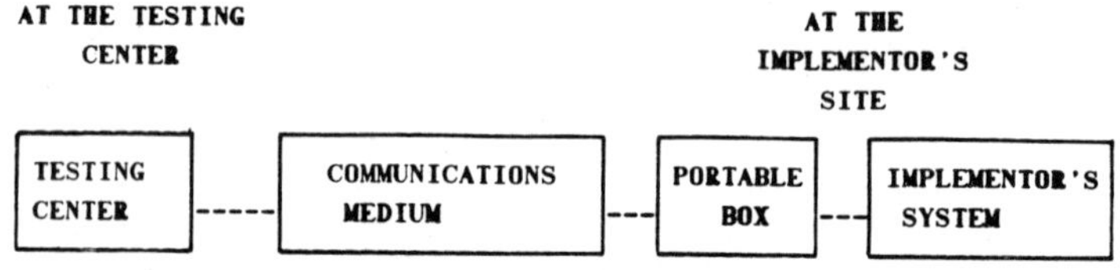

Figure 14: Physical architecture including the portable unit

7.2 Test Sequences Selection

A test sequence is an input request to the IUT generated by the TD or TR. Since the source of the IUT is typically not provided by the implementor, the selection of test sequences at the testing center can only be derived from the service and protocol specification of the protocol under consideration. Test sequences could be specified simply as sequences of commands, as state tables describing the various states of testing and the events and associated actions for each state, or using a test specification language that might be then translated into state tables [Rayn 82].

Testing is said to be *complete* if all the possible requests that could be applied to the IUT are covered by the test sequences. Unfortunately, theoretical results [Piat 80] show that without knowledge of the protocol internal state the size (measured as the number of distinct sequential inputs applied to the IUT) of a complete test sequence has an upper bound of $O(n^3)$ where n is the size of the state set of the protocol reference model. Otherwise, with an access to the protocol internal state this figure comes down to $O(n^2)$. These bounds could be very large for complex protocols such as those involving sequence numbers.

However, there are other methods for near complete tests sequence selection [Sari 82, Ural 83]. As an example, we will use the ***transition tours*** method described by Sarikaya and Bochmann [Sari 82] to calculate a test sequence for the send-and-wait protocol. This method is used to derive test sequences from a protocol specified formally as a state machine but using only its FSM part. A transition tour sequence is an input sequence starting at the initial state and covering all the transitions at least once. The length of the sequence for our protocol example (see Fig. 11) is 8 and the sequence is given by

$$\underline{m}_{C,S}\ \overline{m}_{S,M}\ \mathrm{T}\ \overline{m}_{S,M}\ \underline{m}_{M,R}\ \overline{m}_{R,D}\ \overline{a}_{R,M}\ \underline{a}_{M,S}$$

In general, the upper bound on the sequence length is q + (q-1)(n-1), where q is the number of possible transitions. This is the worst case where a traversal of all (n-1) states is required to include each transition in the test sequence. This method detects all operation errors (errors in the output function of the state machine), but it does not detect all transfer errors (errors of the next state function).

8 Conclusions

In surveying the various protocol development tools, their dependency on the specification tool used has been demonstrated. Based on our taxonomy of specification tools described in section 2.3, we can conclude that behavioral specifications are better suited for synthesis, implementation, performance analysis and testing tools. Assertional specifications, on the other hand, offer better support for verification tools. Belonging to the latter class are temporal logic specifications which can adequately describe both static and temporal requirements of protocol behavior. We expect future proposals of specifications tools to combine the temporal logic framework with other specification models. In addition, since specification-based performance analysis tools are starting to attract much interest, specification tools should offer better support for the specification of protocol timing requirements and performance measures.

Most of the past research on protocol validation tools has ignored the specification and verification of such protocol timing requirements. We believe that such requirements are essential for the correct functioning of most protocols. Integrating the analysis of timing requirements in functional validation tools, i.e., verification and testing tools, would exclude unrealistic protocol behavior and thus simplify their functional validation.

In addition to the surveyed works on individual protocol development tools, there has been recently a growing interest in integrating them into development environments. An ideal development environment should provide a consistent user interface to the various tools supported. Also, recognizing the visual attraction, clarity and wide acceptance of graphical descriptions of protocols, we expect the user interfaces to employ state-of-the-art technology in supporting such descriptions. Technological advances of graphical display devices with colors, multiple window displays, high resolution, and numerous pointing aids (e.g., tablet, mouse and light pen) can be used to aid the protocol developer in constructing and validating complex real-life protocols.

The integration of specification-based development tools in environments would facilitate both the functional and performance validation of protocols starting from early development phases. Thus the costs incurred in iterations through the development phases after post-implementation detection of errors, would be reduced. Furthermore, as more protocol standards are developed, more experience will be required in the application of current and future tools and environments to these standards.

[Ande 84] D.Anderson and L.Landweber.
Protocol Specification By Real-Time Attribute Grammars.
In *Proceedings of the Fourth IFIP International Workshop on Protocol Specification, Testing and Verification.* North-Holland, June, 1984.

[Ansa 81] J.Ansart.
Test and Certification of Standardised Protocols.
In *Proceedings of the First International INWG/NPL Workshop : Protocol Testing - Towards Proof?*, pages 119-126. 1981.

[Ansa 82] J.Ansart.
GENEPI/A -A Protocol Independent System for Testing Protocol Implementation.
In *Proceedings of the Second IFIP International Workshop on Protocol Specification, Testing and Verification.* 1982.

[Ayac 81] J.Ayache, P.Azema, J.Courtiat, M.Diaz and G.Juanole.
On the Applicability of Petri Net-Based Models in Protocol Design and Verification.
In *Proceedings of the First International INWG/NPL Workshop : Protocol Testing - Towards Proof?*, pages 349-370. 1981.

[Azem 78] P.Azema, J.Ayache, and B.Berthomieu.
Design and Verification of Communication Procedures: A Bottom-Up Approach.
In *Proceedings of the Third International Conference on Software Engineering*, pages 168-174. 1978.

[Bart 69] K.Bartlett, R.Scantlebury, and P.Wilkinson.
A Note on Reliable Full-Duplex Transmission over Half-Duplex Lines.
CACM 12(5):260-261, May, 1969.

[Bart 80] K.Bartlett and D.Rayner.
The Certification of Data Communication Protocols.
In *NBS Trends and Applications Conference*, pages 12-17. May 29, 1980.

[Baue 82] W.Bauerfeld.
A Hybrid Model for Protocols and Services: Verification and Simulation by a Modified Depth-First Search Algorithm.
In *Proceedings of the Second IFIP International Workshop on Protocol Specification, Testing and Verification*, pages 451-464. May, 1982.

[Berg 82] H.Berg, W.Boebert, W.Franta, and T.Moher.
Formal Methods of Program Verification and Specification.
Prentice-Hall, 1982.

[Bert 82] G.Berthelot and R.Terrat.
Petri Nets Theory for the Correctness of Protocols.
IEEE Transaction on Communications COM-12:2476-2505, Decmber, 1982.

[Bill 82] J.Billington.
Specification of the Transport Service Using Numerical Petri Nets.
In *Proceedings of the Second IFIP International Workshop on Protocol Specification, Testing and Verification*, pages 77-100. May, 1982.

[Blum 82] T.Blumer and R.Tenney.
A Formal Specification Technique and Implementation method for Protocols.
Computer Networks 6:201-217, 1982.

[Boch 77a] G.Bochmann and J.Gecsei.
A Unified Method for the Specification and Verification of Protocols.
In *Proceedings of IFIP Congress*, pages 229-234. August 8-12, 1977.

[Boch 77b] G.Bochmann and R.Chung.
A Formalized Specification of HDLC Classes of Procedures.
In *Proceedings of the NTC*, pages 03A:2_1-03A:2_11. December, 1977.

[Boch 78] G.Bochmann.
Finite State Description of Communication Protocols.
Computer Networks 2:361-372, October, 1978.

[Boch 79] G.Bochmann and T.Joachim.
Development and Structure of an X.25 Implementation.
IEEE Transactions on Software Engineering SE-5(5):423-439, September, 1979.

[Boch 80a] G.Bochmann and C.Sunshine.
Formal Methods in Communication Protocol Design.
IEEE Transactions on Communications COM-28(4):624-631, April, 1980.

[Boch 80b] G.Bochmann.
A General Transition Model for Protocols and Communication Services.
IEEE Transactions on Communications COM-28(4):643-650, April, 1980.

[Boch 82] G.Bochmann et al.
Some Experience with the Use of Formal Specifications.
IEEE Transaction on Communications COM-12:2476-2505, Decmber, 1982.

[Boch 83a] G.Bochman.
Distributed Systems Design.
Springer-Verlag, 1983.

[Boch 83b] G.Bochmann and P.Merlin.
On the Construction of Communication Protocols.
ACM Transactions on Programming Languages and Systems 5-1:1-25, January, 1983.

[Boch 84] G.Bochmann.
Formal Description Techniques for OSI: An Example.
In *Proceedings of INFOCOM.* IEEE, 1984.

[Boeh 76] B.Boehm.
Software Engineering.
IEEE Transaction on Computer C-25(12):1226:1241, 1976.

[Bolo 84] T.Bolognesi and H.Rudin.
On the Analysis of Time-Dependent Protocls by Network Flow Algorithms.
In *Proceedings of the Fourth IFIP International Workshop on Protocol Specification, Testing and Verification*. North-Holland, 1984.

[Bran 78] D.Brand and W.Joyner,Jr.
Verification of Protocols Using Symbolic Execution.
Computer Networks 2:351-360, October, 1978.

[Bran 80] D.Brand and P.Zafiropulo.
Synthesis of Protocols for an Unlimited Number of Processes.
In *NBS Trends and Applications Symposium*, pages 29-40. May, 1980.

[Bran 82] D.Brand and W.Joyner.
Verification of HDLC.
IEEE Transactions on Communications COM-30(5):1136-1142, May, 1982.

[Bran 83] D.Brand and P.Zafiropulo.
On Communicating Finite-State Machines.
Journal of the ACM 30:433-445, April, 1983.

[Brin 84] E.Brinksma and G.Karjoth.
A Specification of the OSI Transport Service in LOTOS.
In *Proceedings of the Fourth IFIP International Workshop on Protocol Specification, Testing and Verification*. North-Holland, 1984.

[Bux 80] W.Bux, K.Kummerle, and H.Truong.
Balanced HDLC Procedures: A Performance Analysis.
IEEE Transactions on Communications COM-28(11):1889-1898, November, 1980.

[Bux 82] W.Bux and K.Kummerle.
Data Link-Control Performance: Results Comparing HDLC Operational Modes.
Computer Networks 6:37-51, 1982.

[Cork 83] R.Cork.
The Testing of Protocols in SNA Products - an Overview.
In *Proceedings of the Third IFIP International Workshop on Protocol Specification, Testing and Verification*. North-Holland, 1983.

[Dant 80] A.Danthine.
Protocol Representation with Finite State Models.
IEEE Transactions on Communications COM-28(4):632-643, April, 1980.

[Diaz 82] M.Diaz.
Modeling and Analysis of Communication and Coopeartion Protocols Using Petri Net Based Models.
In *Proceedings of the Second IFIP International Workshop on Protocol Specification, Testing and Verification*, pages 465-510. May, 1982.

[Dick 80a] G.Dickson.
State Transition Diagrams for One Logical Channel of X.25.
In *Switching and Signalling Branch Paper 23,Australian Telecommunications Commission.* July, 1980.

[Dick 80b] G.Dickson.
Formal Specification Technique for Data Communication Protocol X.25 Using Processing State Transition Diagrams.
Australian Telecommunication Research 14(2), 1980.

[Dijk 75] E.Dijkstra.
Guarded Commands, Nondeterminacy and Formal Derivation of Programs.
Communications of the ACM :453-457, August, 1975.

[Divi 82] B.Divito.
Verification of Communications Protocols and Abstract Process Models.
PhD thesis, Univ. of Texas at Austin, August, 1982.

[Ecma 80] ECMA/TC23/80/18.
3rd. Draft of Transport protocol.
Technical Report, European Computer Manufacturer Association, 1980.

[Falt 83] U.Faltin et al.
TESDI Manual: Testing and Diagnosis Aid for Higher Level Protocols.
In *IFV-IK-RZ, GMD, Darmstadt, Germany.* 1983.

[Floy 67] R.Floyd.
Assigning Meanings to Programs.
Mathematical Aspects of Computer Science 19:19-32, 1967.

[Gele 78] E.Gelenbe.
Performance Evaluation of the HDLC Protocol.
Computer Networks 2:409-415, 1978.

[Genr 79] H.Genrich and K.Lautenbach.
The Analysis of Distributed Systems by Means of Predicate/Transition Nets.
Semantics of Concurrent Computation, Evian, G. Kahn (ed), Lecture Notes in Computer Sciences.
Springer-Verlag, 1979, pages 123-146.

[Good 78] D.Good and R.Cohen.
Verifiable Communications Processing in Gypsy.
In *Compcon*, pages 28-35. 1978.

[Good 82] D.Good.
The Proof of a Distributed System in Gypsy.
Technical Report 30, The Univ. of Texas at Austin, September, 1982.

[Goud 76] M.Gouda and E.Manning.
Protocol Machine: A Concise Formal Model and its Automatic Implementation.
In *Proceedings of the Third ICCC*, pages 346-350. 1976.

[Goud 84a] M.Gouda and Y. Yu.
Synthesis of Communicating Finite-State Machines with guaranteed Progress.
IEEE Transactions on Comunications COM-32(7):779-788, July, 1984.

[Goud 84b] M.Gouda and Y. Yu.
Protocol Validation by Maximal State Exploration.
IEEE Transactions on Comunications COM-32:94-97, January, 1984.

[Grat 68] G.Gratzer.
Universal Algebra.
Springer-Verlag, 1968.

[Gutt 78] J.Guttag, E.Horowitz, and D.Musser.
Abstract Data Types and Software Validation.
CACM 21(12):1048-1064, December, 1978.

[Hail 80] B.Hailpern and S.Owicki.
Verifying Network Protocols Using Temporal Logic.
In *NBS Trends and Applications Symposium*, pages 18-28. May, 1080.

[Hail 81] B.Hailpern.
Specifying and Verifying Protocols Represented as Abstract Programs.
IBM Journal of Research and Development RC 8674 (37908), February, 1981.

[Haje 78] J.Hajek.
Automatically Verified Data Transfer Protocol.
In *Proceedings of the Fourth International Computer Communications Conference*, pages 749-756. September, 1978.

[Hara 77] J.Harangozo.
An Approach to Describing a Link Level Protocol with a Formal Language.
In *Proceedings of the Fifth Data Communications Symposium*, pages 4.37-4.49. September, 1977.

[Hoar 69] C.Hoare.
An Axiomatic Basis for Computer Programming.
Communications of the ACM 12(10):576-583, October, 1969.

[Holz 82] G.Holzmann.
A Theory For Protocol Validation.
IEEE Tranactions on Computers , August, 1982.

[Iso 83a] ISO TC97/SC16 N1347 .
A FDT based on an extended state transition model.
Technical Report, ISO, July, 1983.

[Iso 83b] ISO TC97/SC16 N1347 .
Draft Tutorial Document on Temporal Ordering Specification Language.
Technical Report, ISO, August, 1983.

[Jurg 84] W.Jurgensen and S. Vuong.
Formal Specification and Validation of ISO Transport Protocol Components, Using Petri Nets.
In *Proceedings of SIGCOMM Symposium.* ACM, 1984.

[Kell 76] R.Keller.
Formal Verification of Parallel Programs.
Communications of the ACM 19(7), July, 1976.

[Klei 75] L.Kleinrock.
Queueing Systems.
Wiley Interscience, 1975.

[Koba 78] H.Kobayashi.
Modeling and analysis: An Introduction to System Perfromance Evaluation Methodology.
Addison-Wesley Pub. Co, 1978.

[Krit 84] P.Kritzinger.
Analyzing the Time Efficiency of a Communication Protocol.
In *Proceedings of the Fourth IFIP International Workshop on Protocol Specification, Testing and Verification.* North-Holland, 1984.

[Krog 78] S.Krogdahl.
Verification of a Class of Link-Level Protocols.
BIT 18:436-448, 1978.

[Kuro 82] J.Kurose.
The Specification and Verification of a Connection Establishment Protocol Using Temporal Logic.
In *Proceedings of the Second IFIP International Workshop on Protocol Specification, Testing and Verification*, pages 43-62. May, 1982.

[Lam 82] S.Lam and A.Shankar.
An Illustration of Protocol Projections.
In *Proceedings of the Second IFIP International Workshop on Protocol Specification, Testing and Verification.* 1982.

[Lamp 77] L.Lamport.
Proving The Correctness of Multiprocess Programs.
IEEE Transactions on Software Engineering SE-3:125-143, 1977.

[Lamp 80] L.Lamport.
'Sometime' is Sometimes 'Not Never'.
In *Proceedings of the ACM POPL Conference*, pages 174-185. 1980.

[Lamp 83] L.Lamport.
Specifying Concurrent Program Modules.
ACM Transactions on Programming Languages and Systems 5(2):190-222, April, 1983.

[Lehm 80] M.Lehman.
Programs, Life Cycles, and Laws of Software Evolution.
In *Proceedings of the IEEE*, pages 1060-1075. September, 1980.

[Lond 80] R.London and L.Robinson.
The Role of Verification Tools and Techniques.
Software Development Tools, W.Riddle and R.Fairley ed.
Springer-Verlag, 1980, pages 206-212.

[Mann 81] Z.Manna and A.Pneuli.
Verification of Concurrent Programs: The Temporal Framework.
Technical Report STAN-CS-81-836, Stanford Unversity, June, 1981.

[Meli 82] J.Melici.
The BX.25 Certification Facility.
Computer Networks 6:319-329, 1982.

[Merl 76] P.Merlin and D.Farber.
Recoverability of Communication Protocols - Implications of a Theoretical Study.
IEEE Transactions on Communications COM-24:1036-1043, September, 1976.

[Miln 80] R. Milner.
A Calculus of Communicating Systems.
Springer Verlag, 1980.

[Moll 81] M.Molloy.
On the Integration of Delay and Throughput Measures in Distributed Processing Models.
PhD thesis, Univ. of California Los Angeles, 1981.

[Muss 80] D.Musser.
Abstarct data Type Specifications in the AFFIRM System.
IEEE Transactions on Software Engineering SE-6(1), January, 1980.

[Nigh 82] J.Nightingale.
Protocol Testing Using A Reference Implementation.
In *Proceedings of the Second IFIP International Workshop on Protocol Specification, Testing and Verification.* 1982.

[Noun 84] N.Nounou and Y.Yemini.
Algebraic Specification-Based Performance Analysis of Communication Protocols.
In *Proceedings of the Fourth IFIP International Workshop on Protocol Specification, Testing and Verification.* North-Holland, June, 1984.

[Noun 86] N.Nounou.
Specification-Based Performance Analysis of Protocols.
PhD thesis, Columbia Univ., 1986.

[Nutt 72] G.Nutt.
Evaluation Nets for Compuetr System Perfromance analysis.
AFIPS Conference Proceedings 41,Part 1:279-286, 1972.

[Oste 80] L.Osterweil.
A Software Lifecycle Methodology and Tool Support.
Software Development Tools, W.Riddle and R.Fairley ed.
Springer-Verlag, 1980, pages 82-118.

[Pete 77] J.Peterson.
Petri Nets.
ACM Computing Surveys 9(3):224-252, September, 1977.

[Piat 80] T.Piatkowski.
Remarks on ADCCP Validation and Testing Techniques.
NBS Trends and Applications Symposium , May 29, 1980.

[Pnue 77] A.Pnueli.
The Temporal Logic of Programs.
In *The Eighteen Annual Symposium on Foundations of Computer Science*, pages 46-57. October, 1977.

[Post 76] J.Postel and D.Farber.
Graphic Modeling of Computer Communications Protocols.
In *Proceedings of the Fifth Texas Conference on Computing Systems*, pages 66-67. 1976.

[Prad 79] B.Chezaviel-Pradin.
Un Outil Grphiquw Interactif pour la Validation des Systemes a Evolution Parallele Decrits par Reseaux de Petri.
PhD thesis, Universite Paul Sabatier, December, 1979.

[Rayn 82] D.Rayner ed.
A System for Testing Protocol Implementations.
Technical Report 9/82, NPL, August, 1982.

[Razo 84] R.Razouk.
The Derivation of Perfromance Expressions for Communication Protocols from Timed Petri Net Models.
In *Proceedings of the SIGCOMM Symposium*, pages 210-217. ACM, June, 1984.

[Regh 82] H.Reghbati.
Performance Analysis of Message-Based Systems.
In *Proceedings of the Second IFIP International Workshop on Protocol Specification, Testing and Verification*, pages 321-324. May, 1982.

[Reis 82] M.Reiser.
Perfromance Evaluation of Data Communication Systems.
In *Proceedings of the IEEE*, pages 171-196. February, 1982.

[Ridd 80] W.Riddle and R.Fairley.
Introduction.
Software Development Tools, W.Riddle and R.Fairley ed.
Springer-Verlag, 1980, pages 1-8.

[Rock 81] A.Rockstrom and R.Sarraco.
SDL CCITT Specification and Description Language.
In *Proceedings of the NTC*, pages G6.3.1-G6.3.5. 1981.

[Rubi 82] J.Rubin and C.West.
An Improved Protocol Validation Technique.
Computer Networks 6:65-73, 1982.

[Rudi 84] H.Rudin.
An Improved Algorithm for Estimating Protocol Performance.
In *Proceedings of the Fourth IFIP International Workshop on Protocol Specification, Testing and Verification*. North-Holland, 1984.

[Sabn 82a] K.Sabnani and M.Schwartz.
Verification of a Multidestination Protocol Using Temporal Logic.
In *Proceedings of the Second IFIP International Workshop on Protocol Specification, Testing and Verification*, pages 21-42. may, 1982.

[Sabn 82b] K.Sabnani.
Multidestination Protocols for Satellite Broadcast Channels.
PhD thesis, Columbia University, 1982.

[Sari 82] B.Sarikaya and G.Bochmann.
Some Experience with Test Sequence Generation for Protocols.
In *Proceedings of the Second IFIP International Workshop on Protocol Specification, Testing and Verification*. 1982.

[Schi 80] S.Schindler.
Algebraic and Model Specification Techniques.
In *Proceedings of the Hawaii International Conference on System Sciences*. 1980.

[Schi 81] S.Schindler.
The OSA Project: Basic Concepts of Formal Specification Techniques and of RSPL.
In *Proceedings of the First International INWG/NPL Workshop : Protocol Testing - Towards Proof?*, pages 143-176. 1981.

[Schw 81a] D.Schwabe.
Fromal Techniques for the Specification and Verification of Protocols.
PhD thesis, Univ. of California Los Angeles, April, 1981.

[Schw 81b] R.Schwartz and P.Melliar-Smith.
Temporal Logic Specification of Distributed Systems.
In *Proceedings of the IEEE Distributed Computer Systems Conference*, pages 446-454. 1981.

[Schw 82] R.Schwartz and P.Melliar-Smith.
From State Machines to Temporal Logic: Specification Methods for Protocol Standards.
IEEE Transaction on Communications COM 12:2476-2505, Decmber, 1982.

[Schw 83] R.Schwartz, P.Melliar-Smith and F.Vogt.
Interval Logic: A Higher-Level Teporal Logic for Protocol Specification.
In *Proceedings of the Third IFIP International Workshop on Protocol Specification, Testing and Verification*. North-Holland, 1983.

[Shan 84] A.Shankar and S.Lam.
Specification and Verification of Time-Dependent Communication Protocols.
In *Proceedings of the Fourth IFIP International Workshop on Protocol Specification, Testing and Verification.* North-Holland, 1984.

[Sloa 83] L.Sloan.
Meachanisms That Enforce Bounds on Packet Lifetimes.
ACM Transactions on Computer Systems 1(4):311-330, November, 1983.

[Sten 76] N.Stenning.
A Data Transfer Protocol.
Computer Networks (1):99-110, 1976.

[Suns 75] C.Sunshine.
Interprocess Communication Protocols for Computer Networks.
PhD thesis, Stanford University, Digital Sytems Laboratory TR 105, December, 1975.

[Suns 81] C.Sunshine.
Formal Modeling of Communication Protocols.
In *Proceedings of the First International INWG/NPL Workshop : Protocol Testing - Towards Proof?*, pages 29-58. 1981.

[Suns 82a] C.Sunshine, D.Thompson, R.Erickson, S.Gerhart, and D.Shwabe.
Specification and Verification of Communication Protocols in AFFIRM Using State Transition Models.
IEEE Transactions on Software Engineering SE-8(5):460-489, September, 1982.

[Suns 82b] C.Sunshine.
Experience with Automated Verification Systems.
In *Proceedings of the Second IFIP International Workshop on Protocol Specification, Testing and Verification.* 1982.

[Suns 83] C.Sunshine.
Experience with Automated Verification Systems.
In *Proceedings of the Third IFIP International Workshop on Protocol Specification, Testing and Verification.* 1983.

[Symo 80] F.Symons.
Representation, Analysis & Verification of Communication Protocols.
Technical Report 7380, Australian Telecommunication Research, 1980.

[Tane 81] A.Tanenbaum.
Network Protocols.
Computing Surveys 13(4):453-489, December, 1981.

[Teng 78] A.Teng and M.Liu.
A Formal Model for Automatic Implementation and Logical Validation of Network Communication Protocol.
In *NBS Computer Networking Symposium*, pages 114-123. 1978.

[Tows 79] D.Towsley and J.Wolf.
On the Statistical Analysis of Queue Lengths and Waiting Times for Statistical Multiplexers with ARQ Retransmission Schemes.
IEEE Transactions on Communications COM-27(4):693-702, April, 1979.

[Ural 83] H.Ural and R.Probert.
User-Guided Test Sequence Generation.
In *Proceedings of the Third IFIP International Workshop on Protocol Specification, Testing and Verification.* North-Holland, 1983.

[Vogt 82] F.Vogt.
Event-Based Temporal Logic Specifications of Services and Protocols.
In *Proceedings of the Second IFIP International Workshop on Protocol Specification, Testing and Verification*, pages 63-74. May, 1982.

[Wass 81] A.Wasserman.
Tutorial: Software Development Environments.
Software Development Tools, W.Riddle and R.Fairley ed.
IEEE Computer Society, 1981, pages 1-2.

[Weir 78] F.Weir, W.Prater, and X.Dam.
X.25 Test Facilities on Datapac.
In *Proceedings of the Fourth ICCC*, pages 273-279. September, 1978.

[West 78a] C.West.
An Automated Technique of Communications Protocol Validation.
IEEE Transactions on Communications COM-26(8):1271- 1275, August, 1978.

[West 78b] C.West.
General Technique for Communications Protocol Validation.
IBM Journal of Research and Development 22(4):393-404, July, 1978.

[West 78c] C.West and P.Zafiropluo.
Automated Validation of a Communications Protocol: the CCITT X.21 Recommendation.
IBMJRD 22(1):60-71, January, 1978.

[West 82] C.West.
Applications and Limitaions of Automated Protocol Validation.
In *Proceedings of the Second IFIP International Workshop on Protocol Specification, Testing and Verification.* 1982.

[Wolp 82] P.Wolper.
Specification and Synthesis of Communicating Processes using an Extended Temporal Logic.
In *Proceedings of the Ninth Symposium on Principles of Programming Languages.* January, 1982.

[X.21 76] CCITT.
Recommendation X.21 (Revised).
Technical Report, Geneva, Switzerland, March, 1976.

[X.25 80] CCITT.
Recomendation X.25 Packet Switch Data Transmission Services.
Technical Report, Geneve, Switzerland, 1980.

[Yelo 82] L.Yellowitz, S.Gerhart and G.Hilborn.
Modeling a Netwprk Protocol in AFFIRM and Ada.
In *Proceedings of the Second IFIP International Workshop on Protocol Specification, Testing and Verification*, pages 435-450. May, 1982.

[Yemi 82] Y.Yemini and J.Kurose.
Towards the Unification of the Functional and Performance Analysis of Protocols, or is the Alternating-Bit Protocol Really Correct?
In *Proceedings of the Second IFIP International Workshop on Protocol Specification, Testing and Verification.* 1982.

[Yu 79] L.Yu and J.Majthia.
An Analysis of One Direction of Window Mechanism.
IEEE Transactions on Communications COM-27(5):778-788, May, 1979.

[Zafi 80] P.Zafiropulo, C.West, H.Rudin, D.Cowan, and D.Brand.
Towards Analyzing and Synthesizing Protocols.
IEEE Transactions on Communications COM- 28(4):651-661, April, 1980.

[Zimm 80] H.Zimmermann.
The ISO Model of Architecture for Open System Interconnection.
IEEE Transactions on Communications COM-28(4), April, 1980.

Compiling Path Expressions into VLSI Circuits

T. S. Anantharaman
E. M. Clarke
M. J. Foster†
B. Mishra
Carnegie-Mellon University
Pittsburgh, Pennsylvania 15213

†Current address: Department of Computer Science, Columbia University, New York, New York 10027.

This research was partially supported by NSF Grant MCS-82-16706, and the Defense Advanced Research Projects Agency (DOD), ARPA Order No. 3597, monitored by the Air Force Avionics Laboratory Under Contract F33615-81-K-1539.

Portions of this chapter also appear in the article "Compiling Path Expressions into VLSI Circuits" by Michael Foster to appear in a future issue of *Distributed Computing*, published by Springer-Verlag, New York, New York.

Abstract: Path expressions were originally proposed by Campbell and Habermann [2] as a mechanism for process synchronization at the monitor level in software. Not surprisingly, they also provide a useful notation for specifying the behavior of asynchronous circuits. Motivated by these potential applications we investigate how to directly translate path expressions into hardware.

Our implementation is complicated in the case of multiple path expressions by the need for synchronization on event names that are common to more than one path. Moreover, since events are inherently asynchronous in our model, all of our circuits must be self-timed.

Nevertheless, the circuits produced by our construction have area proportional to $N \cdot \log(N)$ where N is the total length of the multiple path expression under consideration. This bound holds regardless of the number of individual paths or the degree of synchronization between paths. Furthermore, if the structure of the path expression allows partitioning, the circuit can be laid out in a distributed fashion without additional area overhead.

1. Introduction

As the boundary between software and hardware grows less and less distinct, it becomes increasingly important to investigate methods of directly implementing various programming language features in hardware. Since many of the problems in interfacing hardware devices involve some form of process synchronization, language features for synchronization deserve considerable attention in such investigations. In this paper we consider the problem of directly implementing path expressions as self-timed VLSI circuits. Path expressions were originally proposed by Campbell and Habermann [2] for restricting access by other processes to the procedures of a monitor. For example, the simple readers and writers problem with two reader processes and a single writer process is solved by the following multiple path expression:

path R_1 + W **end**,
path R_2 + W **end**.

The first path expression prohibits a read operation by the first process from occurring at the same time as a write operation. The second path expression enforces a similar restriction on the behavior of the second reader process. In a computation under control of the multiple path expression, the two read operations may occur simultaneously, but a read and write operation cannot occur at the same time.

A *simple path expression* is a regular expression with an outermost Kleene star. The only operators permitted in the regular expression are (in order of precedence) "*", ";", and "+". The "*" operator is the Kleene star, ";" is the sequencing operator, and "+" represents exclusive choice. Operands are event names from some set of events Σ that we will assume to be fixed in this paper. The outermost Kleene star is usually represented by the delimiting keyword **path** ... **end**. Thus $(a)^*$ would be represented as **path** a **end**. Roughly the sequence of events allowed by a simple path expression must correspond to the sequences in the language of the regular expression.

A *multiple path expression* is a set of simple path expressions. As we will see shortly, each additional simple path expression further constrains the order in which events can occur. However, we cannot simply take as our semantics for multiple path expressions the intersection of the languages corresponding to the individual path expressions; two events whose order is not explicitly restricted by one of the simple path expressions may be concurrent. For example, in the multiple path expression for the readers and writers problem discussed earlier the two read events R_1 and R_2 may occur simultaneously.

Path expressions are useful for process synchronization for two reasons: First, the close relationship between path expressions and regular expressions simplifies the task of writing and reasoning about programs which use this synchronization mechanism. Secondly, the synchronization in many concurrent programs is finite state and thus, can be adequately described by regular expressions. For precisely the same reasons, path expressions are useful for controlling the behavior of complicated asynchronous circuits. The readers and writers example above could equally well describe a simple bus arbitration scheme. In fact, the finite-state assumption may be even more reasonable at the hardware level than at the monitor level.

Which brings us to the topic of this paper: What is the best way to translate path expressions into circuits? Lauer and Campbell have shown how to compile path expressions into Petri nets [7], and Patil has shown how to implement Petri nets as circuits by using a PLA-like device called an asynchronous logic array [13]. Thus, an obvious method for compiling path expressions into circuits would be to first translate the path expression into a Petri net and then to implement the Petri net as a circuit using an asynchronous logic array. However, careful examination of Lauer and Campbell's scheme shows that a multiple path expression consisting of M paths each of length K can result in a Petri net with K^M places. Thus, the naive approach will in general be infeasible if the number of individual paths in a multiple path expression is large.

For the case of a path expression with a single path their scheme does result in Petri net which is comparable in size to the path expression. However, direct implementation of such a net using Patil's ideas may still result in a circuit with an unacceptably large area. An asynchronous logic array for a Petri net with P places and T transitions will have area proportional to $P \cdot T$ regardless of the number of arcs in the net. Since the nets obtained from path expressions tend to have sparse edge sets, this quadratic behavior may waste significant chip area.

Perhaps, the work that is closest to ours is due to Li and Lauer [10] who do indeed implement path expressions in VLSI. However, their circuits differ significantly from ours; in particular, their circuits are synchronous, and synchronization with the external world (which is, of course, inherently asynchronous) is not considered. (This means that the entire circuit, not just the synchronization, must be described using path expressions.) Furthermore, their circuits use PLA's that result in an area complexity of $O(N^2)$. Rem [15] has investigated the use of a hierarchically structured path expression-like language for specifying CMOS circuits. Although he does show how certain specifications can be translated into circuits, he does not describe how to handle synchronization or give a general layout algorithm that produces area efficient circuits.

In contrast, the circuits produced by the construction described in this paper have area proportional to $N \cdot \log(N)$ where N is the total length of the multiple path expression under consideration. Furthermore, this bound holds regardless of the number of individual paths or the degree of synchronization between paths. As in [4] and [5] the basic idea is to generate circuits for which the underlying graph structure has a constant separator theorem [8]. For path expressions with a single path the techniques used by [4] and [5] can be adapted without great difficulty. For multiple paths with common event names, however, the construction is not straightforward, because of the potential need for synchronization at many different points on each individual path. Moreover, the actual circuits that we use must be much more complicated than the synchronous ones used in ([4], [5]). Since events are inherently asynchronous in our model, all of our circuits must be self-timed and the use of special circuit design techniques is required to correctly capture the semantics of path expressions.

The paper is organized as follows: A formal semantics for path expressions in terms of partially ordered multisets [14] is given in section 2. In sections 3, 4, and 5 we give a hierarchical description of our scheme for implementing path expressions as circuits. In section 3 we first describe how the complete circuit interfaces with the external world. We then show how to build a *synchronizer* that coordinates the behavior of the circuits for the individual path expressions in a multiple path expression. In section 4 we describe a circuit for implementing single path expressions which we call a *sequencer.* In section 5 we show how the arbiter circuit used in section 3 can be implemented. We also argue that these circuits are correct and can be laid out efficiently. The conclusion in section 6 discusses the feasibility of our implementation and the possibility of extending it to other synchronization mechanisms like those used in CCS and CSP.

2. The Semantics of Path Expressions

In this section we give a simple but formal semantics for path expressions in terms of partially ordered multisets (*pomsets*) of events [14]. An alternative semantics in terms of Petri Nets is given by Lauer and Campbell in [7]. A a pomset may be regarded as a generalization of a sequence in which certain elements are permitted to be concurrent; this is why the concept is useful in modeling systems where several events may occur simultaneously.

Definition 1: A *partially ordered multiset* (pomset) over Σ is a triple $(Q, \leq, F)$ where $(Q, \leq)$ is a partially ordered set and F is a function which maps Q into Σ. □

An example of a pomset is shown in Figure 2-1. We use subscripts to distinguish different elements of Q that map to the same element of Σ. In this case $Q = (A_1,A_2,A_3,B_1,B_2,B_3,C_1,C_2,C_3)$ and $\Sigma = (A,B,C)$. Note that we could have alternatively defined a pomset as a directed acyclic graph in which each node is labeled with some element of Σ.

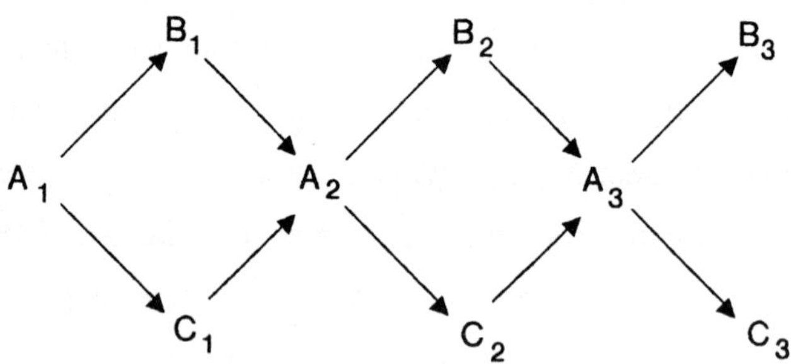

Figure 2-1: An example pomset

If the ordering relation of a pomset P over Σ is a total order, then we can naturally associate a sequence of elements of Σ with P; we will use S(P) to denote this sequence.

Definition 2: If $P = (Q, \leq, F)$ is a pomset over Σ and $\Sigma_1 \subseteq \Sigma$, then the *restriction* of P to Σ_1 is the pomset $P|_{\Sigma_1} = (Q_1, \leq_1, F_1)$ where $Q_1 = \{d \in Q \mid F(d) \in \Sigma_1\}$ and $\leq_1$, F_1 are restrictions of $\leq$, F to Q_1, respectively. □

If P is a totally ordered pomset over Σ and $\Sigma_1 \subseteq \Sigma$, then $S(P|_{\Sigma_1})$ is just the *subsequence* of S(P) obtained by deleting all of those elements of Σ which are not in Σ_1. If R is an ordinary regular expression over Σ, then $\Sigma_R \subseteq \Sigma$ will be the set of symbols of Σ that actually appear in R and $L_R \subseteq \Sigma_R^*$ will be the regular language which corresponds to R.

Definition 3:

Let Σ be a finite set. A *trace* over Σ is a pomset $T = (Q, \leq, F)$ over Σ such that every infinite chain of the partially ordered set $(Q, \leq)$ is an ω-sequence[1] . We say that $i \in Q$ is an *instance* of an event $e \in \Sigma$ if $F(i) = e$. An instance i_1 of event e_1 *precedes* an instance i_2 of event e_2 if i_1 precedes i_2 in the partial order $\leq$. An instance i_1 of event e_1 is *concurrent* with an instance i_2 of event e_2, if neither instance precedes the other. □

In the example above A_1 precedes A_2, but B_1 and C_1 are concurrent.

Definition 4: Let R be a simple path expression with event set Σ_R. A trace T is *consistent with R* iff $T|_{\Sigma_R}$ is totally ordered and every finite prefix of $S(T|_{\Sigma_R})$ is a prefix of some sequence in L_R, the language of regular expression R. If M is a multiple path expression, then a trace T is *consistent with M* iff it is consistent with each simple path expression R in M. $Tr_\Sigma(M)$ is the set of all traces which are consistent with M. □

Consider, for example, the multiple path expression M:

path A;B **end**,
path A;C **end**.

---

[1]In absence of fairness, finite sequences are sufficient. In order to talk about fairness however, we require infinite sequences. An ω-sequence is the shortest infinite sequence that captures the semantics of fairness and has the advantage that all of its prefixes are finite.

with $\Sigma = \{A, B, C\}$. It is easy to see that the trace in Figure 2-1 is consistent with each of the simple path expressions in M and hence is in $Tr_{\Sigma}(M)$.

3. Synchronizers for Multiple Path Expressions

This section describes our implementation of synchronizers for multiple path expressions. Figure 3-1 illustrates the interface between a synchronizer and the external world. Each event *e* is associated with a request line REQ_e and acknowledge line ACK_e. The synchronizer cooperates with the external world to ensure that these request and acknowledge lines follow a 4-cycle protocol:

1. The external world raises REQ_e to indicate that it would like to proceed with event *e*.

2. The synchronizer raises ACK_e to allow the external world to proceed with event *e*.

3. The external world lowers REQ_e, signifying completion of event *e*.

4. The synchronizer lowers ACK_e, signifying the end of the cycle and permission to begin a new one.

In this implementation, an event will occur during the period between cycles 2 and 3 in this protocol, where both REQ and ACK are high. Thus, multiple occurrences of any event *e* are non-overlapping in time, since any two occurrences are separated by the lowering of ACK and the raising of REQ.

In a distributed system each of the devices in the system would be a *client* of the synchronizer; only a subset of the REQ and ACK lines would go

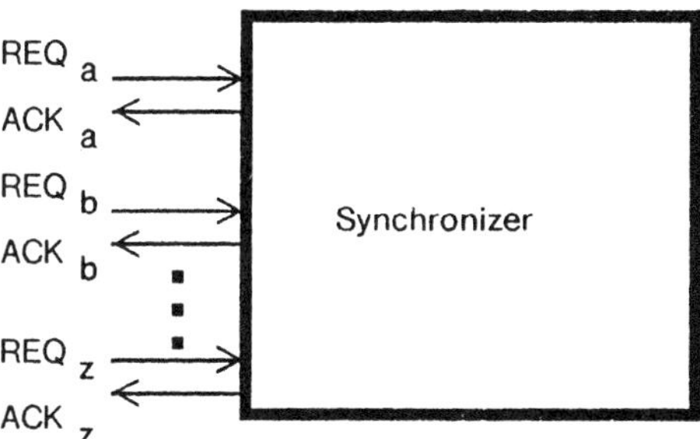

Figure 3-1: A synchronizer

to each device. Before performing an action, each client would request permission from the synchronizer and wait until permission was granted. In this way, harmonious cooperation could be ensured with only a small amount of inter-device communication. Because of the symmetric nature of the protocol any *client* could act either as a master or a slave relative to other *clients.* A slave would always assert all REQ's and wait for a response through the ACK's telling it what to do, whereas a master would assert REQ's only for those events it wishes to proceed with and use the ACK's only to get its timing correct.

An overview of a synchronizer circuit is shown in Figure 3-2. The circuit shown is self timed but not delay independent as it makes certain assumptions about gate delays which will be described later. Some of the building blocks in the circuit are described below.

The C gate in Figure 3-2 is a Muller C-element; the output of a C-element remains low until all inputs are high and thereafter remains high until all inputs are low again. Its behavior then cycles. For an implementation see [16].

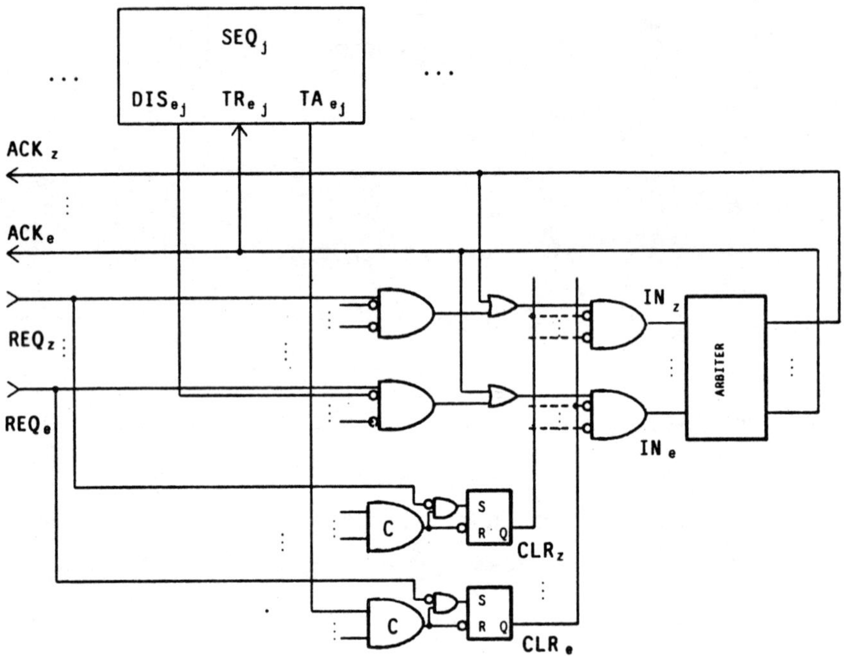

Figure 3-2: A synchronizer circuit

The arbiter in Figure 3-2 enforces pairwise mutual exclusion over the outputs corresponding to pairs of events which occur in the same path expression.In addition to enforcing mutual exclusion the arbiter tries to raise any output whose input is high. Many implementations of arbiters will have metastable states during which fewer signals than possible may be high at the output. Despite the metastable states, however, once an output signal has been raised, it must remain high as long as the corresponding input remains high. The implementation of such an arbiter is discussed in detail in section 5.

Each sequencer block in Figure 3-2 ensures that the sequence of events satisfies one of the simple path expressions that comprise the multiple path expression, and will be described in the next section. The synchronizer circuit contains one sequencer for each simple path expression, so that each simple path expression is satisfied by an execution event trace. For each event *e* that appears in a simple path, the corresponding sequencer has three connections: a request TR_e, an acknowledge TA_e, and a disable DIS_e. Events are sequenced by executing a 4-cycle protocol over one pair of the TR/TA lines. The DIS outputs of the sequencer are only valid between these cycles (when all TR and TA are low), and indicate which events would violate the simple path. The synchronizer will not initiate a cycle for any event whose DIS line is high.

We now describe how the components of the circuit are interconnected. Refer to Figure 3-2. Let SEQ_e denote the set of sequencers for simple paths that contain event *e*. Every sequencer in SEQ_e has its DIS_e signal connected to a NOR gate for *e*, its TA_e signal connected to a C gate for *e*, and its TR_e signal connected to ACK_e. The output of the latch at the end of the C gate for *e*, which is labeled CLR_e, is connected to each of the NOR gates in front of the arbiter which corresponds to event *e* or to some event mutually exclusive to *e*.

Notice that there is no intrinsic need for the synchronizer to be centralized as long as the constraints themselves do not require it. Whenever the multiple path expression can be partioned into disjoint sets of paths so that paths in different sets do not refer to the same event, then each set can be implemented as a circuit independently of the others.

The following is an informal description of how the circuit works. The circuit behaves as shown in the timing diagram in Figure 3-3. When REQ_e is raised, event e is not allowed to proceed unless each sequencer in SEQ_e signals that at least one e type transition is enabled by negating DIS_e. Once this happens IN_e is raised, provided no mutually exclusive event is executing the second half of its cycle (and hence has its CLR high). If the arbiter decides in favor of some other pending event mutually exclusive to e, the above process repeats until e again gets a chance at the arbiter. Otherwise ACK_e will be raised and latched by the NOR gate arrangement in front of the arbiter. At this point the external world may proceed with event e. Simultaneously each sequencer in SEQ_e will find TR_e high and after some time raise TA_e. When all sequencers in SEQ_e have raised TA_e and the external world acknowledges completion of event e by lowering REQ_e, CLR_e will be raised. This causes ACK_e to be lowered. Each sequencer in SEQ_e will find TR_e low and after some time lower TA_e. When all such sequencers are done, CLR_E is lowered, and the cycle is completed.

To formally establish the correctness of our circuit , we must establish two things: First, we must show that the circuit allows only semantically correct event traces; second, that the circuit will allow any semantically correct event trace for some behavior of the external world. These properties of the circuit are often called *safeness* and *liveness* respectively.

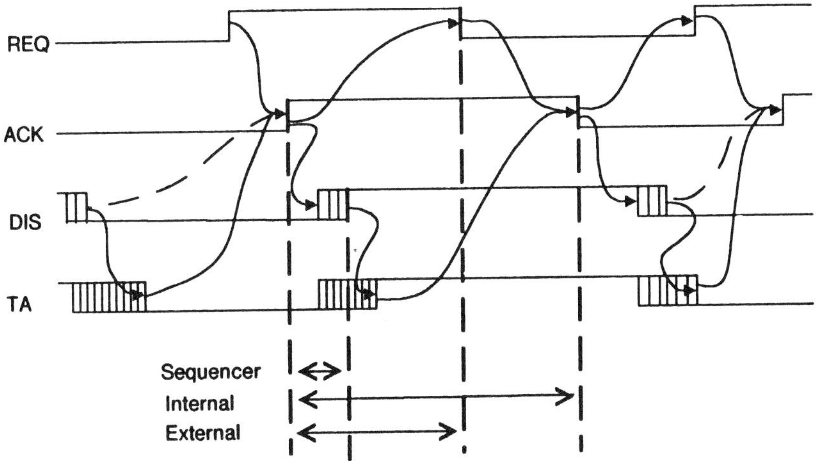

Figure 3-3: Synchronizer timing

A third important property, *fairness*, is dealt with in a separate section. Our proof will make use of properties of the various circuit components shown in Figure 3-2. We list the most important of these properties as propositions, namely those relating to the sequencer, the arbiter, and the external world. Properties of other circuit components such as SR Flip-Flops, NOR gates, etc., are assumed to be well known and are used without further discussion. The proof also makes certain assumptions about the delays of the components:

1. The delay of the main NOR gate plus the 2-input OR gate is less than that of the main Muller-C element plus the SR Flip-Flop.
2. The maximum variation in delay for the NOR gates in front of

the arbiter is less than the minimum delay of the arbiter.

We begin by introducing some notation that will be needed in the proof. Let the sequencers be denoted by SEQ_1 ... SEQ_p corresponding to the path expressions R1 ... Rp $\in$ M, and let Σ_{R1} ... Σ_{Rp} be the subsets of Σ that actually appear in R1 ... Rp respectively. Let I be a set of time intervals, which may include semi-infinite intervals extending from some finite instant to infinity. Each element in I is labeled by an element in Σ. Define T(I) to be the trace which has an element for each element in I and has the obvious partial order defined between elements whose time intervals are non-overlapping. Referring to Figure 3-3, let

- **Ext** = set of time intervals labeled 'external',
- **Int** = set of time intervals labeled 'internal',
- **Seq(j)** = set of time intervals labeled 'sequencer' for sequencer SEQ_j.

For every interval in **Int** with label *e* there are corresponding intervals with the same label in **Ext** and in every **Seq(j)** such that $e \in \Sigma_{Rj}$, namely those which start at the same time. We assume that the starting points of intervals in **Int** lie within some finite time period of interest, and the intervals in **Ext** and **Seq(j)** are restricted to intervals corresponding to those in **Int**.

With this notation in place we state some propositions, or axioms, that describe the properties of the circuit of Figure 3-2. These properties will be used to prove that the circuit is safe and live. The propositions should be viewed as specifications for the correct behavior of lower level circuit modules and the external world, and will be justified in later sections.

Proposition 5: (External world protocol): For all events *e*,

1. REQ_e is raised only if ACK_e is low.
2. REQ_e is lowered only if ACK_e is high. □

Proposition 6: (Arbiter safety and liveness):

1. For any events *e1*,*e2* that are mutually exclusive, ACK_{e1} and ACK_{e2} are never high simultaneously.
2. For any event *e*, ACK_e is raised only if IN_e is raised.
3. For any event *e*, ACK_e is lowered only if IN_e is low,and within a finite time of IN_e being lowered.
4. Consider any set of events $\Sigma' \subseteq \Sigma$, such that no two events in Σ' are in the same path expression. Then if all IN_e, $e \in \Sigma'$, are raised, within a finite time all ACK_e, $e \in \Sigma'$, must be raised. □

Proposition 7: (Sequencer protocol): For any sequencer SEQ_j,

1. TA_e is raised only if TR_e is high.
2. TA_e is lowered only if TR_e is low.
3. DIS_e is stable while all TR's and TA's are low. □

Proposition 8: (Sequencer safety and liveness) : For any sequencer SEQ_j, assume that at all times,

- no two TR's are high simultaneously,
- TR_e is raised only if DIS_e and all TA's are low,
- TR_e is lowered only if TA_e is high.

Then the following hold :

1. TA_e is raised within a finite time of TR_e being raised.
2. TA_e is lowered within a finite time of TR_e being lowered.
3. For any sequencer SEQ_j, whenever all TA's and TR's are low, exactly those events *e* will have DIS_e low, for which S(T(Seq(j))) can be extended by *e* to give a prefix of some sequence in L_{Rj}. □

Proposition 9: (Initialization)

1. Sequencers are initialized with all TA's low.
2. The synchronizer circuit SR flip-flops are initialized to make all CLR's high. □

The following theorem states that a synchronizer satisfying Propositions 5 through 9 is provably safe.

Theorem 10: (Synchronizer Safety) : $T(\mathbf{Ext}) \in Tr_{\Sigma}(M)$.

proof: See the appendix. □

As a converse to theorem 10 we would like to show that our circuit can produce any valid trace **Ext**, such that $T(\mathbf{Ext}) \in Tr_{\Sigma}(M)$ for at least some behavior of the external world. However for some traces $T \in Tr_{\Sigma}(M)$, there does not exist any **Ext** such that $T(\mathbf{Ext})=T$, so there is no way any circuit can produce the required trace **Ext**. This happens when T does not sufficiently constrain the order in which the elements may occur so that any actual set of time intervals will have fewer concurrent elements than T. Given such a T it is necessary to constrain its partial order relation further, by adding additional (consistent) precedence relationships. It is easy to show using definition 4 that this will never remove T from the set $Tr_{\Sigma}(M)$. We shall show that whenever T is sufficiently constrained so that it falls in a class of traces we call *layered*, then for some behavior of the external world T(**Ext**) for our circuit will equal this modified T.

Definition 11: A trace $P = (Q,\leq,L)$ is called *layered*, if Q can be subdivided into a sequence of *subsets*, such that for any *i1*, *i2* $\in$ Q, *i1* precedes *i2* iff the *subset* in which *i1* lies precedes the *subset* in which *i2* lies. □

The trace in Figure 2-1 is layered, since its elements can be subdivided into the sequence of *subsets* $\{(A_1),(B_1,C_1),(A_2),(B_2,C_2),(A_3),(B_3, C_3)\}$ with the above property. If the size of each *subset* were one, then the trace would be totally ordered.

In general, any trace P will have a corresponding layered trace T which preserves most of the parallelism of P. It is easy to show that for any trace P,there exists a layered trace T, which differs from P only in that the partial order relation of P is a restriction of that of T.

Theorem 12: (Synchronizer Liveness): Given any layered trace $P \in Tr_{\Sigma}(M)$, our circuit will produce an event trace Ext, such that T(Ext) = P for some behavior of the external world. □

proof: See the appendix. □

4. Implementing the Sequencer for a Simple Path Expression

This section shows how to construct a sequencer that enforces the semantics of a simple path expression. The sequencer circuit is constructed in a syntax-directed fashion based upon the structure of the simple path expression. We show that a compact layout for the sequencer exists, so that circuits of this type can be implemented economically in VLSI.

Since a simple path expression is a regular expression, the sequencer for a simple path expression is similar to a recognizer for the regular expression. Although schemes for recognition of regular languages have been proposed that avoid broadcast [4], we will use a scheme that requires broadcast of events throughout the sequencer [5, 12]. Because our scheme for interconnecting sequencers (see section 3) requires broadcast, the broadcast within an individual sequencer carries no additional penalty. A sequencer for a simple path expression is built up from primitive cells, each corresponding to one character in the path. The syntax of the path determines the interconnection of the cells in the sequencer. In this section, we first describe the behavior of a sequencer for a simple path expression, then give a syntax-directed construction method.

As noted in Section 3, a synchronizer communicates with each of its sequencers using three lines for each event:

- TR_e: a signal to the sequencer that event *e* is about to commence in the outside world;
- TA_e: an acknowledgement from the sequencer that the execution of event *e* has been noted by the sequencer.
- DIS_e: a status line indicating that action *e* would violate the path constraints so that TR_e should not be asserted by the outside world. It is valid when TR and TA are both low.

These communication lines interact in a complex way. For a single type of event, the signals TR_e and TA_e follow the four-cycle signaling convention (for an example see Section 3). For different types of events, the outside world must guarantee the correct interaction of TR signals by ensuring that only one TR signal for an event satisfying the simple path expression is asserted at any time. The outside world can use the DIS status lines to determine which requests to send to the sequencer.

The sequencer also has a part to play in ensuring the correct interaction of TR, TA and DIS. Besides generating a TA signal that follows the four cycle convention with TR, it must ensure that the signal DIS_e is correct as long as no TR or TA signal is asserted. This guarantee means that if neither TA nor TR is asserted, and neither DIS_{e1} nor DIS_{e2} is true, then the outside world may choose arbitrarily between *e1* and *e2*, letting either of them through to the simple path sequencer. On receiving a TR_e signal, then, the sequencer must assert TA_e, adjust its internal state to reflect the occurrence of event *e*, assert the proper set of DIS lines while awaiting the negation of TR_e before negating TA_e.

Now that the behavior of a sequencer has been described, we show how to construct a sequencer for any simple path expression. A sequencer has two parts: a controller and a recognizer. The controller is connected directly to the rest of the outside world and generates both the TA signals and some control signals for the recognizer. The recognizer keeps track of which events in the path have been seen and generates the DIS signals.

Figure 4-1 shows the controller for a simple path P. The controller accepts the signals TR_e from the synchronizer for each event *e* that appears in P. It generates the signals TA_e along with **Start** and **End**. The meaning of TA_e is that all actions caused by TR_e have been completed. In this realization, TA is just a delayed version of TR, where the delay is long enough to let the sequencer stabilize. An upper bound on this delay can be computed from the layout of the rest of the circuit. Thus the sequencer is self-timed but not delay insensitive. A more complicated, delay insensitive circuit will be described in a separate paper [1] . **Start** and **End** are essentially two phase clock signals that control the movement of data through the recognizer for P. Roughly **Start** is true from the time one TR is asserted until the corresponding TA is asserted, while **End** is true from the time TR is deasserted until TA is also deasserted. The element labeled M.E. (Mutual Exclusion) is an interlock element as shown in fig 5-2. It is required to guarantee that the two clock phases are strictly non-overlapping.

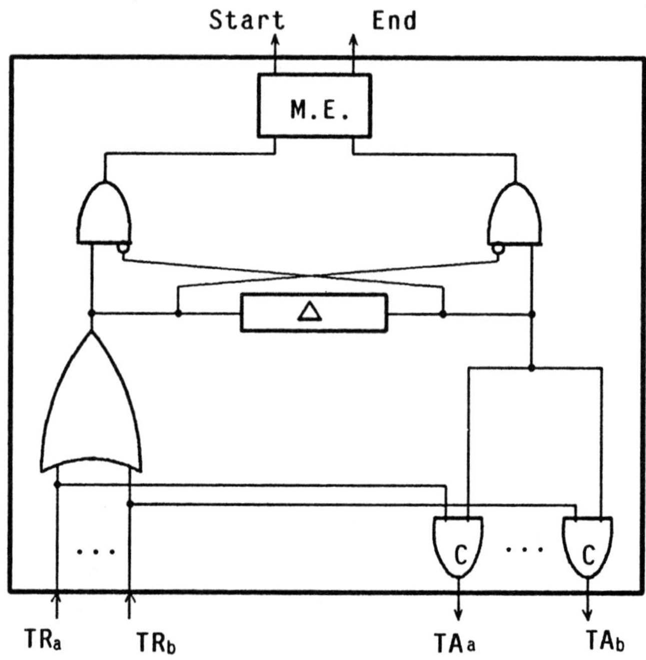

Figure 4-1: The controller for path P

The recognizer for a path accepts the TR_e signals and generates the DIS signals. It is made up of sub-circuits corresponding to subexpressions of the path. To construct the recognizer for a path, we parse the path using a context-free grammar. Productions that are used in parsing the path determine the interconnections of sub-circuits to form the recognizer. Non-terminals that are introduced in the parse correspond to primitive cells used in the circuit.

Recognizers are constructed using the following grammar for simple path expressions.

S → **path** R **end**
R → R;R | (R + R) | (R)* | <event>.

The terminal symbols in the grammar correspond to primitive cells; there is one type of cell for the "+" symbol, one for the "*" symbol, one for the ";" symbol, and one for each event. The non-terminals correspond to more complex circuits that are formed by interconnecting the primitive cells. Using the method described in [3], semantic rules attached to the productions of the grammar specify how the circuits on the right of each production are interconnected to form the circuit on the left.

To keep track of which events in the path have occurred and which are legal, the sub-circuits of a recognizer communicate using the signals ENB (enable) and RES (result). If ENB is asserted at the input of a circuit for a subexpression at the beginning of a cycle (when START is asserted), the subcircuit begins keeping track of events starting with that cycle, and asserts RES after a cycle if the event sequence so far is legal for the subexpression. The ENB input may be asserted before any cycle, and the subcircuit must generate a RES signal whenever any of the previous ENB inputs by itself would have required it. At the top level ENB is asserted only once, before the first cycle. Between cycles each subcircuit deasserts the DIS signal for an event, if the occurance of that event during the next cycle is legal (this is the case if the subcircuit would assert DIS for some subsequent sequence of events even if ENB were not asserted any more). These event signals from all subcircuits are combined to generate the external DIS signals.

Figure 4-2 shows the cell for event *e*. Two latches, clocked by **Start** and **End**, control the flow of ENB and RES signals. The latches are transparent when their enable is asserted and hold their previous value otherwise. The latch pair forms a level triggered master - slave D-Flip-Flop, clocked by the non-overlapping clock signals **Start** and **End**.

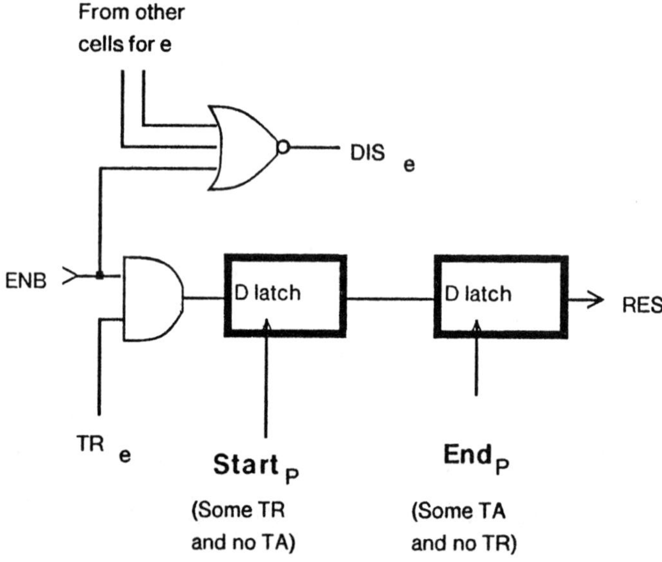

Figure 4-2: Cell for event *e* in path P

The event cell in Figure 4-2 propagates a 1 from ENB to RES only if event

e occurs. When this cell is used in a recognizer for a path expression, the ENB input will be true if and only if event e is permitted by the expression. Thus, if ENB is true it negates DIS_e for the path, as shown in the figure. When a request TR is made, the output of the AND gate is loaded into the leftmost latch. If this request is TR_e, this output is 1; otherwise it is 0. In either case the output of the AND gate is propagated to RES through the latch when TR is lowered.

Figures 4-3 and 4-4 show the cells for the ";" (sequencing) and "+" (union) operators. These are strictly combinational circuits. The circuit for ";" feeds the RES signal from the circuit at its left into the ENB signal for the circuit to its right. The circuit for "+" broadcasts its ENB signal to its operands and combines the RES signals from its operands in an OR gate.

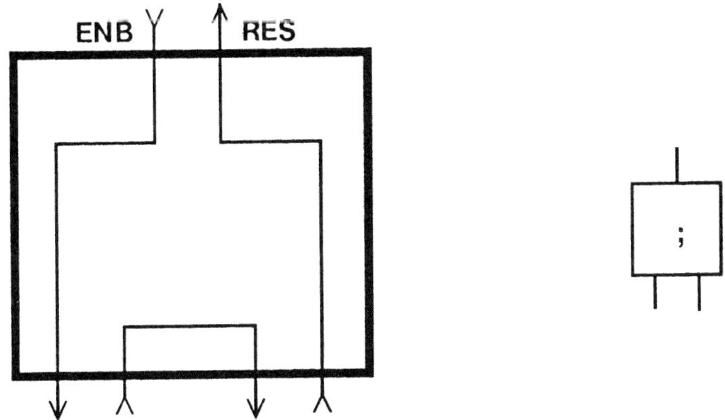

Figure 4-3: Cell for ";"

Figure 4-5 shows the cell for the "*" operator. The cell enables its operand after receiving either a 1 on either its own ENB or its operand's RES. Every time the operand is enabled the "*" cell also puts out a 1 on its

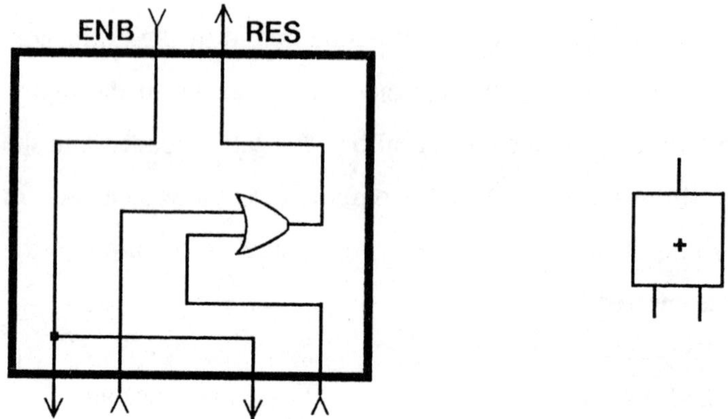

Figure 4-4: Cell for "+"

own RES. It therefore outputs 1 on RES after 0 or more repetitions of its operand's expression. The additional AND gate sets the output to 0 momentarily after each event, thereby preventing the formation of a latch when two or more "*" cells are used together. This cell is responsible for making the minimum cycle duration depend on the path expression. During the first phase of a cycle the sequencer has to perform an ε-closure of the simple path expression. This delay is directly reflected in the gate delay between the ENB input and RES output of the "*" cell. These delays will add up for an expression like $((a^* ; b^*) ; (c^* ; d^*))$.

When larger circuits are made from these cells, the RES and ENB signals retain their meanings. Each event cell or sub-circuit formed from several cells accepts one input ENB and produces one output RES. In general we define a pair of ENB and RES to be correct if the following applies at the beginning of each cycle (just before START is asserted):

- ENB is true if and only if the sequence of events so far can be

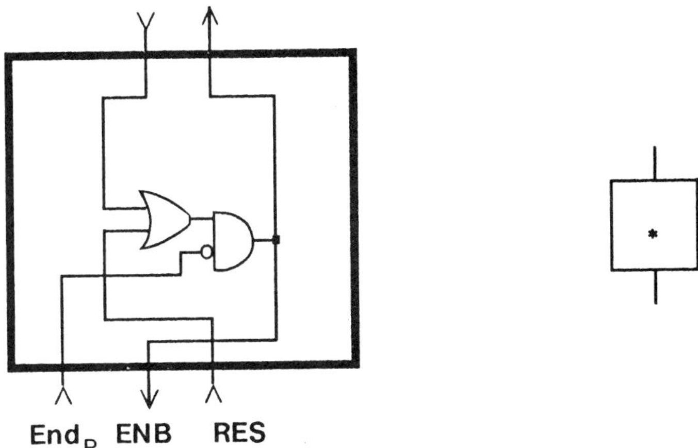

Figure 4-5: Cell for "*"

extended by any sequence of events satisfying the regular expression of the subcircuit controlled by the ENB/RES pair, to give a prefix of some sequence in L_{Rj}.

- RES is true if and only if some sequence of events satisfying the subexpression has just completed, and ENB was true just before the beginning of that sequence.

In addition, a sequencer has a signal INIT, not shown in the figures, which clears the RES outputs of all event (leaf) cells and generates the ENB input for the root cell (which must a "*" cell, if there is an outermost implied Kleene Star) during the first cycle (an RS flip-flop set by the INIT signal and reset by END can be used to generate this ENB signal).

Figure 4-6 shows a recognizer for the path **path** a;(a+b);c **end** constructed using this syntax-directed technique.

All recognizers constructed by the previously described procedure perform the correct function, as required by Propositions 7 and 8. The

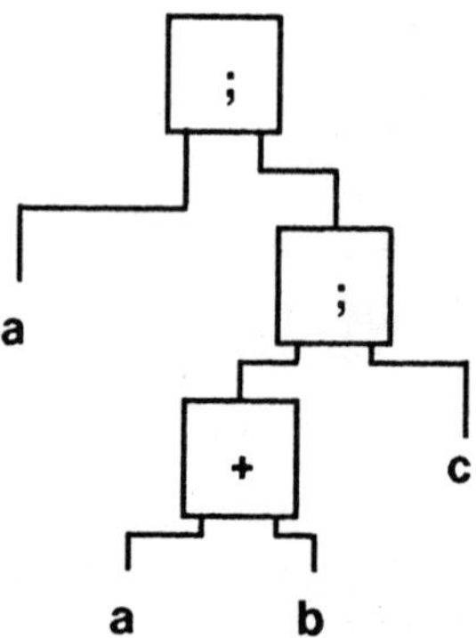

Figure 4-6: A recognizer for **path** a;(a+b);c **end**

former follows directly from the control circuit while the latter is equivalent to the following : If a recognizer is initialized and some sequence of events 'clocked' into the circuit, the recognizer will output 1 on DIS_e between cycles for precisely those events *e* that are forbidden (as the next event) by the simple path expression. To prove this we show that the ENB input of an event cell in the recognizer is 1 if and only if the event corresponding to this cell is permitted by the path. As shown in Figure 4-2, DIS_e is 1 if and only if none of the cells for event *e* is enabled. Therefore, proving that an event cell has its ENB signal set if and only if the corresponding event is permitted in the path will show that the recognizer is functionally correct. In other words, we wish to prove that all ENB signals for event cells are correct, according to the definition of ENB above.

We outline a proof of the stronger statement that all ENB signals in the recognizer are correct. This proof is based upon the structure of the recognizer. An ENB signal in a recognizer is set by one of four sources:

- The operand port of a "+" or "*" cell;

- The left operand port of a ";" cell;
- The right operand port of a ";" cell;
- The INIT signal.

In the first and second cases the signal is correct if and only if ENB for the operator cell is correct. In the third case the signal comes from the RES port of a recognizer for an initial subexpression. Therefore it is correct if and only if the RES signal for the subexpression is correct. In the fourth case the signal is asserted only at the start of the recognition and is correct by definition. Thus, to prove that the circuits are correct, we need only prove that if the ENB signal for any recognizer is correct then so is the RES signal.

Once again, the proof of correctness is based upon the structure of a recognizer. In a correct recognizer the RES signal is true at time t_1 if and only if the ENB signal is true at some preceding time t_0 and the events between t_0 and t_1 obey the path. A recognizer that is a single event cell is clearly correct. A recognizer for path **a;b** built by composition of correct subrecognizers for **a** and **b** is also correct, since if $\text{RES}_\mathbf{b}$ is true at time t_2 then there must be some time t_1 when $\text{RES}_\mathbf{a}$ was true, with all intervening events satisfying path **b**. But then there must have been a time t_0 when $\text{ENB}_\mathbf{a}$ was true and all events between t_0 and t_1 must satisfy path **a**. By definition of composition, then, the events between t_0 and t_2 satisfy **a;b**. A recognizer for path **(a)*** is correct if its subrecognizer is correct, since it outputs 1 and enables its operand if and only if ENB or $\text{RES}_\mathbf{a}$ is true. Finally, a recognizer for path **a** + **b** is correct if both subrecognizers are correct, since if RES is true then one of $\text{RES}_\mathbf{a}$ or $\text{RES}_\mathbf{b}$ must be true, and if one of ENB_a or ENB_b is true then ENB must be true. Since all methods of constructing recognizers have been shown to lead to correct circuits, recognizers constructed using this procedure are functionally correct.

Finally, we give a compact floor plan for the circuit. The floor plan for a sequencer, shown in Figure 4-7 has the cells that make up the recognizer arranged in a line with the controller to one side. The TR signals flow parallel to the line of recognizer cells to enter the controller, and the **Start** and **End** signals emerge from the controller to flow parallel to the line of cells. The ENB and RES signals that are used for intercell communication also flow parallel to the line of cells.

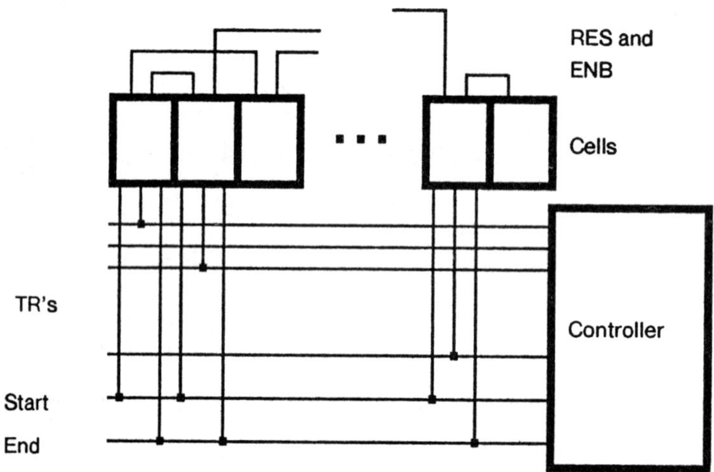

Figure 4-7: The floor plan for a sequencer

The layout in Figure 4-7 is fairly small. If the sequencer for a path of length n that has k types of input events is laid out in this fashion, the area of the layout is no more than $O((n+k)(\log n + k))$. This is due to the structure of the recognizer circuits. All recognizer circuits are trees, which can be laid out with all nodes on a line and edges running parallel to the line using no more than O(log n) wiring tracks [8]. Thus the height of the circuit in Figure 4-7 is O(log n + k) while its width is O(n+k).

5. Implementation of the Arbiter

In this section we elaborate on the arbiter shown in Figure 3-2 to show that the conditions assumed for it can be met. In older literature the term arbiter refers to a device that selects a single event from a mutually exclusive set of requests. In this paper the term is used in a somewhat less restrictive sense. All events need not be mutually exclusive and the arbiter may select more than one event concurrently, as long as the mutual-exclusion conditions are satisfied. We first show how such an arbiter can be built. Later we discuss ways to ensure that the arbiter is *fair* when forced to chose between events. This is much harder to achieve than just the mutual exclusion requirement.

We shall make use of the following terms : An event is *pending* from the time the external world asserts the request until the time the circuit asserts the acknowledge for the event. An event is *enabled* if it is pending, and it is not currently disabled by any path.

The following observation helps to simplify the arbiter: a pair of events occurring in any single path expression must be mutually exclusive. This is due to the role that each event plays in enforcing synchronization among a set of multiple path expressions, all containing the same named event. The arbitration function can thus be represented by a *conflict graph*, in which each event is denoted by a vertex and the relation between a pair of mutually exclusive events is denoted by an undirected edge. From our observation , it follows that the resulting conflict graph for a set of path expressions consists of a set of overlapping cliques, where a clique of k nodes, $A_1, A_2, \ldots, A_k$, corresponds to a simple path expression R, with $\Sigma_R = \{ A_1, A_2, \ldots, A_k \}$. The conflict graph represents the static structure of a multiple path expression. Figure 5-1 shows a multiple path expression and its conflict graph.

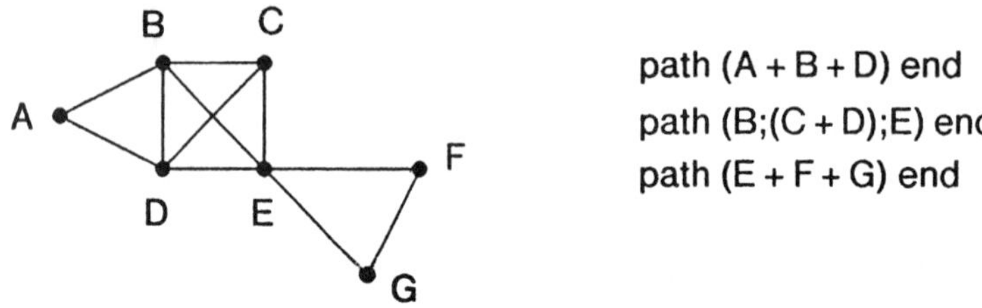

Figure 5-1: The conflict graph of a path expression

The dynamic behavior of the arbiter depends on the conflict graph together with the set of events that are *enabled* at any instant. The dynamic structure of a multiple path expression is represented by an *active* subgraph of the conflict graph induced by the set of vertices corresponding to the events enabled at that instant. The function of the arbiter is to select an independent set of this subgraph, thus ensuring that only one of any pair of mutually exclusive events is enabled. In this paper we require the arbiter to respond whenever it can and not introduce deliberate wait states. More formally we define a *maximally parallel set* of events to be an independent set of the active subgraph, such that it is not a subset of any other independent set of the active subgraph. We require the arbiter to respond with a maximally parallel set without introducing deliberate delays. In general there will be more than one possible maximally parallel set, and the arbiter need not choose the largest one.

Before proceeding further, let us consider the path expression **path** A + B **end**, where the conflict graph is $G = (V, E) = (\{A, B\}, \{[A, B]\})$. Seitz [16] has shown how to build an arbiter for such a structure using an interlock-element, as shown in Figure 5-2.

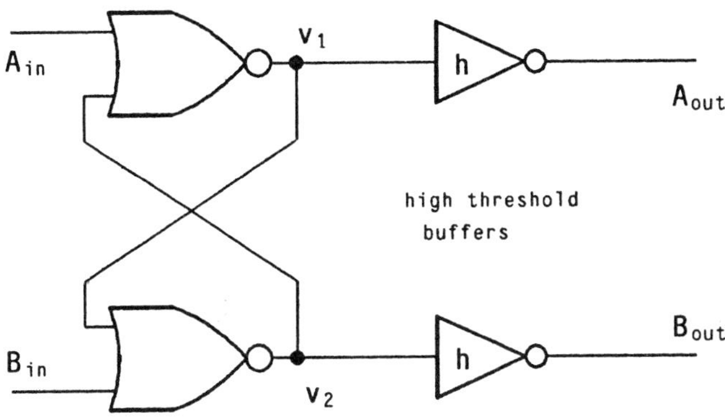

Figure 5-2: Seitz's Interlock Element

Circuit operation in Figure 5-2 is most easily visualized starting with neither client requesting, v_1 and v_2 both near 0 volts, and both outputs high. If any single input, say A_{in}, is lowered then v_1 is driven high, resulting in A_{out} being lowered — B_{out} remains unaffected. Moreover, once A_{out} is lowered, and as long as A_{in} is kept low, the interlock element remains in this stable state irrespective of what happens to B_{in}. If A_{in} is now raised high, then the element returns to its initial condition, if B_{in} is still high; or B_{out} is lowered, if B_{in} is lowered in the meantime.

However, the interesting situation occurs when both A_{in} and B_{in} are both lowered concurrently, *i.e.* within a very short interval of time. In this case the cross-coupled NOR gates enter a metastable state, which is resolved after indeterminate period of time in favor of either A or B. Since this resolution depends on the thermal noise generated by the gates, it is inherently probabilistic. In this case the outputs of the NOR gates themselves cannot be used as the outputs. High threshold inverters between the NOR gates and the outputs prevent false outputs during the metastable condition.

Seitz's idea can be extended by generalizing it to the conflict graph for an arbitrary set of path expressions. Roughly speaking, we may transform the conflict graph to a circuit by replacing each vertex with a NOR gate and each edge with a cross-coupling of NOR gates corresponding to the pair of vertices on which the edge is incident. Consider the circuit for the readers-writers path expression:

path $R_1 + W$ **end**
path $R_2 + W$ **end**

where the pair R_1 and W and the pair R_2 and W are mutually exclusive. The conflict graph and the circuit for this expression are shown in Figure 5-3.

The above arbiter is quite satisfactory if we do not require the arbiter to be fair. In certain applications, however, it is required that the arbiter should be fair when faced with a choice. So far we have not defined what we mean by fairness. The most commonly used definitions of fairness that

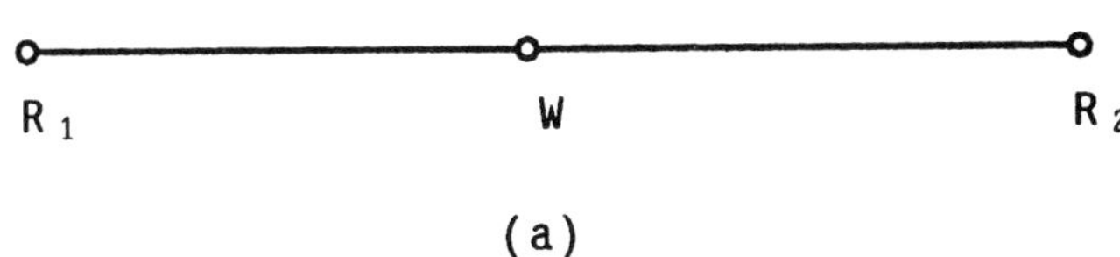

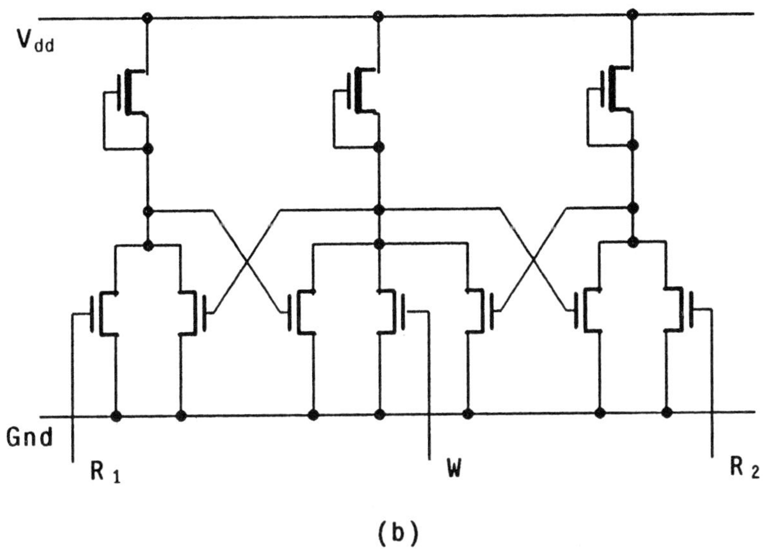

Figure 5-3: (a) The Conflict Graph and (b) The Arbiter in NMOS.

allow pending events to be disabled are due to Lehman, Pneuli and Stavi [9] . The definitions apply to total extensions of infinite execution traces. An arbiter is fair if every total extension of any infinite execution trace, is fair. Only events that are continuously requesting ('continuously pending') are considered.

1. **Impartiality**: Each event is *infinitely often* acknowledged. (Must be fair to all events).

2. **Fairness**: Each event is either *infinitely often* acknowledged or *almost everywhere* disabled. (Need be fair only to events that are *infinitely often* enabled).

3. **Justice**: Each event is either *infinitely often* acknowledged or *infinitely often* disabled. (Need only be fair to events that are continuously enabled.)

The order of these definitions is such that if an arbiter is fair according to one definition it will also be fair according to any succeeding definition, but not the converse. Note that these definitions do not require different events to be acknowledged with equal promptness, all that is required is that no event is starved.

Let us digress for a moment, and see why the arbiter described earlier fails to enforce any of these forms of fairness. The arbiter implementation based on the extension of Seitz's interlock element does make arbitrary choices at times, but such an implementation in NMOS has some problems, even if it is assumed that all equal sized transistors are perfectly balanced. Consider the circuit for the readers-writer problem illustrated in fig 5-3. Consider the situation when the circuit is in the none-requesting condition and all three requests, R_1, R_2 and W, arrive concurrently. An infinitesimally short interval Δt after all three requests arrive, let us assume that the voltages at the outputs (of the NOR gates) have increased by an infinitesimally small value $\Delta v \ll v_{th}$. The pull-down MOS transistors may be assumed to be operating in their linear region. If all pull-ups are assumed to provide equal active resistance, the output of the NOR gate corresponding to W will grow less rapidly than those corresponding to R_1

or R_2. The cumulative effect of this imbalance will result in a low output for W's NOR gate and high outputs for R_1's and R_2's. Hence if R_1, R_2 and W request continuously then the request for W will never go through, resulting in W's starvation. It is easy to see that this violates all three definitions of fairness.

Since we do not allow deliberate wait states it is not possible for an arbiter for path expressionsto be fair according to the first definition. Consider for instance the following path expression:

path (A + B); C **end**,
path D; (A + E) **end**

Suppose that each event takes the same amount of time to execute externally and that new requests for each event are forthcoming as soon as allowed by the protocol. Then simultaneous execution of D and B will alternate with simultaneous execution of C and E without the arbiter ever having to block any event. Yet, event A will never execute even if it remains continually ready. If, however, the first request for event B is delayed by the time it takes to execute an event, then initial execution of event D may be followed by alternate executions of A and (D,C) ! Note that neither the duration of external events nor the occurrence of external requests is under the control of the circuit.

The second (and therefore third) definition of fairness can be enforced using a simple LRU type deterministic arbitration algorithm. Assume there are k events. We assign a priority number from 0 to k-1 to each event, where the priority corresponds to the number of times the event is *blocked*, i.e. the number of times the event is enabled but not selected by the arbiter. At any instant the arbiter selects from the set of enabled events in order of priority. When an enabled event is selected its priority number is reinitialized to the lowest value. On the other hand, if the enabled event is not selected its priority number is incremented by one. Since each event must be enabled an infinite number of times, since any particular event can have at most k-1 neighbors in the conflict graph, and since each time it is blocked at least one of its neighbors is selected with a resulting increment in its own priority, after the kth attempt it will have a priority of k-1, the highest possible. It is possible to show (using induction on k) that no more than one event can ever get a priority of k-1. Hence when the event gets enabled next it will have the highest priority and get selected. Since this will happen an infinite number of times, this ensures fairness according to the second definition. The LRU algorithm has the added advantage that the response time to different events is approximately balanced.

The following simple circuit can be used to implement the LRU algorithm. It uses the arbiter circuit described previously to enforce the mutual exclusion. However each input is preceded by k switchable delay lines (k^2 delay lines in all). Each delay line can be switched off digitally, for instance by selectively bypassing the delay line. The delays are chosen large enough, and their variation made small enough, so that if one input is delayed by fewer delay lines than another, it will be selected by the arbiter (because the arbiter didn't notice the other one in time). The delay lines for any event are controlled by priority of the event: each time an event is blocked, an additional delay line is switched off for it, whereas if the event is acknowledged all its delay lines are switched on again, reducing its priority to the lowest level. A complete arbiter circuit based on this idea requires just $O(k^2)$ area.

The second definition is not the strongest possible form of fairness that can be enforced for path expressions. Consider for instance the path expression **path** ((A;C) + (B;A)) **end**. As before assume that all events are pending at all times. The execution sequence BABABA... is fair according to this definition even though event C is starved (event C is never enabled). We could have done better, however, since ACBAACBA... is also a legal execution sequence.

Although we do not know the strongest form of fairness enforcible for path expressions, it obviously lies somewhere between definitions 1 and 2. Intuitively, the fairest arbiter would only cause starvation for the least number of events possible. The problem can be greatly simplified by requiring the arbiter to be *oblivious* of the sequencing constraints and therefore equate a disabled event with an event not requesting. This restriction will also tend to simplify the logic since the arbiter size need not depend on the size of the path expressions, but only on the alphabet size. It should be kept in mind however that like our previous restriction requiring prompt response, this restriction limits the kind of arbiters possible. It may be noted that the LRU arbiter described previously is oblivious.

We shall describe a probabilistic arbitration algorithm for an oblivious arbiter whose infinite execution traces will be "fair" with probability 1 where "fair" is defined by either of definitions 2 and 3. It also holds for stronger forms of fairness and therefore realizes a type of fairness between definitions 1 and 2. The algorithm is as follows: Whenever the set of currently executing events is not a maximally parallel set, find all ways of extending this set with enabled events so that the new sets are maximally parallel, choose one of them at *random*, and then acknowledge the events in the selected extension. Every time an event is no longer disabled there is a non-zero probability that it will be acknowledged, and if this is the case infinitely often the event will be infinitely often acknowledged. It follows that this algorithm ensures fairness in the sense of the the second or third definition above. It will also prevent starvation for event C in the last example above.

Although we do not know of any direct implementation we shall describe a way of implementing this arbitration algorithm using an oracle for generating random bits. The oracle can be practically realized in a separate isolated circuit that uses amplified thermal noise to generate a random bit pattern. Again we use the extension of Seitz's interlock element, described previously, as the starting point and add a delay element at each input. The delay elements can be digitally switched on or off (by bypassing them), and are large enough so that if two conflicting events are enabled at the same time, and one is delayed by the delay element, the other is sure to be passed by the arbiter. This means that the delay should exceed the gate delay of the arbiter (when no conflicts occur). The delay elements are each controlled by a 1 bit register, which determines if the delay is on or off. A new value is loaded into each register from a (separate) oracle each time the corresponding event gets enabled. This means whenever a new set of events gets enabled, their 'priorities' are randomly 1 or 0. It is easy to show that any maximally parallel set then has a nonzero probability of being selected (when just its events have priority 1 and all others have priority 0), which is just what the probabilistic algorithm requires. To ensure that the random bits clocked into the different registers are largely uncorrelated, the oracle is split into multiple oracles by clocking it into a shift register at a high rate. A tapped delay line could be used instead of the shift register.

Finally, we show that no deterministic oblivious arbiter can do as well as our probabilistic arbiter. We show that every deterministic oblivious arbiter gives rise to starvation of an event which is continually requesting for some path-expression for which the probabilistic algorithm (described above) does not cause such starvation.

The difficulty of building a fair deterministic arbiter that matches the probabilistic arbiter can be illustrated by an example. Consider the following path expression:

path (A;C) + (B;(A + B)) **end.**

Assume the LRU algorithm, described previously, is being used, and that the external clients always request permission to perform all three events A, B and C. Let the priorities of all three be 0's initially. As a result, initially A and B are enabled. Assume that B is selected, making B's priority 0 and A's priority 1. In the next instant, A and B will again be enabled. But now A has the higher priority and will be selected, so that A's priority becomes 0 and B's becomes 1. Continuing in this fashion, it is easy to see that the sequence chosen will be B A B A B A .... The trouble with this scheme is that C will never be enabled even if its request is pending. Increasing the number of levels of priority will not help. This example can be extended to the following lemma.

Lemma 13: Let M be a deterministic finite-state transducer implementing an oblivious deterministic arbiter. Then there exists a path expression over $\Sigma = \{ A, B, C \}$ such that one event, say C, will be starved even though its request is continually pending. Moreover the probabilistic algorithm does not cause such starvation for this path expression.

Proof: Let M be a deterministic finite-state transducer whose alphabet is $\Sigma = \{ A, B, C \}$. Let the states of M be $S = \{ s_1, s_2, \ldots, s_m \}$. Let the conflict graph, G, for the path expression be the complete graph on the vertices A, B and C. We construct a path expression P with the conflict graph G such that M causes the starvation of the event C. Notice that because of the nature of the conflict graph G, if at any instant A and B (but not C) are enabled then at most one of A and B may be selected by M.

Let s_1 be an arbitrarily chosen state of M. We conduct an experiment on M by continuously providing A and B as the enabled inputs, starting with M in the state s_1. If we present a string of inputs $\{ A, B \}, \{ A, B \}, \ldots, \{ A, B \}$ of length m then we notice that at the 1st input $\{ A, B \}$, the transducer deterministically goes from the state $s(1) = s_1$ to a state $s(2)$ while outputting A or B. Let $s(1)$, $s(2)$, $\ldots$, $s(m + 1)$ be the sequence of states and $\sigma \in \{ A, B \}^m$ be the output string produced as a result of the experiment. As a consequence of the pigeon-hole principle, some two states in the sequence of states will be the same . Of all such pairs, let $s(i)$ and $s(j)$

be two such states closest to s_1. Assume that $i < j$ and k the smallest multiple of $(j - i)$ such that $k \geq i$. Without loss of generality assume that M outputs B when in state $s(i)$ with the input { A, B }.

Let P be the path expression

$$\textbf{path } (A + B)^{i-1};((A;C) + B); (A + B)^{k-i} \textbf{ end}$$

It is easy to see that P has G as the conflict graph and if the requests for A, B and C are continuously pending then the sequence of outputs will be a string in $\{ A, B \}^{\omega}$ and C will never be enabled.

The probabilistic algorithm would have no problem with the path-expression since from any state (of the path expression) it could reach the state enabling C with non-zero probability, and hence enable C an infinite number of times in an infinite trace. □

The result of the above lemma can also be stated as follows: A deterministic oblivious arbiter needs at least N/2 states to do as well as one using the probabilistic algorithm, where N is the size of the path-expression, whereas the probabilistic algorithm requires a constant number of internal states. The actual bound on the minimum number of states required may be much larger.

However, for many path expressions the LRU algorithm is just as fair as the probabilistic algorithm and has the advantages that the response times are approximately balanced, instead of being a complex function of the conflict graph as in the probabilistic algorithm. For such path expressions the use of the LRU algorithm is preferable. The problem of determining just which path expressions satisfy this property, and well as more direct ways of combining the advantages of the LRU algorithm with those of the probabilistic algorithm remain to be investigated.

6. Conclusion

Since our circuits have the constant separator property, a more compact O(N) layout is possible using the techniques of [5]. However, while it is definitely possible to automatically generate the $O(N \cdot \log(N))$ layout that we propose, it is much more difficult in practice to generate the O(N) layout of [5]. Furthermore, the O(N) layout will occupy less area only for very large N. We suspect that ease of generating the layout will win over asymptotic compactness in this case. One of the authors (M. Foster) is currently implementing a silicon compiler for path expressions, based on the ideas in this paper.

Finally, we plan to investigate extensions of our construction to appropriate finite state subsets of CSP [6] and CCS [11]. In the case of CSP the subset will only permit boolean valued variables and messages which are signals. If the number of message types is fixed, we conjecture that area bounds comparable to those in section 4 can be obtained. Arrays of processes in which the connectivity of the communication graph is low can be treated specially for a more compact layout. Such a finite-state subset of CSP may even be more useful than the path expression language discussed in the paper for high level description of various asynchronous circuits.

7. Acknowledgements

The authors wish to acknowledge the help of K. Karplus. His comments on an early draft of this paper contributed significantly towards improving the clarity of the paper.

References

1. Anantharaman, T. A. "A delay insensitive regular expression recognizer." (1985).

2. Campbell, R. H. and A. N. Habermann. The Specification of Process Synchronization by Path Expressions. In *Lecture Notes in Computer Science, Volume 16*, G. Goos and J. Hartmanis, Ed.,Springer-Verlag, 1974, pp. 89-102.

3. Foster, M. J. *Specialized Silicon Compilers for Language Recognition.* Ph.D. Th., CMU, July 1984.

4. Foster, M. J. and Kung, H. T. "Recognize Regular Languages with Programmable Building-Blocks." *Journal of Digital Systems VI*, 4 (Winter 1982), 323-332.

5. Floyd, R. W. and Ullman, J. D. "The Compilation of Regular Expressions into Integrated Circuits." *Journal of the Association for Computing Machinery 29*, 3 (July 1982), 603-622.

6. Hoare, C. A. R. "Communicating Sequential Processes." *Comm. ACM 21*, 8 (1978).

7. Lauer, P. E. and Campbell, R. H. "Formal Semantics of a Class of High-Level Primitives for Coordinating Concurrent Processes." *Acta Informatica 5* (June 5 1974), 297-332.

8. Leiserson, C.E. *Area-Efficient VLSI Computation.* Ph.D. Th., Carnegie-Mellon University, 1981.

9. D.Lehman, A. Pnueli, J. Stavi. "Impartiality, Justice and Fairness: The Ethics of Concurrent Termination." *Automata, Languages and Programming,* (1981), 265-277.

10. Li, W. and P. E. Lauer. A VLSI Implementation of Cosy.. Tech. Rept. ASM/121, Computing Laboratory, The University of Newcastle Upon Tyne, January, 1984.

11. Milner, Robin. *A Calculus of Communicating Systems.* Volume 92: *Lecture Notes in Computer Science.* Springer-Verlag, Berlin Heidelberg NY, 1980.

12. Mukhopadhyay, A. "Hardware Algorithms for Nonnumeric Computation." *IEEE Transactions on Computers C-28*, 6 (June 1979), 384-394.

13. Patil, Suhas S. An Asynchronous Logic Array. MAC TECHNICAL MEMORANDUM 62, Massachusetts Institute of Technology, May, 1975.

14. Pratt, V. R. On the Composition of Processes. Symposium on Principles of Programming Languages, ACM, January, 1982.

15. Rem, Martin. *Partially ordered computations, with applications to VLSI design.* Eindhoven University of Technology, 1983.

16. Seitz, C. L. "Ideas About Arbiters." *LAMBDA First Quarter* (1980), 10-14.

Appendix : Proof details

Refer to section 3:

Lemma 14: If the same assumptions as in proposition 8 are satisfied, then T(Seq(j)) is consistent with R_j.

Proof: From proposition 8 it follows that **Seq(j)** consists of non concurrent time intervals. The result is therefore easy to prove by induction on the number intervals in **Seq(j)**, using the same proposition. □

Lemma 15: For each element *i* in **Int** with label *e*, the corresponding elements in **Ext** and **Seq(j)** are subintervals of *i*.

Proof: Follows from the properties of the circuit in fig 3-2) (see also fig 3-3). □

Lemma 16: For any Rj ∈ M, $T(\textbf{Int})|_{\Sigma_{Rj}}$ is a totally ordered multiset.

Proof: It is easy to show that $T(\textbf{Int})|_{\Sigma_{Rj}} = T(\textbf{Int}|_{\Sigma_{Rj}})$. But $\textbf{Int}|_{\Sigma_{Rj}}$ consists of 'internal events' of the path expression Rj, during each of which the corresponding ACK is high. Hence by proposition 6, no two such events overlap, and therefore $T(\textbf{Int})|_{\Sigma_{Rj}}$ is a totally ordered multiset. □

Lemma 17: For any Rj ∈ M, $T(\textbf{Int})|_{\Sigma_{Rj}} = T(\textbf{Ext})|_{\Sigma_{Rj}}$.

Proof: For any element *i* of T(**Int**), that is also in $T(\textbf{Int})|_{\Sigma_{Rj}}$, the corresponding element of T(**Ext**) will be in $T(\textbf{Ext})|_{\Sigma_{Rj}}$ (definition 2) since they must map to the same alphabet $e \in \Sigma_{Rj}$. Hence these traces have the same number of elements. Also from lemma 15 it follows that if *i1* and *i2* are two elements of $T(\textbf{Int})|_{\Sigma_{Rj}}$ satisfying one or none of "*i1* precedes *i2*" and "*i2* precedes *i1*", the corresponding elements of $T(\textbf{Ext})|_{\Sigma_{Rj}}$ will satisfy at least the same relationships. In other words the partial order of T(**Int**) is a restriction of that of T(**Ext**). But by lemma 16 $T(\textbf{Int})|_{\Sigma_{Rj}}$ is a totally ordered multiset. Hence from the above $T(\textbf{Ext})|_{\Sigma_{Rj}}$ will have the same partial order relationship and, therefore, be the same totally ordered multiset. □

Lemma 18: For any Rj ∈ M, $T(\textbf{Seq}(j)) = T(\textbf{Int})|_{\Sigma_{Rj}}$.

Proof: Follows from lemma 15 and 16 in the same way as in the proof of lemma 17. The only difference is that $T(\textbf{Seq}(j))|_{\Sigma_{Rj}} = T(\textbf{Seq}(j))$.

□

Lemma 19: For any sequencer SEQ_j , no two TR's are high simultaneously.

Proof: The two TR's would be two ACK's of events in the same path expression Rj, which cannot be high simultaneously by proposition 6. □

Lemma 20: For any sequencer SEQ_j , TR_e is raised only if DIS_e is low and all TA's are low.

Proof: By induction on the number of rising transitions of TR's :

1. (First transition): Let the corresponding event be *e*. By proposition 9 initially all TA's are low, and all CLR's are high, hence all TR's are low initially. By proposition 7 all TA's will remain low until the first rising transition of TR_e. By the same proposition DIS_e will not change until the first rising transition of TR_e. If DIS_e were not low, IN_e would remain low (see Figure 3-2). Hence by proposition 6, TR_e would remain low, a contradiction.
2. (For a succeeding transition): Let the corresponding event be *p* and that of the previous transition *q*. While TR_q is high no TA or TR other than TA_q or TR_q can be high (proposition 6 and lemma 19). Until CLR_q goes high, TR_q must remain high (see Figure 3-2). Once CLR_q goes high, all IN_a, with $a \in \Sigma_{Rj}$, will be low after a short delay (see Figure 3-2). Assuming the variation in this delay for different *a*'s is less than the delay of the arbiter in lowering TR_q, all TR_a with $a \neq q$ will continue to remain low until CLR_q is lowered (see Figure 3-2). All TA_a, with $a \neq q$, also continue to remain low (proposition 7). But CLR_q remains high at least until TA_q is lowered (see Figure 7). Hence by the time TR_p is raised all TA's will be low. Also TR_p could not have been raised if IN_p were low (proposition 6). But if DIS_p was high when TA_p was last lowered then IN_p would now be low (see Figure 3-2), assuming the main NOR gate plus the 2-input NOR gate have a lesser delay than the Muller-C element plus

the SR Flip-Flop. Moreover, DIS_p cannot change before TR_p is raised (proposition 7). Hence DIS_p must be low when TR_p is raised.

□

Lemma 21: For any sequencer SEQ_j, TR_e is lowered only if TA_e is high.
Proof: The NOR gate arrangement in front of the arbiter insures that once TR_e is high it remains high until CLR_e is raised, and this can occur only if TA_e is high (see Figure 3-2). Moreover once TA_e is high it will remain high until TR_e is lowered (proposition 7). □

Theorem 10

Proof: Lemmas 19,20,21 satisfy the preconditions of proposition 8. Hence T(**Seq**(j)) is consistent with Rj for any Rj ∈ M. By lemma 18 and definition 4, T(**Int**) is consistent with Rj for any Rj ∈ M. By lemma 17 and definition 4, T(**Ext**) is consistent with Rj for any Rj ∈ M. Hence by definition 4, T(**Ext**) ∈ $Tr_\Sigma(M)$. □

Lemma 22: If T ∈ $Tr_\Sigma(M)$ is layered, then each *subset* (*cf.* definition 11) of T has the property that no two elements in it are instances of events in Σ_{Rj} for any Rj ∈ M.
Proof: Any two elements *i1*,*i2* (corresponding to events *e1*,*e2*) in the same *subset* of T must be concurrent (definitions 3,11). Suppose *e1*,*e2* ∈ Σ_{Rj} with Rj ∈ M. Then $T|_{\Sigma_{Rj}}$ will include *i1*,*i2* which will be concurrent (definition 2). Hence $T|_{\Sigma_{Rj}}$ cannot be a total order and therefore T ∉ $Tr_\Sigma(M)$ (definition 4) -- leading to a contradiction.

Hence the result. □

Theorem 12

Proof: The behavior we require of the external world is that it simultaneously raise REQ for all events in the first *subset* of T, wait until all corresponding ACK are high, then simultaneously lower all REQ, wait until all ACK are low, then repeat this *cycle* for the next *subset* of T, and so on. We need to show that under these conditions the circuit responds within a finite amount of time in each *cycle*. The result then follows directly.

As shown in the proof of lemma 20, all ACK's are initially low. Hence they are low at the beginning of each of the *cycles* mentioned in the previous paragraph. At the beginning of each such *cycle*, **Ext**,**Int** and every **Seq**(j) with Rj $\in$ M, get redefined. Let Tp denote T restricted to subsets before the current cycle. It is easy to show by induction on the number of cycles and definition 4 that at the beginning of each cycle T(Ext) = Tp and Tp $\in Tr_{\Sigma}$(M). Hence for any Rj $\in$ M, S(Tp$|_{\Sigma_{Rj}}$) is a prefix of some element in L_{Rj}. If the next *subset* contains an instance *il* of event *el*, then for each Rj $\in$ M such that *el* $\in \Sigma_{Rj}$, S(Tp$|_{\Sigma_{Rj}}$) can be extended by *il* to give a prefix of some sequence in L_{Rj}; in fact this extension gives the next value of Tp$|_{\Sigma_{Rj}}$ (see lemma 22). But by lemmas 18,17, for any Rj $\in$ M, T(Seq(j)) = T(Ext) $|_{\Sigma_{Rj}}$ = Tp$|_{\Sigma_{Rj}}$. Hence for each Rj $\in$ M, such that el $\in \Sigma_{Rj}$, T(Seq(j)) can be extended by *il* to give a prefix of some sequence in L_{Rj}. Thus by proposition 8, the corresponding sequencers SEQ_j, with *el* $\in \Sigma_{Rj}$, will have DIS_j low. This applies to any *el* in the next *subset* of T.

Therefore at the beginning of any cycle, when REQ_{el} for any event *el* in the next subset of T is raised, all DIS_{el} inputs to the NOR gate for event *el* (see Figure 3-2), will be low. Also within a finite amount of time all relevant TA_{el}'s must go low by proposition 8, since the corresponding TR_{el}'s are already low. Hence CLR_{el} will go low, and IN_{el} will go high for each *el* in the next subset of T. It follows from proposition 6 and lemma 22 that all ACK's corresponding to events in the next *subset* of T will be raised within a finite amount of time.

The proof for the second half of the cycle is more straightforward. By lemma 8 once all REQ's are lowered, within a finite time all relevant TA's will be raised, causing the corresponding CLR's to go high. As a result all relevant IN's go low (see figure 3-2) and hence by proposition 6 all ACK's go low within a finite time, completing the cycle. □

Parallel Processing and Computer Aided Programming in Crystal

Marina C. Chen
Department of Computer Science
Yale University
New Haven, CT 06520

1. Introduction

Crystal is a general purpose language for parallel programming. From the standpoint of programming languages, it might look unconventional; however, it consists mainly of formalized mathematical notations. Along the same line as SETL [6] in providing set-theoretical notation as a means of very high level programming, **Crystal** places its emphasis on recurrences and is intended for very high level programming of parallel systems. In the linguistic aspect, language **Crystal** consists of:

- *sets* for data types;
- *functions* for abstraction, where a function may be implemented either by sequential code or by an assemblege of parallel processes;
- *recursion equations*, which is the main construct for parallelism;
- *bounded range*, which is basically a for loop constuct;
- and *unbounded minimalization*, as in recursive function theory, which is basically a while loop construct.

With these constructs, **Crystal** is able to express homogeneous or inhomogeneou parallel systems of any network connectivity.

We have some experience in expressing problems in various application domains in **Crystal**, and we found that problems in scientific computing and physics can be expressed very fluently, perhaps due to mathematical nature of the language. On the side of symbolic computation, the kernal of a VLSI switch level simulator [1] has been described in **Crystal** as three levels of recursion equations [2]. Graph algorithms, such as finding connected components, minimum spanning trees, bi-connected components, etc. [8], can easily be expressed in **Crystal** as well. **Crystal** also serves as a hardware description langauge for various computer aided design tools: VLSI arithmetics, logic designs, and machine architectures [2], etc., described in **Crystal**, serve as precise functional definitions of the hardware.

In the algorithmic aspect, **Crystal** has a set of design and synthesis methods which compile problem definitions to efficient parallel algorithms, map them to target architectures, and then optimize the code according to the characteristics of the target machines. Pipelining is automatically compiled into parallel implementations. Efficient algorithms generated this way include the class of all systolic algorithms and numerous VLSI architectures. A variety of different architectures are generated for a given problem and their relative merits can be systematically evaluated.

In this paper, we shall first state several key ideas and viewpoints that underlie **Crystal**'s synthesis approach to parallel processing. In Section 3, several examples of **Crystal** programs, along with a general definition, are given. In Section 4, we illustrate how to interprete a problem definition in **Crystal** so as to reveal its large scale parallelism. In Section 5, we describe briefly how to infuse constraints into the definition so that an efficient parallel algorithm can be obtained. In Section 6, we incorporate pipelining by *space-time* mapping, and present the many possible algorithms or architectures obtained from the same algorithm by space-time mapping.

2. Parallel Processing from Crystal's Viewpoints

1. **We start from problem definitions.** A sequential program very often over specifies a problem in the sense that extraneous data dependency is introduced due to the constraint imposed by the sequential model of computation. The mathematical definition of a given problem, however, is often a description infused with the least amount of such extraneous data dependency. Without the presence of such artificial constraints, a mathematical definition can be interpreted as an algorithm which exhibits as much parallelism as the problem allows.

2. **We do not merely extract parallelism from sequential programs.** A sequential program also under specifies a problem for which an efficient parallel solution is sought, in particular, in the case of locality of communications and load balancing, which are of central concern in parallel processing. That is to say, mere recovery of parallelism by discarding the extraneous dependency will gain some parallelism, but not enough for seeking efficient parallel algorithms.

3. **We infuse constraints imposed by parallel hardware.** The parallel implementation media impose their own set of constraints on the design of algorithms, and the extreme parallelism exhibits in the definition may not be most efficient from their standpoint. For instance, bounded fan-in and fan-out degrees, and locality of communications, are often imposed by realistic parallel machines such as a network of parallel processors. These constraints, which must be taken into account in order to devise an effi-

cient parallel algorithm, imply the serialization of some of the computations and communications specified by the definition. As a consequence, the heart of the synthesis approach described here lies in harnessing the extreme parallelism exhibit in the definition by infusing suitable data dependencies, as opposed to the approach which extracts parallelism from sequential programs.

4. **The programming space is now multi-dimensional**, not the one-dimensional space as in sequential programming. The programming space for parallel algorithms has been enlarged from the one-dimensional space of sequential programming to multi-dimensional space in which processors can be arranged in a variety of different ways. The number of possible solutions to a given problem can be different not only in the algorithmic sense, but the same algorithm can have many different realizations in the multi-dimensional space and time. These different space-time realizations have different properties and a suitable one shall be chosen depending on the context.

5. **We compile for parallelism, not coding by hand.** Efficient task distribution is hard for the programmer. Besides, any hand-coded parallel program binds an algorithm to a particular space-time realization, and therefore it is not necessarily suitable for it to be used in a different context. We therefore generate all of the possible space-time realizations from an abstract specification, compiling for parallelism. We also automatically incorporate pipelining into programs, and evaluate the relative merits of the different realizations systematically.

3. Crystal Programs

Each parallel program in **Crystal** consists of a system of recursion equation(s). For example, the number of partitions of an integer k into integers less than or equal to m can be obtained by applying the following recursively defined function C to the pair of integers (m,k).

$$C(i,j) = \begin{cases} i = 1 \to 1 \\ i > 1 \to \begin{cases} i > j \to C(i-1,j) \\ i = j \to C(i-1,j)+1 \\ i < j \to C(i-1,j)+C(i,j-i) \end{cases} \end{cases} \tag{3.1}$$

In Equation (3.1), we call i and j recursion variables and C a functional variable of the equation.

The definition of dynamic programming can be posed in a general form where $C(i,j)$ is some cost function which is to be minimized.

$$C(i,j) = \min_{i<k<j} f(C(i,k),C(k,j)) \text{ for some function } f \text{ of the costs, and}$$

$$C(i,i+1) = C_i \text{ for all } i, \text{ the individual costs,} \tag{3.2}$$

where recursion variables i and j range over integers $0 < i < j \leq n$, for some constant integer n. Another similar example,

$$C(i,j) = \sum_{k=1}^{n} A(i,k) \times B(k,j) \text{ for } 0 \leq i,j < n. \tag{3.3}$$

is a specification for the matrix multiplication, with functional variable C for the resulting product and recursion variables i and j for, respectively, the row and column index.

In general, a parallel program is defined by a system of recursion equations

$$\begin{aligned} F_1(\mathbf{v}) &= \phi_1(F_1(\tau_{11}(\mathbf{v})), F_2(\tau_{12}(\mathbf{v})), \ldots, F_n(\tau_{1n}(\mathbf{v}))) \\ F_2(\mathbf{v}) &= \phi_2(F_1(\tau_{21}(\mathbf{v})), F_2(\tau_{22}(\mathbf{v})), \ldots, F_n(\tau_{2n}(\mathbf{v}))) \\ &\cdots \\ F_n(\mathbf{v}) &= \phi_n(F_1(\tau_{n1}(\mathbf{v})), F_2(\tau_{n2}(\mathbf{v})), \ldots, F_n(\tau_{nn}(\mathbf{v}))), \end{aligned} \tag{3.4}$$

where:

- $\mathbf{v} \stackrel{\text{def}}{=} [v_1, v_2, \ldots, v_n] \in A$, and A is a discrete structure which is a cartesian product $A_1 \times A_2 \times \cdots \times A_n$, where each A_i, say, is a subset of the set of integers or the set of rationals, and $(A_i, \sqsubseteq)$ is a flat lattice, where "$\sqsubseteq$" is the approximation order [12];
- function τ_{ij} maps from A to A;
- functional variables $F_1, F_2, \ldots, F_n$, range over continuous functions mapping from $(A, \sqsubseteq)$ to $(D, \sqsubseteq)$, where D can be some value domains such as the set of integers, reals, etc., or it can be some domain of functions, functions of functions, etc., and $(D, \sqsubseteq)$ is a continous complete lattice;
- functions $\phi_1, \phi_2, \ldots, \phi_n$, are continuous functions over the domains $(D, \sqsubseteq)$. Thus (3.4) is a system of fixed-point equations, and on its right hand side,

  $$\lambda(F_1, F_2, \ldots, F_n).\lambda\mathbf{v}.[\phi_1(\cdots), \phi_2(\cdots), \ldots, \phi_n(\cdots)]$$

  is a continuous function mapping from E^n to E^n, where $E \stackrel{\text{def}}{=} [(A, \sqsubseteq) \rightarrow (D, \sqsubseteq)]$, the domain of continuous functions from $(A, \sqsubseteq)$ to $(D, \sqsubseteq)$.

Such a system of equations embodies a parallel computation on a discrete structure A with multiple data streams F_i, processing functions ϕ_i, and communication functions τ_{ij}, where $1 \leq i,j \leq n$. The discrete structure A is in general some n-dimensional space, it ranges from the degenerate case (0 dimensional) where a piece of straight code (without any iteration or recursion construct) is executed on a uniprocessor, to a two-dimensional case where a systolic program is running on a linear array, or to a multi-dimensional case with programs running on butterfly, tree, or hypercube machines. A set of communication functions is often associated with each particular process structure A. Each processing funciton ϕ_i is a composition of base functions (e.g. "+" in (3.1)) from some value domain $(D_1, \sqsubseteq)$ to another value domain $(D_2, \sqsubseteq)$.

The outermost base function in the composition is often a "case" function, as is the one with four cases (flattened from the nested conditionals) in Equation (3.1). Each equation in (3.4) can be written structurally in more detail as k cases:

$$F_i(\mathbf{v}) = \begin{cases} p_{i1}(F_1(\tau_{i11}(\mathbf{v})), F_2(\tau_{i12}(\mathbf{v})), \ldots, F_n(\tau_{i1n}(\mathbf{v}))) \rightarrow \\ \quad \phi_{i1}(F_1(\tau_{i11}(\mathbf{v})), F_2(\tau_{i12}(\mathbf{v})), \ldots, F_n(\tau_{i1n}(\mathbf{v}))) \\ p_{i2}(F_1(\tau_{i21}(\mathbf{v})), F_2(\tau_{i22}(\mathbf{v})), \ldots, F_n(\tau_{i2n}(\mathbf{v}))) \rightarrow \\ \quad \phi_{i2}(F_1(\tau_{i21}(\mathbf{v})), F_2(\tau_{i22}(\mathbf{v})), \ldots, F_n(\tau_{i2n}(\mathbf{v}))) \\ \ldots \\ p_{ik}(F_1(\tau_{ik1}(\mathbf{v})), F_2(\tau_{ik2}(\mathbf{v})), \ldots, F_n(\tau_{ikn}(\mathbf{v}))) \rightarrow \\ \quad \phi_{ik}(F_1(\tau_{ik1}(\mathbf{v})), F_2(\tau_{ik2}(\mathbf{v})), \ldots, F_n(\tau_{ikn}(\mathbf{v}))) \end{cases}$$

where $p_{i1}, \ldots, p_{ik}$ are boolean predicates

The number of cases k depends on the homogeneity of the processing functions and the uniformity of the communication functions over structure A. Since the predicates are functions of F_i's, both the processing and communication (or data flow) of each element in A might be data dependent and change dynamically during a computation. The classification of parallel machines can be borrowed here, corresponding to the so-called single instruction multiple data (SIMD) type of machine architectures, where the processing and communication functions of all elements of the process structure are the same, and the recursion equations are of a simple form. For the MIMD type of architectures, the recursion equations are usually composed of many cases.

Note that the system (3.4) is in the form of simultaneous, course-of-values recursion, which is primitive recursive. Thus unbounded minimalization is an absolute necessity rather than a mere convenience for specifying computations which are recursive but not primitive recursive.

4. Parallel Interpretation of Crystal Programs

4.1. Process structure

A mathematical definition can be interpreted as a parallel program. Take the straightforward definition given in Equation (3.2) for dynamic programming as an example: each pair of indices (i_0, j_0) is interpreted as a *process* in the *process structure* $P \stackrel{\text{def}}{=} \{(i,j) : 0 < i < j \leq n,\ i,j \text{ are integers}\}$. The process structure P is ordered by a data dependency relation. We say that a process $\mathbf{u}$ precedes $\mathbf{v}$ ($\mathbf{u} \prec \mathbf{v}$), or $\mathbf{v}$ depends on $\mathbf{u}$ ($\mathbf{v} \succ \mathbf{u}$), for instance, when datum $C(\mathbf{v})$ appears on the right-hand side of the System (3.2) and datum $C(\mathbf{u})$ appear on the left-hand side of (3.2).

4.2. Data dependency relation

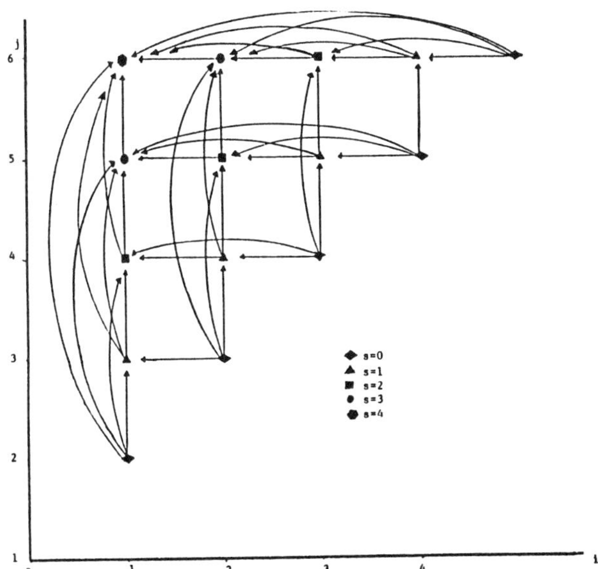

Figure 1: The DAG describing the data dependency of dynamic programming.

The process structure can be depicted by a data dependency graph, and it can either be a DAG (Directed Acyclic Graph) as shown in Figure 1 or a DCG (Directed Cyclic Graph) as shown in Figure 2. It consists of nodes, where each node corresponds to a process (i,j) in the set P, and directed edges, where an edge is emitting from node $\mathbf{u}$ to node $\mathbf{v}$ if $\mathbf{u} \prec \mathbf{v}$. Those nodes that have no incoming edges are called *sources*. For dynamic programming, the sources are $(1,2), (2,3), \ldots, (n-1,n)$.

If the system of recursion equation is such that the transitive closure "$\overset{*}{\prec}$" of relation "$\prec$" on all processes is a partial order, then a DAG will be obtained. If, furthermore, there is no infinite decreasing chain from any process (i,j), i.e., the set $(P, \overset{*}{\prec})$ is a well-founded set. The existence of any source is necessary for the data dependecy relation "$\overset{*}{\prec}$" to be well-founded.

Similarly, the DAG in Figure 3 for the integer partition is obtained, where nodes $(1,j)$ are sources. For matrix multiplication we obtain a DCG as in Figure 2, which implies that the data dependency relation as defined is not a partial order. Note that it does not contain any source. The DCG can be interpreted as a parallel algorithm which completes the computation in a single step, as with those in combinational circuits.

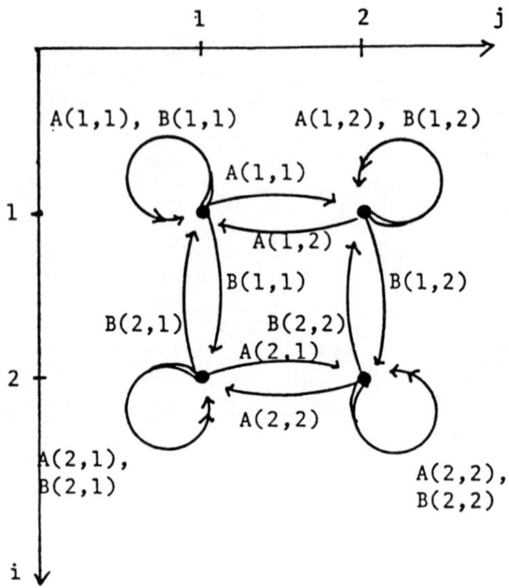

Figure 2: The DCG describing the data dependency of the multiplication of 2-by-2 matrices

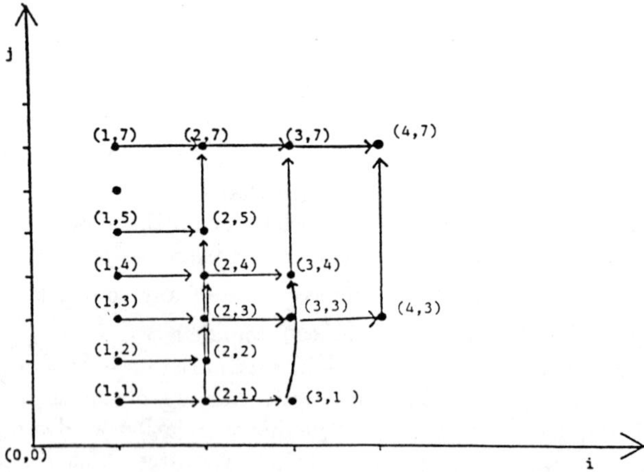

Figure 3: The DAG describing the data dependency of integer partition.

4.3. Execution wavefront

The processes are parallel in nature. For a system that yields a DCG as data dependency graph, the computation is defined to be completed in a single step. For a system that yields a DAG as a data dependency graph, a computation starts at the sources, and is followed by other processes each of which starts execution when all of its required inputs, or dependent data, become available. By this definition, a DAG without any source can never start a computation.

A sequence of *execution wavefronts* $s = 0, 1, 2, \ldots$ can be defined. All sources belong to the zero'th wavefront ($s = 0$) in the sequence, a process belongs to the n'th wavefront if all of its dependent processes belong to wavefronts $n - 1$ or less and there is at least one dependent process belonging to wavefront $n - 1$. Clearly, processes belonging to the same execution wavefront do not depend on one another. For dynamic programming, the execution wavefront number s is described by the expression $j - i - 1$, and this can be seen from Equation (3.2) that any cost $C(i,j)$ cannot be computed until the costs $C(k,j)$ and $C(i,k)$ for all $i < k < j$ are computed, in particular, $C(i,j-1)$ and $C(i+1,j)$, due to the inherent data dependency. In other words, each cost $C(i,j)$ associated with an interval of length $j - i$ depends on some costs associated with intervals of length $j - i - 1$. The wavefronts are shown by the dotted line in Figure 4.

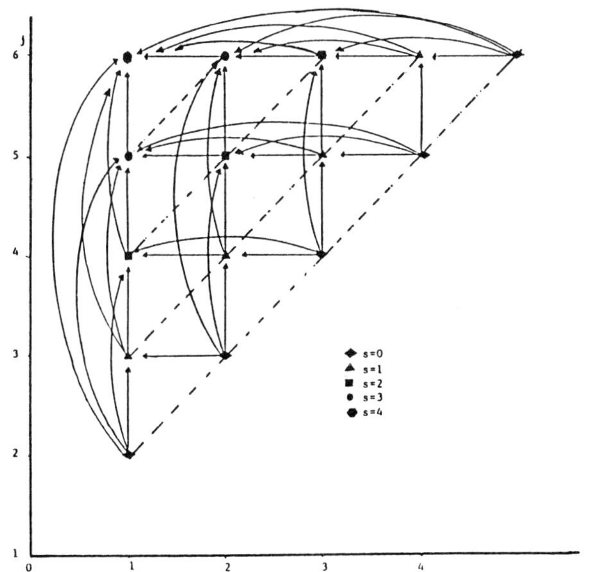

Figure 4: The execution wavefronts in the parallel interpretation of dynamic programming.

4.4. Complexity of the naive parallel algorithm

Using one processor for each process in, say, System (3.2), we obtain immediately a naive parallel algorithm for dynamic programming in which the local processing at each processor, and the communications between processors, are obtained from the definition as described above. For this example, altogether $O(n^2)$ number of parallel processors are needed. The number of time steps needed, i.e., the total number of execution wavefronts is n. However, for each time step, there associated some delay that is not independent of the problem size, which might increase the total time complexity significantly. Such a directly interpreted parallel algorithm turns out not to be a very efficient one.

5. Implementation Constraints in Parallel Systems

5.1. Communication: an implicit cost

In each execution wavefront, some processor must communicate with other processors. The time it takes for a processor to complete a communication, unfortunately, is not entirely independent of the number of destinations to which data must be sent, nor of the sources from which data must be received. The time complexity of a parallel algorithm, therefore, cannot be determined by the number of execution wavefronts alone; the communication time must also be taken into account.

Let the amount of time for completing a single processor (single source) to processor (single destination) communication be called *unit communication time*, denoted by δ.

5.2. The Problem with Large Numbers of Fan-ins and Fan-outs

Due to the inherent physical constraints imposed by the driving capability of communication channels, power consumptions, heat dissipations, memory bandwidth, etc., data cannot be sent or received to or from a large number of destinations or sources in a unit communication time. Putting such constraints in algorithmic terms: The time it takes to communicate between two processors is proportional to the fan-in and fan-out degrees, often linearly proportional, where the *fan-in degree* of a datum is defined as the number of data items it depends on, and *fan-out degree* is the number of data items dependent upon it. Suppose an algorithm which takes $O(n)$ steps to complete has a large fan-in or fan-out degree, say degree $O(n)$; then it is $O(n)$ number of unit communication time incurred for each step. As a consequence, the total time complexity amounts to $O(n^2)$. Such is the case for the naive parallel interpretation of the dynamic programming definition in Equation (3.2).

5.3. Cost for bounded fan-in and fan-out degrees

Can the fan-in and fan-out degrees of an algorithm be decreased so as to decrease its total time complexity? On the other hand, is there any alternative cost one must pay for the new algorithm with bounded fan-in and fan-out degrees? In some cases, it turns out that it is possible to derive, from the original definition, a bounded degree algorithm which increases the number of execution wavefronts only by a constant factor. In other cases, such as when a naive parallel interpretation yields a single step algorithm, the number of execution wavefronts must be increased to $O(n)$ or $O(\log n)$ in order to reduce to bounded degrees the large number of fan-ins and fan-outs which are say, of $O(n^2)$ complexity. Such possibility is exactly the point of restricting the fan-in and fan-out degrees: reduction of the high degrees result in reduction of the total time complexity of the algorithm.

How to reduce the fan-in and fan-out degrees? Reduction of the fan-in degree can be achieved by serializing the computation of an n-ary associative function, which takes n arguments, as the composition of a number of k-ary functions, where k is bounded. On the other hand, reduction of the fan-out degree can be achieved by serializing an n-destination communication as a series of local communications. The new algorithm, even infused with new data dependencies due to such serializations, may well maintain the same time complexity as the original algorithm, as is the case with dynamic programming[3] or LU decomposition [4].

Since an algorithm with bounded fan-in and fan-out degrees only incurs a constant number of the unit communication time δ at each execution step of the algorithm, the time complexity of the algorithm is within a constant factor of the order of its execution wavefronts.

5.4. Counting fan-in and fan-out degrees

For the dynamic programming, the fan-in degree of process (i,j) is $2s$ where $s \stackrel{\text{def}}{=} j - i - 1$. Its fan-out degree is $n - s - 2$, because $C(i,j)$ is needed by $C(i,k)$ for $k = j+1, \ldots, n$ (there are $n - j$ such terms), and $C(k,j)$ for $k = 1, \ldots, i-1$ (there are $i - 1$ such terms).

Taking matrix multiplication as an example, it is obvious that every node (i,j) in the DCG, as shown in Figure (2), has fan-in degree $2n$ where n of them are from nodes in row i and the other n of them are from nodes in column j. Conversely, its fan-out degree is also $2n$. In the following, we use matrix multiplication to illustrate the reduction of fan-in and fan-out degrees.

5.5. Reduction to bounded fan-in and fan-out degrees

We want to reduce fan-in and fan-out degrees, however, we must keep in mind that such transformation on the definition might result in a new algorithm with increased time complexity. Since the definition of matrix multiplication gives a single step parallel algorithm, a increased time complexity seems inevitable. Choices can be made here to either increase the time complexity by a logarithmic factor or by a linear factor. Since the fan-in and fan-out degrees of each process is of order n, the algorithm has logarithmic time complexity requiring a network with fan-in fan-out degrees logarithmic of the problem size. In fact, multiplication of two n-by-n matrices can be completed on networks such as a mesh of trees [10] and hypercubes in $O(\log n)$ time steps using $O(n^3)$ number of processes. Alternatively, the fan-in and fan-out degrees can be reduced to a constant, yielding systolic algorithms that use $O(n^2)$ number of processes.

It is obvious that replacing the summation over n pair of numbers by $n-1$ successive binary additions reduces the fan-in degree to three. Algebraically, Equation (3.3) is transformed to

$$c(i,j,k) = \begin{cases} k = 0 \rightarrow 0 \\ 0 < k \leq n \rightarrow c(i,j,k-1) + A(i,k) \times B(k,j) \end{cases} \tag{5.1}$$

Note that the new equation defines a three-dimensional process structure and yields a DAG, with processes $(i,j,0)$ being the sources. The execution wavefront is counted by k, ranging from 0 to n and yielding a linear time complexity. We note that if the expression for counting wavefronts are linear expressions of the recursion variables, and the ranges of these variables are linear of the problem size, then the time complexity is also linear. This observation suggests that to reduce the $O(n)$ fan-out degree of Equation (3.3), the serialization may be performed as recursion in variables i and j.

As described by the following two new equations, two new functional variables a and b are introduced so that for each j, $a(i,j,k)$ replaces $A(i,k)$, and for each i, $b(i,j,k)$ replaces $B(k,j)$, and the large fan-out of $A(i,k)$ and $B(k,j)$ is now eliminated.

$$a(i,j,k) = \begin{cases} j = 0 \rightarrow A(i,k) \\ 0 < j \leq n \rightarrow a(i,j-1,k) \end{cases}$$

and similarly,

$$b(i,j,k) = \begin{cases} i = 0 \rightarrow B(k,j) \\ 0 < i \leq n \rightarrow b(i-1,j,k) \end{cases} \tag{5.2}$$

and substitute these two equations into Equation (5.1)

$$c(i,j,k) = \begin{cases} k = 0 \rightarrow 0 \\ 0 < k \leq n \rightarrow c(i,j,k-1) + a(i,j,k) \times b(i,j,k) \end{cases}$$

System (5.2) is a now **Crystal** program with fan-in and fan-out degree three.

5.6. Communication Costs and Low-order Recursion Equations

A remaining criterion for a good parallel algorithm is that the range of communications must be local. The more local the range of a communication, the less area and time in hardware must be dedicated for its completion. The range of communications occurring in an algorithm, again, can be recognized algebraically from the defining **Crystal** program.

As mentioned earlier, the process structure of a **Crystal** program is a discrete domain. Without loss of generality, assume the index tuples appearing on the two sides of a equation differ by some integer values. A communication function τ is called a first order difference operator when $\tau(\mathbf{u})$ appears on the right hand side of a equation and it differs from $\mathbf{u}$ in exactly one index by one. Clearly, a first order differerce operator specifies a nearest neighbor communication. The order of a system of recursion equations is defined to be the maximum number of times a given set of first order difference operators must be applied to the index tuple $\mathbf{u}$ to obtain every communication function appearing in the system. A high order system must contain some long range communications, which are routed via many nearest neighbor communications. Due to the high cost of communication in current technology, the delay for communications of the high order terms can undermine the efficiency of an algorithm. If it is at all possible, the order of a system of recursion equations should either be kept constant or grow very slowly (e.g., logarithmically) with respect to the problem size.

In the matrix multiplication example, System (5.2) is first order; therefore all communications are between nearest neighbors and no more transformations are needed to reduce the order of equations. Thus far, we have achieved in bringing a definition to a practically efficient algorithm. The steps of transformations on the definition are shown in Figure 5.

6. Incorporating Pipelining by Space-time Mapping

A naive implementation of System (5.2), derived above could use one processor for each process; however, after the execution of a process, a processor would be sitting idle, wasting resources. It turns out that only $O(n^2)$ number of processors are needed, i.e., each processor can be re-used by $O(n)$ number of processes. In general, a system of low-order recursion equations with bounded fan-in and fan-out degrees defined on a d-dimensional process structure with the size in each dimension of $O(n)$ requires only $O(n^{d-1})$ number of processors. The space-time mapping procedure described in this section achieves the saving of $O(n)$ number of processors.

6.1. Space-time recursion equations

From the standpoint of implementation, a process $\mathbf{v}$ in a system of recursion equations will be mapped to some physical functional unit, or processor s during execution, and once the process is terminated, another process can be mapped to the same processor. In fact, such re-use of the resource is the essence of

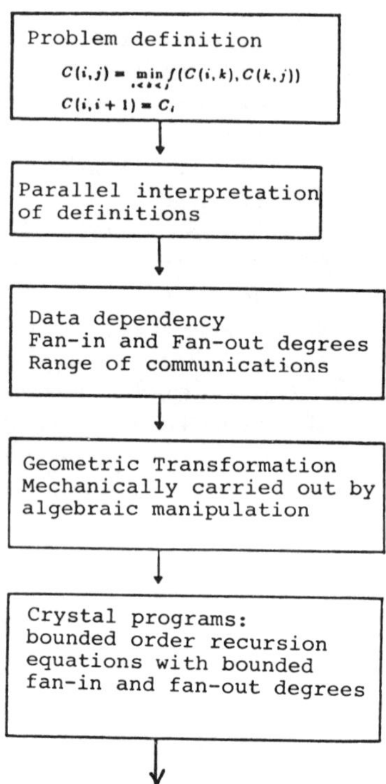

Figure 5: Algorithm transformation.

pipelining. We call each execution of a process by a processor an ***invocation*** of the processor. Let t be an index for labeling the invocations so that the processes executed in the same processor can be differentiated, and let these invocations be labeled by strictly increasing non-negative integers. Then for a given implementation of a program, each process $\mathbf{v}$ has an alias $[s,t]$, telling when (which invocation) and where (in which processor) it is executed.

How shall the process name $\mathbf{v}$ be related to its alias? One of the key issues in devising an efficient parallel algorithm is to find a suitable one-to-one function that maps a name to its alias. Once such a function is obtained, it can be substituted into the program to yield another system of recursion equations which has the property that (1) the time component t must always be non-negative, and (2) the time component of any invocation on the right-hand side of an equation must be strictly less than the time component of the invocation on the left-hand side of the equation. Such equations are called ***space-time*** recursion equations (STREQ) [2] and the function a ***space-time mapping.*** A system of space-time recursion equations specifies completely what code each processor executes at each invocation (its processing function), how the processor communicates with other processors (its communication functions), how communications and computations are controlled locally at each processor (its predicates), how each processor should be initialized (its specification at time zero), and how input streams should be supplied (its specification of processors at the boundary of the process structure).

The goal of **Crystal**'s space-time mapping procedure is to generate, from a given algorithm, a system of space-time recursion equations that embodies a pipelined parallel algorithm or VLSI architecture, optimal with respect to the algorithm. The steps of the space-time mapping procedure are shown in Figure 6.

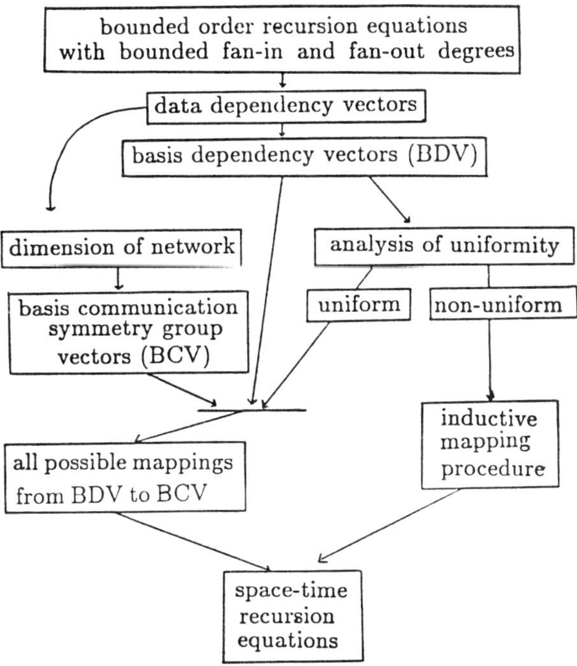

Figure 6: The space-time mapping of a **Crystal** algorithm.

The mapping itself is merely a transformation of the process structure from one coordinate system to another, where the latter could be interpreted as a space-time domain. Thus the dimensionality of the concrete network is one less than that of the process structure. What needs to be resolved is a method to find such mappings.

6.2. Data dependency vectors

By extending the domains of indices for a process to the rationals, a d-dimensional process structure can be viewed as being embedded in a d-dimensional vector space over the rationals. From now on, we can refer to the indices of a process as a vector.

Definition 6.1. A *data dependency vector* is the difference of the vector on the left-hand side of a recursion equation and a vector on the right hand side of the equation.

The data dependency vectors appearing in the recursion equations for matrix multiplication are shown in the Table 1. The process structure is partitioned according to the data dependency. The equivalence relation is denoted by "$\sim$", and $\mathbf{v} \sim \mathbf{u}$ if process $\mathbf{v}$ and process $\mathbf{u}$ have the same data dependency. The four equivalent classes of data dependency of System (5.2) are (1)$(k = 0) \wedge (0 < i \leq n) \wedge (0 < j \leq n)$, (2)$(i = 0) \wedge (0 < j \leq n) \wedge (0 < k \leq n)$, (3)$(j = 0) \wedge (0 < k \leq n) \wedge (0 < i \leq n)$, and (4)$(0 < i \leq n) \wedge (0 < j \leq n) \wedge (0 < k \leq n)$.

	(1)	(2)	(3)	(4)
a	$(0,1,0)$	$(0,1,0)$	sources	$(0,1,0)$
b	$(1,0,0)$	sources	$(1,0,0)$	$(1,0,0)$
c	sources	$(0,0,1)$	$(0,0,1)$	$(0,0,1)$

Table 1: The difference vectors describing the data dependency of streams a, b, c for matrix multiplication.

6.3. Uniformity of a parallel algorithm

The concept of uniformity is introduced to characterize parallel algorithms so that an expedient procedure can be applied to a *uniform algorithm* in seeking the space-time mapping.

Definition 6.2. A uniform algorithm is one in which a single set of basis vectors can be chosen so as to satisfy the following mapping condition: each data dependency vector appearing in the algorithm can be expressed as a linear combination of the chosen basis vectors with non-negative coordinates.

6.3.1. Example of a uniform algorithm

For instance, in the data dependency class (3) in Table 1, the two data dependency vectors $(0,0,1)$ and $(1,0,0)$ are expressed as the following linear combinations with non-negative coordinates, $(0\cdot \mathbf{d}_1 + 0\cdot \mathbf{d}_2 + 1\cdot \mathbf{d}_3)$ and $(1\cdot \mathbf{d}_1 + 0\cdot \mathbf{d}_2 + 0\cdot \mathbf{d}_3)$, respectively, where $\mathbf{d}_1 \stackrel{\text{def}}{=} (1,0,0)$, $\mathbf{d}_2 \stackrel{\text{def}}{=} (0,1,0)$, and $\mathbf{d}_3 \stackrel{\text{def}}{=} (0,0,1)$. Clearly, a single set of basis difference vectors, namely, $\{\mathbf{d}_1, \mathbf{d}_2, \mathbf{d}_3\}$ suffices to express each data dependency vector with non-negative coordinates in all of the classes as their linear combinations, hence System (5.2) is a uniform algorithm.

6.3.2. Motivation for the Mapping condition

The mapping condition is motivated by the possibility of using as the space-time mapping a linear transform from the basis dependency vectors to the basis *communication vectors.* A communication vector $[\Delta s, \Delta t]$ is just a data dependency vector of a system of STREQ, which always has a positive time component Δt, and which represents a communication from a processor s to another processor $s + \Delta s$ in Δt time steps. If the mapping between the two sets of basis vectors is determined, then the mapping of each data dependency vector is also determined: its mapping is the same linear combination as itself, except in terms of the corresponding basis communication vectors. If a difference vector has a term with negative coordinates in its linear combination, then the mapping of this term to space-time represents a communication that takes negative time steps, a situation that is not feasible in any physical implementation. For a non-uniform program, more than one set of basis difference vectors must be chosen so as to satisfy the mapping condition, and the space-time mapping might become piece-wise linear, or non-linear. In this case, an inductive mapping procedure is needed [3] to find the space-time mapping for non-uniform algorithms.

6.4. Basis communication vectors

Each network comes with a set of basis communication vectors. For instance, in an n-dimensional hypercube, a processor has n connections to its nearest neighboring processors. Each of the n communication vectors (one for each connection), has $n + 1$ components: the first n ones indicating the movement in space, and the last in time, which is always positive (counting invocations). These n communication vectors, together with the communication vector $[0, 0, \ldots, 0, 1]$, representing the processors's communication of its current state to its next state, form the basis communication vectors. In an n-dimensional network, there can be more than one set of basis communication vectors. Taking a two-dimensional hexagonal network as an example, a diagonal connection has a communication vector $[1, 1, 1]$. The set of vectors $\{[1, 0, 1], [0, 1, 1], [1, 1, 1]\}$ serves as bases as well as the set $\{[1, 0, 1], [0, 1, 1], [0, 0, 1]\}$.

For a uniform algorithm, a mapping of the basis dependency vectors to basis communication vectors determines a parallel implementation. Not only can there be numerous sets of basis communication vectors, but each results in an implementation with different data flow. In other words, for the same algorithm, there result numerous possible implementations. Lin and Mead [11] show that regularly connected networks with nearest neighbor connections and indefinite extensibility can be enumerated by the subgroups of the symmetry groups. In Figure 7, a few of the most often used two-dimensional networks and their associated communication vectors in the three-dimensional space and time are given. The **Crystal** compiler finds for each of these networks a parallel implementation of the algorithm so that the most suitable one for the target application can be chosen.

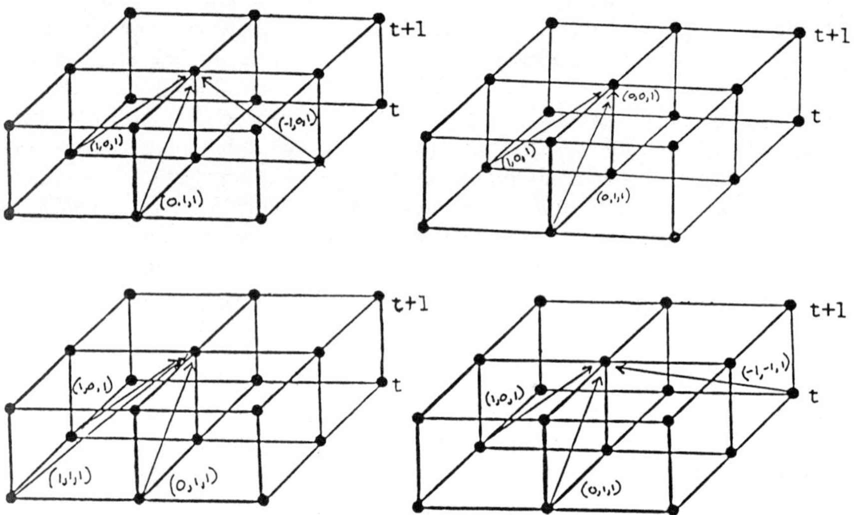

Figure 7: Networks and their associated communication vectors.

6.5. Obtain linear mappings for uniform algorithms

Thus for each set of basis communication vectors obtained from the subgroup enumeration, we immediately obtain the linear mapping from the basis difference vectors to them, and in turn the mapping T from processes to invocations of processors.

Listed in Table 2 are the basis communication vectors for matrix multiplication in System (5.2), three different sets of communication vectors (CV1, CV2, CV3) and the resulting systolic algorithms. Also listed are the systolic algorithms for LU decomposition derived using the same method.

Figure 8 shows the process structure for a two-by-two matrix multiplication in the original coordinate system (from System (5.2)). The new coordinate system after transformation is shown in Figure 9, which illustrates in space and time the invocations of a systolic matrix multiplication using communication vectors CV2. In the case where the communications to the outside world from a network of processors are limited only to those via its boundary processors, the inputs must reside outside the boundaries intially, and then be shifted into the network. For this example, we know where the inputs should appear in the process stucture from System (5.2), as shown in Figure 9. To figure out where they should be outside the network initially, the inputs $A(i,k)$, $B(k,j)$, and

$C(i,j)$ are shifted out from inside the boundaries of the process structure in the directions opposite to $[0,1,1]$, $[1,0,1]$, and $[1,1,1]$ respectively, until each of the inputs reaches the bottom plane in Figure 9. The two-dimensional systolic network and the resulting input streams are depicted in Figure 10.

difference vectors	CV1	CV2	CV3
$\mathbf{d}_1 \stackrel{\text{def}}{=} (1,0,0)$	$[1,0,1]$	$\mathbf{c}_1 \stackrel{\text{def}}{=} [1,0,1]$	$[1,0,1]$
$\mathbf{d}_2 \stackrel{\text{def}}{=} (0,1,0)$	$[0,1,1]$	$\mathbf{c}_2 \stackrel{\text{def}}{=} [0,1,1]$	$[0,1,1]$
$\mathbf{d}_1 \stackrel{\text{def}}{=} (0,0,1)$	$[0,0,1]$	$\mathbf{c}_3 \stackrel{\text{def}}{=} [1,1,1]$	$[-1,-1,1]$
MM	*	[13]	[9]
LU	[7, 5]	[4]	[9]

* this is the obvious systolic algorithm in which partial product are accumulated in place.

Table 2: Data dependecy vectors, communication vectors, and systolic designs for matrix multiplication and LU decomposition.

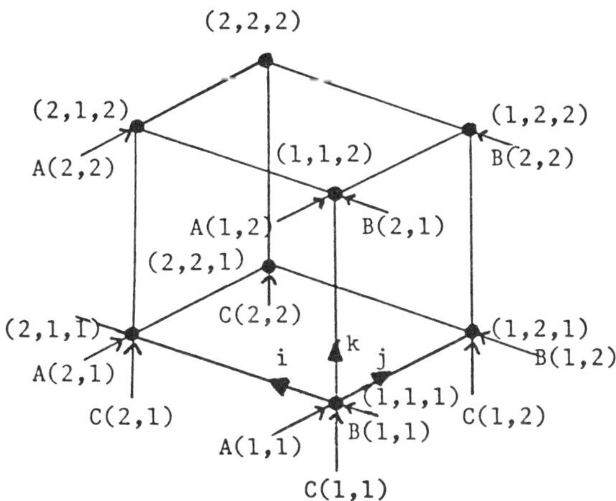

Figure 8: The process structure in the original coordinate system.

6.6. The complexity of the mapping procedure

For uniform algorithms, the linear mapping is immediate with a given mapping between the two sets of basis vectors. To determine that an algorithm is uniform involves examination of the algorithm symbolically, which depends on the number of different data dependency classes and is independent of the problem size. The choices in basis sets and all the possible mappings between them are all proportional to the dimensionality of the process structure; hence they are constant with respect to the size of the problem.

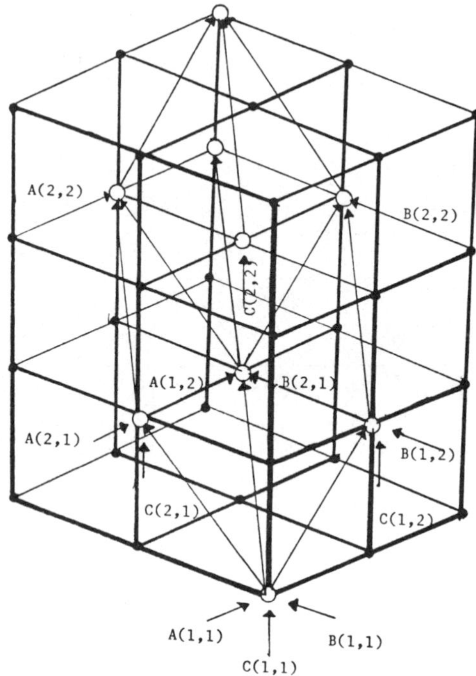

Figure 9: The process structure in the new coordinate systems.

7. Concluding Remarks

The space-time recursion equations obtained after space-time mapping can be interfaced to silicon compilers to produce special-purpose VLSI designs, or else undergo another stage of transformations that map the algorithm using a virtual network (a network with ideal size and connectivity) to a machine with a given architecture and size. Some code optimization is also needed at this stage. The steps of transformation at this stage are shown in Figure 11.

In short, **Crystal** provides a simple, straightforward, but powerful way of defining computational problems. When interpreted by **Crystal**, the definition naturally discloses a parallel algorithm where the communications between processes and the computation within an individual process become clear. The **Crystal** programming environment takes such definitions, analyses and performs necessary transformations to yield algorithms having bounded degrees of fan-in and fan-out and using only local communications. The resulting algorithms go through the process of space-time mapping to yield pipelined algorithms and architectures. Thus, based on the language **Crystal**, a unified theory for understanding and generating any systolic architectures comes into existence.

From a programmer's point of view, **Crystal** is easy to use because the programmers does not need to specify explicit communications in a program; the specification is a functional definition that is natural to the problem rather

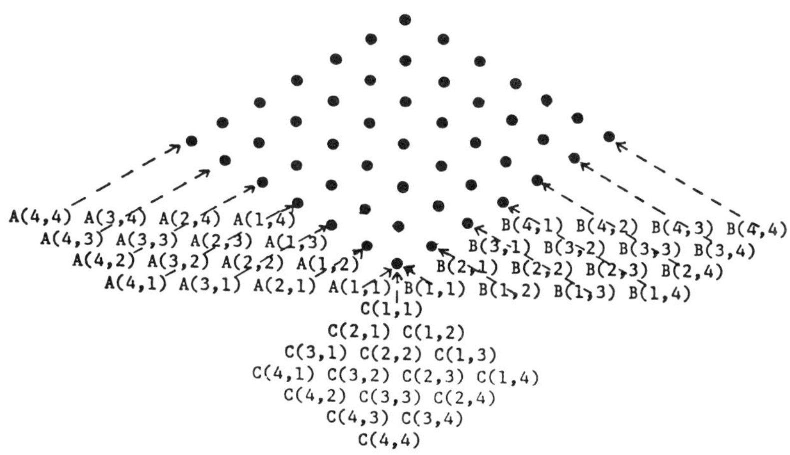

Figure 10: The systolic network using basis communication vectors CV2.

than tailored to machine execution. The correctness of a **Crystal** program is easy to ensure because first of all, it has a precisely defined fixed-point semantics. Secondly, **Crystal** encourages large scale parallelism, but at the same time allows a complex system to be specified by a hierarchy of parallel sub-systems by composition and abstraction. Thirdly, the **Crytal** compiler generates all possible space-time implementations from a functional and deterministic definition by using a set of powerful synthesis methods, as opposed to allowing programmers to use non-deterministic programming constructs to specify possible alternative implementations. The high level notation and algebraic properties language **Crystal** enjoys allow programmers to use **Crystal** not only as a means to interact with computer systems, but as a way of communciation among themselves. On the other hand, they make **Crystal** amenable to algebraic manipulation; thus all algorithm transformations described above can be carried out mechanically.

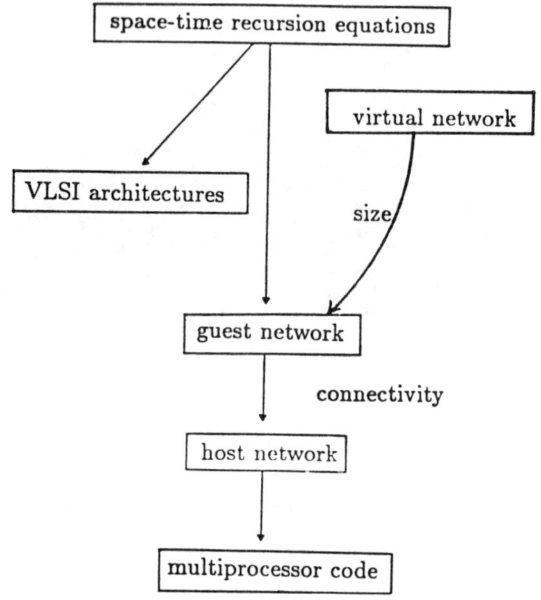

Figure 11: Mapping parallel algorithms to multiprocessors.

Last but not least is the portability issue. Notice that in this approach to parallel processing, successive transformations are performed on algorithms all written in the same language — **Crystal** — including the code optimization step which takes the machine characteristics as parameters. Only at the last code generation step do different machines require different code generators and routing schemes. Such a high level of portability is especially important in an age where larger, better and ever more different machines are built.

References

[1] Bryant, R. E., *A Switch-Level Simulation Model for Integrated Logic Circuits,* Ph.D. Thesis, Massachusetts Institute of Technology, March 1981.

[2] Chen, M. C., *Space-time Algorithms: Semantics and Methodology,* Ph.D. Thesis, California Institute of Technology, May 1983.

[3] ———, *Automatic Generation of VLSI Architectures: Synthesis by Algorithm Transformation,* Technical Report 427, Yale University,, October 1985.

[4] ———, Synthesizing Systolic Designs, *Proceedings of the Second International Symposium on VLSI Technology, Systems, and Applications,* May 1985, pp. 209–215.

[5] Delosme, J., Morf M., Scattering Arrays for Matrix Computations, *Proceedings of SPIE, Real time signal processing IV,* August 1981, pp. 74–91.

[6] R.B.K. Dewar et al, *Programming by Refinement, as Exemplified by the SETL Representation Sublanguage,* ACM TOPLAS, January (1979), pp. 27–49.

[7] Gentleman, W.M., Kung, H.T., Matrix triangularization by Systolic Arrays, *Proceedings of SPIE, Real time signal processing IV,* August 1981, pp. 19–26.

[8] Ming-Deh A. Huang, Solving some graph problems with optimal or near-optimal speedup on mesh-of-trees networks, *Proceedings of FOCS,* IEEE, Oct 1985, pp. 232–240.

[9] Kung H. T. and Leiserson C. E., Algorithms for VLSI Processor Arrays, *Introduction to VLSI Systems by Mead and Conway,* Addison-Wesley, 1980.

[10] F. T. Leighton, *Complexity Issues in VLSI: Optimal layouts for shuffle exchange graph and other networks,* MIT Press, Cambridge Massachusetts, 1983.

[11] Lin, T.Z., Mead, C.A., *The Application of Group Theory in Classifying Systolic Arrays,* Display File 5006, Caltech, Mar 1982.

[12] Scott, D.S. and Strachey, C., Toward a Mathematical Semantics for Computer Languages, Fox, J. ed., *Proceedings of the Symposium on Computers and Automata,* Polytechnic Institute of Brooklyn Press, New York, 1971, pp. 19–46.

[13] Weiser, U., and Davis, A., A Wavefront Notation Tool for VLSI Array Design, *VLSI Systems and Computations,* Computer Science Press, 1981.

AUTHOR INDEX

CHARLES R. ARNOLD, PH.D
ARNOLD ASSOCIATES
P.O. BOX 1151
NEW LONDON, CT 06320